The Resettlement of British Columbia

Cole Harris

The Resettlement of British Columbia: Essays on Colonialism and Geographical Change

With cartography by Eric Leinberger

UBCPress / Vancouver

09 08 07 06 05 04 03   5 4 3

Printed in Canada on acid-free paper

National Library of Canada Cataloguing in Publication Data

Harris, R. Cole.
The resettlement of British Columbia

Includes bibliographical references and index.
ISBN 0-7748-0588-9 (bound); ISBN 0-7748-0589-7 (pbk.)

1. British Columbia – History. 2. British Columbia – Geography. 3. British Columbia – Colonial influence. I. Title.

FC3811.H37 1996   971.1   C96-910706-4
F1088.H38 1996

Canadä

UBC Press gratefully acknowledges the financial support for our publishing program of the Government of Canada through the Book Publishing Industry Development Program (BPIDP), and of the Canada Council for the Arts, and the British Columbia Arts Council.

The BC Heritage Trust has provided financial assistance to this project to support conservation of our heritage resources, gain further knowledge, and increase public understanding of the complete history of British Columbia.

Set in Stone by Laura Ball
Printed and bound in Canada by Friesens
Copy editor: Nancy Pollack
Proofreader: Dallas Harrison
Cartographer: Eric Leinberger

UBC Press
The University of British Columbia
2029 West Mall
Vancouver, BC V6T 1Z2
604-822-5959 / Fax: 604-822-6083
E-mail: info@ubcpress.ca
www.ubcpress.ca

To the Bosun Ranch and some of its inhabitants: my grandparents Margaret and Joseph, my parents Ellen and Dick, and my uncle Sandy.

Contents

Figures and Illustrations

Figures

Illustrations

Introduction

In the preface to a book on French rural life, one of the great French historians reflected on the village of his youth and the worn stone path, sculpted by the feet of centuries, that led from his house to the village brook. In a sense, he had followed that path through most of his scholarly life, tracing it back into an age-old peasant world and a material civilization remote from his own. The path left the industrial and the modern, and entered their own long European antecedents – his own history leading from his own doorstep in the form of a worn stone path.

Few British Columbians can live with the past in this way. Most are immigrants, occupiers of spaces that recently belonged to others. Longer pasts are not here, and most ways have been brought from afar. Here was a place to make lives and futures, and yet in some basic way, I think, people live somewhat perched, far from various homes, in a place that is not quite their own. An immigrant society has hardly come to terms with where it is in the world, this Pacific corner of North America that just over 200 years ago no outsiders knew anything about, and that since has become a crossroad of colonialism and the modern world. Brought into outside focus so recently and then changed so rapidly, it is not an easy place to know.

In these circumstances, immigrant British Columbians fall back on simple categories of knowing and the exclusions they entail. They assume that British Columbia was wilderness and that they are bearers of civilization. Living within this imaginative geography, they associate colonialism with other places and other lives – a racially segregated South Africa, Joseph Conrad's fear-ridden Congo – where they can easily condemn its brutalities, yet are largely oblivious to its effects here. They turn the Fraser Canyon into a gold rush trail, a place where rugged land and sturdy miners met; a gondola gives them scenery and a touch of 'gold pan Pete.' The equation is simple and powerful, but leaves out thousands of human years and lives. The Fraser Canyon was not empty when the miners arrived; it had as dense an early-contact, non-agricultural population as anywhere in the Western Hemisphere. The ancestors of these people had been there for thousands of years. They defended this territory against enemies to the north and south and, when Europeans arrived, debated how best to deal with them. However, the peoples of the canyon were up against not only superior fire power, but also well-developed strategies of colonialism worked out in the course of Europe's worldwide advance into the non-European world. In detail colonialism took many forms, but it turned on common assumptions about the superiority of European civilization to the ways of the non-European world and, for all the kindly intentions of some of those who were caught up in it, depended on force to achieve its essential purpose: the transfer of land from one people to another. This was as true in British Columbia as anywhere else. Broadly, we are here, most of us, because we have imposed ourselves.

This imposition is recent, well within what some would call the project of modernity. Modernity may be thought of as a form of social organization characterized by a heightened capacity for the surveillance and management of individuals and populations, capitalist enterprise and industrial production, and the centralized control of the means of violence. As such, modernity was accompanied by the changing time-space relations associated with the technologies of transportation and communication that have evolved over the last two centuries. It may also be thought of as the frame of mind associated, some would say, with disenchantment and rational progress. I use the term even more loosely, and with more cultural relativity, to imply the gamut of developments within western European societies and their offshoots that, by the late nineteenth century, had made these societies much the most powerful on earth. It was this complex of meaning and power, derived particularly from Britain, that accompanied and sustained colonialism in British Columbia.

But British Columbia, a territory outlined by British diplomacy and named by Queen Victoria, was not Britain. Much of it had been Coyote's or, along the coast, Raven's creation. These tricksters had animated the world. Stories about them gave land and people meanings that had nothing whatever to do with western European civilization or the project of modernity. Yet from the late eighteenth century on, these two complexes of meaning and power were in touch with each other; before the end of the nineteenth century, Coyote and most of what he represented had been overridden – never completely, never without resistance – and a complex of power of outside origin was squarely in charge in a new geopolitical space. The essays in this book are about the uneven intersection of colonialism and modernity with Coyote and his world. Essentially, they deal with some of the strategies and tactics by which Coyote and his kind were decentred and marginalized in their own land.

Conceived this way, the study of British Columbia leads well beyond the boundaries of one Canadian province. Colonialism was a worldwide phenomenon, and the analytical literature on colonialism, particularly in its more generalized and theoretical aspects, is an obvious source of ideas about colonialism here. Similarly, the literature on modernity, broad and diverse as it is, comprises a large part of the intellectual background for the analysis of a modernizing British Columbia, however the modern is conceived. To try to understand British Columbia without recourse to the thought in these literatures is to ask too much of oneself – rather like trying to make a violin without experience or assistance. On the other hand, British Columbia is unique in many ways, and to understand it only in the light of ideas imported from elsewhere is either to ignore what is unique or turn it into an instance of what is thought to be general. I have no intention of doing either. The challenge, rather, is to soak oneself in a place and also in the broader literatures that may be expected to yield ideas about it, and to think hard about the relationships between the findings of these two experiences.

This is not easily done. I am a British Columbian and have lived here most of my life, but for years my research went into early Quebec, and for more years I edited a volume of the *Historical Atlas of Canada*. Only in the last few years has time emerged for much serious consideration of early British Columbia. Compared to those who have worked for years in British Columbia's archives, I am a neophyte, and compared to those (usually much younger) who have given years to social theory and find it far easier to read the post-colonial literature than I do, I am a neophyte too. Yet theory detached from empirical considerations gathers an increasingly irrelevant momentum, while empirical work detached from theory ignores both its own assumptions and many useful ideas. The essays in this book are my inherently rather cautious exploration at this interface, sustained by scholars who know the archives, on the one hand, and social theory, on the other, far better than I.

To deal with colonialism and modernity is necessarily, I think, to write into an interdisciplinary discussion. I have certainly wished to do so, and hope that the essays in this book will appeal to historians, anthropologists, sociologists, political scientists, and cultural and colonial theorists, as well as historical geographers and the interested public. Disciplinary boundaries are receding, and probably should; I am not even sure that there needs be a distinction between academic and non-academic writing. In any event, I have tried to minimize the difference, while knowing the difficulty of doing so.

At the same time, it is well to remember where one has come from. I come from a tradition of scholarship that lies at the interface of geography and history. I have always considered myself a historical geographer sensitive to human space and place: the geographical context of human life. That context is important not, a priori, as the stage on which human life takes place, but because it, itself, is an ongoing human creation that, in the language of social theory, constitutes and is constituted by human structures and agency. Societies and their places and spaces exist in ongoing, reciprocal relation with each other; it is impossible to understand one very well without coming to terms with the other. Nowhere is this more obvious than in modernizing British Columbia, where new settlements and landscapes were among immigrants' principal creations, and issues of power characteristically turned on the control of land. Land was the new opportunity; life here was about occupying, controlling, and managing it, about establishing who could do what where. In the process settlements were created and space was reconfigured. It is this dimension of the British Columbian past that a geographer finds weakly represented in existing academic literature. Some of these essays are more explicitly geographical than others, but they all have geographical edges; otherwise, at least for me, British Columbia does not quite come into focus.

In the 1970s, I wrote a pair of essays about the synthesizing habit of mind inherent in historical geography, contrasting it, favourably, with the abstracting, simplifying, and, it seemed to me, a-geographical tendencies inherent in theory. In the early 1990s, I wrote an essay urging historical geographers to pay more attention to social theory, and many of them concluded that I had become a convert to recent fad. But what had changed, I think, was our understanding of theory. In the 1970s, positivism was still in the air, and part of its baggage was theories conceived as candidates for covering laws. I thought, and still do, that the search for such theory was misguided and dangerous. Ideas, however, are a different matter, and if theories are conceived as sets of interrelated ideas that are used suggestively rather than deductively, then they can only contribute to the challenge of synthesis that, as much as ever, I feel is at the heart of my work. For those who want to see them that way, these essays are an attempt in the 1990s to catch, in the borderlands of several academic disciplines and theoretical literatures, the opportunity for historical geographical synthesis.

This collection of essays is a set of related soundings that, rather like spot checks for Atlantic cod, may not be enough to reveal very much of what has been going on. A great deal has been left out. The missionaries and the increasingly pervasive bureaucracy of the Department of Indian Affairs barely figure, yet both were critical aspects of late-nineteenth-century colonialism in the province. None of the province's large industrial workplaces is analyzed. There is little explicit treatment of women, a glaring omission when set against the achievements of feminist theory. Even more serious, given my emphasis on colonialism, is the lack of a sustained analysis of Native resistance. There are several reasons for this: an archival record that, overwhelmingly, is by and about white immigrants; my own unfamiliarity with ethnology and its ways; my lack of confidence that, without a great deal more work than I have had time for, I either could or should begin to represent a very different, politically oppressed people whose own voices have been heard much less than they should. I do not subscribe to the view that one cannot speak for others, but I do know that when a privileged white who is likely to be considered an authority speaks for those who have been the victims of privileged whites, that speaking should be more informed than I now can be. So these essays deal largely with colonial strategies and other modern ways introduced to British Columbia, and touch only a few dramatic responses from the Native world they were displacing. There is an altogether other set of stories to tell.

Some soundings are much more premeditated than mine. Robert Galois, friend and research colleague, and I had intended at one stage to write a historical geography of British Columbia before the Canadian Pacific Railway, but that book, when finally I had time to confront the archives, seemed premature and overwhelming. I then planned, and still plan, to write a book on the Fraser River, and several of the essays in this volume grew out of forays for that project. It was when I tried to establish who had lived where and in what numbers along the lower and middle Fraser in the late eighteenth century that I ran into the echoes of a smallpox epidemic. Magnified a little, those echoes became 'Voices of Smallpox around the Strait of Georgia,' published in *Ethnohistory* (December 1994) and republished here with some additions.

Reading the Fort Langley and Fort Kamloops journals while I was also reading Michel Foucault on sovereign and disciplinary power interested me in the strategies of power in the land-based fur trade, and led to the second essay. A portion of 'Strategies of Power in the Cordilleran Fur Trade' appeared in the *Canadian Geographer* (June 1995), but the full essay is published here for the first time. 'The Making of the Lower Mainland,' my first writing on the Fraser River, was prepared for a book entitled *Vancouver and Its Region* (1992), edited by Graeme Wynn and Timothy Oke, and written by members of my department at the University of British Columbia. I have brought parts of this essay up to date, and have rewritten the conclusion; otherwise, it is included as first written. 'The Fraser Canyon Encountered,' a drastic rewriting of an article in *BC Studies* (summer 1992), explores a region to which, some years ago, I began to take students on field trips. The canyon has increasingly fascinated me, as I realized the size of its pre-contact population, and the extent to which it bore the focused brunt of immigrant energy, capital, and government. It is here that, very tentatively, I begin to deal with strategies of Native resistance. 'A Population Geography of British Columbia in 1881' is tied to Robert Galois's careful survey of the nominal census of 1881 for a map in Volume II of the *Historical Atlas of Canada*. Co-authored with him, it is our attempt to provide a comprehensive, albeit introductory, analysis of the social structure of British Columbia on the eve of the CPR. It was published in the *Canadian Geographer* (spring 1994), and is republished here unchanged. 'The Struggle with Distance,' written for this volume, explores some of the relationships between introduced technologies of transportation and communication and the reach of colonialism and modernity.

The next two essays deal with some of the settlements and societies that, in a sense, were the culmination of colonialism. 'Industry and the Good Life around Idaho Peak' is the most focused of the collection, and the one in which I am the most steeped, for my family and my wife's family have been bound up with that mountain for the last 100 years. I reprint the essay as first published in the *Canadian Historical Review* (September 1985), partly because it contains an egregious error that reflects the mind-set of colonialism. When I wrote that there was no evidence of Native settlement near Idaho Peak, I did not know about the smallpox epidemics of 1782 and 1862, or about the measles epidemic of 1848, or about influenza in 1849, or about James Teit's ethnographic report, based on conversations with elderly people living near Colville, Washington, of several Native villages on Slocan Lake. Mine is another example, from one who should have known better, of the substitution of wilderness for an erased Native world. The penultimate essay, 'Farming and Rural Life,' considers the fifty years before World War II, and is co-authored with David Demeritt, whose knowledge of the North American agricultural literature in this period is far greater than mine. We wrote the essay for a book on the changing Canadian countryside, but publish it here for the first time, to mark a late phase of what all these pieces are about: the processes of colonization and modernity in this corner of North America.

The final essay, and by a good margin the most abstract, is an attempt to describe the social structure of immigrant British Columbia, the society for which space had been made by the processes described in this book. 'Making an Immigrant Society' deals with cultural replication and change, and with the balance, in any immigrant society, between the tendency to simplify immigrants' particular traditions and to introduce new dimensions of complexity in the form of unfamiliar peoples and places. I draw on arguments I published years ago about early European settlements in eastern North America, but recontextualize and considerably expand them. At the end of a book that turns around the colonial encounter, this final essay deals with what, from the point of view of the colonized, must be the most invidious of all forms of colonialism: the creation of a new society with its own values and momentum in their territory. Colonialism in a place like British Columbia is not so much a set of tactics that others employed at some time in the past as an ongoing set of relationships based on the fact that newcomers established themselves here, and refashioned a strange place, making it their own. Most British Columbians today, I as much as anyone else, are heirs of and continuing participants in a pervasive, ongoing colonialism.

When I give talks about my work, I am often asked about its relevance to current political arguments over Native land. In response I usually point out that I am more interested in understanding than in prescription but, if pressed, usually say something like this: Immigrant British Columbians, particularly males of British background, were extraordinarily lucky to encounter a bounteous, depopulated land just when railway, telegraph, and post had brought it within relatively easy reach of the outside world. Our luck has been built on others' misfortune, and we should appreciate the havoc our coming has wrought. Colonialism is not pretty, neither here nor anywhere else. We took away, often quite inadvertently, most Native people's opportunity to live with dignity, and I think we have to give that opportunity back. There is a perverse irony in the claim, made too frequently these days, that current attempts to somewhat redress two centuries of racism and colonialism are themselves racist. Native people deserve some special considerations because we took their land and victimized them. Moreover, they have now a good deal of power. Active, non-violent Native resistance would win the support of world opinion and bring this province to its knees. For both reasons, in my view, we have little choice but to negotiate in good faith with Native peoples about access to resources. While doing so, perhaps all parties can remember that those resources themselves have been badly damaged, especially by the last 100 years or so; and that many non-Natives, ordinary people without much power or influence, came here because there seemed to be opportunity, worked exceedingly hard, perhaps got a little way ahead, and – they or their progeny – have long since considered this adopted place their home. Add to this the various agreements, many of them unwise in my view, that governments have made with capital, and the cost of buying them out, and the nature of our predicament becomes clear. There are no simple solutions, least of all to try to maintain the politics of colonialism.

I have dedicated this collection to the Bosun Ranch at New Denver, British Columbia, and to some of my relatives who lived there, and should explain myself. My English grandfather and Scottish grandmother created this farm out of a forested mountainside overlooking Slocan Lake. The youngest of the numerous progeny of a wealthy Wiltshire meatpacker, but judged to have no head for business, my grandfather was sent to the Agricultural College in Guelph. From there he came west to farm for a few years in the Cowichan Valley in southern Vancouver Island before heading to the Slocan in 1896, drawn by the prospect of supplying fruit and vegetables to a burgeoning mining district, and bringing as a hired hand, so the story goes, a boatswain who had escaped from the Royal Navy (hence the name of the farm – 'ranch' was an affectation). On a trip back to England in 1897, he met and married my grandmother, she from a yeoman farming background near Aberdeen. The farm became an orchard, but the mines closed, other markets were far away, and the Canadian Pacific Railway would take fruit only by the boxcar load. My grandfather, who had planted a variety of species with the intention of supplying a local market over as long a season as possible, was stuck. Eventually he pulled out a prime young orchard and turned the land to sheep pasture, refusing to admit that he was developing a cougar ranch. By the 1930s, dairy cattle had replaced sheep, but few in New Denver or Silverton, the villages nearby, could afford milk. My grandfather had a milk wagon and delivered it anyway, though by this time the Bosun Ranch had long since consumed an English inheritance, and there was no more money there than anywhere else in the valley. Then the war came, my grandmother died, my grandfather was too old to farm, and the Securities Commission took over the

Bosun Ranch, c. 1910. The man is my grandfather, the boy my father.

place, making it one of the destinations for Japanese evacuated from the coast. After the war it returned to the family. My uncle Sandy lived there all his life.

My father, who was born on the ranch in 1900 and eventually studied English at McGill (MA thesis on the prefaces of Bernard Shaw), was a high school teacher in Vancouver and so, most years, our family, my parents, my sister Susan, and I, spent the better part of two summer months at the ranch. It is the site of my most vivid childhood memories, partly of a remarkable collection of people, partly of endless political talk – Fabian socialism and the Social Gospel were part of the ranch air – but also of the ranch itself and its remarkable setting on a narrow terrace between a mountain and a long, narrow mountain lake. The ranch bore the remains of the main attempts to turn an idyllic setting for a young Canadian family into a commercial farm, but much more. There were traces of the trail that, in the early 1890s, was the overland link between New Denver and Silverton, traces of the old wagon road, built by my grandfather and the boatswain in 1897, leading from the farmhouse to the lake and a small stone pier, largely broken up by the waves, where the lake steamer, the *SS Slocan*, had once put in. More mysterious, because my sister and I were forbidden to enter them, were the adits and stopes of the defunct and partly collapsed Bosun mine. In a couple of places, where the stopes broke the surface, we could peer into a cramped underground world of rickety ladders angling up close, dark walls of rock. My grandfather and the boatswain had located this prospect on the ranch in 1896, and my grandfather, having no interest in mining, had promptly sold options on it for $7,500, then a considerable sum. With this money he built a theatre in New Denver (the Bosun Hall, still there) and put in the village's first water works. The mine, like many in the Slocan, was short-lived, but successful for a time. At its peak it employed more than fifty men, and one year it was the principal Slocan shipper. The ruins of the mine ran in a line across the ranch; adits, one above the other, a dump at the mouth of each, ore car tracks on some of the dumps, a blacksmith's shop, the remains of a bunkhouse, and, jutting out over the lake on piles, a considerable structure from which ore was loaded into boxcars on barges. At the edge of the field, not far from the line of adits, were several granite boulders riddled with practice drill holes made by two powerful Swedes, Canadian rock-drilling champions, while a small boy, my father, held the watch and counted their strokes. And the old ranch house itself, a sprawling gingerbread affair, was empty and in ruin by my late teens. When I was small, the house was lived in by fifty-two elderly Japanese men, each of whom had a small garden along the little creek behind the house, and they turned it into a patchwork of flowers, lawns clipped with scissors, tiny ornamental bridges, and wave-sculpted stones gathered from the beach. Everywhere on this magic ranch there were stories.

The ranch affected virtually everyone who spent any time on it. Men came to work and stayed, not because they were paid much, but because the place was welcoming and my grandmother's cooking was good. A shed near the ranch house is still called the cathedral because the man hired to build it took so long. In the Depression there was no reason to leave. The Japanese appreciated my grandfather's and my uncle's kindnesses and the beauty of the place where war and deportation had dropped them. After the war several of the old men asked to stay on, and did; they were the ranch house's last inhabitants until, in the early 1970s, the family demolished much of it and restored the remainder. About this time the 'hippies' arrived in the Slocan, and they loved my uncle Sandy for the intimate way he lived with a place, its stories, and its wild animals.

The ranch has always been near the heart of my life, and more than anything else, I think, made me a historical geographer. Most of the essays in this volume probably revolve around it. It is my western Canadian counterpart of an ancient French village. But in this case the path goes back a known 100 years, then stops. There was a known beginning, either in 1890 when silver was found in the mountains, or in 1896 when my grandfather arrived. And there was a remarkable opportunity. No one else was interested in farming, and he had his pick of land; he chose a beautiful, well-watered terrace, probably the best farmland in the valley, though there were only about sixty potentially arable acres. There had been a mining claim on it, and he was required to do some prospecting. The showing that became the Bosun mine took one morning to find, and the English company that bought it turned it into a mine that produced silver-lead ore valued at four million turn-of-the-century dollars. My grandfather struggled all his life to make the farm pay – he wanted to turn it over to a manager so he could organize a political party (The Useful People's Party) and write radical political tracts – but could not, however hard he worked.

Everybody worked. My grandfather was not good with horses, and farm machinery was just coming in. The place was developed largely by hand. But he participated in what he considered a God-given opportunity. When I was a small boy and quite sick, he came to my room one day to ask if I wanted to know his views about life, and when, somewhat startled, I said 'Yes, granddad, I do,' he unwound his long, once-powerful frame slowly along my bed and told me that life was about making a contribution, especially in a beautiful new place, made by God. God had given us a beautiful land and with it the opportunity to start again and right past wrongs. At the end of his life he was not sure that civilization had budged very much, but the very idea that it might be able to start again because it had found a new, empty place for itself, was a form of the opportunity that the ranch, and British Columbia more broadly, seemed to offer.

My grandfather did not know about the smallpox epidemic of 1862. When he arrived there were no Native people in the valley. Had there been, he would have treated them with interest and kindness, but it would never have occurred to him that he, himself, might not belong there. In fact, the ranch grew out of an extraordinarily short-lived opportunity, a lens of time in which the Native population had disappeared, silver had been found in the Slocan Valley, modern systems of transportation brought in the outside world, and Britons moved freely and confidently within the empire. There had never been an equivalent spatial opportunity before, and there never would be again. Out of it came the ranch and the lives that, over four generations now, have circled around it. Broadly, these lives are part of the larger project of colonialism, but my grandparents (so far as I knew them), my parents, and my uncle Sandy lived as attractively as I have known people to live. And yet ... There are house pits in a lovely, isolated spot along the Slocan River south of Slocan Lake, and the last time I tried to see them I was turned away by Natives who did not want to have anything to do with whites, least of all there. Some may have come from Colville and had ancestors in the Slocan Valley. Perhaps I understood.

My other point of attachment for the last many years has been the Department of Geography in the University of British Columbia. It is a privilege to be part of a good department in a good university; whatever I have brought to these essays has been enormously augmented by the setting in which they were written and discussed. Individual acknowledgments are made after each essay, but here I want particularly to thank Olav Slaymaker and Timothy Oke, heads of my department while these essays were brewing; my colleagues Trevor Barnes, Derek Gregory, Daniel Hiebert, David Ley, Gerry Pratt, Graeme Wynn, and particularly Robert Galois, whose vast knowledge of the archives and of the interactions of Natives and newcomers in early British Columbia I have constantly relied on. Even more, I want to thank and acknowledge the graduate students with whom I have worked most closely these last years. They have shared their excitements and findings, and have taught me far more than I have taught them: Brett Christophers, David Demeritt, Ken Favrholdt, Averill Groeneveld-Meijer, Cathy Kindquist, Richard Mackie, Dan Marshall, Richard Phillips, Nadine Schuurman, Matthew Sparke, Lynn Stewart, Stephen Wilcockson, Bruce Willems-Braun, and, most particularly, Daniel Clayton, who, more than anyone else in his years here as a masters, then doctoral, student, led me from the exhausted aftermath of a historical atlas to many of the literatures, ideas, and data engaged in these essays. Eric Leinberger, cartographer, has been a pleasure to work with throughout.

I also thank the Social Sciences and Humanities Research Council of Canada for its support, my wife Muriel, who is my most honest critic, and a Canadian public who, I much hope, will provide something of the opportunity to a next university generation that it has provided to mine.

The Resettlement of British Columbia

1
Voices of Smallpox around the Strait of Georgia

Well, it's a good thing to study these things back, you know. Like the way the people died off.

– Jimmy Peters, Chawathil, 1986[1]

The old Indians grow quite pathetic sometimes when they touch upon this subject. They believe their race is doomed to die out and disappear. They point to the sites of their once populous villages, and then to the handful of people that constitute the tribe of today, and shake their heads and sigh.

– Charles Hill-Tout, 1904[2]

Demographic collapse, in short, led to widespread settlement discontinuity. To grasp the implications of such discontinuity, one must imagine what almost total depopulation would mean in Italy or Spain ca. 1500 – silent villages, decaying cities, fields lying waste, orchards overgrown with brush.

– Karl W. Butzer, 1992[3]

It is now clear that Europeans carried diseases wherever they went in the Western Hemisphere, and that among genetically similar peoples with no immunity to introduced viruses and bacteria, the results were catastrophic.[4] In the century or so after Columbus, the population of the Western Hemisphere fell by some 90 per cent according to current estimates.[5] For all the tyrannies of conquerors and colonists, diseases apparently had far more telling demographic effects.

In British Columbia, little enough is known about contact-related disease and depopulation. Whites have told other stories, ethnographers have encouraged Native informants to describe 'traditional' ways, and the few recorded Native accounts of disease have been treated as myths. Today, as political debates about Native government and land claims intensify, and as appeals proceed through the courts, questions of disease and depopulation are explicitly repoliticized – which does not make listening easier.[6] For a society preoccupied with numbers, scale, and progress, more people imply fuller, more controlled occupation of land. Thus, it has been in the interest of non-Natives to suggest small pre- or early-contact Native populations, and in the interest of Natives to suggest much larger ones. A disinterested position may not exist. Yet there are Native accounts of disease, many of them long pre-dating current political and legal calculations, as well as numerous references to disease by white explorers and traders.

In this chapter, I consider Coast Salish accounts of pre-contact smallpox around the Strait of Georgia, the body of water between southern Vancouver Island and the mainland, and in adjacent parts of Puget Sound and the lower Fraser Valley (Figure 1.1). Even today there may be more smallpox stories in circulation, or fragments of stories partly remembered, but these are the ones that have been recorded and made public. A comparison of these Native stories with early white accounts suggests that, in different ways and from different vantage points, they describe the same events. From this insight, coupled with information from the Plains, I conclude that smallpox reached the Strait of Georgia in 1782 and that its effects were devastating. I then consider whether useful estimates of immediate pre-smallpox population are possible, and end by asking why this epidemic has been so invisible: What does it mean that whites have lived for several generations alongside the Coast Salish without understanding – without apparently wanting to understand – that Native people had been decimated by smallpox before Vancouver and Galiano sailed into the Strait of Juan de Fuca?

Although the introduction of smallpox to the Strait of Georgia was part of a hemispheric tragedy, there is no simple line from the Caribbean at the end of the fifteenth century to the Northwest Coast at the end of the eighteenth. The course, effects, and social construction of disease were different in different places. The Strait of Georgia and the larger Northwest Coast have their own stories to tell, to which I come as a geographer mindful of another geographer's adage that one cannot know a place very well without locating its people.[7] To enquire where people lived in what is now southern British Columbia at the beginning of the nineteenth century is to encounter smallpox; ongoing continental debates about disease, depopulation, and the contact process; and the politics of land in contemporary British Columbia.

Surviving Native accounts of the arrival of smallpox are scattered and fragmentary. The great late-nineteenth- and early-twentieth-century ethnographers of Northwest Coast cultures did not work among the Coast Salish; the major ethnographic collections of stories do not come from these peoples. Nor did the ethnographers have pre- and early-contact diseases in

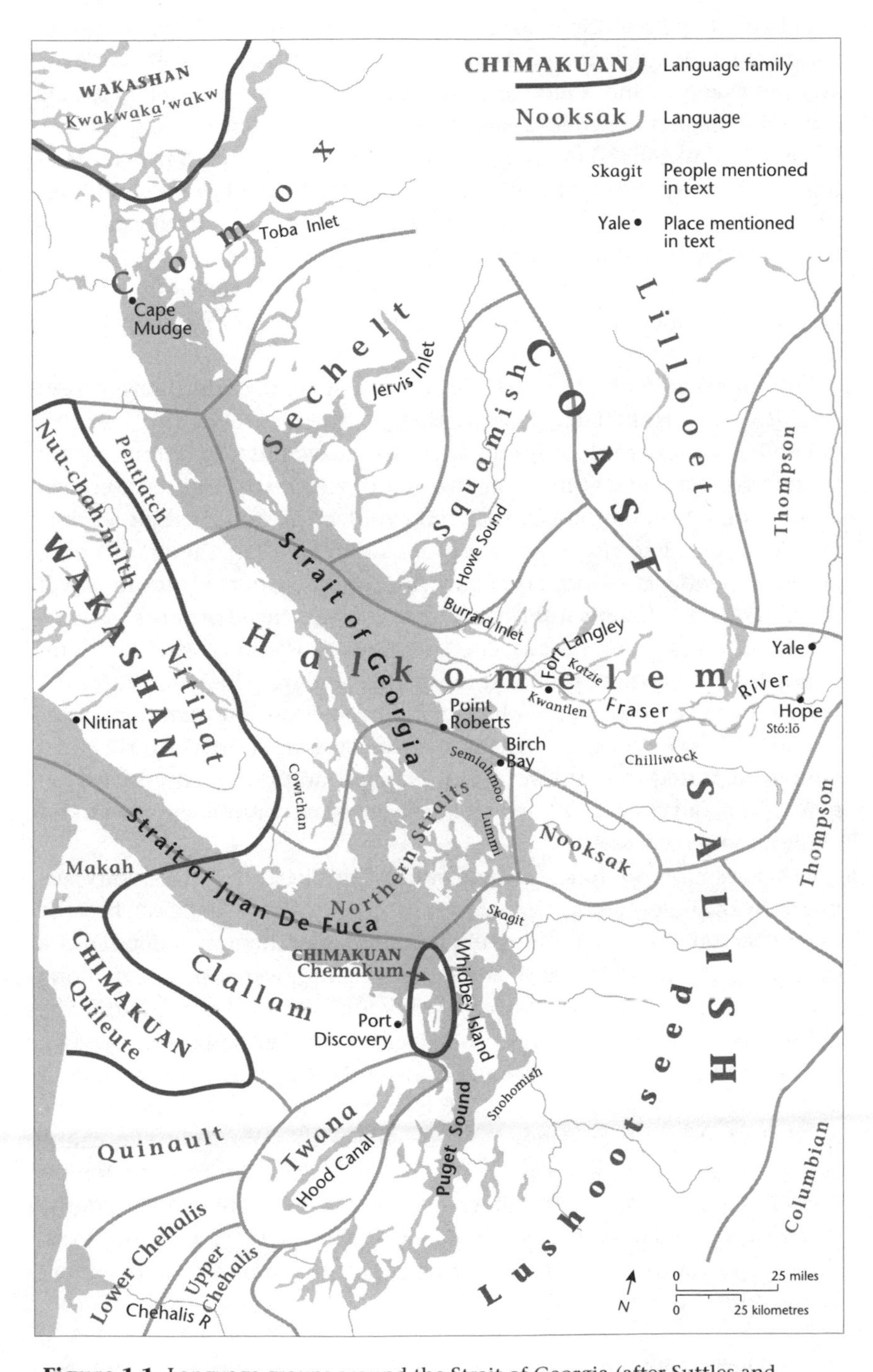

Figure 1.1 Language groups around the Strait of Georgia (after Suttles and Kinkade)

mind and, therefore, they did not ask questions that would have elicited information about them. Generation after generation of the elderly died, cultures changed, and, eventually, oral traditions thinned. What is left are a number of short references and, condensed and often rephrased, a few whole accounts. All the material cited here has been written down, and it is impossible to reconstruct the circumstances of the stories or the intentions of the tellers. Often an account has been translated by one person, and then recorded in summary form by another. In Jan Vansina's phrase, they are 'mutilated messages' that present every opportunity for misunderstanding.[8] And yet, these surviving fragments are powerful and generally consistent with each other.

Erna Gunther, writing on the Clallam (south coast of the Strait of Juan de Fuca), and Homer Barnett, writing on the Coast Salish of British Columbia, either heard no stories about early epidemics or did not record them.[9] Wilson Duff, writing on the Stó:lō (along the lower Fraser well above its mouth), considered that early epidemics probably had reached the Stó:lō, but had no information about them.[10] On the other hand, W.W. Elmendorf, ethnographer of the Twana (Hood Canal in Puget Sound), learned that his informants' grandparents 'lived at times of disastrous epidemics.' The most severe, he was told, was very early, 'perhaps about 1800,' and came from the south via the lower Chehalis; 'from the Twana it passed north to the Klallam and peoples on southern Vancouver Island.'[11] Wayne Suttles, writing on the Lummi (northeastern Puget Sound), reported that according to 'Native tradition' smallpox arrived before Vancouver in 1792; 'several villages were completely wiped out, while all suffered losses.'[12]

Other accounts are fuller, though somewhat filtered by white constructions. In the mid-1890s a Vancouver woman, Ellen Webber, asked the Kwantlen about a large unoccupied midden approximately a quarter of a mile long, 100 feet wide, and, at its centre, some twenty feet deep along the north bank of the Fraser River, twenty-four miles from its mouth. She published her findings 'as they were given to me' (but largely in her own words) in the *American Antiquarian*. Apparently the village was more than 600 years old and had contained 600 prosperous people. Attacks from the north had always been fended off, usually with stones piled in cairns along the river bank in front of the village.[13] But one year the raiders came in such numbers that their canoes blackened the river. Even so, the Kwantlen defended their village ferociously. The river ran red with blood. Then, as a Kwantlen victory seemed assured, some of their enemy attacked from the rear.

> Now all was confusion. Many were killed, and many women were taken slaves. A few escaped to the woods, where they remained in hiding two

> or three days. Then, with the children, they came out, and with sad hearts they laid away their dead ... But misfortune followed the little band of survivors. In the swamp, near the village lived a fearful dragon with saucer-like eyes of fire and breath of steam. The village was apparently regaining its former strength when this dragon awoke and breathed upon the children. Where his breath touched them sores broke out and they burned with the heat, and they died to feed this monster. And so the village was deserted, and never again would the Indians live on that spot.[14]

Almost until Webber's day, people 'remembered and respected the dragon,' and when passing the swamp, crossed to the other side of the river and paddled softly and silently so as not to waken it. 'Accursed is the one who awakens the dragon, he and all his people; for the sore-sickness will surely be their punishment.'[15]

In 1896, Charles Hill-Tout, former theology student at Oxford and then master of an Anglican college in Vancouver, visited the Squamish 'through the kindness of the Roman Catholic bishop' to record their history and cosmology.[16] The chiefs produced 'the old historian of the tribe.' This was Mulks, decrepit, blind, and 'about 100 years old.' Mulks spoke only archaic Squamish, which Hill-Tout could not understand, and which Mulks uttered 'in a loud, high-pitched key' that his Squamish listeners followed with rapt attention. Every ten minutes or so, the translator offered a precis, but not even a fifth, Hill-Tout estimated, of what the old man had said. The story began with the creation of the world out of the water, and continued with accounts of a flood from which only one couple survived, and of a winter that did not end and during which all but two, a man and his daughter, died of starvation. In each case the land was re-peopled, and 'the people learned to forget the terrible punishment the Great Spirit had sent upon their forefathers.' Then,

> one salmon season the fish were found to be covered with running sores and blotches, which rendered them unfit for food. But as the people depended very largely upon these salmon for their winter's food supply, they were obliged to catch and cure them as best they could, and store them away for food. They put off eating them till no other food was available, and then began a terrible time of sickness and distress. A dreadful skin disease, loathsome to look upon, broke out upon all alike. None were spared. Men, women and children sickened, took the disease and died in agony by hundreds, so that when the spring arrived and fresh food was procurable, there was scarcely a person left of all their numbers to get it. Camp after camp, village after village, was left desolate. The remains of which, said the old man, in answer to my queries on this

> head, are found today in the old camp sites or midden-heaps over which the forest has been growing for so many generations. Little by little the remnant left by the disease grew into a nation once more, and when the first white men sailed up the Squamish in their big boats, the tribe was strong and numerous again.[17]

In 1936, Old Pierre, then about seventy-five years old, told the ethnographer Diamond Jenness a very similar story, though more influenced by the missionaries.[18] Old Pierre, a Katzie, lived along the Pitt River, a tributary of the lower Fraser two days' paddle from the Squamish. The time came, he said, when the land was 'overcrowded.' When people 'gathered at the Fraser River to fish, the smoke from their morning fires covered the country with a pall of smoke.' Then the 'Lord Above' sent rain that fell until most of the mountains were covered and most people had drowned. After the flood, the population multiplied again and 'the Lord Above ... saw that once more they were too numerous in the land.' 'Then in the third month (October) of a certain year snow began to fall.' Soon every house was buried. Nine months passed 'before the snow melted completely from the house-tops.' Half the people died of starvation. A third time the population grew, and then came smallpox. Old Pierre's account is the most explicit surviving pre-contact description of the disease around the Strait of Georgia.

> After many generations the people again multiplied until for the third time the smoke of their fires floated over the valley like a dense fog. Then news reached them from the east that a great sickness was travelling over the land, a sickness than no medicine could cure, and no person escape. Terrified, they held council with one another and decided to send their wives, with half the children, to their parents' homes, so that every adult might die in the place where he or she was raised. Then the wind carried the smallpox sickness among them. Some crawled away into the woods to die; many died in their homes. Altogether about three-quarters of the Indians perished.
>
> My great-grandfather happened to be roaming in the mountains at this period, for his wife had recently given birth to twins, and, according to custom, both parents and children had to remain in isolation for several months. The children were just beginning to walk when he returned to his village at the entrance to Pitt Lake, knowing nothing of the calamity that had overtaken its inhabitants. All his kinsmen and relatives lay dead inside their homes; only in one house did there survive a baby boy, who was vainly sucking at its dead mother's breast. They rescued the child, burned all the houses, together with the corpses that lay inside them, and built a new home for themselves several miles away.

> If you dig today on the site of any of the old villages you will uncover countless bones, the remains of the Indians who perished during this epidemic of smallpox. Not many years later Europeans appeared on the Fraser, and their coming ushered in a new era.[19]

Farther upriver, among the Stó:lō, echoes of similar events linger to this day. Albert Louis heard of a flood before the whites came, then smallpox. 'It killed, oh, half the Indians all around the Fraser River there.'[20] Dan Milo, almost 100 years old in 1962, spoke of a village (Kilgard) where everyone died save one boy who settled down with a girl who was the only survivor from a village nearby.[21] In the village of Sxwoxwiymelh ('a lot of people died at once'), according to Susan Peters, twenty-five to thirty people died each day and were buried in one of the larger pit houses.[22] Patrick Charlie said that everyone there died of smallpox, and that the houses were burned down.[23] In 1986, Jimmy Peters, who grew up after World War I in the village of Yale at the foot of the Fraser Canyon, remembered elders who tried to keep children away from the houses collapsed on the dead and the burial grounds, and the children who, curious and uncomprehending, sneaked off there anyway.

> Things that the old timers did years ago, we're not supposed to touch it even kickwillie houses. And where they were buried. A lot of them died in that place. And just buried in there ... Chickenpox, smallpox, killed them all off. And they just died there. And we're not supposed to go there and touch them. A lot of times we used to go up there and dig out and see what they used to use years back. Like rock bowls, or rock knives, wood chisels, you know. But they'd tell me. 'Don't you go there. Somedays, some nights you'll dream about that, and you might not live long,' he says. They're too sacred. You leave them there. You're not supposed to touch anything that they owned years back.[24]

Sometime in the 1920s, Ayessic, chief at Hope, a village fifty kilometres below Yale on the Fraser, told the antiquarian and collector C.F. Newcombe about the first whites to descend the river. 'News came from above ... that men of different race were coming.' Troubled, 'the people came together and it was decided to try to please the newcomers.' After they had painted their bodies 'with red fungus paint (soquat),' messengers were sent to invite the strangers at Big Canyon 'to come down.' 'They found them there camping with a number of boxes and packs which were thought to hold smallpox or miracle medicine.'[25]

In the 1960s, fisherman Nick Stevens, living at the mouth of the river, remembered his Native grandfather's account of smallpox among the

Cowichan on Saltspring Island. There, 'according to the stories handed down,' smallpox came on the south wind, and the people could not get 'the clean north wind to blow the foul disease away.' The south wind blew all winter 'until most of the tribe were dead and there were too few left to bury their bodies.' The survivors took the corpses to a small island near Fulford Harbour, 'placing their remains in crevices in the rocks, covering them with flat stones.' When, as boys, Stevens and his brother found a skull on this island, their grandfather flew into a rage. 'Take it back where you found it, he roared. It will bring us bad luck.'[26] In a slightly different category is *Indians of Skagit County* (1972), by Martin Sampson, a Swinomish chief. Relying partly on oral tradition, Sampson describes a 'first epidemic in the 1700s,' which he identifies as smallpox, that killed a great many coastal people but did not reach the upper Skagit.[27]

Ample ground exists for disagreement about the meaning of these fragments. They may not all refer to the same epidemic, their dating would be expected to be uncertain, some of their elements (for example, floods) recur in stories told in many cultures, and some of their analytical categories are anachronistic introductions. At the same time, many point to an eighteenth-century epidemic, and two have an explicit chronological marker: the epidemic preceded whites. Descriptions of the disease fit smallpox, though measles is probably not excluded. Yet these fragments, coming from many different performance situations, appear to describe the same event and are broadly congruent with other evidence from outside the oral tradition.

The European record of the lands and peoples around the Strait of Georgia begins in 1790 when the Spaniard Manuel Quimper sailed through the Strait of Juan de Fuca as far as the San Juan Islands. Encountering small numbers of Natives almost everywhere he went, Quimper estimated there were 500 people in the strait, and 1,000 at its southwestern entrance near Nunez Gaona (Neah Bay). Some of these people, he thought, had been drawn from the outer coast by the great quantities of 'seeds' – possibly camas – available in the strait.[28] The next year, the commander at Nootka, Francisco Eliza, continued the Spanish survey through most of El Gran Canal de Nuestra Sra del Rosario (the Strait of Georgia). Again, he saw many people at the entrance to the Strait of Juan de Fuca, and mentioned Native settlements here and there around the Gran Canal del Rosario. Along the south shore of the Strait of Juan de Fuca, Natives 'from outside' came from time to time 'to trade boys'; at the edge of all the beaches were 'skeletons fastened to poles.'[29] The next year, both British (Vancouver) and Spanish (Galiano, Valdes) expeditions circumnavigated Vancouver Island, surveying and mapping as they went.

The Spanish wrote appreciatively about the Natives, but offered few comments on Native settlements or numbers. They found both deserted and inhabited villages in the Gulf Islands, and inhabited villages near rivers at the head of some inlets and at several other places. Beyond Johnstone Strait, on the northeast coast of Vancouver Island, the Nuchaimuses (Nimpkish) were a 'populous tribe.'[30]

The British, who had more officers and a little more time than the Spaniards, and who were more inclined to treat Natives as objects for investigation, provided a good deal more information. Reaching the southeastern end of the Strait of Juan de Fuca, Vancouver began to find deserted villages, and human skeletons 'promiscuously scattered about the beach, in great numbers.' After local surveys in the ships' boats, similar reports came back from his officers; it seemed, Vancouver wrote, as if 'the environs of Port Discovery were a general cemetery for the whole of the surrounding country.' In some deserted villages, 'the habitations had now fallen into decay; their inside, as well as a small surrounding space that appeared to have been formerly occupied, were overrun with weeds.' There were also 'lawns' on eminences fronting the sea, which Vancouver thought might have been sites of former villages; in a few, the framework of houses remained. In Vancouver's mind, 'each of the deserted villages was nearly, if not quite, equal to contain all the scattered inhabitants we saw.'[31] As the expedition continued into Puget Sound, more of the same was found.

winter, readily distributed smallpox among its inhabitants.

> During this Expedition we saw a great many deserted Villages, some of them of very great extent and capable of holding many human Inhabitants – the Planks were taken away, but the Rafters stood perfect, the size of many a good deal surprized us, being much larger in girth than the Discovery's Main mast. A Human face was cut on most of them, and some were carved to resemble the head of a Bear or Wolf – The largest of the Villages I should imagine had not been inhabited for five or six years, as brambles and bushes were growing up a considerable height.[32]

In a 'favoured' land that was 'most grateful to the eye,'[33] there were not many people. 'We saw only the few natives which are mentioned, silence prevailed everywhere, the feathered race, as if unable to endure the absence of man, had also utterly deserted this place.'

The expedition continued northward, finding more deserted villages along the eastern shore of the Strait of Georgia. At Birch Bay, there was 'a very large Village now overgrown with a thick crop of Nettles and bushes.'[34] There were deserted villages in Burrard Inlet, Howe Sound, and Jervis Inlet, and only occasional 'small parties of Indians either hunting or fishing [that] avoided us as much as possible.'[35] Farther north, Toba Inlet 'was nearly destitute of inhabitants,' though there was a deserted but well-fortified village that 'seemed so skillfully contrived and so firmly and well executed as rendered it difficult to consider the work of the untutored tribes we had been accustomed to meet.'[36] Only as the expedition got well into and through Johnstone Strait did it encounter a country that was 'infinitely more populous than the shores of the gulf of Georgia.'[37]

While Vancouver considered that deserted villages and numerous human skeletons 'do not amount to a direct proof of the extensive depopulation they indicate,'[38] he and his officers thought that the lands around Puget Sound and the Strait of Georgia recently had been severely depopulated.[39] Archibald Menzies, the expedition's botanist, estimated that 'the inhabitants of this extensive Country [apparently Puget Sound] did not appear to us on making every allowance of computation from the different Villages and strolling parties that were met with to exceed one thousand in all, a number indeed too small for such a fine territory.'[40] Puget gave the same figure.[41] All agreed that the cause or causes of depopulation could not be established, but variously speculated that they might have been disease, warfare, or population movements associated with seasonal hunting and fishing and with the maritime fur trade on the outer coast.

Disease

Captain Vancouver reported near Port Discovery that 'Several of their stoutest men had been seen perfectly naked, and contrary to what might

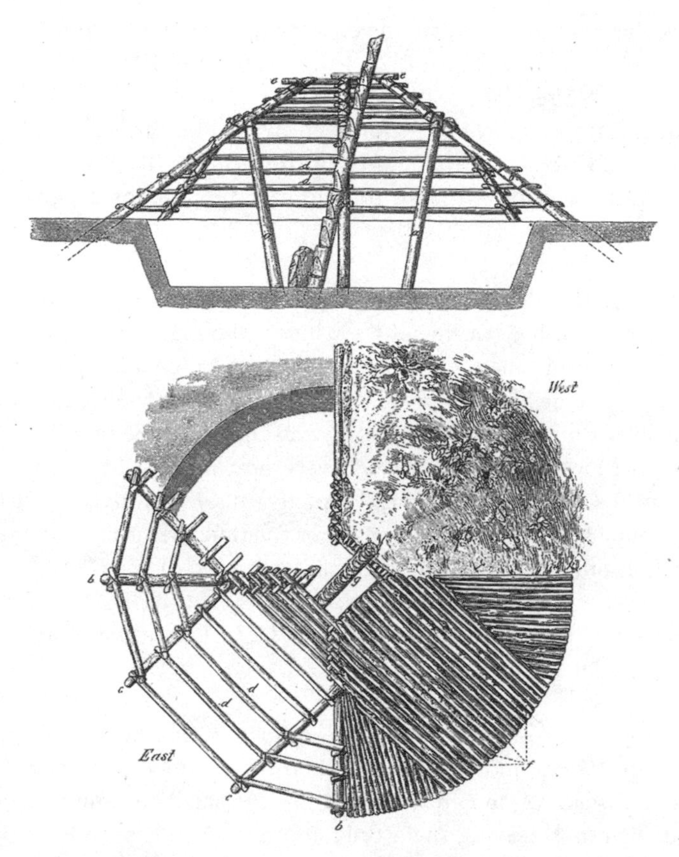

Interior pit house. An estimated winter population density of 1 person/2.5m^2 exposed all inhabitants to any contagious disease.

have been expected of rude nations habituated to warfare their skins were mostly unblemished by scars, excepting such as the smallpox seemed to have occasioned, a disease which there is great reason to believe is very fatal amongst them.'[42] Farther south, in Hood Canal, he recognized 'one man, who suffered very much from the small pox. This deplorable disease is not only common, but it is greatly to be apprehended is very fatal amongst them, as its indelible marks were seen on many; and several had lost the sight of one eye, which was remarked to be generally the left, owing most likely to the virulent effects of this baneful disorder.'[43] Later, near Whidbey Island, Vancouver reported that Peter Puget had met some very unwelcoming Indians: 'In their persons they seemed more robust than the generality of the inhabitants; most of them had lost their right eye, and were much pitted with the small pox.'[44] Puget himself wrote: 'the Small pox most have had, and most terribly pitted they are; indeed many have lost their Eyes and no Doubt it has raged with uncommon

Inveteracy among them but we never saw any Scars with wounds, a most convincing proof in my Mind of their peaceable Disposition.'[45] The Spaniards did not report signs of smallpox.

The next Europeans in the region were the American overland explorers, Lewis and Clark. Near the mouth of the Willamette, a few miles from the present-day city of Portland, they found the remains of 'a very large village.'

> I endeavored to obtain from those people the situation of their nation, if scattered or what had become of the natives who must have peopled this great town. an old man who appeared of some note among them and father to my guide brought forward a woman who was badly marked with the Small Pox and made signs that they all died with the disorder which marked her face, and which she was very near dieing with when a girl. from the age of this woman this Distructive disorder I judge must have been about 28 or 30 years past, and about the time the Clatsops inform us that this disorder raged in their towns and distroyed their nation.[46]

A year later, David Thompson wrote from Kootenay House in the Rocky Mountain Trench:

> these people the Kootenaes were once numerous, but being continually at war with Nations more powerful and far better armed than themselves, they diminished continually, 'till at length the Small Pox almost entirely rooted them out, leaving them only about 40 Families, and now they may count about 50 Families of 6 & 7 to a Family.[47]

On the lower Columbia three years later, he was asked: 'is it true that the white men ... have brought with them the Small Pox to destroy us ... is this true and are we all soon to die.'[48] Descending the Fraser River in 1808, Simon Fraser mentioned smallpox once: 'the small pox was in the camp [a Native village some 200 kilometres from the mouth of the Fraser River] and several natives were marked with it.'[49] Fur trader Ross Cox, who spent two months at the mouth of the Columbia River in 1814, said that the Natives remembered smallpox with 'a superstitious dread.'[50] John Work, a member of a Hudson's Bay Company (HBC) expedition sent from the Columbia in 1824 to explore the lower Fraser River, noted that an old chief near the mouth of the Fraser seemed to be marked with smallpox.[51] The next year, Scottish botanist John Scouler visited the Strait of Georgia in a HBC ship and saw an elderly, pockmarked Native in the retinue of Cowichan Chief Chapea at Point Roberts, just south of the Fraser's mouth. Scouler had seen no other direct evidence of smallpox on the Northwest Coast.

> The rarity of such an occurrence at once indicated the fatality of the disease and the dread they entertain of it. This epidemic broke out among them in 17__ and soon depopulated the eastern coast of America, and those on the Columbia were not secure behind the Rocky Mountains, and the ravages of the disease were only bounded by the Pacific Ocean. The Cheenooks to the present time speak of it with horror, and are exceedingly anxious to obtain that medicine which protects the whites, meaning vaccination. Such is the dread of this disease that when about to plunder the tribes of the interior, they have been deterred by the threat of disseminating smallpox among them.[52]

Three years later, the HBC established Fort Langley on the lower Fraser. In the fort journal (1827-30) and in the correspondence associated with the fort's early years, physical evidence of smallpox is not mentioned.[53]

Raiding

At the time of the Fort Langley journal, the peoples around Georgia Strait and Puget Sound lived in terror of raids from the Yaclewtas (Lequiltok), a Kwakwaka'wakw people from northern Vancouver Island. Armed with muskets obtained directly or indirectly from Nawitte, a centre of the maritime fur trade at the northern end of Vancouver Island, the Lequiltok killed or captured many Coast Salish people in the 1820s. The fact that the Vancouver journals mention fortified villages and beacons, possibly watchtowers, 'so frequently erected in the more southerly parts of New Georgia,' and that there is abundant archeological evidence of fortified, pre-contact sites around the Strait of Georgia implies that raiding had been common before 1792.[54] The many Native accounts of these raids are difficult to date, but in the Kwantlen story reported by Ellen Webber, a raid from the north was followed by smallpox, which in turn was followed by the coming of whites. Myron Eells, a missionary in Puget Sound, reported a story, which he probably heard sometime between 1875 and 1879, of a pitched and apparently pre-contact battle near Victoria between warriors from most of the Puget Sound tribes and 'the British Columbia Indians' (probably the Lequiltok). The British Columbia Indians won, and 'only a few of the defeated Indians ever lived to return; in some cases only three or four of a tribe.'[55] There can be little doubt that raiding was widespread in the region before 1792, with often drastic local effects. Whether raiding could lay waste to a region as large as the lands around Puget Sound and the Strait of Georgia, especially before 1792 when few if any raiders had firearms, is another matter.

Population Movements

Twentieth-century ethnographies of people such as the Clallam (Gunther), Twana (Elmendorf), and Lummi (Suttles) – all of whom occupied territories where the Vancouver expedition found many deserted villages – describe seasonal migrations.[56] Early in the spring, people left coastal winter villages in small groups to fish, dig clams, gather edible plants, and hunt along nearby coasts. The Lummi went to the eastern San Juan Islands to dig camas and clams, fish for spring salmon and halibut, and hunt; the Twana dispersed around the shores of Hood Canal. Some old people usually remained in the winter village where, through the spring and summer, groups returned intermittently and briefly to leave dried fish or roots. In late July, some eastern Clallam went to Hood Canal to take dog salmon. In September, most Lummi gathered at fishing weirs a short distance up the Nooksack River. Such seasonal rounds did not take most people far from their winter village or the coast. The Twana named the shores of Hood Canal in great detail and the interior very sparsely. To be sure, the ethnographies describe early-nineteenth-century practices that, it has been argued recently, were even more local in the 1790s.[57] In either case, almost everyone who wintered around Puget Sound and the Strait of Georgia would have been scattered in small groups along the coast fairly near their winter villages when the Vancouver expedition passed through.

John Scouler was the first to suggest that a failure to understand the Native seasonal round was 'the cause of the mistake into which the very accurate C.[aptain] Vancouver fell, concerning the apparent depopulation of the coast.'[58] Scouler himself thought, incorrectly, that Natives 'retreat to the interior of the country' from the end of September to the beginning of April, and then returned to the coast where, by Scouler's own logic, Vancouver should have found them. There is no evidence that Native seasonal rounds took people away in May and June from the coastlines that Vancouver and his officers explored and mapped.

Another possibility, however, is raised in the journals: that peoples from these inland waters had moved to the outer coast to trade directly with Europeans. If they had, there is no record of it in the ethnographies. Nor would peoples along or en route to the outer coast readily make room for intruding traders, much less for entire communities. The characteristic continental pattern of the fur trade is the opposite; groups well placed to trade directly with Europeans sought to monopolize such contacts by keeping others away.[59]

Native oral traditions and the texts of European explorers and traders provide different and largely independent records of late-eighteenth-century disease and depopulation around the Strait of Georgia. Besides their distinct cultural contexts, the two accounts are differently positioned in relation to the events they describe. The one grows out of the intimacy of experience and the shifting nature of oral tradition; the other out of the curiosity and ignorance of outsiders and the durability of writing. Yet the contents of one set of accounts seem to be broadly reproduced in the contents of the other. The two sets are mutually reinforcing and undoubtedly address the same horrendous event: late pre-contact depopulation around the Strait of Georgia and Puget Sound caused principally by smallpox.

This outbreak of smallpox was part of a pandemic that started in central Mexico in 1779 and quickly spread.[60] In 1780 and 1781, it devastated the Guatemalan Highlands; a decade later, it reached southern Chile, enabling the Spaniards to expand into an area they had been unable to conquer for 250 years.[61] Smallpox was in the New Mexican pueblos in 1780 and from there, transported indirectly by horse, diffused rapidly northward to affect all groups on the northern Plains. By early 1782, it reached the forest Cree north and west of Lake Manitoba.[62] From there it soon reached the Chipewyans. According to David Thompson, who was on the Plains a few years later, 'From the Chipeways it extended over all the Indians of the forest to its northward extremity and by the [Dakota] Sioux over all the Indians of the Plains and crossed the Rocky Mountains.'[63] The same epidemic affected groups around the Great Lakes. Thompson, who estimated that half to three-fifths of the peoples on the northern Plains died, talked with an Orcadian employee of the HBC who had witnessed the devastation: stinking tents in which all were dead, bodies eaten by wolves and dogs, 'survivors in such a state of despair and despondence that they could hardly converse with us.' 'The countries were in a manner depopulated.'[64] Twenty-three years later, when Lewis and Clark reached the middle Missouri, they found the 'fallen down earth of the houses,' and the scattered bones of men and animals in empty villages.[65]

An elderly man at Fort Cumberland on the North Saskatchewan River told Thompson that a war party of Nahathaway (Upper Churchill and Saskatchewan River Cree) Indians had contracted the disease from the Snake (Shoshone).[66] William Tomison, the trader at Cumberland House on the North Saskatchewan River, understood that the disease had reached the Shoshone from the Spaniards.[67] Certainly, smallpox was among the Shoshone in 1781. From a major rendezvous in southwestern Wyoming, the Shoshone traded with the Flathead, Nez Perce, Walla Walla, and various peoples along the Snake River.[68] Any of these trading connections could have brought smallpox to the lower Columbia. So could parties of Flatheads, Pend d'Oreille, Nez Perce, and others who crossed the Rockies to hunt and raid along the upper Missouri.[69] In 1840,

Asa Smith, a Congregational missionary, reported that smallpox had reached the Nez Perce sixty or seventy years earlier by this means, with 'very few surviving the attack of the disease.'[70] In 1829, HBC trader John Work reported 'a dreadful visitation of smallpox' on the Columbia Plateau near Fort Colvile that, he estimated, had occurred fifty or sixty years earlier. Jesuit missionary Gregory Mengarini reported smallpox among the Flathead at about the same time.[71]

It is clear, as Scouler reported in 1825, that smallpox reached the lower Columbia from the east. Ross Cox, on the Columbia a decade earlier, drew on the same body of common knowledge.

> The disease first proceeded from the banks of the Missouri. It travelled with destructive rapidity as far north as Athabasca and the slaves of Great Slave Lake, crossed the Rocky Mountains at the sources of the Missouri, and having fastened its deadly venom on the Snake Indians [Shoshone], spread its devastating course to the northward and westward, until its frightful progress was arrested by the Pacific Ocean.[72]

So, in the 1840s, did John Dunn, another fur trader. Smallpox, he said, 'had nearly dispeopled the whole of the northern continent of its native inhabitants.'[73] Breaking out 'between the sources of the Missouri and the Mississippi ... it spread its devastations northward as far as Athabasca, and the three horns of the Great Slave Lake; and westward across the Rocky Mountains to a short distance along the shores of the north Pacific ... Numbers of tribes were totally swept away; or reduced to a few scattered and powerless individuals. The remnants of many others united; and formed a new and heterogeneous union.'[74]

As James Mooney suggested years ago, diffusion from this direction probably dates smallpox's arrival along the lower Columbia to 1782.[75] From the lower Columbia, the disease spread north, probably via the Cowlitz and lower Chehalis rivers, to Puget Sound; in 1782-3, it struck most if not all the peoples around Puget Sound and Georgia Strait.[76] The epidemic extended as far north as Nitinat on the west coast of Vancouver Island, to perhaps Cape Mudge on the east coast of Vancouver Island, and up the Fraser River well into the canyon (Figure 1.2).[77] It may have stopped because it struck in winter; devastated populations may no longer have been infectious when mobility increased in the spring. The mortality rate will never be known, but given evidence from the Plains that this was hemorrhagic smallpox, and the dense, previously unaffected populations it encountered on the West Coast, Old Pierre's estimate of three-quarters may well be conservative.[78]

In my view, and contrary to Robert Boyd,[79] who has recently and usefully reopened the study of epidemics on the Northwest Coast, there was

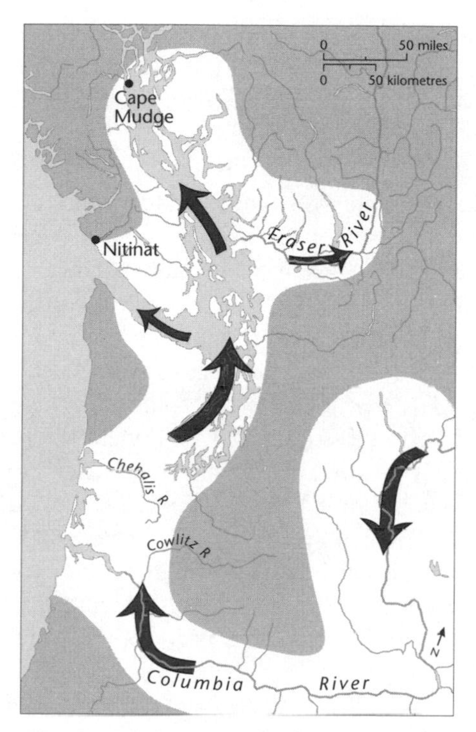

Figure 1.2 Approximate distribution of smallpox, 1782

not a second smallpox epidemic in Puget Sound and around the Strait of Georgia in 1801. Boyd's evidence for a second epidemic about 1801 – Elmendorf's informants, Old Pierre, Fraser's report – is consistent with a single epidemic in 1782. Moreover, visible evidence of smallpox was rare by the mid-1820s. Ross Cox, at Fort George in 1812 and for several years thereafter, reported that those bearing traces of smallpox were 'nearly extinct.'[80] John Scouler saw only one such face during a year on the lower Columbia and the Northwest Coast in the 1820s; John Work saw one pockmarked face on the Fraser River in 1824.[81] HBC traders, who usually reported evidence of smallpox, did not mention smallpox in the Fort Langley journal (1827-30) or in fort correspondence because they saw no trace of it; this suggests a particularly high mortality rate in 1782 among affected children, or that the peoples who came to trade and fish along the lower Fraser had not brought the elderly with them. Had there been a smallpox epidemic in 1801, evidence would still have been abundantly at hand in the 1820s, and would have been reported.

In a sense, however, Boyd is right about the limited coastal range of 'the epidemic of 1801,' though his map approximately describes the epidemic of 1782. Smallpox had appeared among the Tlingit in the 1770s, but, as pointed out below, there is no evidence that there was a coastwide epidemic in 1775. There certainly was in 1862, but this time government officials and missionaries had vaccinated most of the Coast Salish, few of whom died.[82]

It might now appear possible to estimate the regional population just prior to smallpox, especially as Archibald McDonald, chief trader at Fort Langley, compiled a census of the peoples around Puget Sound and the Strait of Georgia in 1830.[83] Positing a sexually balanced population and a normal age distribution after 1782, no ecological constraints on population growth, and cultural pressure to build up the population (therefore, high birth rates), it would seem possible to work back from 1830 to an estimate of the population just after the epidemic. This figure multiplied by the rate of population loss in 1782 would yield the pre-epidemic population. However, it is not known whether other European diseases reached the region soon after 1782 (gonorrhea came with the traders to Fort Langley in 1827, but may already have reached the area). It is not known whether raiding was a major demographic factor, though in this period there is reason to think it was. The mortality rates for 1782 are only estimates. The census of 1830 is very approximate. And so on. No solid ground exists anywhere.

Other approaches to estimating pre-contact populations are not more promising.[84] It hardly seems possible, in this region of great ecological variety, general abundance, and occasional dearth, to usefully estimate the ecological carrying capacity for peoples of late-eighteenth-century Coast Salishan technology. Perhaps it can only be said that, given a mild, humid climate, the resources of river and sea, and the capacity of migrating salmon to transfer a portion of the food chain of the whole north Pacific Ocean to local fishing sites, there was more non-agricultural food on the Northwest Coast than anywhere else on the continent, and perhaps more in and around the lower Fraser River than elsewhere on the Northwest Coast. Nor, given the methodological problems of inferring population density from archeological evidence, can archeology readily provide reliable estimates.[85] If the diseases that shortly followed smallpox were known (they are not), medical predictions of rates of infection and mortality could be made. The rate of population decline around the Strait of Georgia inferred from the nineteenth-century censuses (1830, 1839, 1852, 1876, 1877, 1881) could be projected back to 1780, but this takes no account of the disastrous first effects of European infectious diseases. In short, none of these approaches suggests a calculation or a research strategy that might be expected to yield a fairly reliable estimate of the pre-smallpox population around the Strait of Georgia.

I return, therefore, to opinions from the past. Captain Vancouver and his officers thought the region was depopulated. Thirty-five years later,

HBC traders at Fort Langley were amazed at the numbers of people about. Canoes passed up and down river 'by Hundreds,' or 'in great numbers.'[86] In 1828, 550 canoes of Cowichan and 200 of Squamish came down from the Fraser Canyon. A three-quarter-mile-long Cowichan fishing village sat on the south bank of Lulu Island,[87] and a Nanaimo village, only somewhat smaller, was a few miles below the fort. Often, from the trader's perspective, 'a great many Indians' were hanging around.[88] Archibald McDonald, chief trader at Fort Langley, noted 'The Indian population in this part of the world is very great.'[89]

The census he submitted in 1830 reported Native men around the Strait of Georgia, Puget Sound, and along the lower Fraser River. It had been made 'by repeated examination of the Indians themselves,' and particularly, for Fraser populations, of Sopitchin, a chief from a village at the foot of the Fraser Canyon. McDonald was surprised at the high figures in the canyon. But as he had seen many people there in 1828, when descending the river with Governor Simpson, and as he knew Sopitchin's estimates for the lower Fraser to be reliable, he was inclined to accept them. This census, combined with the 1835 census of the Kwakwa̲ka̲'wakw by HBC trader W.F. Tolmie, yields a map – the indirect product of two HBC traders and several Native chiefs – of the distribution of population from the foot of Puget Sound to the northeastern end of Vancouver Island in the 1830s (Figure 1.3).[90]

Although the map omits some peoples altogether, its general patterns are clear. There were dense populations in the Fraser Canyon and in parts of Queen Charlotte Sound. Elsewhere, the numbers were modest. Along the lower Fraser River, a rich source of food, there were few winter residents.[91] Most of the peoples the traders commented on came to the river seasonally from around the strait. Around Puget Sound, the region that had so charmed Vancouver and his officers and in which there was such a quantity and diversity of accessible foods, the population was less than 2,500, well above Menzies' and Puget's estimates of 1,000, but still small in so favoured an area.[92] The map is what, in hindsight, it could only be: an approximate picture of populations that had recovered somewhat from a devastating smallpox epidemic fifty years before. Estimates of population density are relative. For HBC traders accustomed to sparse boreal populations, there were a lot of people around; for those who knew what the population had been, there were few.

In the Native memory, there was a time when the land was densely settled. Even before the flood, according to Old Pierre, 'Families settled on the mountains, on the plains, and on the sea-shore, wherever they could find food, for the land was overcrowded.' After recovering from the flood, the people were again 'too numerous on the land.'[93] According to Bob Joe, a Stó:lō, the population in the Chilliwack area was

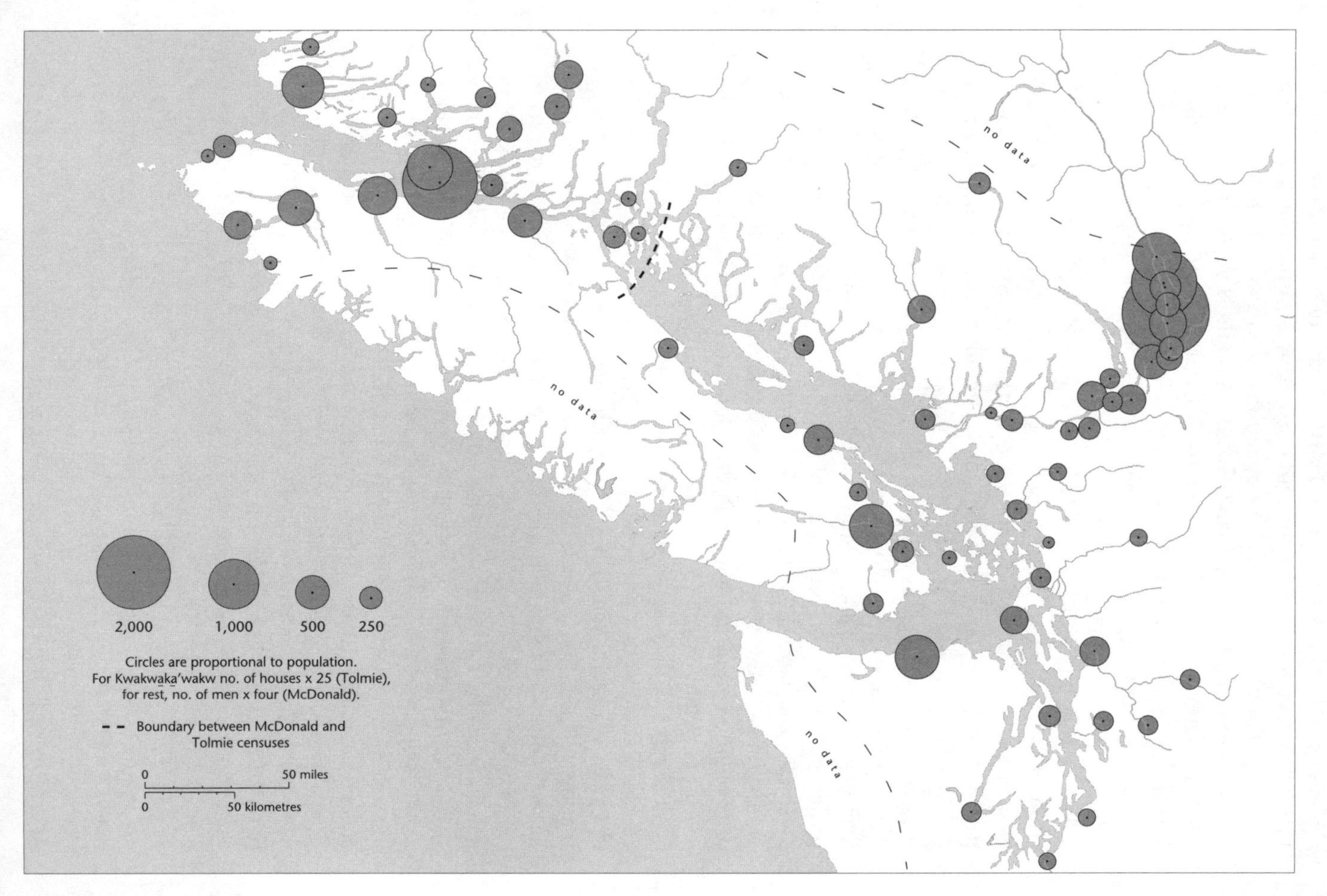

Figure 1.3 Population around the Strait of Georgia and extensions in the 1830s (after HBC censuses)

formerly 'a thousand to one, comparing the population today.'[94] Agnes Kelly said there had been 'thousands' of people nearby at Agassiz.[95] More substantial is an inventory of former Stó:lō and Southern Thompson villages from which a map of winter villages from Koia'um in the north (where Fraser saw evidence of smallpox in 1808) to just below the modern city of Chilliwack can be prepared (Figure 1.4).[96] The data in the inventory are largely from ethnographic sources, collected over the years and supplemented by archeological site surveys. Although the map has been prepared cautiously, it is uncertain whether all village sites were occupied each winter; if they were not, then the map probably exaggerates the density of late-eighteenth-century winter settlement along this stretch of the Fraser River.

Yet the village map is intriguing, especially when considered in relation to data from the 1830 census (Figure 1.5). The distribution of population in 1830 does not correspond to the earlier distribution of villages. The Chilliwack River, along which, apparently, there had been some twenty-five villages, was largely deserted in 1830. Calculations are tempting. If the average population of a village was 150 people, then before the smallpox epidemic at least 15,000 people inhabited the area shown on Figure 1.4. There are obvious ambiguities, but it seems clear that this section of the Fraser River once supported far more people than indicated in the census of 1830, or than white settlers and ethnographers have supposed.

The demographic outlines of the fifty years after 1780 around the Strait of Georgia and Puget Sound are, I think, fairly clear. A large, dense, and probably demographically quite unstable population was devastated by smallpox in the winter of 1781-2 or 1782-3.[97] The great majority of the people died. Although recovery was retarded by Lequiltok raiding and, perhaps, by other European diseases, the regional population had risen substantially by 1830, but not nearly to its pre-smallpox level.

Depopulation created vacuums that drew in surrounding people. Groups, for example, that had been unable to live on the Fraser River could now do so. The evidence is unclear, but some surviving Katzie may have moved out of the Pitt River to settle on the Fraser; surviving upriver Chilliwack may have moved down to the rich sloughs on the Fraser floodplain.[98] It is quite possible – there is no evidence one way or another – that space opened on the lower Fraser at this time for the Cowichan and Nanaimo fishing villages reported in the 1820s. The people in Mud Bay, just south of the Fraser, were wiped out, and the Semiahmoo moved northward, occupying this territory. Similar relocations occurred on the San Juan Islands and on the south coast of Vancouver Island.[99] More generally, depopulation contributed to inter-regional political instability as the depleted Coast Salish became more vulnerable to Lequiltok raiding.[100] In the longer run, the Coast Salish,

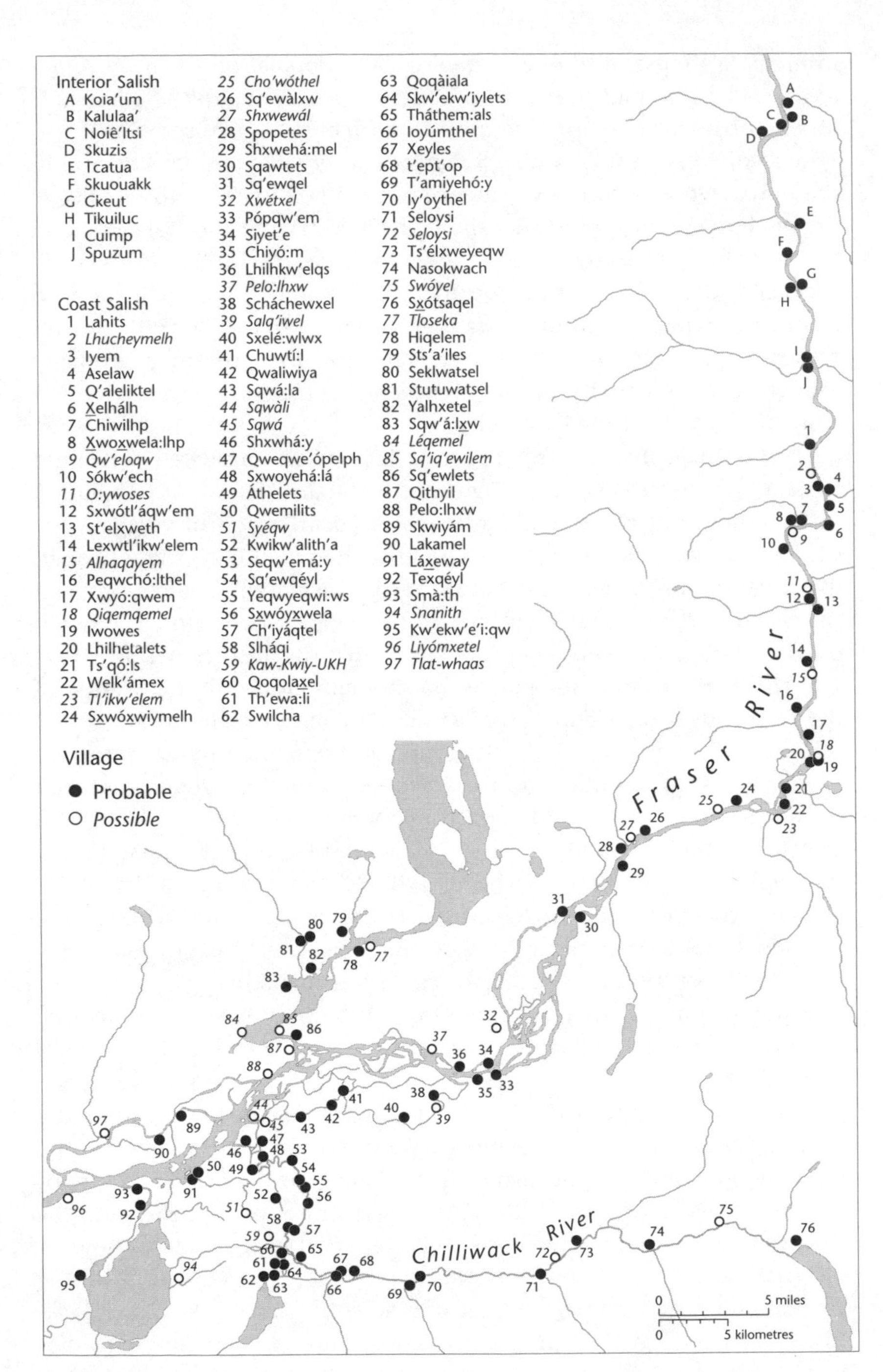

Figure 1.4 Winter villages along the Fraser River, mid-late eighteenth century

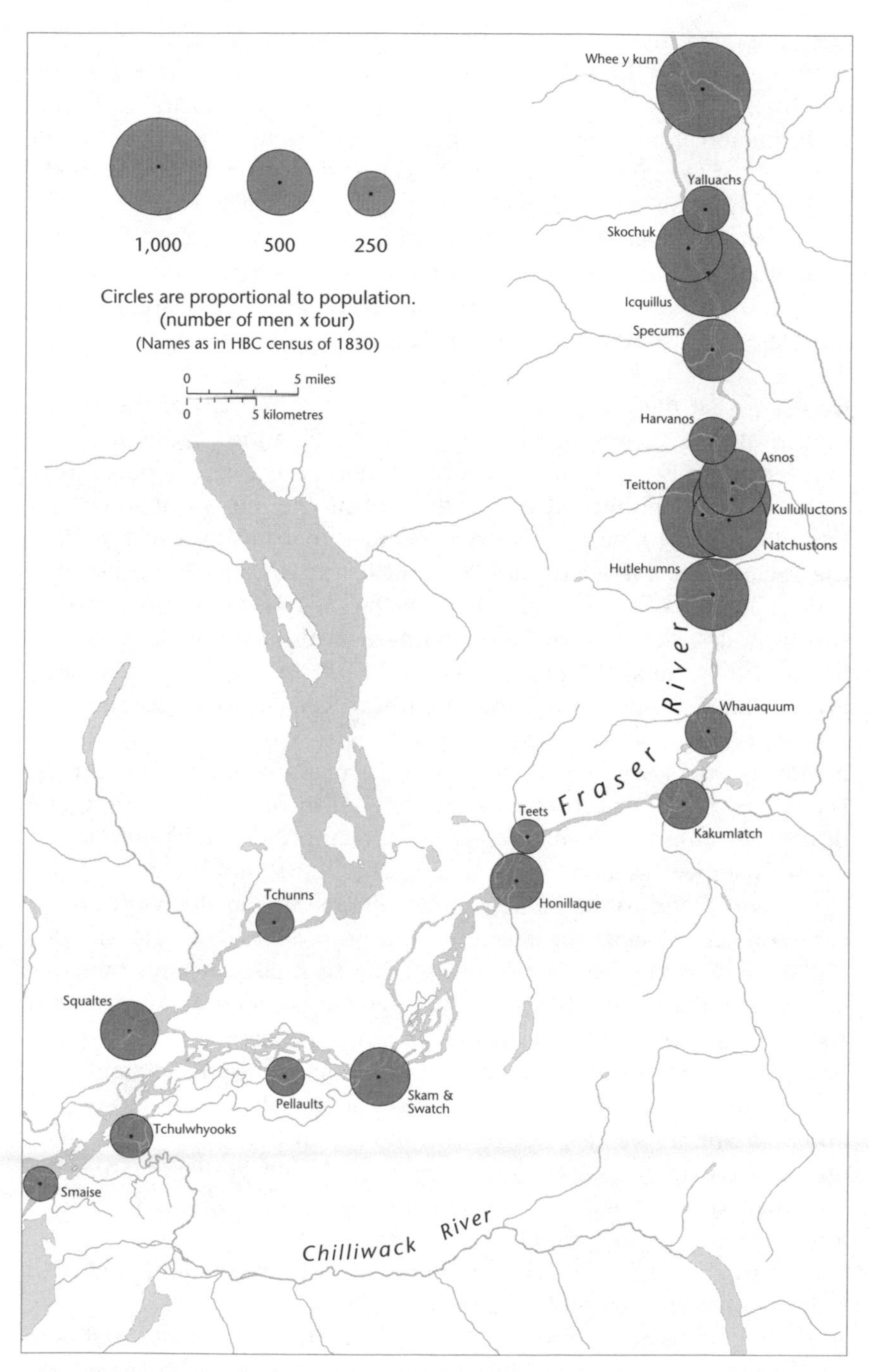

Figure 1.5 Smaise to Whee y kum, 1830 (after HBC census)

once the most numerous people on the Northwest Coast, became relatively invisible in their own territory. Other peoples came to exemplify Northwest Coast culture both to the outside world and to the newcomers in the towns and countrysides that emerged around Puget Sound and the Strait of Georgia. The relative neglect of the Coast Salish has partly to do with urbanization patterns; the particular secrecy with which the Coast Salish treated their stories, songs, and ceremonies; and the influence of Franz Boas. But it has also to do with early, profound depopulation. As the Swinomish chief Martin Sampson put it, the whites encountered 'a people trying to recover from a devastating blow.'[101]

How is it that the smallpox epidemic of 1782 is not part of the lore of modern British Columbia, especially as it was identified, quite precisely, more than eighty years ago? In a short piece on the Native population of North America published in the *Bulletin* of the Bureau of American Ethnology in 1910, James Mooney concluded that smallpox had reached the Pacific from the Plains in 1782; and in his considerably elaborated survey, published posthumously in 1928, he suggested that this epidemic was 'very destructive throughout southern British Columbia.'[102] Yet as late as 1964, the anthropologist Wilson Duff, in *The Indian History of British Columbia*, used HBC and Dominion censuses to calculate that 70,000 people lived in what is now British Columbia in 1835.[103] Although Duff knew that there had been smallpox among the Tlingit, Haida, and Coast Tsimshian, and suspected it in the south, his estimate of the pre-contact population of British Columbia – 'at least 80,000 and probably somewhat more' – largely discounted smallpox as a demographic influence. Most earlier ethnographers ignored the possibility of pre- or early-contact epidemics of infectious European diseases; as late as 1965, Philip Drucker thought 'the first devastating smallpox epidemic probably occurred in the middle 1830s.'[104] Among contemporary scholars, Robin Fisher doubts much of the evidence for early smallpox.[105] James Gibson has spelled out the archival case for smallpox among the Tlingit and adjacent peoples in 1835-8,[106] and, as noted above, Robert Boyd has argued an important, if jumbled, case for smallpox epidemics in 1775 and 1801. Overall, academic scholarship has approached with great hesitation the idea that Native societies were decimated by disease just before or soon after Europeans arrived on the Northwest Coast.

But why this hesitation? The question has wide ramifications, and I can only sketch components of an answer.

It is important to recognize that the early-contact Northwest Coast does not have a common epidemiological history, unlike the Plains where, with the advent of the horse, diseases could be carried quickly over great distances. On the coast, people lived geographically circumscribed lives, travelling to local or regional resource procurement and trading sites, but not, until the establishment of Fort Victoria, drawn into contact with most other coastal peoples. When smallpox broke out in Victoria in 1862 and nervous officials sent Natives home, a mechanism was at hand as never before for the diffusion of smallpox throughout the length and breadth of the Northwest Coast. Smallpox had broken out among the Tlingit in the 1770s, and had reached the lower Columbia from the east in 1782, but the two outbreaks were unconnected. Cook saw no signs of smallpox at Nootka in 1778, nor did the Spaniards in 1789-92. Nor did the maritime fur traders. Smallpox was neither there nor, from the evidence, anywhere else on the west coast of Vancouver Island north of Nitinat in the late eighteenth century.[107] Nor had it reached the northeast coast of the island. In 1841, Governor Simpson, travelling through Johnstone Strait in the HBC steamer the *Beaver*, found that the Quakeolths (Kwagulths, Kwakwa̱ka̱'wakw) 'had been exempted from the smallpox,' a conclusion supported by the Vancouver journals and by Robert Galois's recent study of Kwakwa̱ka̱'wakw settlement.[108]

To grossly simplify the geography of early-contact disease, there were, at least, three broad, epidemiological regions along the Northwest Coast: the Alaskan panhandle and north coastal British Columbia; the west coast of Vancouver Island and around Queen Charlotte Sound and Johnstone Strait; and the Strait of Georgia to the Columbia River. If a common coastal pattern is assumed, then argument about different findings in different locations obscures both the complex geography of depopulation and particular demographic disasters, such as the smallpox epidemic of 1782-3. Eventually, 100 years or more after contact, the demographic effects of introduced diseases among different populations may everywhere have been much the same – those who missed smallpox in 1782 succumbing, they or their progeny, to later European introductions – but, if this were so, there were many different local histories of depopulation.

Until the last generation, estimates of particular pre-contact populations, and therefore of particular epidemics and depopulations, have been approached within the widely held assumption that the contact population of North America (north of the Rio Grande) was about one million. Mooney divided his 1910 estimate of 1,150,000 people as follows: United States: 846,000, Canada: 220,000, Alaska: 72,000, Greenland: 10,000.[109] In his more elaborated estimates, he 'conservatively' estimated the pre-contact population of British Columbia at 86,000.[110] There were no other careful continental estimates. The influential Berkeley anthropologist, Alfred Kroeber, writing in 1939, thought that 'until a new, equally systematic survey has been done, Mooney's figures should be accepted in toto,' though in Kroeber's view they were 'too high rather than too low' and would probably 'shrink to around 900,000, possibly somewhat farther.' Moreover, for Kroeber 'the outstanding fact [about Mooney's figures] is the exceptional density on the Pacific coast.'[111] This powerful orthodoxy survived well into the 1960s and beyond. Therefore, if early censuses pointed to a Native population in British Columbia in the 1830s of about 70,000 (and if this was an 'exceptional density' in a country with a contact population of 220,000), precontact totals could not have been much higher. Such was the box in which Wilson Duff and Philip Drucker found themselves. Given Mooney's, then Kroeber's, assumptions about Canadian and continental populations, there was not much demographic space for contact diseases on the Northwest Coast.

Nor, in a sense, was there ethnographic space. Salvage ethnography in the style of Franz Boas assumed traditional Native cultures yielding to modern Western cultures without much of interest between. Therefore, ethnographers in quest of the former sought out elderly people with good memories, and wrote down as much of what they were told as possible, capturing, they believed, vanishing traditional ways. When field notes were worked up into books, an academic datum plane was created: traditional Northwest Coast culture. If the ethnographers asked their questions at the end of the nineteenth or early in the twentieth century, as many of them did, their informants remembered and described early- to mid-nineteenth-century societies. This was the slice of time that ethnography transformed into timeless traditional culture.

Smallpox and other contact diseases posed two basic challenges to such procedures. First, they raised the possibility that informants' memories did not quite reach the traditional world. If smallpox and other diseases had disrupted societies before the most elderly informants remembered them, then traditional societies were simply out of ethnographic range. Ethnographic notebooks contained information about societies that were already somewhat transformed. Second, and even more telling, the concept of pre- or early-contact epidemics introduced the idea of time and began, however crudely, to situate Native people historically. Native societies before and after a devastating smallpox epidemic could not, presumably, be quite the same. In short, the farther back in time epidemics were pushed, along with the concept of change associated with them, the more the epidemics interfered with the idea of traditional culture, and the more impetus they gave to the idea of history. At the very least, the Eurocentrism inherent in the assumption that Native cultures were static would give way to another Eurocentrism: that Native history began with a devastating European introduction. Beyond this was another assumption: that Native societies changed like any others, and generated multiple histories in which epidemics were embedded; yet the ethnographers' view of Native culture was far more static, and deflected them from any serious consideration of pre- and early-contact epidemics along the Northwest Coast.

More generally, the idea of disease-induced depopulation runs counter to the long-held conviction that Europeans brought enlightenment and civilization to savage peoples.[112] It turns the story of the contact process away from the rhetorics of progress and salvation and towards the numbing recognition of catastrophe. Progress wrestled from the wilderness by hard, manly work and registered by expanding settlements and populations is suddenly qualified by population losses. The rhetoric of development begins to pale. The Western idea of property, coupled with an expanding world economy, appears as an agent of destruction as much as of creation. A linear view of progress fails. It becomes harder to believe that European goods and a European God had rescued Native peoples from want and ignorance. Ideologies and values that trans-Atlantic expansion had so powerfully reinforced lose authority. The whole European engagement with a New World, which was not new after all, begins to appear in a different light.

These sober thoughts were not what modern British Columbians or other recent North Americans, proud of their achievements and intent on their futures, wanted to hear. It was far more convenient to think that the Native population had always been small, and that those who remained would soon die off. In the late nineteenth and early twentieth centuries, as railways were built, speculations proliferated, boosterism filled the air, and Native populations dwindled, there was ample ground to think that both were true. By this time, most Natives lived on reserves as wards of the state, segregated from the mainstream of white society. To all intents and purposes they had become invisible, and their pasts, reduced to curious fragments in museums, were even more so. An immigrant, racist white society was not interested in such pasts, scholarship was blinkered, and only a few elderly Natives told stories that were easily construed as myths.

Now, some of the constraints are lifting. Hemispheric and continental pre-Columbian population estimates are far higher than in Mooney's or Kroeber's day; in this light, there is now room to consider that there may have been many more people in British Columbia than what seemed possible only a few years ago. Native peoples have not died out, and the continuing vitality of Native societies, coupled with their growing political and academic influence, has considerably undermined the salvage ethnographers' bipolar model of culture. The broad critique of meta-theory, positivist science, and one-point perspective, sustained over the last generation, has encouraged scholarship to articulate the long-hidden or suppressed accounts of relatively powerless people: women, ethnic minorities, peasants, refugees, as well as Natives.[113] In addition, archival sources are more accessible. For all these reasons, it is easier now than it was even a short generation ago to discern infectious diseases in early-contact British Columbia.

The picture that emerges is hardly surprising. Native people in the province were not spared what Natives in the rest of the continent and hemisphere experienced. In the century or so after the first arrival of European infectious diseases, Native populations throughout the Western Hemisphere commonly declined by some 90 per cent. In all probability, that was the magnitude of population decline in British Columbia. If so, then the population of the province on the eve of the first epidemics was well over 200,000 people, of whom more than 50,000 lived around the Strait of Georgia and up the Fraser River to the limit of Coast Salish territory.[114] If population decline was in the order of 95 per cent, then these figures are doubled.

In southern British Columbia, the process of disease-related depopulation probably began with the smallpox epidemic of 1782.[115] Eventually, in recurring epidemics over approximately a century, smallpox visited all Native groups in the province, some several times. However, smallpox was only the most spectacular of a complex of European infectious diseases that together were far more devastating than any one of them. The eventual result, everywhere, was severe depopulation at precisely the time that changing technologies of transportation and communication brought more and more of the resources of the northwestern corner of North America within reach of the capitalist world economy. Here was an almost empty land, so it seemed, for the taking, and the means of marketing many of its resources. Such was the underlying geographical basis of the bonanza that awaited immigrants to British Columbia.

Passing through the province by train just before World War I, Rupert Brooke, a poet as English as the ancient village of Grantchester where he lived, missed the dead and 'the friendly presence of ghosts.' Mountain breezes, he said, 'have nothing to remember and everything to promise.' This was a stranger's conceit. Jimmy Peters, who poked as a lad in the graves of his ancestors, knew otherwise. So did Charles Hill-Tout, who listened to Mulks, the old Squamish historian, and the Scowlitz elders who believed 'their race is doomed to die out and disappear.' Brooke was travelling through a profound settlement discontinuity, measured not, as it would have been in Europe, by decaying cities, wasted fields, and overgrown orchards, but by the abandonment of countless seasonal settlement sites, the unnaming and renaming of the land, and the belief of some that their world was coming to an end, and of others that it was opening towards a prosperous future.

2
Strategies of Power in the Cordilleran Fur Trade

On 23 June 1790, Don Manuel Quimper, ensign of the Royal Armada, landed near Sooke on Vancouver Island, planted a large wooden cross, and took possession of the coast 'in the name of His Catholic Majesty Carlos IV.' He buried documents of possession, fired a twenty-one gun salute, and left.[1] When he returned a few weeks later, Native people had removed the cross; his crew made another that Quimper hoped would be more secure, this time by topping and limbing a small 'pine' and nailing on a cross beam. Two years later in Puget Sound, Captain George Vancouver, following the 'usual formalities,' took possession of the coast 'from that part of New Albion, in the latitude of 39 20' north, and longitude 236 26' east,' to the Strait of Juan De Fuca, 'in the name of His Present Majesty and for his heirs and successors.'[2] Twenty years later, in 1813, the captain of the British sloop *Racoon* arrived at Fort Astoria on the Columbia River, ran up a British flag at the fort, broke a bottle of Madeira on the flagpole, and in a loud voice 'took possession of the establishment and the country in the name of His Britannic Majesty and named it Fort George.'[3]

On the other hand, consider this: Arriving overland in September, 1828, at Fort St. James in north central British Columbia from York Factory on Hudson Bay, George Simpson, Governor of the Hudson's Bay Company (HBC) in North America, and his party contrived to enter the fort 'in the most imposing manner we could for the sake of the Indians.' When within hearing of the fort, a gun was fired, a bugle sounded, and a piper began 'the celebrated march of the clans – *'Si coma leum cogadh na shea'* (Peace; or war, if you will otherwise).' The guide led the party, carrying the British flag; then the bugler and piper; then, mounted, the governor followed by two traders riding abreast; then twenty men in a line on foot with their loads; then a loaded horse; and, finally, another trader. As the party neared the fort, it was welcomed by 'a brisk discharge of small arms and wall pieces.' Three days later, James Douglas, the trader in

Astoria (Fort George) in 1813, as illustrated in Gabriel Franchère, *Narrative of a Voyage to the Northwest Coast of America, 1811-1814*. The fort was soon enlarged, but its defensive aspect remained unchanged.

charge at the fort, sent for the principal Indians 'and introduced [them] to the Governor described as the Great Chief.' As there had been killings of HBC personnel and reprisals in the area,

> the Governor could not do less than deprecate such proceedings. He represented to them how helpless their condition would be at this moment were he and all his people to enter into hostilities against them. That a partial example had already been made of the guilty parties, but that the next time the Whites should be compelled to imbrue their hands in the blood of Indians, it would be a general sweep; that the innocent would go with the guilty, and that their fate would become deplorable indeed. The war on the sea coast this season was also represented to them in the most formidable light – and that it was hard to say when we would stop; never, in any case, until the Indians gave the most unqualified proof of their good conduct in the future ... At the close of the harangue, the chief had a glass of rum, a little tobacco, and a shake of the hand from the Great Chief, after which the piper played then the song of peace. They dispersed, to appearances quite sensible of all that was said to them.[4]

Here were two strategies of white power in the Cordillera: one by representatives of the Crown, a discourse of sovereign power; the other by a business manager of a trading company, a discourse of the fur trade.[5] The former claimed possession of the land in the name of a distant sovereign, intending to incorporate territories and their peoples in the imperial reach of the state. The latter, making no territorial claims or reference to external authority, was about 'good conduct' and the means of achieving it. Its message was simple and direct: either Natives would give the most unqualified proof of their 'good conduct' (i.e., would neither attack whites nor steal their property), or swift, drastic retaliation would follow. The 'war on the sea coast' in which, in retaliation for the killing of a HBC clerk and four men, the company ship razed two villages in the Strait of Juan de Fuca and killed more than twenty people,[6] was a pale indication of the revenge whites could and would mete out. Accompanying this threat was the decorum of the fur trade: a little tobacco, a little rum, a handshake from the Great Chief.

The older and, in the long run, more enduring of these discourses was about sovereign power. But between the formal acts of possession that states were not yet able to enforce and the establishment of British colonies or American territories was approximately half a century in which fur trading companies represented European power in the northern Cordillera. Traders would obey the orders of their governments,[7] but in most of the northern Cordillera throughout most of the first half of the nineteenth century, the state was absent, held off by sheer physical isolation and unresolved territorial claims. Formal acts of possession had not been conclusive. Russian and Spanish interests had pulled back, but conflicting British and American claims remained. In 1818, Anglo-American diplomacy created 'Oregon Territory,' its sovereignty still to be negotiated, its lands still open to traders of either nationality, between the southern limit of Russian America (54°40′ N) and the northern limit of Spanish Mexico (42° N); the convention was extended in 1827 after negotiations failed to produce a border agreement. Oregon Territory was a bilateral free-trade zone, not a colony. The geopolitical arguments over territory were not settled until 1846. On the mainland north of the 49th parallel, the fur trade held until the gold rush to Fraser River and the creation of the colony of British Columbia in 1858.

For approximately fifty years, therefore, the land-based fur trade in the northern Cordillera operated beyond the protective reach of the state. An army was not at hand. The law of the state, available in principle, was absent in fact. An act of 1803 stipulating that offenses in Indian territories were to be 'tried in the same manner and subject to the same Punishments, as if the same had been committed within the provinces of Lower and Upper Canada'[8] and extended west of the Rockies after the merger of the Hudson's Bay and North West companies in 1821, was not enforceable. The British government advised the HBC governor in London that company officers should continue 'to preserve the Peace and good Government of that part of North America under the Jurisdiction of the Hudson's Bay Company.' In effect, without courts and justices, the HBC operated beyond British legal practice, subject only to the constraint of possible parliamentary investigation. Moreover, the fur trade had entered a territory in which the intricate geographical configuration of settled European society was absent. There were no towns, no countrysides, no roads, and no people whose lives were enmeshed in these geographies and in the power relations that flowed through them. Instead, there were other peoples inhabiting otherwise organized lands. By the time the fur trade reached the Cordillera, it had some 150 years of North American experience with such strangeness. Coping strategies had been worked out, and an elaborate, considerably taken-for-granted discourse of the fur trade – of which Simpson's performance at Fort St. James was a part – was in place. This was a discourse of commercial capital, its object profit, tied to the particular exigencies of a trade that operated among Native peoples and across huge, unfamiliar distances.

The discourse of commercial capitalism turned around management, order, and property. As much as possible, it avoided irregularity and uncertainty, and encouraged system. It tended to regulate time, and to commodify nature and work. It valued hard work, thrift, and steady reliability. Such were the best ways to control complex transactions in uncertain markets. And so Governor Simpson sought out and promoted men of 'system and regularity,' efficient managers, as he was himself, of a commercial empire. Such men managed the fur trade in the northern Cordillera. To manage the trade, they had to manage their employees and, to a degree, the Native peoples among whom they lived and on whose trade goods and labour they relied. They had to do this in territory beyond the reach of the state, unstructured by prior conventions of European power, and peopled by those an increasingly global European experience categorized as savages, the alter-ego of civilized Europeans.[9] Essentially, the traders had a huge problem of geographical organization on their hands: how to reconfigure an alien territory and discipline its peoples so that an ordered, profitable trade was possible therein. The discourse of the fur trade addressed this problem and, in so doing, created a proto-colonial presence in the Cordillera.[10]

The first problem for European fur traders in the northern Cordillera was to create familiar, safe spaces for themselves. To do so, they had to Europeanize and defend patches of land and, as almost from the beginning of the North American fur trade, they did so by establishing forts. Usually palisaded, the forts were islands of relative security amid unfamiliar, potentially hostile people inhabiting territories that Europeans did not control. They were also nodal points in circuits of trade and communication (Figure 2.1). Interior posts were connected to each other and to the outside world by canoes, river and lake boats of various sorts, and pack horses, and to coastal posts by ship and, in some places, boats and canoes. Such carriers moved furs, European trade goods, supplies, despatches, accounts, letters, books, and gossip. Forts connected by such circuitry were a minimal but sufficient human geography for the land-based fur trade, enough to enable it to operate in the Cordillera.

When traders in the Cordillera did not build palisaded, well-defended forts, they took risks. In 1814, for example, two undefended posts at either end of the Northwest Company's far western operations – one on the upper Liard, one probably on the Snake – were overrun.[11] Initially unfortified posts like Fort Okanagan and Nisqually (Figure 2.2) were soon well defended.[12] A characteristic fort in the Cordillera contained approximately the following defensive equipment: A rectangular palisade of cedar, fir, or pine logs, usually squared on two surfaces (to fit tightly), planted four feet in the ground, standing fifteen to eighteen feet above it, and pegged to cross-pieces four feet from the top. A gallery six to seven feet wide on the inside of the palisades, four and a half feet below the top, and running the length of the front and back walls (in some cases, all four walls), from which men could fire through loopholes. Two bastions at opposite corners of the rectangle, usually square two-storey structures measuring twelve to

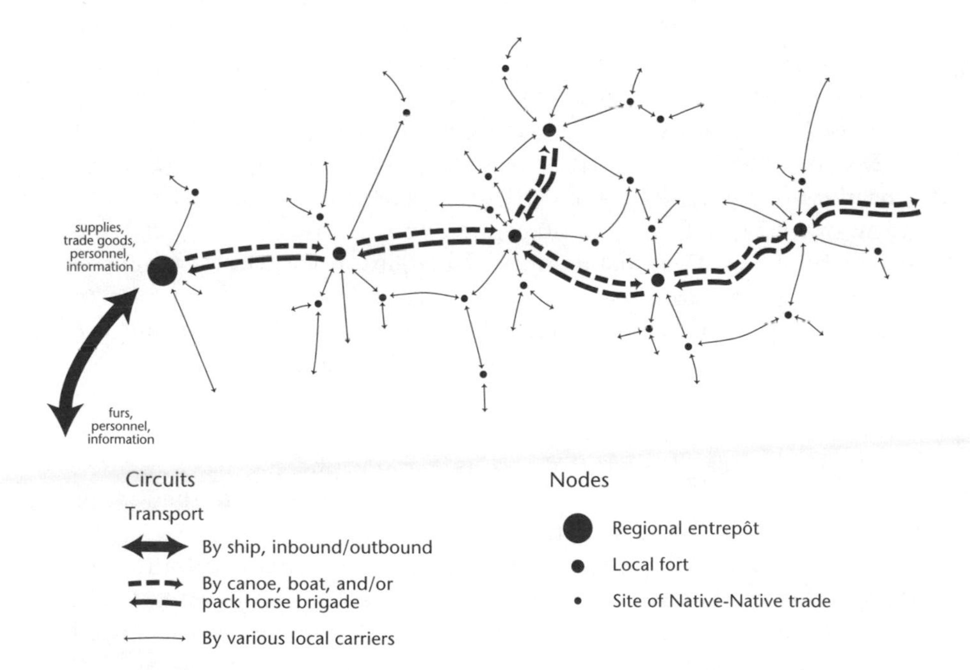

Figure 2.1 Diagram of fur trade circuits

fifteen feet per side, each outfitted with at least four cannon, two aimed along the walls and two aimed outwards. Massive paired gates, front and back, eight to ten inches thick and ten feet wide, made of layers of planks bolted and studded with nails, within which were small doors that admitted one person at a time. A considerable armament: cannon of from one to, in some forts, twelve or more pounds, and variously including carronades (short, large-calibred cannon) intended to fire round shot and grape, to inflict broad damage at close range; and culverins (long, narrow-bored cannon) intended for longer range accuracy; blunderbusses (short, large-bored guns also for firing round shot and grape) mounted on swivels at points along the palisades; stands of muskets, bayonets, and ammunition in the bastions, ready for use; and, in some forts, boarding pikes and grenades. A low, thick-walled powder house was usually close to the Big House, the residence of the officer in charge. There was always a sentry at the main gate, which was always locked by the officer in charge at 9:00 P.M., always a watch on the galleries at night to make rounds of the buildings and call 'All's well' every half hour.[13] With any suggestion of trouble, men slept in the bastions. Figure 2.3, a plan of Fort George (formerly Fort Astoria) in 1818, is fairly characteristic.

Confident that, with normal precautions, they could hold such forts, traders and their men felt safe within them. The construction of a small palisade was the work of about a month; along the coast, such work usually took place under the protection of a ship's guns. When the palisade was up, bastions built, and armament in place, traders had secured a space. Three years after the building of Fort Langley, the chief trader could consider a 'war of extermination'[14] against a large Native village nearby because he was confident that a few men could hold the fort against a general uprising of numerous, 'brutally disposed' Natives.[15] On the other hand, a fire that destroyed a building at Fort George reminded traders of their vulnerability; the whole fort could easily have gone up, in which case 'we should have been left at the mercy of barbarous Indians, without the means of helping ourselves.'[16] The commander of the British sloop *Racoon* scoffed at Fort Astoria in 1813; he could 'batter it down in two hours with a four pounder.'[17] 'The place was not fit to resist anything but savages'[18] – but that was its purpose, and for that purpose it served. Under the protection of such forts, traders established farms where soils and climate permitted.

Inside the palisades, the number and arrangement of buildings, depending on the size of the fort, was approximately as shown in Figure 2.3. The arrangement was ordered and somewhat military, with an open central space (parade square, mustering ground), and a Big House overlooking the establishment from, if possible, higher ground at the back. Buildings were of timber-frame construction infilled with squared logs,

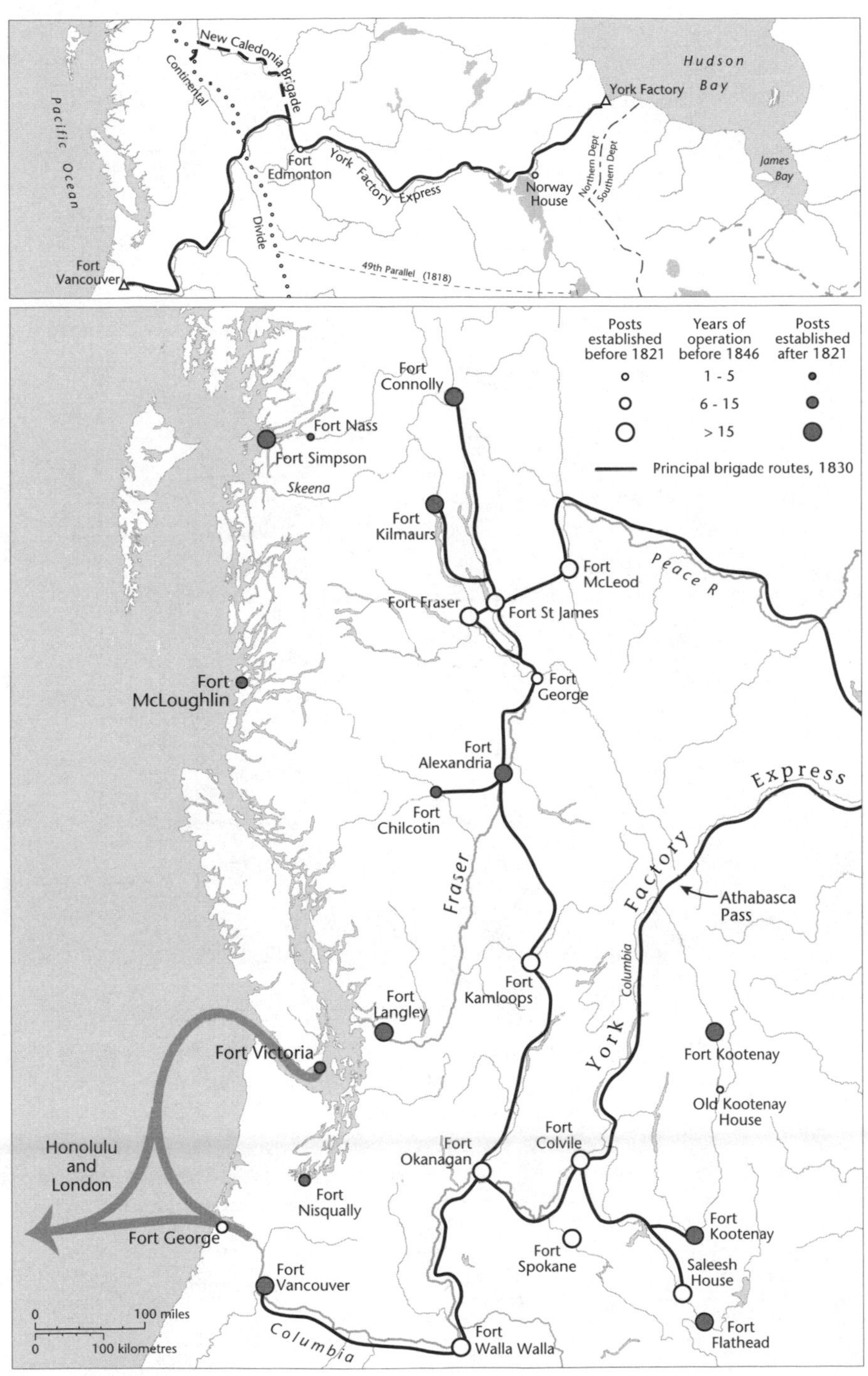

Figure 2.2 Northwest and Hudson's Bay Company posts in the Cordillera, 1805-46

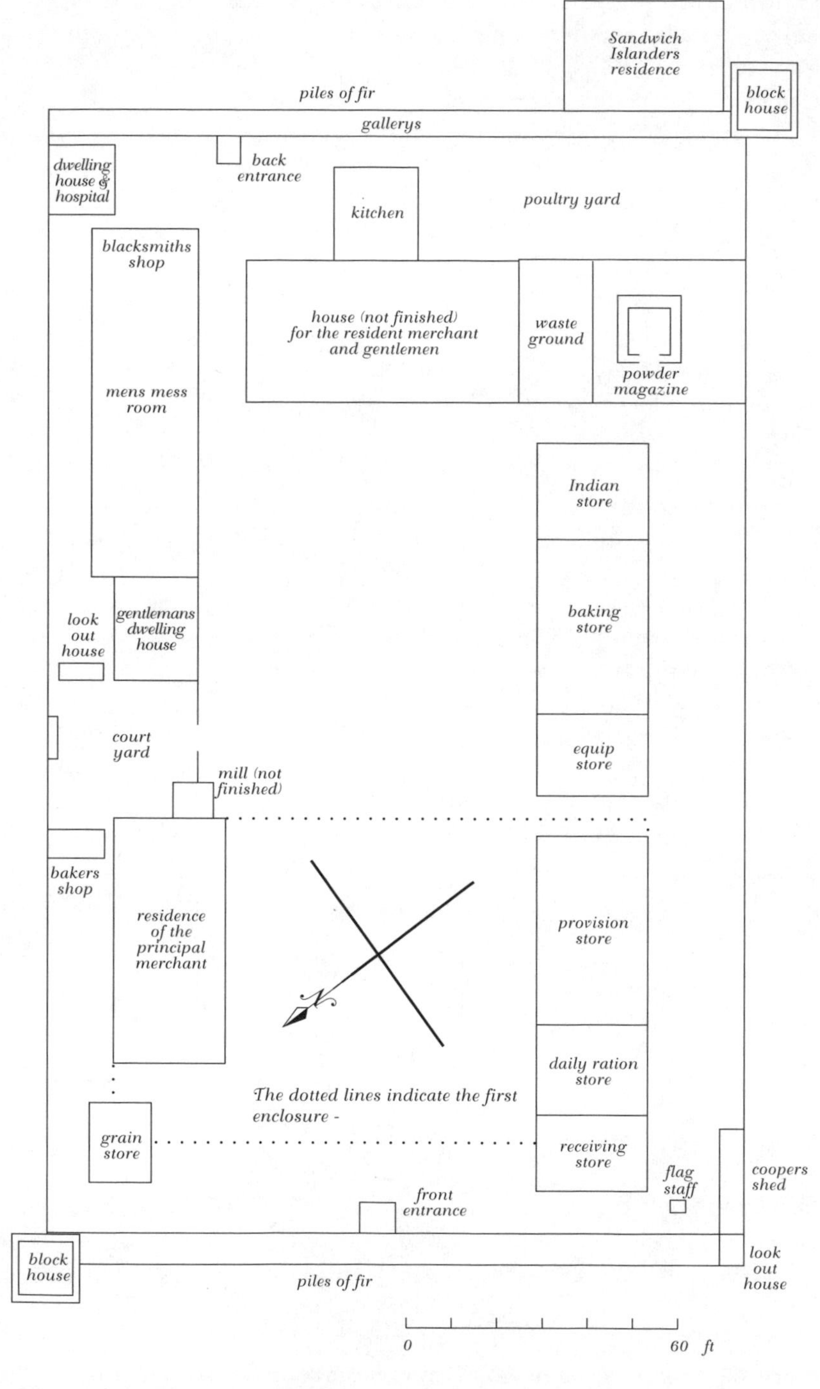

Figure 2.3 Plan of Fort George

known as Red River frame in Manitoba, and as *pièce sur pièce en coulise* in Lower Canada, whence came this method of construction. Built in an austere, frontier Georgian style with vernacular traces from Lower Canada, the structures were usually whitewashed.

The number of officers and men in the forts varied from as few as six or seven in the smaller establishments to forty or fifty in the larger. Most of the men kept Native women in the fort, and some of these women brought slaves. The forts, then, were complex societies, divided by the social hierarchies of the fur trade and, to a lesser extent, of Native society, and by sharp differences in culture, language, and race. The officers were almost always of British background, the men more diverse – primarily French Canadians, Métis of various ancestries (usually French Canadian on the male side), Iroquois, and Hawaiians (Kanakas) – and the women were Natives, usually from a nearby group. French and, more comprehensively, Chinook, a trading language that evolved along the lower Columbia, were the linguas franca of such establishments.

The forts were the 'power containers' of the fur trade,[19] loosely analogous to borderland castles or walled towns in Europe. A closer analogy is a ship at sea; the complement of men who made the long voyage to the Northwest Coast and built the first fort there had exchanged one bounded, hierarchical setting for another. In the longer run, the 'crews' were very different, and one was far less self-contained than the other. Yet, when the HBC put a steamer, the *Beaver*, on the coast in the mid-1830s, it functioned somewhat as a mobile fort, and the men, whether on land or sea, were subject to much the same work discipline.

Local, regional, and external circulation linked these forts together. Small parties travelled between adjacent forts carrying information and country produce (local resources for local consumption) along navigable waterways and horse trails as supply and demand permitted. Fort Kamloops, roughly in the middle of the HBC's cordilleran operations before 1846, exchanged horses and dried fish with its nearest accessible neighbours, Fort Alexandria in the north and forts Okanagan and Colvile in the south, each some 300 kilometres away (Figure 2.4).[20] The posts in New Caledonia (north-central British Columbia), located on different rivers with different salmon cycles, relied on exchanges of fish. Natives also carried mail between posts. A letter was bartered by one carrier to the next, gaining in value as it passed through several hands to its destination, where the trader redeemed it with presents. Apparently, letters usually got through, sometimes remarkably quickly, a reflection, according to one trader, of the Natives' superstitious veneration of literacy, and a cheap, effective means for traders in adjacent posts to keep in touch with each other.[21]

Annual shipments outward of furs, accounts, and mail, and inward of supplies, instructions, and mail, were organized in brigades, parties of

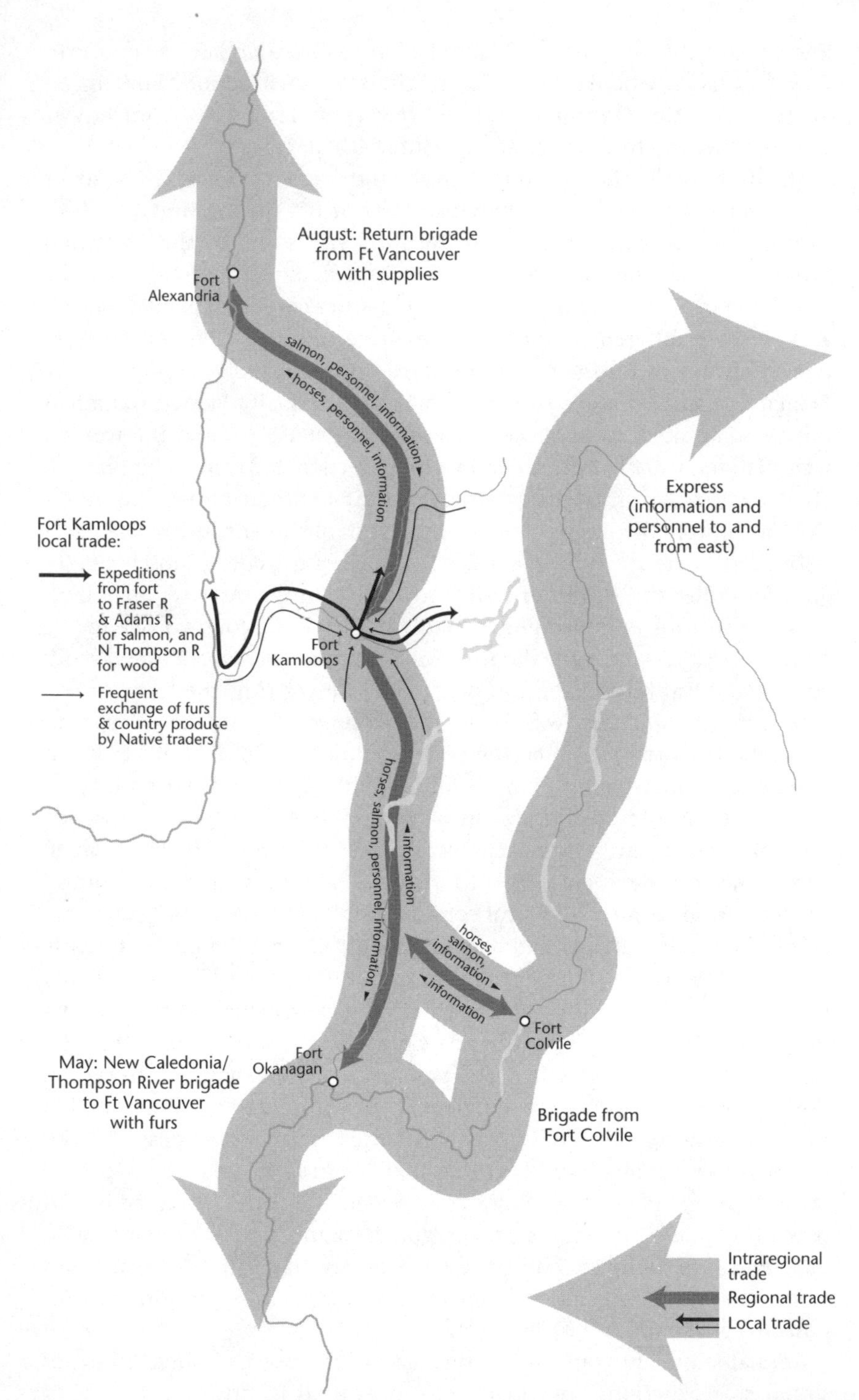

Figure 2.4 Trade from Fort Kamloops

well-armed officers and men, that linked individual posts to the main cordilleran depot on the lower Columbia. Wherever Native hostility was anticipated, the brigades were reinforced, as much as possible, with additional men and firepower; in the early years, small cannon and swivels (blunderbusses) were deployed at the main portages on the Columbia. Departing at much the same time each year and following established routes to established camping places, the brigades were compact, defensible bodies of men passing through Native territory. The route of the annual brigade from New Caledonia to the central depot on the lower Columbia is shown in Figure 2.2. It left Fort St. James by boat about April 20 with furs traded the previous year and accounts company clerks had 'methodized to a high degree.'[22] At the junction of the Stuart and Nechako rivers, the brigade met boats from Fort Fraser, picking up furs and accounts; similar 'returns' were picked up at Fort George on the Fraser before it carried on to Fort Alexandria. At Fort Alexandria, boats were left behind, and the brigade travelled overland to Fort Kamloops – from which, in most years, the Thompson River brigade had already departed – and then through the Okanagan Valley to Fort Okanagan on the Columbia, to a rendezvous with the Fort Colvile brigade. The enlarged brigade proceeded by boat under the senior officer to Fort Vancouver, arriving about June 15. It returned a month later, moving more slowly upriver and reaching Fort St. James in October.[23] For most interior posts, the annual going and coming of these brigades was the main event of the year. Shipping between coastal forts was the coastal equivalent of the brigade.

From the lower Columbia River, there were two main links to the outside, non-cordilleran world. Both the Astorians and the Northwesters tried to send a ship around the Horn to the Columbia each year. After 1821, in the early years of HBC control, one ship a year sailed from London, leaving in January and arriving on the Columbia in mid-June.[24] By the 1830s, as HBC trade expanded into the Pacific, sailings to and from Pacific ports, principally Oahu (Honolulu), also relayed outside information and goods.[25] The other route was by the spring express, which left Fort Vancouver in late March, bound for the annual council of the HBC at Norway House at the north end of Lake Winnipeg, and York Factory on Hudson Bay, some 3,000 kilometres away.[26] Usually led by the chief accountant at Fort Vancouver, and carrying the accounts of the whole Columbia Department – based on data from the various forts assembled the previous year, and reworked by company clerks at Fort Vancouver during the winter – as well as officers and men on furlough, the spring express was barely fitted between the spring break-up and fall freeze-up of northern rivers. It comprised two boatloads of men along the lower Columbia, to assist with portages and strengthen the party, and but one thereafter as far as Boat Encampment on the upper Columbia (Figure 2.2). From there, the party crossed Athabasca Pass on snowshoes to connect with horses brought to the other side, then with canoes or boats on the Athabasca River as far as Fort Assiniboine, travelling as the river ice broke up. The spring express then continued by pack horse to Fort Edmonton, then by boat on the North Saskatchewan River to Norway House, reached in mid-June. Finally, it reached York Factory, from where, in mid-July, the fall express originated. This express carried despatches and mail from London, picked up more despatches and mail at Norway House, some originating in the council there and some coming by express from Montreal, and was back on the lower Columbia at the end of October, just ahead of freeze-up in the north. By European standards, methods of travel were atavistic, but accounting followed current procedures, and the close coordination of land transportation over long distances anticipated the railway to some extent.

Such was the stark geography European traders imposed on the Cordillera. In essence, it was a minimal construction of nodes and circuits intended to facilitate trade in an isolated corner of the world, and to make connections to distant managers and markets. In outline, it was hardly original, but rather the product of a long adaptation, beginning early in the French regime along the lower St. Lawrence, of European trading methods to North American peoples and environments. Within this introduced geography, and extending their influence beyond it, were European systems of power, essential components of the operation of trade. Indeed, the forts and the circuits connecting them should be thought of as part and parcel of the discourse of the fur trade, a particular discourse of power that made it possible for traders to control their men and, to some extent, the surrounding Native populations. I now turn to the strategies that made up this discourse, beginning with those intended to control company servants before turning to those intended to control Natives.

Entering the fur trade as 'hired servants,' men signed contracts that bound them to the bidding of their employers for specified periods. They were to obey orders, work as required, adhere to company rules and regulations, refrain from independent trade, and go where they were sent. The HBC contract of engagement – a standardized document with spaces left for biographical information, dates, and wage rates – stipulated, among other things, that a servant was to devote 'the whole of his time and labour' for the service and benefit of the company, was to 'perform all such work and service, by day or by night, for the said Company as he shall be required to do,' and was to 'obey all orders, which he shall receive from the Governors of the Company in North America, or ... their Officers or Agents,' and 'all laws, orders and regulations established or made by the said Company for the good government of their settlements and territories.' Moreover, he was to defend company property 'with courage and fidelity,' and was neither to 'absent himself from the said service, nor engage, or be concerned in any trade or employment whatsoever, except for the benefit of the said Company and according to their orders.' The company could dismiss a servant at any time, terminating his wages at that date. By contrast, a servant had to give a year's notice, otherwise he could be retained on the agreed terms for an additional year. If he deserted, he would lose all his wages, without 'relief either in law or equity.'[27] Except for the duration of service, such contracts set no limits to a company's power over its men. In the absence of other law they set the legal terms of ordinary work and life in the fur trade.

With such a contract in the background, a hired servant lived day by day within the more pervasive discipline imposed by the routine, spatial organization, and spectacle of fort life. In summer, the fort bell rang at 5:30 A.M. and again at 6:00, when the officer in charge assigned the work for the day. At 8:00 A.M., work stopped for breakfast, then resumed from 9:00 to 12:00, when there was an hour off for dinner. A bell at 6:00 P.M. ended the working day. Saturday was a half day, and Sunday a day off, though the HBC required everyone to attend divine service, which was to be 'publicly read with becoming solemnity.'[28] Such routine was a disciplinary strategy; even women and children, according to HBC Standing Rules and Regulations, were to be given 'such regularly useful occupation' as is 'best calculated to suppress vicious and promote virtuous habits.'

Moreover, fort routine and work were inserted in a close theatre of power, with calculated disciplinary intent. Men ate rations issued every Saturday, dried fish and potatoes more often than not, which they or Native women prepared in their quarters. Officers and clerks ate in the dining room of the officers' residence, the Big House, where they sat in order of rank and dined handsomely. Men were issued striped cotton shirts and a few yards of cloth; officers often dressed elegantly. Men paddled canoes and officers rode in them; sometimes, it was said, they were lifted in and out. Officers in some of the larger forts kept riding horses. Officers' quarters were spacious and commanded the fort; men lived in barracks along the lateral walls, several men to a room if they were single, in small rooms of their own if they lived with Native women.[29] The Hawaiians at Fort George in 1818 were relegated to a location just outside the wall (Figure 2.3). And so it went; position in the hierarchy of the fur trade was constantly displayed.

The polyglot, multiracial labour force of the fur trade was also a tactic of control. The HBC favoured Orkney men ('prudent, quiet people') and Canadians ('active, capable of undergoing great hardships')[30] and, according to Ross Cox, brought up on 'the principles of passive obedience and nonresistance.'[31] By the mid-1820s, however, the company had difficulty recruiting enough of either.[32] Other men, less trusted, were distributed in small numbers among various forts. Scots and Irish were clannish and difficult to manage; a few of them could be scattered around. Red River Métis were unreliable, but the 'danger from their misconduct' could be mitigated by 'distributing them throughout the country.'[33] So with the Iroquois. When Iroquois plotted to kill the Northwester Donald McKenzie because he stopped them from trading independently with the Shoshone, his response was to disperse them. 'One was sent to ... Oakinachen [Fort Okanagan], two to Spokane House, and the rest placed on a separate hunting ground in the neighbourhood under the eye of an influential chief, where they would do no harm.'[34] Hawaiians, part of the labour force of the cordilleran fur trade from the beginning, were always a minority at any fort, as traders sought to forestall harmful 'combinations'[35] by mixing ethnicities and races.

If such tactics failed, corporal punishment was in reserve. Traders' response to perceived insolence or disobedience was often immediate and violent. At Kamloops in 1812, Alexander Ross dealt with a Canadian who wanted to buy a 'squaw' and then, when Ross refused the trade goods he needed, threatened to remain with the 'savages.' 'Provoked at his conduct, I suddenly turned round and horsewhipped the fellow.'[36] William Tolmie, who could put the stone farther than anyone at Nisqually, found that when he only threatened 'lickings,' men mistook his 'forbearance for fear,' so he waded in with fists and feet – the cure, in his eyes, for insolence, and a clear example to others. 'The custom of the country,' he wrote, 'renders it [such physical assertion of dominance] almost necessary for a newcomer.'[37] Father Morice maintained that club, whip, and fist were the common responses to misconduct in New Caledonia. Cruelty, he thought, was pervasive; occasionally men died from beatings administered in 'fits of passion.'[38] The process was somewhat more formal when an officer fixed a punishment and someone else carried it out. Such was the fate of William Brown, an Orkney man at Fort Vancouver who refused to return to Fort Langley. Sentenced to receive two dozen lashes, 'he was stripped and tied up to one of the Great Guns'; after six lashes he was ready to go 'whither they pleased to send him.'[39] Such was the fate of a Hawaiian at Fort Victoria who failed to give the 'All's well' while on watch, and was found trying to get into the storehouse. 'He was lashed up to a tree the next day and given 3 dozen lashes, which was his whole punishment.'[40] Such was the fate of two men who refused to sail on a company ship, and of the boatswain who refused to make a cat to whip them. The men received a dozen lashes; the boatswain was demoted. John McLoughlin, chief factor at Fort Vancouver, reported to the Governor and Committee of the HBC: 'I told them ... that we did not bring men to the country to Flog them, but to perform certain Duties, and if they would not do their Duty by fair means, we would try if other means would not do, as I was determined they would do their Duty.'[41]

Such procedures and assumptions were part of a British disciplinary environment in which flogging was still an accepted punishment for many military and civil offenses. Even so, it was held, the circumstances of the fur trade justified, or at least explained, a particular severity. Father Morice thought that the problem of subsistence in northern posts prevented punishment by long detention.[42] John McLoughlin claimed that, whereas in the civilized world a man who refused his duty could be dismissed and replaced by another, fur traders were stuck with the men they had, and therefore had 'no alternative but to make them do their duty.'[43] James Douglas felt that obedience among men in the fur trade stemmed neither from 'upright principle' nor 'dread of legal penalties,' but 'from a high degree of respect for [i.e., fear of] their officers ... when that feeling is deficient, we are often compelled to use strong measures in repressing violence, and arresting the dangerous process of insubordination.'[44] From the traders' perspective, all these observations were valid. It was difficult to incarcerate men, though a Hawaiian at Fort Vancouver spent at least five months in irons and one of the bastions at Fort Victoria served as a prison; there were not alternative workers; and the varied crews that comprised the contracted labour force of the fur trade were not subject to the rule of law.

At times, discipline disintegrated. In the early 1790s, the HBC trader Philip Turnor thought that anarchy pervaded all the interior HBC posts above York Factory, a condition which he thought only more men and proper officers could correct.[45] McLoughlin's son was killed by his men at Fort Stikine in 1842.[46] According to Father Morice, a Canadian from Fort Kamloops dropped a tree on a particularly brutal officer, killing him instantly.[47] Such were the dangers, to which the antidote, in Turnor's words, was 'a necessary steady Subordination.' A variety of disciplinary strategies usually served, and when they did not, physical violence was always an alternative. When Governor Simpson told McLoughlin that kindness was the best disciplinarian, McLoughlin retorted that he had spent forty years in the fur trade, and that Simpson wrote for outside effect.[48] McLoughlin was right. The fur trade did require that men 'respect' their officers, and respect, as the traders understood the word, rested on fear.

Men could desert, and did from time to time. It was relatively easy to drop over the palisade at night and disappear into the forest; it was even easier to get away from a work party outside the walls. Where to go was another matter. Natives currying favour and presents from officers at the forts often brought deserters back. Sometimes they killed them. When

Native people were suspected of harbouring deserters, traders retaliated by taking hostages, stopping trade, or threatening violence. Often they sent out parties to track down deserters, usually with success. Alexander Ross reported a spectacular desertion at Fort George in 1816, and a characteristic response to it.[49] A Russian named Jacob convinced eighteen men, mostly Hawaiians, to desert and strike out for California, all of them eluding the watch and getting over the palisade one night. Chase was given and the tentative Hawaiians were quickly caught, but Jacob got away. He returned twice: at night to scale the palisade and rob the storehouse, and in broad daylight disguised as a Native woman, to plot an attack on the fort. Learning where he was, the traders sent out a party of forty, and in a surprise, pre-dawn attack on a Native village, captured him. Jacob was shipped in irons to Hawaii. Deserters had some chance of success where there were rival European traders to desert to; otherwise, a deserter could not survive on his own, while Natives known to aid deserters faced the full array of disciplinary tactics (discussed below) that traders could throw at them.

Fort society was the most disciplined creation of the western fur trade. But even in the forts, surveillance was far from total, and discipline was always sporadic and limited. Lives were not tucked away from each other, nor were they entirely exposed. The officers saw much, but not all that went on in a fort – and much of what they did see rarely figured in the journals and letters that are the principal records of these places. Traders were responsible for trade and for the deployment of contracted workers; domestic arrangements did not preoccupy them unless they impinged on the business of the fort. And so most of the Native women who lived in the forts, linking them in myriad ways to societies beyond the walls and considerably transforming the local culture of working life, were, in the details of their lives, largely outside the traders' ken. So were most of the innumerable small acts of resistance – the procrastinations and prevarications – of the work force they sought to manage.

In small posts, and particularly during long winters with inadequate provisions, discipline tended to give way to a more elemental psychological and physical struggle for survival. In 1811, Daniel Harmon at Stuart's Lake Post (later Fort St. James) wrestled with extreme isolation and turned to God; W.F. Wentzel, on the Mackenzie River that year, watched several of his men, and almost himself, die of starvation.[50] In times of severe stress, fort discipline was bent in various ways, depending largely on the personalities involved. Otherwise, traders and men stationed in different forts apparently lived under a fairly standard umbrella of disciplinary practices, part of the well-tested discourse of the western fur trade.

Beyond the fort, discipline weakened. Even a small party sent out to cut wood was no longer supervised. Traders complained, as centuries before had overseers of Atlantic fisheries when men went off in small boats to fish,[51] that not enough work was being accomplished. It was harder to discipline men on a brigade than in a fort. Brigade desertions complicated the problem of capture. Essentially, traders' power dropped off away from forts because they did not manage this space and, therefore, found it more difficult to manage their employees' time and their employees' relations with Natives and rival non-Native traders.

Most employees in the forts lived with Native women. As time went on, they learned Native languages and had kin in Native villages. In fur trade letters and journals, almost all written by officers of British background, Native names and places are commonly gallicized, a reflection of the considerable interaction between fort men, many of whom were Métis, and surrounding Native societies. Just how men got away into the Native world can only be surmised – by staying out a few extra days when sent off to trade provisions, by turning a trapping party to another purpose, by some tacit understanding that they could slip away for a few days – but certainly they did. A Shuswap informant told James Teit, ethnographer of the Interior Salish, about HBC half-breeds who brought welcome new stories to pit houses on winter nights.[52] A rough Catholicism was perhaps introduced this way, as well as favourable and unfavourable foretellings of the 'black robes.' Data are sparse, but not entirely absent. Here may be the cultural middle ground between Europeans and Natives in the northern Cordillera that Richard White has described in the Great Lakes basin.[53] To the extent that these relationships stabilized dealings with Natives and channelled information, they were useful to the fur traders. Useful or not, officers did not control them.

Finally, monopoly was one of the preconditions of discipline, and when monopoly broke down away from the forts, traders were helpless. Such, in the 1820s, was Peter Skene Ogden's predicament in the Snake Country, where he commanded large, multiracial trapping parties and American traders circulated. Orders were disobeyed; men said it was too dangerous to go where Ogden led, and took their own routes. Ogden could do nothing: 'I did not think it good policy to use any threats towards them in case of our again meeting with the Americans but if God Spares my life until the Fall an example Shall Certainly be made of some of them' – that is, some would be whipped at the fort. Others wanted to steal horses from the Snakes, and Ogden could not stop them either: 'in this cursed and ill fated Country no man Can enforce obedience to his commands.'[54] A group of Iroquois defected to the Americans, leaving with a speech that would have been impossible under monopoly conditions: 'I must now tell you that all the Iroquois as well as myself have long wished for an opportunity to join the Americans, and if we did not sooner it was entirely owing to our bad luck our not meeting them ... but now we go and all you can say or do will not prevent us from going.'[55] Monopoly and discipline had broken down together. Later, monopoly would be challenged by settlement in the Willamette Valley. Settlement offered accessible, alternative workplaces where, among many former employees of the fur trade, a deserter might hide. As settlement expanded in the Willamette Valley during the last HBC years on the lower Columbia, desertions from the brigades increased.[56]

From the traders' point of view, the control of Natives posed a different set of problems. Some women apart, Natives did not live in the forts, but across territories that traders hardly knew and could not oversee. In such circumstances, surveillance of Natives was impossible; the machinery was lacking. Moreover, traders were interested in profit, not in the management of people – unless profit was at stake. Consequently, they did not involve themselves in inter-Native quarrels except when the safety of their own property and personnel was threatened. They did not try to direct Native cultural change, though they assumed it would occur, except occasionally when a trader tried to curtail Native tortures of captives[57] or, when traders sought, apparently with little effect, to direct Natives away from warfare or, in their word, 'indolence,' and towards the steady pursuits of trapping and trading.

Traders sought predictability, stable trade environments, and safety. In effect, they sought to extend something of the order and security they had created behind palisades to the larger territory of the fur trade so that, at least along their habitual routes, personnel and goods could move about unharmed. Space they did not control, occupied by people they considered barbarous and were in no position to manage, had somehow to be rendered safe. From the traders' perspective, the challenge of Native management in the Cordillera boiled down to securing the conditions for their own survival, mobility, and profit. Many of the techniques they used to achieve these ends were variants of those they used to manage men.

In this case, too, their strategy rested on a politics of fear – 'respect' or 'terror' were the traders' common words. Natives were to understand, as Simpson told the chiefs at Fort St. James, that quick, violent retribution would follow any attack on the personnel or property of the fur trade. This was not a theoretical proposition: over and over again, the traders demonstrated its tangible effects. Their motives, as reiterated, were that 'untill an example and a severe one be made of them there will be no peace and rest ... ,' that Natives would be 'restrained from Committing acts of atrocity and violence by the dread of retaliations,' or, simply, that the example of the traders' quick violence would be 'a terror to others.'[58] Natives, the traders thought, mistook kindness for weakness, and were restrained only by the threat, backed by the demonstrated reality, of retribution that was fearless, implacable, and severe.[59] As far as possible, trader violence was to be public, a spectacle of power intended to impress and dissuade within a pervasive theatre of power in which Natives, like company servants, were audience and actors.

There were other tactics, all part of the discourse of the fur trade, all intended less to shape Native lives than to give traders the tools to manage their own agendas among people they considered barbarous and untrustworthy. Interracial sexual partnerships were one such tactic: they calmed the men, provided links to and allies in Native societies and channels of information about them, and took place quickly whenever a new fort was established. Traders also knew and exploited the fact that Native societies were factionalized and local; more or less adroitly, they practised a politics of divide and rule, using presents, rewards, flattery, spies, and boundless duplicity. They could exploit the huge disjunction between Native and European spheres of knowledge by threatening to call up natural disasters. Literacy, which Natives seem to have treated as a manifestation of spirit power, was used as an instrument of control, especially when combined with the extended spatial system of the fur trade and juxtaposed to local, oral cultures. And they could threaten to stop trading, a threat that, in proportion to Native dependence on firearms to ward off similarly armed enemies and Native reliance on powder and shot from a particular fort, could threaten the survival of Native societies.

In short, the officers of the cordilleran fur trade, almost all of whom had worked in the trade for years in various capacities and knew its ways, had access to a repertoire of violent and non-violent strategies to protect their interests. Using them, they were able to consolidate a European position in the Cordillera, a crucial proto-colonial phase of European influence. I now consider these strategies more closely.

There were no fixed rules about corporal or capital punishment of Natives beyond the assumption, held by every trader, that, in the interests of successful trading, both would be required from time to time. Authority rested with the trader in charge, who was free to punish as he wished. Occasionally, traders were reprimanded by their superiors for being too severe with their men, but never, apparently, for being too severe with Natives. Natives were another category of humans – savages living in a state of barbarism – to whom European assumptions about justice and fair play, such as they were, did not apply. Natives could be useful in various ways, but had to be 'made to behave.' Within the broad discourse of the fur trade, how traders did this was up to them. And so similar 'offenses' met various responses within a hierarchy of violence ranging from impromptu beatings or whippings, to time in irons, to more formal whippings, to shootings or hangings, to raids intended to wipe out villages and populations. In general, corporal and capital punishment were most resorted to and most severe where traders felt least secure – where they had recently established themselves or where there was competition from other traders – and less resorted to and less severe where time and monopoly allowed other forms of coercion to work. But traders always understood that violence, threatened and meted out, was central to the security of the fur trade.

Much of the hierarchy of fur trade violence came quickly into play in the tense early years along the lower Columbia. Natives were beaten for petty thefts;[60] at Fort Astoria in 1811, they were put in irons.[61] On the brigades upriver, punishment was more severe. A man who had taken a silver goblet was hanged, though he returned it and therefore, by the terms of Native law, thought himself safe; he was a victim not of a different conception of the law, but of European power.[62] At the Dalles, where traders had to fight their way through a Native trading monopoly, thefts brought hostage-takings and threats, backed by cannon and men in military formation, to destroy villages. Usually the goods came back.[63] Killers were killed if caught. The presumed killers of three Pacific Fur Company men, caught two years later by North Westers and Natives, were shot.[64] Natives who mauled three men just outside the walls of Fort George were also shot in a macabre piece of fur trade theatre:

> The prisoners were confined in the bastion, and next morning led out, blindfolded, to be shot. They were placed opposite a 6-pounder, while a party of rifle-men were in the bastion ready to fire through the loopholes, which manoeuvre was made use of in order to make the Indians believe that they were shot by the great gun. The dead bodies were taken down to the wharf in coffins, and exposed for some days, till their friends were allowed to carry them away.[65]

Another Native thought to have killed a woodcutter was shot after a contrived jury trial and a show of force by apprehensive traders:

> Immense numbers of Indians belonging to the various surrounding nations were in attendance; some on shore, and others in canoes. The guns on the battery and in the bastions were loaded with grape, and attended by men with slow matches. The remainder of our people were drawn up in front of the fort, all armed with muskets and bayonets.[66]

Often, as traders were part of a system they could not always control, violence was less premeditated. Iroquois employees of the North West Company (NWC) went on the rampage in 1818 after some Cowlitz killed one of them for molesting Cowlitz women. The Iroquois fired on an unsuspecting Cowlitz camp, killing twelve people, taking scalps, and forcing the North Westers to turn to the Willamette for furs. There, according to Alexander Ross, the bloodshed was repeated. A large trapping party, apparently mostly Iroquois but led by two Métis, killed fourteen Natives while trying to steal their horses. Premeditated or not, violence was pervasive along the lower Columbia in the NWC years, as it apparently was along the Mackenzie, another remote theatre of NWC activity.

NWC trade appears to have been calmer in what is now north-central British Columbia, which traders called New Caledonia. The environment was broadly familiar to traders coming from the northeast, the Native population much smaller than along the Columbia, competition absent, and personalities perhaps less belligerent. Stuart Lake Post, later called Fort St. James, was not palisaded when Daniel Harmon arrived in November 1810. When a Native lad cut a hole in a parchment window two feet from Harmon's bed and took some clothing, Harmon, perhaps the gentlest officer in all the cordilleran trade, did no more than retrieve the clothes from 'the young Rascal,' and tell him that a second offense would be severely punished. But even Harmon could administer a beating, though with enough remorse to note that he had not done so for eleven years.[68] His victim was the Carrier chief, Quas (Kwah), who apparently wanted credit for a friend and, when it was refused, offered this remarkable speech (in Harmon's precis) on the differences between them:

> He then told me, that he saw no other difference between me and himself, but this only: 'you,' said he, 'know how to read and write; but I do not. Do not I manage my affairs as well, as you do yours? You keep your fort in order, and make your slaves,' meaning my men, 'obey you. You send a great way off for goods, and you are rich and want for nothing. But do not I manage my affairs as well as you do yours? When did you ever hear that Quas was in danger of starving? When it is the proper season to hunt the beaver, I kill them; and of their flesh I make feasts for my relations. I, often, feast all the Indians of my village; and, sometimes, invite people from afar off, to come and partake of the fruits of my hunts. I know the season when fish spawn, and, then send my women, with the nets which they have made, to take them. I never want for any thing, and my family is always well clothed.'[67]

When Quas went on to talk of his war exploits, Harmon was 'strongly tempted to beat him, as his object manifestly was, to intimidate me.' Finally, when Quas refused several small pieces of cloth for a breech cloth, Harmon assumed that Quas was picking a quarrel.

> I, therefore, threw down the cloth, and told him, if he would not have that, he should have this, (meaning a square yard stick which I had in my hand) with which I gave him a smart blow over the head, which cut it, considerably. I then sprang over the counter, and pelted him, for about five minutes, during which time he continually called to his companions, all of whom had knives in their hands, to come and take me off. But, they replied that they could not, because there were two other white people in the room, who would prevent them.

A few days later, Quas invited Harmon to a feast, and, rather than be thought afraid, Harmon went. At the feast, Quas announced that he considered himself Harmon's wife, 'for ... that was the way he served his women ... when they misbehaved.' In reply, Harmon adjusted the metaphor: he would treat Natives as his children and 'chastise them when they behave ill, because it was for their good.'

After the merger of the North West and Hudson's Bay Companies in 1821, most officers of the former company were employed by the latter, and the broad discourse of the fur trade, as it bore on Native management in the northern Cordillera, continued unchanged. Some HBC officers were known to be particularly severe in their dealings with Natives; some thought that the common practices of the fur trade were too lenient. After his experiences in the Snake Country, Peter Skene Ogden held that the way to pacify Natives was to kill a dozen or so when whites first entered a new trading territory. So treated, Natives would not 'murder' whites, and 'Trappers would make hunts and Traders become rich men.'[69] But company policy remained, rather, to retaliate quickly and visibly, taking blood for blood, thereby instilling 'respect' and allowing traders and their employees to move about safely in Native territory. When other whites were present, the point was generalized. In response to the Indian killing of a HBC trader near Fort George, John McLoughlin at Fort Vancouver raised a mixed force of British and American settlers, American missionaries, and ships' crews as well as HBC servants to track down the presumed killer, and hang him 'with a deep sea lead furnished from an American brig in the harbour, every person present [that is, Americans as well as British] handling the line when the Indian was raised off the ground.'[70] Natives in attendance were to understand that whites stood by each other, and that the Willamette was to be safe for all of them.

When HBC traders identified someone they took to be the guilty party, they tried to catch and punish him individually, meting out, as had the North Westers, whippings and irons for theft, and hanging or shooting for killing. A Native presumed to have stolen goods from a company boat was taken to Fort Kamloops where the trader (one Donald McLean, long known for his harshness towards Natives)

> stripped that indian and tied him against the fort and sent for all the indians to see what they were going to do with him. They got all the goods back except some handkerchiefs and shirts. They tied him there and one of the men cut him with a leather until the blood flew. The indian is alive yet. We call him mean Jim.[71]

Retaliation for a killing was as quick as circumstances permitted. The presumed killer of the trader at a fort in New Caledonia was shot at the fort gate as he tried to leave.[72] The presumed killers of a company servant at Fort McLeod in the spring of 1828 'were all cut off ... to a man' the following summer.[73] On the other hand, the punitive party sent out in January 1849 to avenge the murder of a member of the New Caledonia brigade the previous November killed, by one account, two accomplices and, by another, several innocent people, while the presumed culprit fled to the mountains. Apparently he was killed next year by an uncle bribed with 100 beaver skins if he brought in his nephew's scalp, and threatened with death if he did not.[74] The killing a few years before of Samuel Black, chief trader at Kamloops, apparently because some thought his 'evil medicines' had led to the death of a local chief, also had a protracted denouement. After the killing, the men at Kamloops fled to forts Colvile and Vancouver, from where parties converged on Kamloops. Not finding the killer in Native settlements nearby, they took horses and burned canoes and other property. According to John Tod, whom McLoughlin eventually put in charge of the fort, their conduct only incurred the hostility of Native people who regretted the killing as much as whites and who considered it a mistake.[75] On assuming command, Tod returned horses, paid for destroyed property, and offered a sizeable reward. In a few days, information was ventured about the presumed killer's location. After a long chase, the man was captured, and was being brought in irons to Kamloops when he tipped the canoe carrying him across the Thompson River and was shot by Natives from the bank (in some accounts, he drowned). According to Tod, the incident did not perturb the Natives near Fort Kamloops; 'They all acknowledge that he merited death at our hands.' As Tod noted in the fort journal,

> The Indians assembled came into the hall and quietly smoked their pipes. Made them a speech on the death of the murderer. They acquiesced fully to all that was said on the subject. Grand Gule [who a few days before had participated in the ambush that led to the capture] was elected chief and paid the goods he was promised for betraying the murderer into our hands. These he distributed in part amongst a few of his relations.[76]

When traders could not identify a particular culprit, they retaliated against a village or tribe. Such was the case after the killing, apparently by the Clallam along the south shore of the Strait of Juan de Fuca, of Alex McKenzie and party during a trip in 1828 from Fort Langley to Fort Vancouver. McLoughlin assembled a force of more than sixty men at Fort Vancouver, telling them that 'the honour of the whites was at stake' and that if the expedition did not succeed, 'it would be dangerous to be seen by the Natives any distance from the Fort hereafter.'[77] The expedition marched north to Puget Sound, traded eleven canoes, and proceeded on by water, firing at eagles and discharging rockets, killing two families of sleeping Clallam (the head of one was said to be the brother-in-law of the principal murderer), and meeting the HBC vessel *Cadboro* at the east end of the Strait of Juan de Fuca. From there, the combined force proceeded west to a large Clallam village where the *Cadboro* began a cannonade; the Clallam fled into the forest. A landing party broke or burned thirty canoes, burned train oil and other provisions, and burned the lodges; the village was destroyed. On the expedition's return, another village, this one unoccupied, was cannonaded and burned. In different accounts, a total of twenty-one or twenty-five people were killed, though Frank Ermatinger, a HBC clerk who left the fullest account of the expedition, considered such estimates 'a made-up story,' and that the expedition's leader had been soft and indecisive. McLoughlin, however, was satisfied. Had there been no retaliation, 'others by seeing them [the Clallam] unpunished would have imitated their example and whenever an opportunity offered have murdered any of us that fell in their way ...'[78] 'Every one acquainted with the character of the Indians of the North West Coast will allow they can only be restrained from Committing acts of atrocity and violence by the dread of retaliation.'[79]

Perhaps the clearest example of this policy is provided by the affair of the missing Hawaiian during the fishing season at Fort Langley in 1830. The man disappeared after a day in the fish house, and poling the river turned up no trace of him.[80] The other Hawaiians said that, at home, he had frequently wandered off, that he had tried to throw himself overboard during the sailing from Hawaii, and that he was given to melancholy. There matters rested uneasily for a week until the Hawaiian's clothing turned up in the large Nanaimo fishing village just below Fort Langley. The traders were told that the Hawaiian had traded his clothing for fish and then, being taken across the river, had upset the canoe, eluded capture, and got away into the forest. This seemed improbable. When other Natives reported seeing his mutilated body in the Nanaimo village, the traders had all the evidence they needed that the Nanaimo had murdered him, apparently in retaliation for a beating one had received for stealing a key to the fish house. As a person, the Hawaiian meant nothing to the traders, but as a company employee, his murder had to be avenged. The devised plan, later called a 'war of extermination' [81] by Archibald McDonald, in charge at Fort Langley, was this: The schooner *Vancouver*, reinforced with half the men from the fort, would sail up the Fraser River as if on a regular voyage to the fort, but, this time, would fire on and destroy the Nanaimo village. McDonald consulted with his second and third in command at Fort Langley – to ascertain that they could hold the fort in the face of a general Native uprising[82] – and contacted the captain of the schooner. Arrangements were made, the fort was on tenterhooks, and the Natives, apparently knowing that something was up, suddenly stayed away. Then, the evening before the attack, the naked, starving Hawaiian emerged from the forest. His account, pieced together, essentially corroborated what the traders had already been told, minus the rumour about a 'mutilated body.' The attack was off. A couple of days later, when some Nanaimo brought the missing clothing to the fort, they were told that by doing so they had saved 'their village and the lives of their women and children.' McDonald was more than satisfied: the affair could not 'by any possibility have terminated more fortunate for our interests and peaceable repose than it is'; although the attack was narrowly avoided, 'nothing was done rashly or without mature deliberation.'

Later, the HBC would make some limited retaliation when one of its seasonal Native employees was killed. In 1849, a Native lad was shot, apparently by some Cowichan, at one of the company dairies near Victoria. Douglas considered it fortunate that 'none of our people were hurt,' but did respond to 'this glaring insult' by sending out an armed party to chase off the Cowichan.[83] Nothing more, however, was done, as would have been the case had the lad been white.

How is the fur traders' use of violence to be interpreted? Legal historians of the fur trade have recently pointed out that the practice of violent retribution without trial, of blood for blood, is not derived from English common law, and appears to have more to do either with ancient Mosaic law or with Native ways.[84] Without an organized system of European law to fall back on, a reasonable premise is that traders adopted a Native system of vengeance and elements of Native law. The trade was not so much an imposition as a process of cultural encounter with borrowings both ways, and it operated within a territory still largely subject to Native law, that is, to many local systems of law. In a legal and diplomatic sense, the fur traders became another Native group operating in Native territory within, to a considerable extent, Native rules of diplomacy.[85] Implicit in this position is the assumption that traditional fur trade scholarship has underplayed Native agency and, in so doing, has been complicit in the colonization and marginalization of Natives.

This position is attractive, but, at least in the northern Cordillera, I think it is too focused on law per se, and too inattentive to what I would call the geography of power. Perhaps the explanation for a policy of violent retaliation lies neither in Native nor Mosaic law. Certainly, the fur traders thought their retaliations would be meaningful to Natives. That was their didactic point. Certainly, too, some traders thought they could achieve their ends most efficiently by adopting some Native practices. Alexander Ross, for example, was scathing when Natives in the Willamette Valley turned back a large NWC hunting party because, in his view, its members did not know enough to pay tribute. Some tobacco and a pipe of peace, he thought, would have served. He returned with a larger party, camped opposite the Natives, and waited. Eventually he agreed to 'pay for their dead, according to their own laws' – and, presumably, gave some tobacco and smoked the pipe of peace – in return for which the Natives allowed whites into the valley.[86] As the years passed, traders living with Native women and learning Native languages must have been well aware of Native laws, and employed them when, as for Ross, they were tactically convenient. But the corporal and capital punishments traders meted out, variable as they were for similar offenses; variously directed at individuals or at groups when individuals could not be discerned; accomplished by means of whips, irons, and hangings, none of which had been part of Native punishments; and imposed on many different regional cultures, do not strike me as European adaptations of Native systems of vengeance, even less of Native laws. I suspect they have less to do with law, whether British, Mosaic, or Native, than with power, and are better thought of as particular strategies of power, together with the assumptions of social control lying behind them, broadly derived from Europe but framed in the particular circumstances of the fur trade.

These circumstances were that traders were cooped up in forts and dependent on the lifelines between them. Their capacity for the close surveillance of the surrounding Native population was severely limited, and their ability to impose disciplinary regimes – of the sort, for example, that missionaries would later introduce – was virtually nil. They were operating, as they saw it, among 'treacherous savages,' and they sought to make life safe for themselves and their employees. A fundamental way to do so was to demonstrate the cost of any offense against the personnel or property of the trade, a cost measured in the effects of power that Natives could not contain and that, as much as possible, traders displayed before them. People must be made to be afraid of the traders, to witness the spectacle of power and know that, if they did certain things, they would become victims. Once this lesson was learned, Natives would monitor their own conduct towards whites, and the white presence would be secured. Such was the assumption, its value dependent upon people knowing, like the European masses confronted with public executions, 'what unleashing of force threatened them.' This sporadic, local, and highly visible power, a substitute for continual supervision, 'sought a renewal of its effect in the spectacle of its individual manifestations ... [and] was recharged in the ritual display of its reality as "super-power."'[87] In the Cordillera, it did not validate a monarch's authority and a state's laws, as the spectacle of the scaffold was intended to do in Europe. It did not, in itself, force Natives to trade, nor was it intended to.[88] It was intended only to secure the traders' presence and the safety of their trade, and, combined with non-violent strategies, it generally did.

The constant theatre of the fur trade, expressed in dress, conduct, ceremony, and buildings, was a disciplinary strategy directed towards Natives as much as company servants. The fort was an imposing symbol of power to which Natives were never allowed free access; defensive accoutrements were sometimes 'more for the Show and the name of the thing among the Indians than anything else.'[89] Salutes fired by a fort or a ship's guns, welcoming fusillades, trumpet calls, drum rolls, flags, demonstrations of superior marksmanship, and so on were all parts of the show of power. So was a domineering bravado, of which the NWC trader Peter Pond's conduct in the Athabasca country is an extreme example. He would whack Natives with the flat of his sword, telling them that 'the country and the Indians belonged to him and he would do with them as he pleased.'[90] James McKenzie, in Athabasca a few years later, told Natives who wanted the trade in women to stop that 'we would do as we thought proper, for it was not their business to prescribe rules to us ... '[91] Traders understood that they should not reveal 'the least symptom of fear' whether, to judge by some of their accounts, facing timber wolves, truculent servants, or Native people.[92] Lines were undoubtedly forgotten from time to time, but traders had served long apprenticeships for their roles.

Inserted in this theatre of power in times of particular stress were tricks made possible, from the Natives' point of view, by the traders' astonishing command of the natural world. One was to threaten to introduce smallpox. Smallpox had devastated the southern plateau and parts of the south-central coast in 1782, had been on the north coast somewhat earlier, and had reemerged in regional epidemics.[93] Natives well knew its effects, were terrified at the prospect of the disease, and tended to associate it with whites. Knowing this, traders in tight circumstances played on their fears. Duncan McDougall was in charge at Fort George when news arrived that Natives on the west coast of Vancouver Island had captured the NWC ship *Tonquin*. Fearing an attack on the fort, McDougall assembled several chiefs, showed them a small bottle, told them that it contained smallpox, and threatened to release the disease. The chiefs, understanding, said Ross Cox, that 'he held their fate in his hands,' protested that this would kill the good people with the bad and offered every promise of friendship, and McDougall eventually allowed that he would not uncork the fatal bottle as long as Natives neither attacked nor robbed whites. This was a powerful threat; McDougall became 'the Great Small-pox chief.'[94] John Tod, at Kamloops in the 1840s, used a different version of the same threat to diffuse a concerted, considerably premeditated Shuswap attack. Smallpox, he told the Shuswap, had arrived from the south; the news immediately turned warriors into frightened men waiting for Tod to vaccinate them.[95]

The threat to blow everyone up with gunpowder could be used in much the same way.[96] More imaginative was the trader at Fort Chesterfield on the South Saskatchewan River. Wanting to move a large group of Native people away from the fort so his own small party could leave safely, he hoisted a kite, let it hover over the fort until it had been well seen, then hauled it down and showed the chiefs a feigned letter, telling them it came from the 'Master of Life,' and that it ordered them to remove to a place some distance off and not return for several days. If they did return, they would be attacked by an army of Cree and Assiniboine. The Natives left.[97]

The success of the ruse with the kite depended, in good part, on the Natives' association of spirit power with literacy. Literacy enabled whites to know, without apparent intermediary, what was going on far away. This was remarkable spirit power; Harmon reported that the Carrier thought whites able, by looking in books, to take the life of anyone they wanted. They could know all the past and see into the future. Literacy identified whites as supernatural beings, placed on earth, perhaps, by the sun or the moon.[98] How widely such views were held and how long they lasted is impossible to say. In 1847, the artist Paul Kane met a man in Puget Sound who was able to pass unmolested through groups of strange Natives by showing them an old piece of newspaper.[99] In 1864, the leader of the Tŝilhqot'in (Chilcotin) party that allegedly killed twenty-one whites constructing a trail inland from Bute Inlet, stated when sentenced to hang that a white had threatened some Tŝilhqot'in with death and had taken down their names. Two years earlier, most of the Tŝilhqot'in – virtually all in some areas – had died from smallpox, a disease Natives had long associated with whites, and that a white in the area had predicted. The taking down of names, perceived as another form of devastating white spirit power, may have been the immediate cause of the 'Chilcotin war.'[100]

Literacy, ships, and brigades allowed traders to coordinate policies at a subcontinental scale. This, coupled with a tested, widely diffused discourse of power and one overriding motive – gain – for their presence in the Cordillera, allowed traders to superimpose a relatively unitary set of strategies on the complexity and tensions of established Native societies. The fur trade was, in a sense, a system that had penetrated intricate lifeworlds. Along the interface of system and lifeworld were, to put it starkly, traders looking for profit and peoples living within deeply rooted cultures. Traders had an explicit purpose for being in the Cordillera, whereas Native peoples *lived* there; and the Native tendency, as soon as traders appeared, was to contextualize the newcomers and derive advantage from them within ongoing societies and their modes of signification. Native social power tended to be local, residing in house groups and families, and diffused more widely through complex, place-and-name-linked networks of kin in which individuals had little coercive power. Such social power was embedded in intricate local histories – some recounted in public stories, some held very privately – of clan and kin, friendship and feud, and malevolent and protecting spirits. The disjunction between intricate local ways frequently at cross-purposes and the extended system and unitary purpose of the fur trade offered traders many tactical opportunities to assert their influence.

The traders were well aware of tensions and animosities within Native societies, and that, in most situations, some Natives were well disposed towards them and others were not. This was the basis of their common distinction between 'good Indians' and 'bad Indians.' As need be, there were ways of getting information about the 'bad.' Spies could be hired; they were used in the first Snake River expedition to keep track of hostile Shoshone and, though data about them are sparse, were always part of the traders' repertoire.[101] More information came through the Native women in the forts. Although women increased provisioning costs, these liaisons were essential to a successful fort; they kept the men there, bonded the fort somewhat to local society, and provided information. An attack on the second ship to arrive at Fort Astoria was averted by information from a Native woman, on board with one of the sailors. She was 'handsomely rewarded' and moved to the fort. This pattern continued, with traders sometimes virtually arranging marriages for their junior officers. James Murray Yale was married to the daughter of a local chief a month after he arrived at Fort Langley: 'we have thought it good policy in Mr. Yale to form a family Connection with them.'[102] When spies and other information channels gave traders a sense of where trouble was brewing, they could wade in with some combination of the bombast, intimidation, presents, and firepower at their disposal. Whatever they did, there would be some Native people who sided with them against their own enemies.

Given such Native support, the threat, which traders made from time to time, to abandon a fort[103] usually produced the desired result. This was not only because of Native dependence on powder and shot and fondness for tobacco and other European goods, but also because the traders' presence conferred political and strategic advantage. Occasionally, traders did close forts, as along the upper Peace in 1823-4, in retaliation for Native killings of company men. A few years later, in this case, Governor Simpson recommended reopening two of the four closed 'since the Indians had suffered enough for the crimes of a few.'[104]

Native peoples were not passive victims of the varied strategies of this discourse of white power. Whites and their goods were useful to them, and they sought to manipulate traders for their own ends, just as traders sought to manipulate Natives, neither quite understanding the aims and politics of the other. Native people were as eager traders as whites. Chiefs married off daughters to secure alliances; some young women turned down Native men for whites. White and Native agendas interacted in the fur trade, and white power always rested on the alignments it was able to make with particular Native interests. The traders' presence usually served the interest of some Natives full well, and the traders depended on these alignments of mutual interest.[105] Within Native societies, there were protracted arguments – an edge of which appears in traders' writings and ethnographic records – about how best to deal with whites. And there was a good deal of resistance, ranging from women who fled white men and fort life to killings of traders and company servants. What the traders viewed as murders were usually viewed by Native people as retaliations for violations of their customs or territorial rights. Yet if the fur trade was an encounter shaped by Native as well as white agency, it was not, I think, an equal encounter. Whatever Native peoples wanted to do about it, the traders established their presence, and the balance of power in the Cordillera tilted fairly inexorably towards them.

There were a number of reasons for this, among them the different dependence of traders and Natives on the goods they obtained in trade. For European traders, furs were necessary for profitable trade; for Native people, some European goods became necessary for survival, and others for the maintenance of changed ways of life. Almost everywhere in the Cordillera, the differential introduction of firearms suddenly disrupted prior balances of power. As the Lequiltok, a southern Kwakwa̱ka̱'wakw people from northeastern Vancouver Island and adjacent mainland, acquired firearms from Nawittee, an emporium of the maritime fur trade at the northern end of Vancouver Island, their raids into the Strait of Georgia and Puget Sound increased in intensity. As the Blackfoot on the western Plains acquired guns from more easterly traders, all the peoples immediately west of them became vulnerable to their attack. Such peoples were desperate to acquire their own firearms and, when supplied, required powder and shot on a continuing basis. For them, trade became a matter of survival. Firearms were also used for hunting, though probably a chief at Spokane exaggerated when he apparently claimed in 1814 that 'we have broken our arrows and almost forgotten how to use them.' He also claimed that 'the white men made us love tobacco almost as much as we love our children.'[106] Neither guns nor tobacco were easily given up. Nor were knives, kettles, blankets, cloth, or, indeed, most items of trade. With the introduction of new goods, Native ways changed, and luxuries became necessities. Domestic life, for example, was suddenly different with kettles, trade blankets, and iron knives, harbingers of cultural coercion in that they introduced some everyday forms of what would later be seen as a colonizing culture.[107] As Native cultures adjusted across a broad front, there was little inclination – and perhaps, after a time, hardly the capacity – to pull back. Even Native card games changed as European cards and games were introduced.[108] Newly acquired ways could hardly be unlearned. Of course, some white people entering the Cordillera with the fur trade became 'entangled' with Native goods and ways,[109] but their lives were neither at the centre of the white world nor, after a time, in positions of particular influence in British Columbia. There were always other whites, their lives unaffected by the fur trade. There were not other Natives.

Out of the larger historical European experience with the world, traders conceived of themselves as whites of British or, more broadly, European background, and conceived of Native peoples as savages. Although these categories were complicated somewhat by Hawaiians, Native women living in forts, and Métis, traders used the dichotomy between whites and savages to conceptualize their circumstances and devise their strategies. Traders of different nationalities employed by different companies would present a common front to perceived Native threats. Natives, however, could not order the world in this simple, powerful way because they could not draw on a historical experience that enabled them to relativize and categorize themselves as 'Natives.' Rather, they lived in small groups and situated themselves in relation to other such groups within known, regional worlds. To them, there were no 'Natives,' only different peoples associated with different places. When fur traders entered this world, they became part of this complex local equation, and particular groups sought advantage from them. As it became clear that the traders were from outside the Native social world, there was neither a coordinated social organization nor a developed conception of Native to put against them, though the concept began to emerge as soon as the traders were identified as 'other.' Significantly, it was the trading language, Chinook, that required a word, *Siwash*, for Native. The concept slowly emerged – out of the encounter with newcomers and the larger world that enabled different Native peoples to conceive of themselves as a common people – but took time to impose itself over more locally organized and understood worlds. Perhaps early projects to coordinate different groups to drive whites out adumbrated this process, but projects did not materialize, lacking the social organization and conceptual framework to bring them about. In effect, having no word for or conception of themselves as a single people, Natives could not coordinate a response to the challenge that fur traders presented.

Nor did they have the physical power to defy whites for long. There were no Native centres that a determined white presence could not take. Here and there Natives acquired swivels, even small cannon, but a few such arms were no match for a well-defended fort, or defence against concerted white attack. By relying on surprise and local knowledge, Natives could snipe around the edges of white power, killing isolated individuals, occasionally someone in a fort, overwhelming small parties, and occasionally even taking a ship or a poorly defended fort – but the weight of trader disciplinary practice was intended to demonstrate the consequences of doing so. In all these ways, the fur trade was an asymmetrical encounter, and it had the capacity, over time, to establish the preconditions for full-blown colonial regimes.

By the early 1840s, the HBC had established its influence through most of the huge territory from present-day southern Oregon through the Alaskan panhandle. The company's control was probably greatest along the old axis of the fur trade – the lower Columbia to the upper Fraser via the Okanagan – and weakest along the margins of Russian influence, where forts and a HBC monopoly had recently been established. In much of the interior, a network of forts and brigade trails was well in place, and company ships, including the steamer *Beaver*, plied the coast. White competitors had been bested: in the northwest, by an 1839 deal with the Russian American Company to sell foodstuffs and pay a rent in skins in return for the trade of the Alaskan panhandle; in the south and southeast, by severe over-trapping and price competition to drive off American traders operating out of St. Louis; along the coast, by price competition after the depletion of sea otter stocks to discourage American ships looking for land furs.[110] A white presence was established and, in most areas, was not contested. At many forts, life had settled long since into a calm routine punctuated by the seasonal round of food procurement and trade. Fur traders and the rhythms of trade were part of regional life. Near the oldest forts, a few Native people began to live in log cabins, and many wore European clothing. When the colony of Vancouver Island was created in 1849, James Douglas could assure the London secretary of the HBC that settlement began in the 'most favourable auspices' as the only obstacles were those 'the hand of nature has imposed.' Natives were 'not only kind and friendly, but ready and willing to share their labour' and to assist settlers. He could even engage in this mellow reflection, ironic as in some ways it was, given his long involvement in the disciplinary strategies of the fur trade.

> It has been a work of time and labour to bring the Indians to that state of friendly intercourse; and I have endeavoured strongly to impress on the minds of Captain Grant and his followers [first settlers], the incalculable importance, both as regards the future well being of the Colony, and their own individual interests, of cultivating the friendship of these children of the forest.[111]

Statements like this have helped construct an enduring myth about the British fur trade in the Cordillera: that, compared to the American fur trade, it was gentle and benign, an early manifestation of a more managerial, less competitive, and less violent Canadian culture. Recently, an American legal historian, John Reid, has wondered how Canadian scholars can make such claims without embarrassment. For Reid, violence was endemic in the fur trade, with perhaps the difference that the larger company organization of the British trade allowed it to be more systematic, relentless, and violent, killing many in situations where American traders with more limited resources killed few. Reid is substantially right. The fur trade was built on terror and violence that, as much as possible, was implacable and witnessed. Even in 1849 on southern Vancouver Island, the memory of what the HBC had done to the Clallam was in the air, reinforced as it repeatedly had been by other, less spectacular manifestations of company power.

But Reid underestimates the power of a monopoly to manage the fur trade with only occasional direct recourse to violence. Where the HBC gained a monopoly position, it was able to control the distribution of alcohol and firearms. Having established the point that assaults on company personnel or property would bring unavoidable retribution, the HBC could fall back on non-violent strategies of control, notably marriages, its politics of divide and rule, and the bluster and theatre of trade. Along with violent eruptions now and then, these strategies usually worked. This was the stability to which Douglas referred and that, from a fur trader's perspective, was real enough by 1849 in areas where monopoly prevailed. Such areas were a far cry from the competitive Snake Country of the 1820s or, for that matter, from the Mackenzie Valley where the HBC and NWC competed before 1821 and a trader wrote in despair:

> Indolence, robbery and murder are the consequences of an opposition in trade: people would suppose it would rouse their attention to indus-

> try, having goods at a lower price, but far to the contrary; drunkenness, idleness and vice are prefered ... no good can be derived from the turbulent struggles of opposition in this country; it destroys trade, creates vice, and renders people crafty, ruins good morals, and almost totally abolishes every humane sentiment in both Christian and Indian breast.[112]

Allowing for distortions in both views, this was not the fur trade Douglas presided over in 1849, and the difference was neither culture nor nationality, but the passage of time and the effects of monopoly.

Over some fifty years, commercial capital, operating beyond the state and largely outside a system of law, had considerably modified the northern Cordillera. It had established a white presence that, for the most part, Native peoples accepted, whatever they made of whites. In much of the Cordillera, whites could move about safely, though most of their traffic was in a few narrow corridors. Native cultures had been considerably modified, not by deliberate plans to civilize – these would come later – but as Natives responded to the presence of newcomers and their goods. To a degree, Native peoples still controlled most of the territory beyond the forts, as well as their own agendas, but this control was now qualified because they could not exclude whites. They probably could not capture most forts. If, away from the forts, they stopped a party, they could not stop the retribution that would follow. They could not repulse a concerted white attack on any settlement. To this extent, whites were in control; the northern Cordillera had been somewhat colonized before colonies were established, before the border settlement of 1846. When formal colonies were created, the ground had been prepared and there was a large body of experience – the evolving, now two-hundred-year-old discourse of the fur trade – on which colonial administrators could draw. It was not a legal discourse so much as an accumulated experience with the strategies of trade in the North American interior. Colonies would clothe power in the rule of law, but, as far as Native peoples were concerned, the discourse of power long continued to operate, a legacy, partly, of the fur trade.

Insofar as it influenced the traders' management of Natives, this discourse depended approximately on what Michel Foucault called sovereign power, that is, the power of seizure of property or life, exercised episodically and dependent on fear to secure compliance. In Europe, the state, validated by a discourse of rights and law, had become the dominant locus of sovereign power; but such power, Foucault held, was also exercised apart from the state. The western North American fur trade, where sovereign power operated beyond the state and any formal system of legitimacy, is one such example. There, as in Europe, it was clad in theatre and spectacle intended to emphasize its presence and reduce the need for its use – a very particular theatre adapted to the circumstances of a fur trade along a remote interface of the European and the non-European. Unlike sovereign power in Europe, this regime of power was not backed by a discourse of rights. Nor had it yet given way to what Foucault termed disciplinary power, another technology of power, centred on taking charge of life rather than the threat of death, that invented 'normality' and sought conformity, and that, in armies, prisons, asylums, schools, intellectual disciplines, and eventually 'swarming' out into the larger body of society, came to regulate and order many details of everyday lives. Away from the forts, and even there only in rough, much-modified form, the varied machinery of such power was not at hand. Nor were traders interested in normalizing – 'civilizing' – Natives; they sought, rather, a profitable trade and, in pursuit of it, their own security.

The regime of sovereign power that Quimper and Vancouver anticipated in the 1790s began to be imposed on Vancouver Island in 1849, and on the mainland north of the 49th parallel in 1858. With colonies and colonial administrations, instructions came from the Colonial Office as the overall management, such as it was, of much of the northern Cordillera passed from a trading company to the British imperial government. British civil and criminal law were introduced, troops were at hand, and surveyors plotted the outlines of towns and countrysides. Responsibilities for social control once assumed by fur trading companies passed to the Crown. Yet experience in managing Natives lay with the traders, a fact that the British parliament recognized in appointing Douglas governor of both colonies, and that affected official policy well after he retired in 1864.

Two examples. In November 1852, a white shepherd was killed a few miles from Victoria, and the killers were presumed to be two Native men, a Cowichan and a Nanaimo.[113] Douglas, acting quickly to capture them so as to 'prevent further murders and aggressions which I fear may take place if the Indians are emboldened by present impunity,'[114] assembled a force of more than 150 men, largely drawn from a British frigate at Esquimault, and embarked for Cowichan Bay in early January with a flotilla of small vessels and the HBC steamer *Beaver*. En route, he met some frightened Saanich whom he advised were Her Majesty's subjects and who were 'to give up offenders against the laws whenever required to do so.' Douglas apparently later told the Cowichan: 'Give up the murderer, and let there be peace between our peoples, or I will burn out your lodges and trample out your tribes.'[115] At Fort St. James twenty-five years earlier, he had heard Governor Simpson's similar pronouncement. The Cowichan turned over a man. Douglas promised to give him a fair hearing at Nanaimo, and told the Cowichan that 'they must respect Her Majesty's warrant and surrender criminals belonging to their respective tribes on demand of the Court Magistrate and that resistance to the civil power would expose them to be considered as enemies.' There were similar intimidations at Nanaimo, but no one was turned over; the wanted man was captured after a long chase. Both were hurriedly tried on the quarterdeck of the *Beaver* before a jury of naval officers, and hanged the same day in the presence of most of the Nanaimo. The size and composition of the expeditionary force, the rhetoric of law and civil government, and the trial were new (there had not been trials since NWC days), but otherwise the assumptions and tactics of the Cowichan expedition were of the fur trade, even in the spies Douglas hired.[116]

In July 1879, the Nlha7kápmx gathered at Lytton to elect a head chief and council whom, they intended, would oversee their local government. Within the authority of the Queen and terms of the Indian Act of 1876, and encouraged by their Anglican missionary, they sought a limited but defined political authority within an increasingly settler-dominated society.[117] The Indian Reserve Commissioner, Gilbert Malcolm Sproat, was on hand for the meetings, and reported enthusiastically to Ottawa. For the most part, however, white British Columbia was outraged. Confederations of Natives were dangerous, a policy of divide and rule far safer. Taken aback by the intensity of the reaction, Sproat told the superintendent general of Indian Affairs in Ottawa that there is 'a class of "Old Residents" here, whose notion of Indian management is terrorism.'[118] Shortly thereafter, nine old residents, six of them former fur traders, outlined their position in a petition that effectively undermined Sproat's standing in Ottawa, encouraged his resignation, and sealed the fate of the Nlha7kápmx initiative. According to the old-timers, it was 'exceedingly dangerous ... to combine a number of half civilized Natives scattered over a large extent of territory sparsely inhabited by whites, without any controlling influence.' Moreover, 'the past safety and security which we have enjoyed in the Province is owing to the fact that the large Indian population of the Country has been divided into small bands without a head Chief possessing general authority or influence, and without the ability to unite and constitute themselves a powerful and formidable force.'[119] Here, more than twenty years after the creation of the colony of British Columbia, was the lingering voice of the fur trade, still not about the rule of law, to which in this case the Nlha7kápmx more nearly sought to conform, but the tactics of power.

Understandably yet ironically, present-day Native peoples have turned to the courts, where they confront a system of power established less clearly in law than in practice. The fur trade introduced a regime of non-Native power that expanded in the colonial period and continues, imbricated now in law, to the present. This is why the resolution of Native claims will lie less with the courts than with the political process, and why non-Native British Columbians need to understand, as now they hardly do, how non-Native power took root in this province.

3
The Making of the Lower Mainland

Europeans first reached the lands around the estuary of the Fraser River at the end of the eighteenth century, but did not consolidate their hold over the area for almost another seventy years. Until 1858, the year of the gold rush to the Fraser River and the creation of the Crown Colony of British Columbia, these lands were overwhelmingly a Native place in which Fort Langley, the trading post established in 1827 near the mouth of the Fraser, was an island of British control. After 1858, effective Native control of the region collapsed very quickly. In 1881, when peoples were first enumerated in a Canadian census, power lay squarely with governments and their representatives, the courts, the owners of sawmills and fish canneries, and, to an extent, local white leaders. Natives had been allocated small reserves where, their numbers much reduced and their voices unheard, they lived at the margins of a non-Native world. The state, industrial capital, and the cultural values of an immigrant population of predominantly British origin dominated a remade and renamed place, the Lower Mainland.

In a few years, the area had passed through a remarkable transformation: from the local worlds of fishing, hunting, and gathering peoples to a modern corner of the world economy within the British empire and an emerging federal nation-state, the Dominion of Canada. A transition that in Europe took millennia, here took decades, which is why the Lower Mainland presents such interesting analytical opportunities.

Although Spanish and English navigators in the early 1790s, and Simon Fraser in 1808, wrote briefly about the area, the documentary record begins to expand only in the 1820s. This record plus ethnographic accounts permit a consideration of the human geography of the lands around the Fraser estuary circa 1820, when it was still Native. The second section of this chapter describes the intrusion of Fort Langley into this Native territory, the third deals with the momentous geographical changes in the area between 1858 and the first federal census in 1881, and a final section comments briefly on some of the causes and implications of these changes.

A Native Place

In the winters of the early 1820s, there were probably three population clusters near the mouth of the Fraser River: Musqueam on the north arm of the Fraser River, the Kwantlen villages just upriver from modern New Westminster, and Tsawwassen on the western shore of Point Roberts (Figure 3.1). At Musqueam and the Kwantlen villages, the largest of these settlements, there were several hundred people. In the 1930s, the anthropologist Homer Barnett was told that Musqueam had once comprised three adjacent 'villages.' The largest, Male, was a continuous shed structure, 500 yards long, made up of many house segments (Figure 3.2); a second had seventy-six house segments arranged in a circle around a lacrosse field; and another comprised thirteen house segments. Barnett recorded the circular village in his field notes[1] but, doubting his informant on this point, described it as semicircular in his book. Apparently, there were also three adjacent Kwantlen villages. In all three population clusters, buildings were constructed of cedar posts and planks (Figure 3.2).

Within these three clusters, the largest unit of regular authority was the house group, most of whose members were close relatives. Other members were usually slaves, or people who, for one reason or another, were unable to form a house group of their own. One house group might occupy several house segments within a long shed building, or all of one shorter structure. Each group owned house and mortuary sites, some principal resource procurement sites, and names, songs, and rituals. The head of a house group was usually a descendant of a founding family, sometimes a respected elder. But in the matrix of kin within which most people lived, authority depended on esteem and had little coercive power. Except as their actions affected the collective property of the house group, in which case decisions were taken by the head in conjunction with the elders, individual conjugal families did as they wished. Many owned important resource procurement sites. The heads of house groups met frequently, and usually one of them – because of age, eloquence, or the size of his or her house group – was particularly respected. But this person had no institutionalized authority; there was no institutionalized hierarchy of power beyond the house group. Within every village, different house groups were linked by blood ties and by obligations incurred by giving and receiving gifts. Similar ties linked the three winter population clusters at the mouth of the Fraser with each other, and with people elsewhere.[2]

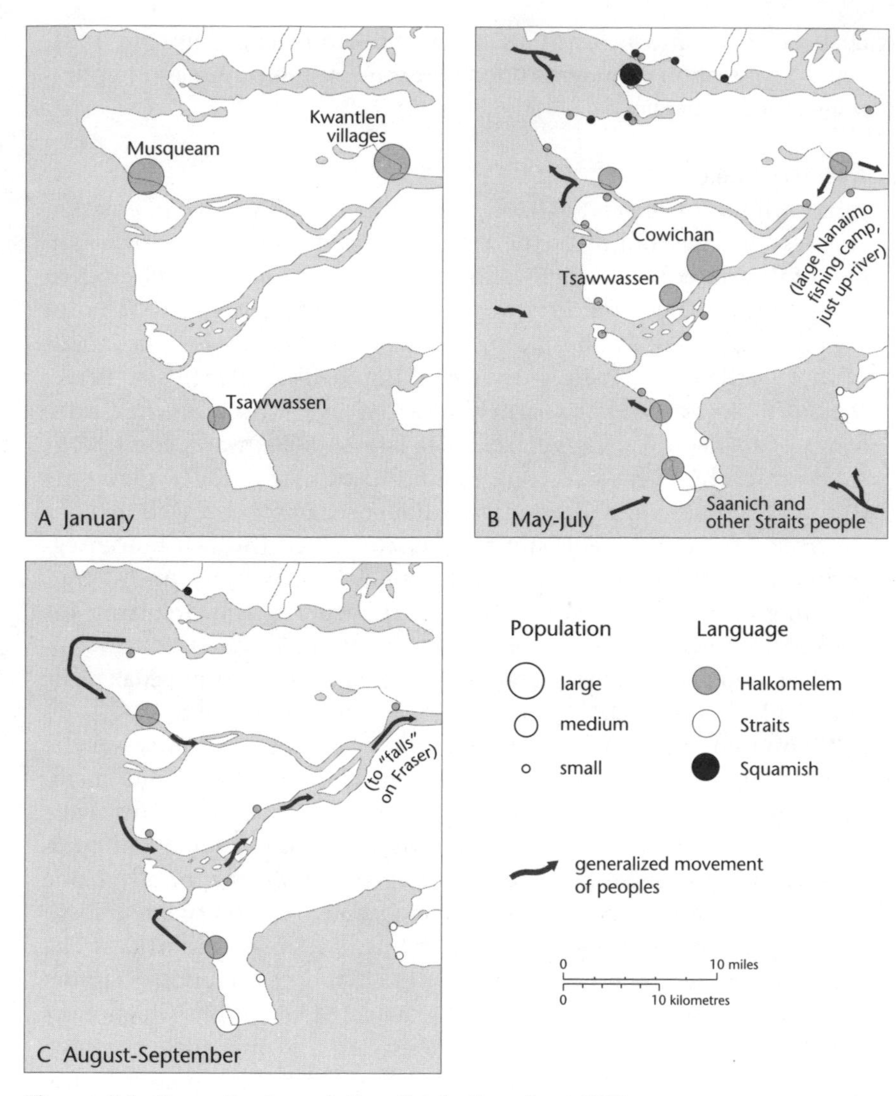

Figure 3.1 Generalized population distribution about 1820

Although winter curtailed movement between settlements, the people at Kwantlen villages, Musqueam, and Tsawwassen participated in a much larger region of social interaction (Figure 3.3). They spoke Halkomelem, the language of the peoples of the lower Fraser Valley, from the Fraser Canyon to southeastern Vancouver Island. Along the coast to the north were speakers of other Coast Salish languages, the nearest being the Squamish, who wintered at the head of Howe Sound, and the Sechelt. The most southerly speakers of a Wakashan language, the Lequiltok, were a good 240 kilometres north of the mouth of the Fraser, around

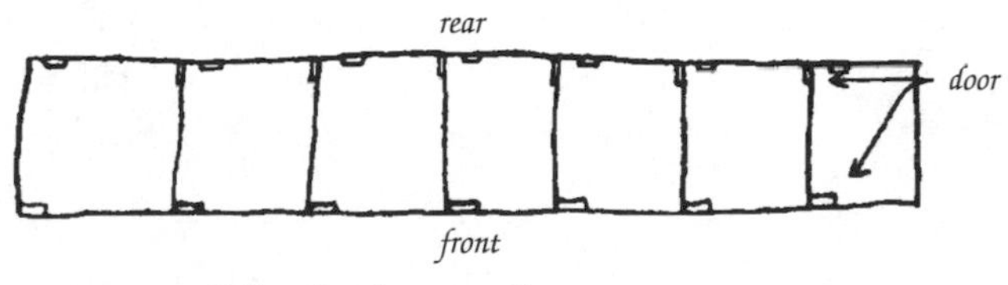

Plan showing seven house segments

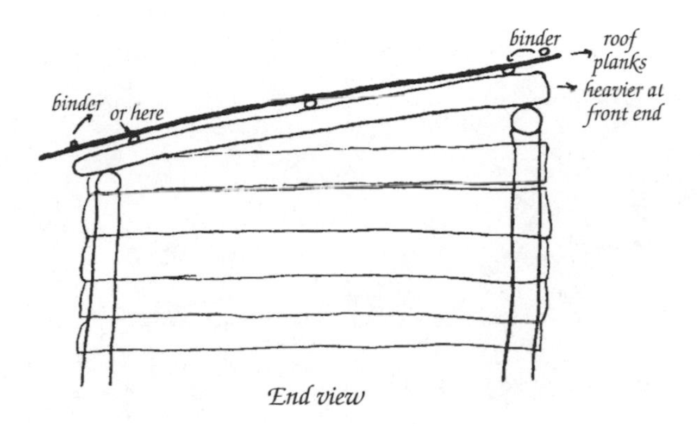

End view

Figure 3.2 Shed house at Musqueam (after Homer Barnett)

Johnstone Strait. Immediately south of the Halkomelem, along the coast, were speakers of other Coast Salish languages: Nooksack, Straits, and a little farther away, Clallam and Lushootseed. Inland, to the north and east, were speakers of Lillooet and Thompson, each an Interior Salish language. The people at Musqueam, the Kwantlen villages, and Tsawwassen knew and, in one way or another, dealt with all these peoples. Many individuals were bi- or trilingual, and someone would understand almost any visitor from afar.

In March, when food supplies were much diminished, the people of the lower Fraser began to move in conjugal families or house groups to resource procurement sites, where they often met other peoples. This, with great variation in detail, was the Northwest Coast pattern. Near the Fraser, the river itself dominated the seasonal round of resource procurement. Ethnographer James Teit concluded that, compared to the Columbia and Skeena rivers, and the largely overland routes from Squamish to Lillooet and from Bella Coola to the upper Fraser, the Fraser was not a major route of coastal-interior trade, due to the canyon. But as one of the largest reservoirs of food on the continent, the river drew people from afar, and supported many more people than lived along it in winter.

Figure 3.3 The Lower Mainland in linguistic context (after Suttles and Kinkade)

Figure 3.1B shows the distribution of population in the lands around the Fraser estuary in early summer.[3] Winter population clusters had dispersed. Musqueam groups were scattered around what are now English Bay and Burrard Inlet and at many fishing or gathering sites on the Gulf Islands and around the Fraser delta; the Tsawwassen had a fishing camp on the south bank of Lulu Island; the Kwantlen were dispersed along the river and its tributaries in locations most of which are not now precisely known. Other peoples came to the area. Squamish groups sought shellfish,

fish, and birds in English Bay and Burrard Inlet. Cowichan people, Halkomelem-speakers from Vancouver Island, occupied plank-house fishing camps along the south bank of Lulu Island where, in spring, they caught oolichan and sturgeon; in 1824, the fur trader F.-N. Annance said there was one mile-long village.[4] Some 500 Nanaimo people, also Halkomelem-speakers from Vancouver Island, had a plank-house fishing camp on the Fraser near the mouth of the Pitt River, where they also took oolichan and sturgeon. By early July, Saanich and other Straits-speakers, together with some Clallam and others from Puget Sound, congregated at the southwestern tip of Point Roberts where, with rows of reef nets in shallow waters, they caught large numbers of salmon as the fish rounded towards the Fraser. Annance considered this settlement, which was uninhabited when he saw it in December, almost as large as the mile-long fishing camp on the south bank of Lulu Island.

The intense, early summer use of the shorelines and river banks around the Fraser estuary diminished abruptly in early August, when most people – though only the Saanich, apparently, among the Straits-speakers – moved some 180 kilometres upriver to take salmon in the rapids at the foot of the Fraser Canyon (Figure 3.1C). People remained at the reef netting sites and at a few other locations, but Burrard Inlet and much of the lower Fraser may have been virtually deserted. Several thousand people congregated at the foot of the lower canyon, just above Yale. Most returned in late September, often transporting their dried salmon on plank platforms laid across two dugout canoes. In the last two weeks of September 1828, the chief trader at Fort Langley recorded 550 canoes of Cowichan and 200 of Squamish passing downriver.[5] In early October, many peoples collected *wapato* – Indian potato (*Sagittaria latifolia*) – from marshes along the lower Fraser and its tributaries prior to a large social and ceremonial gathering of well-fed, well-provisioned peoples at the mouth of the Pitt River (possibly at the eastern end of Lulu Island). Not everyone returned to the population cluster where they had spent the previous winter. Cowichans sometimes overwintered at the foot of the Fraser Canyon; others stayed along the lower Fraser. Apparently, a good many people passed different winters in different villages with different kin.

This flux of peoples, coupled with marriages that were almost always between people from different house groups (often from different population clusters) and with property rights held by house groups and conjugal families, created intricate webs of socio-economic relationships that spread well beyond the region. Social space had few clear boundaries. Individuals could belong by right of birth and marriage to several different house groups. People from different winter population clusters would have rights, therefore, to many of the same resources. Ties of kin crossed dialect and language boundaries that, in any case, were not sharp. The obligations incurred by gift-giving at the feasts added another layer to the web. When, for example, Cowichans came to Lulu Island, or Squamish to Burrard Inlet, or some Musqueam went to the Gulf Islands, they were not entering the territory of another people so much as moving within webs of social and economic relations that connected different individuals and groups to each other, and to each other's places.

Such arrangements did not prevent conflicts. Wrongs were avenged, whether with payments or blood. The cycle of small-scale raids and reprisals was difficult to break, and could occur locally or over considerable distances – anywhere within the range of peoples' contacts. Sometimes sizeable war parties formed, reflecting a consensus among many or all of the heads of house groups in, or even beyond, a population cluster. Led by temporary 'war chiefs,' their attacks were swift and fleeting, usually just before dawn. If possible, men were killed and women and children captured, often to be ransomed by surviving relatives at the cost of most of their possessions. But there was no institutional or logistical support for prolonged assaults. Nor, given the lack of political authority beyond the house group, were alliances formed easily between different population clusters.

In the annual round of resource procurement, conjugal families and house groups fished, hunted, and gathered a large part of what they ate: fish and shellfish primarily, but also birds, land and sea mammals, and a great variety of edible plants. Native peoples fashioned most of their tools, clothing, and buildings from locally available materials. Yet material goods circulated steadily among families and house groups in winter population clusters through informal gift-giving, and through more formal giving to guests at feasts, which were held to maintain status and consolidate social claims: to a name, a marriage, a guardian spirit, a song, or a place. These were frequent winter occurrences. There was little trade as such within population clusters; the circulation of property by giving was, rather, an integral part of the social organization. Feasts involving people from different population clusters – 'potlatches,' as they were known later in Chinook trading jargon – were held in late spring when the weather was fit for travelling. The feasts were large, and gifts were distributed on the basis of rank, generating reciprocal obligations; at subsequent feasts, guests were expected to give more than they had received. The potlatches may have become common, as Homer Barnett surmised, only after Europeans introduced new wealth to the area. Exchanges of property over much longer distances, such as those involving dentalium shells (*haiqua*) from the southwest coast of Vancouver Island, or canoes from Johnstone Strait, apparently involved barter and bargaining combined with gift-giving and kin relations. Raiding may have redistributed more property than did such trade.

Economy and society were not separate categories, nor was the environment. People lived in familiar places, named them intimately, knew the seasonal ways of flora and fauna, and, within the limits of their technology, satisfied most of their material needs from local resources. Subsequent inhabitants of the region would not begin to match this detailed, localized knowledge of a natural world. Nor would they know its spirits. The Native peoples of the Lower Mainland drew no distinction between mind and matter, animate and inanimate, human and natural, subject and object – categories of the modern European mind. The founding figure in a creation story of the Pitt River people had taken a sandhill crane, then a sockeye salmon, to wife. The sockeye, therefore, were relatives, returning to give themselves to their kin. A soft rain on a west wind was a mother weeping. Everything depended on spirit power. At puberty, the young sought a guardian spirit, and their subsequent lives were an unfolding relationship, often mediated by dreams, with that spirit and others – spirits interwoven with society, interwoven with the environment. People lived within a coherent totality, a lifeworld. Life was highly contextualized within experience, and the context was largely shared, with individual stories wrapped around each other and around the creation stories. Everyday life was part and parcel of an experienced, known whole, from which it was impossible for an individual to stand aside.[6]

It is not clear to what extent, in 1820, this Native world had been influenced by white contact. In 1808, Natives at the foot of the canyon, near Yale, told Simon Fraser that white men had already been there. He did not believe them, but David Thompson evidently did, noting on his remarkable map of 1813-14: 'To this place the white man come from the sea.' When Fraser met the Kwantlen, they 'evinced no kind of surprise or curiosity at seeing us, nor were they afraid of our arms, so that they must have been in the habit of seeing white people'[7]; the hostile reception he received from the Musqueam also implies that Europeans were known there. On the other hand, when John Work, exploring for the Hudson's Bay Company (HBC), was on the lower Fraser in 1824, he found very few European goods, and noted that the meadows and small streams south of the river were replete with beaver, indications that the trade in land furs was not under way.[8] The indirect effects of the white presence along the coast had been far more telling. Smallpox, coming from the Plains via the Columbia River, had devastated the peoples around the Strait of Georgia in 1782 (see Chapter 1). To the north, the Kwakwa̱ka̱'wakw in Johnstone Strait were not affected; this, plus the establishment of Nawittee at the north end of Vancouver Island as a major centre of the maritime fur trade, gave a southern Kwakwa̱ka̱'wakw tribe, the Lequiltok, a decisive military advantage over their traditional enemies to the south. In the

1820s, the Lequiltok, armed with muskets, were raiding along the lower Fraser for slaves; the Musqueam and other Fraser River people lived in terror of them.[9]

Fort Langley in a Native World, 1827-57

An American ship was trading well into the Strait of Juan de Fuca in the spring of 1827, a few months before the HBC established Fort Langley. From this time on, Native people of the Lower Mainland had direct, regular access to Europeans.

The establishment of Fort Langley brought an island of outside control and a well-developed system of nineteenth-century British trade into the midst of Native territory.[10] The twenty men who built Fort Langley in the late summer and fall of 1827 were old hands of the Hudson Bay and Montreal fur trades, and knew exactly what they were doing. A first bastion went up in two weeks. It appears, wrote the chief trader, 'to command respect in the eyes of the Indians, who begin, shrewdly, to conjecture for what purpose the Ports and loopholes are intended.'[11] Within six weeks, there were two bastions, a palisade, and gates. The traders had enclosed a small, defensible ground. Then living quarters went up, built of timber-frame construction, like the bastions, with the spaces between the vertical posts filled by squared horizontal timbers. Before winter, a simple fort was finished. On November 26, 'a Flag Staff was cut and prepared, and in the afternoon erected in the South East Corner of the Fort. The usual forms were gone through ... in baptizing the Establishment.'[12] For those who made it, this small, defended settlement, like hundreds built before it in the northern continental interior, was not very remarkable.

Established to extend the HBC's presence along the coast and to thwart American trading vessels, Fort Langley was an outlier of the company's extensive, coordinated trading system. Furs and, by 1829, salted and barrelled salmon were shipped from Langley to Fort Vancouver on the Columbia River. Supplies came from London via the Columbia. Sometimes a Native carrier was given letters to transport upriver to Fort Kamloops, to catch, with luck, the brigade for the Columbia. Local self-sufficiency, encouraged by the company, was quickly achieved at Fort Langley. Sturgeon, salmon, and some game were traded from the Natives, or fished and hunted by company employees. In 1828, potatoes were found to yield well; soon there were other vegetables, grains, and livestock. By 1830, Fort Langley fed itself and had a food surplus for export.[13]

The fort's small society was polyglot and multiracial. The first officers were Scots. Most men were French Canadians or Métis – French and, soon, Chinook were the fort's most frequently spoken languages – but others were British or Iroquois, and one was Hawaiian. All the women were Natives; some came from the Columbia River, but most were local. As noted in Chapter 2, James Murray Yale, who arrived in October 1828, was married a month later to the daughter of a local chief, a marriage that the Natives probably thought would cement an alliance, and that the chief trader thought would be good for business. In principle, the officer in charge of the fort, like the captain of a ship, commanded this society. In fact, his decisions dominated defensive arrangements, the deployment of contract labour, and the commercial economy, but not the fort's domestic world. Some Native women in the fort kept their own slaves, and social networks crossed the palisade to the society beyond the palisade. For thirty years after 1827, there was no mechanism by which a few whites in a fort or on ships could control Native life in an adjacent village, or anywhere else in the Lower Mainland.

Yet HBC introductions into Native life became more numerous and involved more than trade goods such as blankets and firearms. In 1829, Indian women at Fort Langley received 'a good mess of potatoes' for a day's work,[14] and soon potatoes were grown at most Native settlements along the lower Fraser and around the strait. Chickens were also introduced at this time. Dogs killed the first two chickens to reach a Native settlement; their owner returned to Fort Langley with the two dead birds, asking for live ones in exchange. Venereal diseases also diffused from Fort Langley, though they may also have been in the area before 1827. All such introductions affected Native life, as did the process of trade itself. The attentions white traders gave to chiefs probably raised their status in Native society. Native groups that participated directly in the trade had an advantage over those that did not. The Kwantlen largely abandoned their villages at what later became New Westminster, and resettled near the fort; much of this trade soon passed through their hands, establishing a relationship that, in general, had been repeated across the transcontinental span of the fur trade. New wealth undoubtedly increased the scale of gift-giving at the feasts and, as Homer Barnett thought, may have made the larger feasts into intervillage occasions: the historic potlatch.

However, in the last analysis, Fort Langley was a bounded society. Company traders had difficulty extending their control much beyond its walls. If goods were stolen from the fort, every effort was made to retrieve them and to punish the thief. The traders had to be seen as resolute in the protection of property. They would threaten to discontinue trade, and, when they did, both the missing goods and someone who may have been the thief were usually turned over to them. When a fort wife left, claiming that she had not been well treated and 'secured with enough property,' the traders suspected that she departed to be with her Native paramour, and sent a party of five to bring her back.[15] She had become property not so much of her husband as of the HBC. Traders had dealt with Natives for years, and knew the tactics of bluster, threat, and imperturbability. They were more than prepared to play off local Native factions. They could also adjust their prices, particularly to draw Native trade from American ships. And they could sell firearms with deliberate, geopolitical intent, specifically to counteract the power of the Lequiltok. But when a Cowichan chief was rumoured to have traded his arms and ammunition to the very Lequiltok he was supposed to fight, the traders were helpless. They could not establish the truth of the story, and to threaten would be to lose much of the Cowichan trade. The chief trader recorded the simple reality in the fort journal: 'We Cannot undertake to Control them So effectually, and must take them as they Come.'[16] Traders did not attempt to change Native values, they did not actively interfere with the Native subsistent economy, and they did not begin to control Native territory.

In 1839, Fort Langley was moved four kilometres upriver to be closer to its farm. A larger fort was built. In the early 1850s, the fort was less a fur trade post than a hub of a diversified export economy and a supply depot for the interior trade, with connections upriver to forts Yale and Hope, and thence by brigade trail to Kamloops and beyond. More than twenty company servants worked at Fort Langley; its multiracial population must have approached 200. Furs, fish, and cranberries were traded from Native people; grains, butter, and meat from the company farm, whose produce went mainly to the Russians in Alaska, were the fort's principal exports. Native women worked in salmon salteries at Fort Langley, at the mouths of the Chilliwack and Harrison rivers, and at Fort Hope. Other Natives worked in the fields or on the *bateaux* they helped track, pole, and row upriver. Such work was seasonal, and was paid in kind. Trade and, to a lesser extent, seasonal work transferred large quantities of HBC goods to Native hands without, it appears, disrupting the seasonal rounds of most Native communities or undermining their control of their subsistent economies. HBC traders at Fort Langley in the mid-1850s were no more able to control surrounding Native societies than their predecessors had been in the 1830s.

Yet the context of Native life in the region was certainly changing. HBC price competition and coastal shipping (particularly the *Beaver*, a side-wheel steamer introduced in 1836) eliminated American traders from the Strait of Georgia. The company established Fort Victoria on Vancouver Island in 1843; with the border settlement of 1846, the fort became the HBC's main depot on the Pacific. After 1846, the reef net fisheries and seasonal villages at Point Roberts were in American territory. In 1849, Vancouver Island became a proprietary colony. The Cowichan and Nanaimo soon began to learn what this meant. As recounted in Chapter 2, when two Natives were accused of murdering a white shepherd, a force of 150 sailors and marines from the British frigate *Thetis* accompanied

View of Fort Langley, by J.M. Alden. Palisade, guard, and fish sheds in the foreground, Kwantlen village across the river.

Governor Douglas to Cowichan Bay, then to Nanaimo. The two suspects were taken, tried by jury, and publicly hanged. Three years later, a force of almost 450 Royal Marines and seamen returned to Cowichan Bay to apprehend another suspected murderer, try him the next day, and hang him that evening in front of the Cowichan.[17] By this date, a colliery, with up-to-date industrial technology, and the beginnings of an industrial town, British Columbia's first, had been established at Nanaimo. New systems of white power were entering the territory of the Halkomelem-speaking peoples.

The effects of these developments on the peoples of the Lower Mainland are far from clear. Native trapping must have altered some seasonal rounds, but probably not very much as beaver became scarce; everywhere, said a fur trader in 1846, the steel trap had done its work.[18] Some people from the Lower Mainland began to visit Fort Victoria, which had a larger choice of European goods than at Fort Langley as well as a Native market for slaves. After the border settlement, they also dealt with American traders in Puget Sound. With the establishment of Fort Victoria and Nanaimo, the peoples of southeastern Vancouver Island may have come in smaller numbers and/or for shorter periods of time to the Fraser River. As Coast Salish acquired firearms, Lequiltok raiding diminished and stopped; in the 1850s, there was considerable Coast Salish trade with the Lequiltok and other more northerly tribes, principally at Fort Victoria. British military force had not been used against the Musqueam, Tsawwassen, or Kwantlen, but these people undoubtedly heard about it, in oft-repeated detail, from their kin across the strait.

When Simon Fraser descended the river, some Natives in the canyon took him for Coyote, the transformer figure in their accounts of creation (see Chapter 4). By the 1850s, however, most people of the Lower Mainland must have recognized, without, of course, putting it this way, that quite alien sources of power, entirely outside their experience, were affecting life around the Strait of Georgia. Shared experience no longer fully explained their changing lifeworld.

Town, Countryside, and Camps, 1858-81

News of gold along the Fraser, which the HBC had been trading quietly from Natives at Kamloops for a few years, became public in San Francisco in the early spring of 1858. Coupled with the increased capitalization of the California mines, the decline of small-scale, individual opportunity there, and other gold fevers around the Pacific basin in the mid-nineteenth century, the news produced a gold rush to the Fraser River. At least 20,000 miners entered the mouth of the river in the spring and summer of 1858, most coming via Victoria, which suddenly became a city of 5,000, and almost all heading for gold fields that were thought to begin below Fort Hope, 150 kilometres inland, and extend upriver to who-knew-where.

At the beginning of August 1858, the cordilleran mainland north of the 49th parallel became a Crown Colony; Queen Victoria named it British Columbia. Colonel Moody, commander of a regiment of Royal Engineers sent to the new colony, selected 'the first high ground on the north side after entering the [Fraser] river'[19] as the site for a capital; Queen Victoria named it New Westminster. The site, Moody thought, could be rendered 'almost unassailable'; moreover, there were 'great facilities for communication by water, as well as by future great trunk railways into the interior.'[20] It was a defensive site near the head of marine navigation on a river route to the interior: 250 years earlier, Samuel de Champlain had chosen a similar site for similar reasons on the St. Lawrence.

With these developments, the exclusive trading regime of the HBC, the relationships between Natives and Europeans on which it rested, and Native control in their own territory all began to wane. British civil and criminal law suddenly began to be enforced in the colony. A judge and stipendiary magistrates were appointed to interpret it, jails were built for offenders, and, if necessary, gunboats or troops could be used; for the region, this was a new system of administration backed by the most powerful and expansionistic of nineteenth-century nation-states.

The gold rushes also shifted the economic balance towards resource industries that were increasingly dominated by industrial capital. The industrial age was entering British Columbia in specialized work camps that combined an abundant resource, elements of industrial technology, and transportation connections to distant markets. New people came, some from across the Pacific, but more, directly or indirectly, from Europe, particularly from Britain. Most immigrants believed in progress, private property, and the superiority of British civilization. Thousands of miles from home, they defended such assumptions with the vigour of those who are dislocated, yet have the power of government at their disposal. Native and Chinese people, therefore, were excluded from citizenship; the latter were to be kept out or apart; the former, if they did not die off, were to be civilized. Such plans had spatial imperatives, as, indeed, had the entire momentum of British Columbia after 1858. A new human geography was required, and more than anywhere else in the abruptly created colony of British Columbia, this new geographical project began in the lands around the mouth of the Fraser River.

There, essentially, it established the ancient dichotomy between town and countryside and, equally basic in Canada, camps associated with staple trades. More specifically, it created a river-mouth town; farms superimposed on, but not entirely displacing, an older Native world; and canning, sawmilling, and logging operations. Within and among these settlements were particular configurations of power. Beyond them were the world economy, the British empire, cultural values of the late-nineteenth-century English-speaking world, and, less insistently overall, but extremely important individually, the particular settings from which other non-English-speaking peoples had come.

A Town

New Westminster, a capital and also a river-mouth steamboat port, was the creation of both government and gold rush. The Royal Engineers established their camp, Sapperton, on the site of former Native villages, just east of the new townsite, which they surveyed in a grid embellished by crescents, terraces, and public squares (Figure 3.4).[21] They designed and supervised construction of most of the capital's first government buildings: customs house, treasury, assay office, courthouse, jail (gaol), and land registry office. They designed Holy Trinity Anglican church, a dignified Gothic revival church built of wood above the fledgling town at the edge of the forest, on land set aside for a public garden. But the capital created by the Royal Engineers was also a port: a trans-shipment point between ships arriving from Victoria and river steamers. At the height of the Cariboo gold rush in 1862, there were some 400 beds in boarding houses and hotels, many stores selling outfit for the mines, and steamboat captains vying for the river traffic.

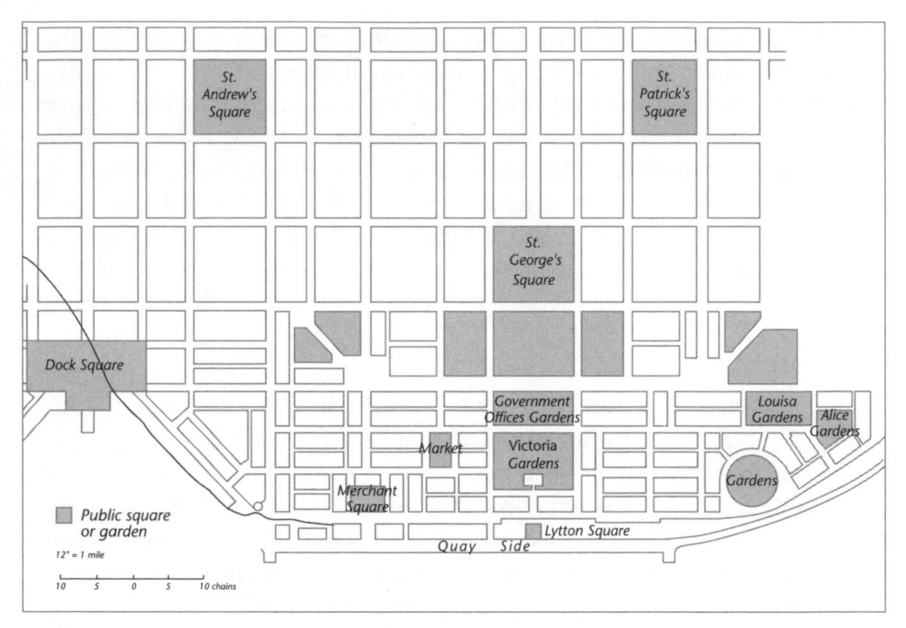

Figure 3.4 Plan of New Westminster, 1862

The officers of the Royal Engineers were well-educated men who held visions of nature shaped by the romantic poets, the writings of John Ruskin, and the broad literary and artistic reaction in England to industrial society. At Sapperton, they laid out a cricket ground and walks into the ravines. At the site of New Westminster, Colonel Moody found a forest 'magnificent beyond description, but most vexatious to a surveyor and the first dweller of a town. I declare without the least sentimentality, I grieve and mourn the ruthless destruction of these most glorious trees. What a grand old park this whole hill would make.'[22] For the eastern Canadians in the town, most of whom were Methodists or Presbyterians, only a generation or two removed from pioneer conditions, forest walks and natural parks were 'useless follies.' These people considered themselves practical, and were the strongest boosters of New Westminster's trade and industry. When the Royal Engineers were recalled in the fall of 1863, their vision of nature went with them, and would hardly reappear in mainland British Columbia for another forty years.

After the engineers left, Moody's house in Sapperton was enlarged for the new governor. When the colonies of Vancouver Island and British Columbia were united in 1866, New Westminster briefly became the capital of an enlarged British Columbia. But with the post-gold rush slump and, in 1868, the conversion of the capital to Victoria, New Westminster's population fell to under 500. The town remained a port of entry to the mainland and a local service centre, and benefitted from industrial developments along the lower Fraser, growing slowly in the 1870s in proportion to the expansion of these activities. By 1881, almost 2,000 people lived in New Westminster. Four canneries and three small sawmills operated in or near the town. It was the urban connection for farm families throughout the lower Fraser Valley and, to an extent, for loggers and sawmills on Burrard Inlet, and it was the gateway for the railway construction beginning in the lower canyon above Yale, the site of the old Native fishery. New Westminster still housed a few government employees – government agents, an Indian agent, a constable, a customs officer, a warden and a prison guard, land agents, and a postmaster – as well as the Oblates, a French Roman Catholic order. The town was the administrative seat of mainland British Columbia and the Queen Charlotte Islands, but its momentum now lay with commerce and industry.

New Westminster's occupational structure was more diverse than any other place on the mainland. It was a small, late-nineteenth-century city of somewhat British cast, though in 1881, some 10 per cent of its inhabitants had been born in the United States, another 10 per cent in China, almost 20 per cent in eastern Canada, and, even excluding Natives, a good third in British Columbia.[23] A large part of the labour force was made up of artisans and workers associated with the port or resource industries, many of whom spoke little or no English. The elite, who controlled the town, reflected bourgeois Victorian values. Their wooden

Two views near New Westminster. *Top*: The English Gothic imagination along the Fraser River. *Bottom*: Institutional upper town, commercial lower town, 1861.

houses frequently copied styles in San Francisco, their gardens were more inclined to be English, and their social conventions, such as ladies' 'at home' days, were parts of a taken-for-granted Victorian image of respectable urban life. There were other, more basic assumptions: the law should serve the interests of property, men should head households, and, with only slightly less unanimity, the Queen should reign and British civilization should be reproduced in British Columbia.

From this perspective, Chinese and Natives were alien and 'other.' In the early 1860s, a few Chinese people lived in shacks at the edge of town; by 1881, there were over 200 Chinese in New Westminster, almost all in a Chinatown situated at the western end of Front Street, near a cannery, two small sawmills, and Native homes. Racism largely created Chinatown, and the existence of Chinatown itself, and its real or imagined pathologies, reinforced the social construction of race.[24] In the early 1860s, Native peoples came for the spring oolichan and sturgeon fisheries, and often stayed a while. 'Decent people,' fulminated a newspaper editor, were subjected to 'the intolerable nuisance of having filthy, degraded, debauched Indians as next door neighbours.' Although 'citizens' tried to keep Natives out – a small river-front reserve, established in 1862, was intended to segregate them – Native people moved easily through New Westminster streets and empty lots until, in the 1870s, they began to settle in shacks beside the fish canneries. For most whites, the Natives were a different, incomprehensible, racially identifiable people whose economic usefulness was acknowledged, but whose social status was not measured by any scale that included whites. Less threatening than the Chinese, they were considered equally alien and other (see Chapter 9).

Most whites in New Westminster kept in regular touch with home and the larger world from which they came. Until 1869, letters, magazines, and newspapers from London came by ship and rail across the isthmus of Panama in less than two months. With the completion of the Union Pacific Railroad to San Francisco in 1869, they took about a month. In 1865, telegraph lines connected New Westminster to the American telegraph system; a year later, the first trans-Atlantic cable extended the link to Britain. Goods came via the Union Pacific and San Francisco, or around the Horn and through Victoria, British Columbia's Pacific port. By such means the outside world was accessible, much more so, really, than was British Columbia itself (see Chapter 6).

In the lower Fraser Valley, the river was virtually the only artery of inland transportation; river steamboats ran to Yale at the foot of the canyon, and a wagon road and trails extended beyond. Away from the routes to the mines, most of the interior was inaccessible, and the range of New Westminster's influence there was extremely limited. Victoria continued to exert its distant authority through gold commissioners, magistrates, and government agents; and the Department of Indian Affairs in Ottawa had begun to create Indian agencies and to appoint Indian agents to administer them. The Oblates had devised a system, based on itinerant priests and Native officials, for the regular surveillance of dispersed, exceedingly isolated populations. But control was hampered by the problems of movement. Even within the Lower Mainland, movement was very restricted. It was difficult to walk in the forest. The government cut trails and seasonal roads – initially, partly for defence – to Burrard Inlet and along the Fraser, but the river itself remained the main avenue of transportation. People were perched in New Westminster within a stretched, internationalized social space that had only begun to come to terms with British Columbia.

A Countryside

As well as links with a town, a settled countryside required a land policy; in British Columbia, this meant that terms had to be worked out to turn land judged to be wilderness into private property. The Colonial Office favoured compact settlement on surveyed lands sold at a good price. Cheap land and lax terms of payment would encourage 'the premature conversion into petty and impoverished landowners of those who ought to be laborers.'[25] Therefore, shortly after they arrived, the Royal Engineers surveyed a number of ranges – at the mouth of the Pitt, opposite New Westminster, and in the Fraser delta – and a few lots, intended for military settlers, along the American border. Each range was divided, as topography permitted, into thirty-six square, numbered, 160-acre sections. These sections were priced at ten shillings an acre or eighty pounds, half payable in advance. Few were sold, in good part because land was available across the border for half the price. Governor Douglas had warned that 'the sturdy yeomen expected this year from Canada, Australia, and other British Colonies might be driven in hundreds across the frontier to seek for homes in the United States territories.'[26] The next year, local officials, with the reluctant support of the Colonial Office, adopted a more American policy of pre-emption, thereby increasing the availability of land by allowing settlement to precede surveys, and reducing its initial cost by allowing payment to follow surveys. In 1861, the Colonial Office accepted a lower price for land: four shillings, two pence – one dollar – an acre.

Pre-emptors of 160 acres could purchase an additional 480 acres, paying half the price at the time of sale, half when the land was surveyed. They were to be, or become, British subjects. With minor changes, such policies remained in effect until 1875, when land began to be surveyed into townships of thirty-six square-mile sections, and offered to British subjects in free grants of 160 surveyed or unsurveyed acres. Additional land could be purchased for one dollar an acre. Implicit in such legislation was the denial of Native rights to land. From 1866, Natives were not allowed to pre-empt land, because, the governor argued, the Crown could not delegate its constitutional trust over Indian lands.[27] Rather, Natives received a few tiny reserves, held for them by the federal government. Figure 3.5, which shows all these land surveys, is, essentially, a map of the new balance of power in an area subdivided into properties and opened for development.

Yet the pace of land acquisition was slow. Figure 3.6 shows the sales and pre-emptions of Crown land in the Lower Mainland before Confederation. Almost no land was sold in 1859, when the price was ten shillings an acre. Lower land prices, pre-emptions, and the expectations of a gold rush to the upper Fraser improved the land market in 1860 and 1861, but the rate of alienation of Crown land declined thereafter. For the most part, lands were taken up along the river, the main artery of transportation, close to New Westminster and around Burrard Inlet. In 1868, just over 1,100 acres were under crops in the entire lower Fraser Valley. Most of the alienated land shown in Figure 3.6 was undeveloped; much of it was held by speculators, but prices for uncleared land were static. Confederation itself did not increase the attraction of land. In 1872, there were 228 pre-emptions in all of British Columbia; in the first full year of free land grants (1875), only 179 such grants were made.[28]

The essential problem, almost as old as the European settlement of Canada, was that isolated settlements created by a staple trade were not easily converted to other pursuits. The development of alternative economies was hampered by small local markets and inaccessible distant ones. As the gold rushes waned in British Columbia, this conundrum loomed everywhere. Agriculture, which seemed to offer both economic security and social stability, was one apparent alternative supported by a spate of agrarian rhetoric. The Lower Mainland was judged to be one of the most promising agricultural areas in British Columbia. But there were no external markets for its agricultural produce; even the Cariboo mines and the cities of Victoria and Nanaimo were better served by farmers closer at hand. Markets, such as they were, were in New Westminster and in the lumber camps and sawmills on Burrard Inlet. Moreover, there were major environmental obstacles to farming: prairies were subject to seasonal flooding, and massive forests were exceedingly difficult to clear.

In this situation, agriculture required some capital and developed slowly. Farming appeared first on the prairies where, despite all the labour of dyking and draining, start-up costs were less than in the forest. Without hired labour, a pre-emption would not become a farm for years, and because white labour was expensive, Chinese or Native labour was

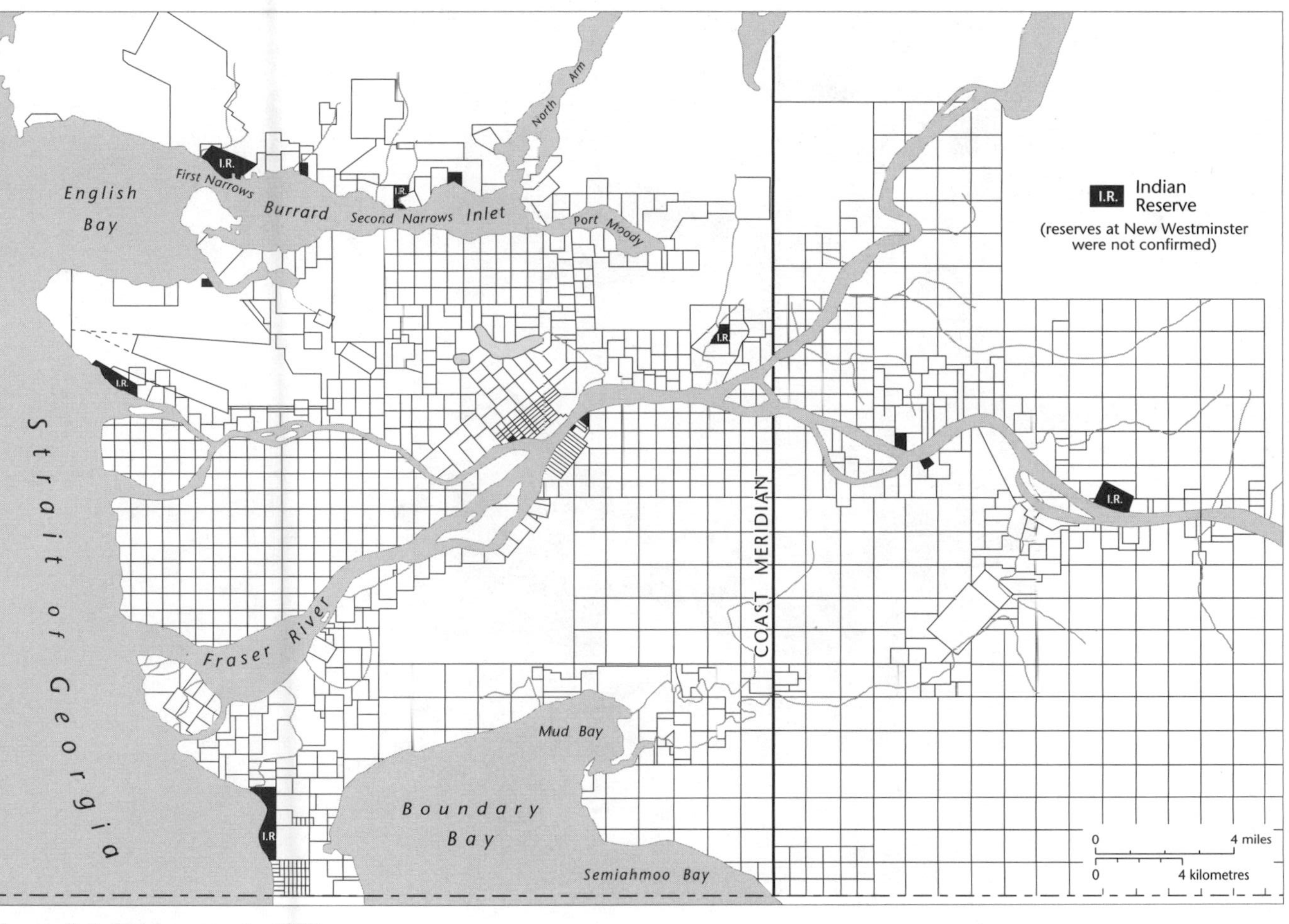

Figure 3.5 Land surveys to 1876

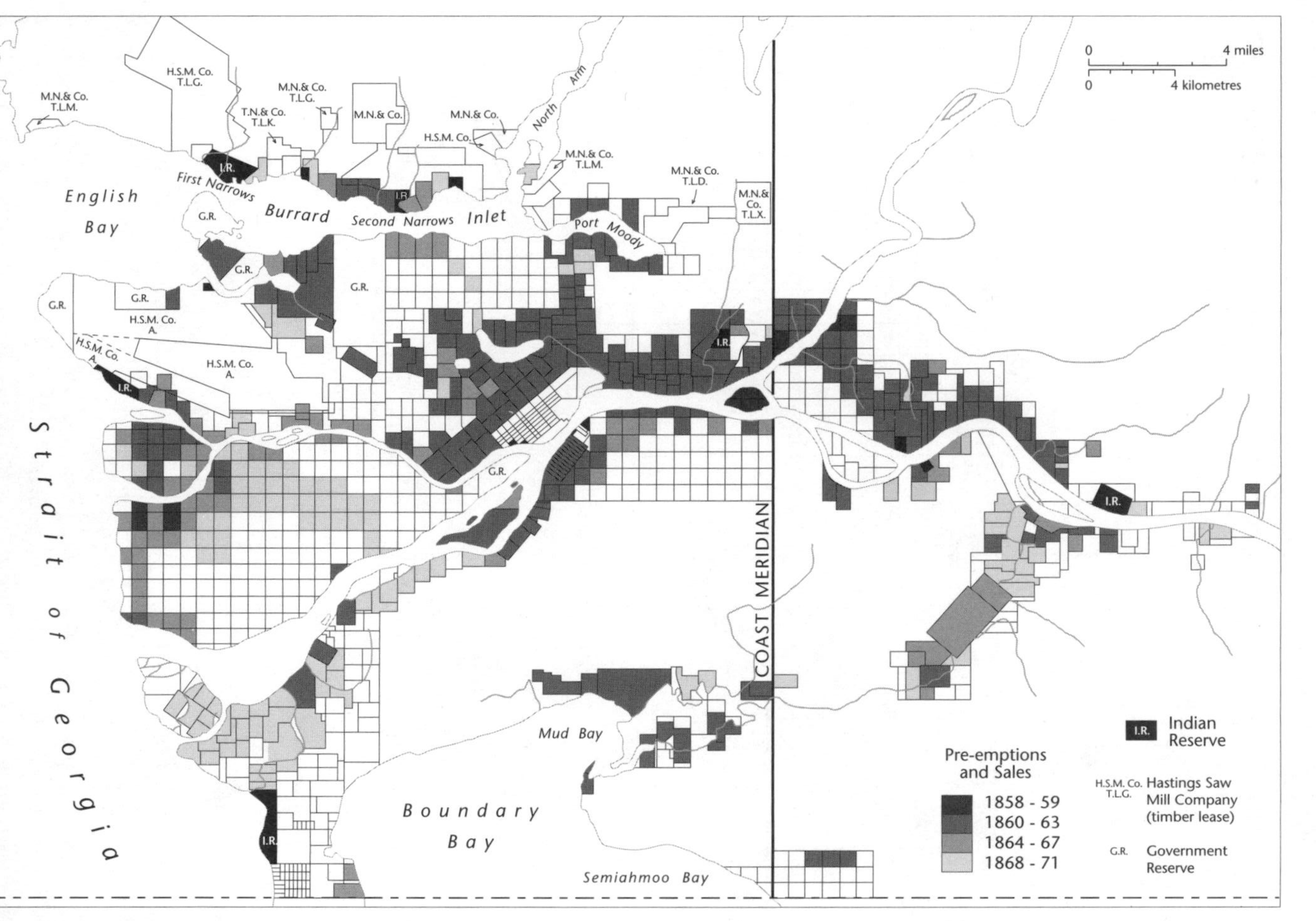

Figure 3.6 Land pre-emptions and sales, 1858-71

commonly used. As farms developed, they became mixed operations, partly because of the diverse requirements of family subsistence, partly because the local market was unspecialized. Therefore, wheat and other cereals were grown on most farms; orchards were common; and roots were raised for domestic use, animal feed, and sale. All farms had land in meadow and pasture, and raised some cattle; the most prosperous in the region sold hay, oxen, and various foodstuffs to the lumber camps. For many, however, farming was essentially a subsistent operation, an interminable labour that men might interrupt by wage work in New Westminster, on a road-building crew, or in a logging camp or sawmill.

Farm settlers in the Lower Mainland were of many backgrounds. At Langley, where there had been a HBC farm for thirty years, most heads of households in the 1860s were former company employees: mostly French Canadians, Orcadians, or other Scots. Their wives were frequently Natives, and their children tended to intermarry with one another. By the 1870s, the Langley population was changing as new settlers arrived, most from eastern Canada (particularly Ontario), some from the British Isles (Irish and English as well as Scots), and only a very few from the United States. There was a good deal of chain migration – people coming to a relative already established – and the links connected east rather than south; although only a few miles from the border, the early agricultural settlement of the Lower Mainland was not by Americans. Seeds, livestock, and farm implements were more likely to come from the United States. Several Lower Mainland farmers went to Oregon to purchase cattle, and then drove them to Puget Sound for shipment to the Fraser. Some settlers imported bulls from Ontario or, occasionally, from England.

In good part, the Ontarian pioneer landscape and experience were being recreated in the Lower Mainland. Family farms were hewed from the forest with simple tools; as farms took hold, log cabins gave way to houses (in Ontario, usually brick construction; in the Lower Mainland, frame, but often of similar style and trim). The mix of peoples and religions – Presbyterians (both Reformed and Church of Scotland), Wesleyans, Church of England, and Roman Catholics – was much the same as in Ontario; the British connection was real. A settler society was emerging, based on family farms and supported by the local rural neighbourhood, churches, schools (with curricula adapted from Ontario), roads, post offices, and commercial and institutional connections with New Westminster. A few pigs, firkins of butter, vegetables, or a cow or two would be taken to New Westminster for sale. There, settlers saw about title deeds for land. Going to New Westminster, small as it was, was 'going to town.' Always, the idea of progress was in the air. If pioneering was a struggle, accidents common, and the outcome by no means foregone, individual and family progress towards economic security and social respectability tended to be measured by establishing a farm. To do so required land and hard work; the commitment to both, therefore, was enormous.

What, then, of the Native peoples? Like many other settlers, Fitzgerald McCleery, who came from County Down, Ireland, and settled on the north arm of the Fraser River near the village of Musqueam, hired Native and Chinese labour. But he knew that his farm was his property, and that he, and his more prosperous uncle across the river, were citizens of a British colony. These were certainties; the winter dances at Musqueam, which McCleery saw occasionally, were curiosities from another world.[29]

Figure 3.7 shows the distribution of Native population around the Lower Mainland in the winter of 1877.[30] Government officials and missionaries had vaccinated Natives in the Lower Mainland just before the smallpox epidemic of 1862. Its effects, therefore, were far less devastating than they were in most of British Columbia. As people from outside the Lower Mainland settled there, the Native winter population may have been higher than it had been fifty years before. Although the old Kwantlen villages at New Westminster no longer existed – the last Natives living there were dislocated by the Royal Engineers in 1859 – some 300 Natives, many undoubtedly Kwantlen, lived in frame shacks near the two canneries in New Westminster. Musqueam and Tsawwassen remained, the former with just under 100 and the latter with just over fifty people. Around Burrard Inlet and False Creek were five small Native villages, each occupied in the main by Squamish-speakers who had come to work in the logging camps and sawmills of Burrard Inlet in the early 1860s. Some 150 Natives lived in Moodyville and Granville, the two sawmill towns on the inlet. As in the 1820s, this winter population was augmented in spring and summer. Cowichan still came to their plankhouse village on the south shore of Lulu Island in 1867, perhaps even later, and in the 1870s many Natives still depended on the Fraser's oolichan, sturgeon, and salmon fisheries. Increasingly, however, they were becoming trespassers on their own former resource procurement sites.

Except at New Westminster, Moodyville, and Granville, all the people shown in Figure 3.7 were now on reserves, patches of land set aside for government through the local Indian agent. The first small reserves had been surveyed by the Royal Engineers. In 1864, however, Governor Douglas instructed surveyors to make reserves as large as Natives wanted, and some of them wanted 100 or more acres per family. Posts were driven, but surveys were not completed, understandings not recorded. After Douglas retired later that year, his successors disavowed the surveyors' authority, and abandoned a policy they judged to be prodigal.[31] Not understanding white law and denied access to white courts, the Native

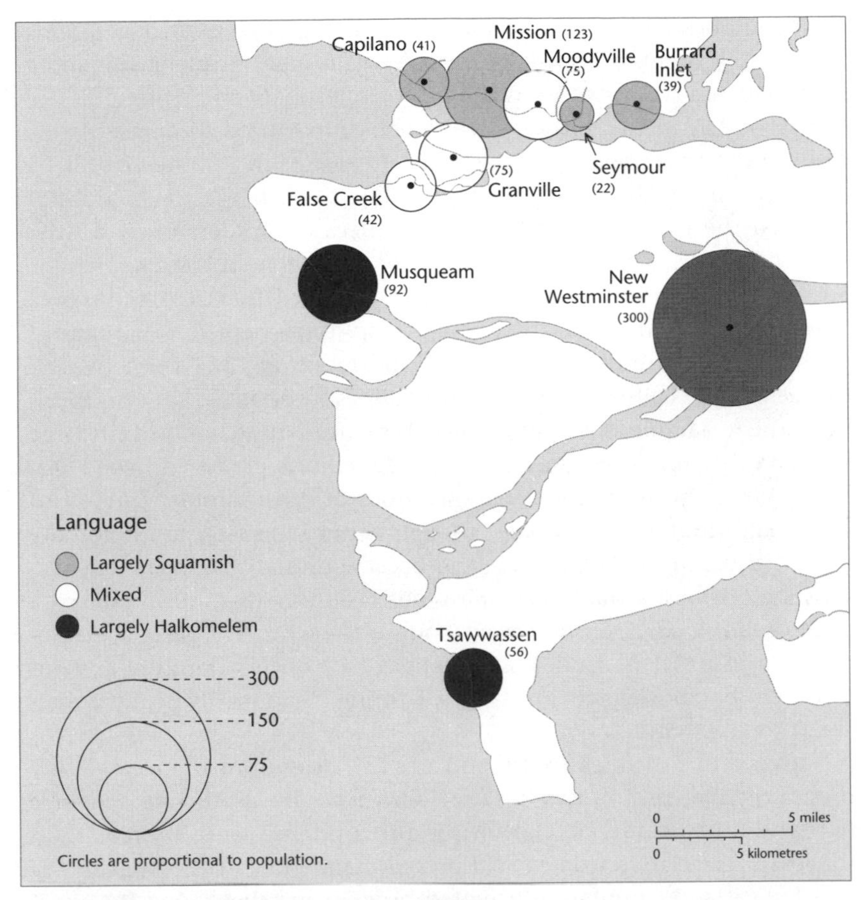

Figure 3.7 Native population, winter 1877

peoples were helpless. But they remembered. Years later, in 1913, a Musqueam chief told a royal commission investigating the Native land question: 'Since these posts were put down by Sir James Douglas for the Indians, the land has been lessened twice. The Indians were not notified or consulted ... and after that three persons came here to Musqueam and told some of the Indians that the posts ... meant nothing at all.'[32] Indeed, by the mid-1870s, government sales and pre-emptions to white settlers largely prevented any expansion of Native reserves (Figure 3.5). In April 1878, Gilbert Malcolm Sproat, Indian Reserve Commissioner, reported a meeting with six chiefs from the lower Fraser Valley: 'The Indians say that their lands are not sufficient in area and that, for several years, white settlers have been coming into the District and, in some cases, have been permitted to take up land which the Indians were hoping to get. They ask that this be no longer permitted ... They consider that they have been quiet and obedient to the law, and have not been well treated as regards their land.'[33] Sproat asked the provincial government to alienate no more land near reserves until he was able to investigate the situation. The request was ignored. In June 1879, when Sproat tried to adjust Native lands in the lower valley, he found that the areas they wanted had been taken up. Although Sproat was sympathetic to their wishes, he did not question the rights of private property. Because holders of land titles could not be dislodged, there was virtually nothing he could do.

Government officials and missionaries intended that Natives become farmers, a civilized pursuit that would help 'turn them into Europeans' and their reserves into countryside. At Musqueam in 1877, some twenty-two acres were cultivated, a third in potatoes, vegetables, oats, and fruit trees, the rest in meadow and pasture. There were nine horses, thirty-one head of cattle, and some poultry.[34] Such agriculture produced a good deal of food to supplement the 'large quantities of dried salmon' the census enumerator found in the village, though neither the Musqueam nor any other Natives in the Lower Mainland became primarily farmers. The reasons are obvious: a traditional subsistent economy that still produced a great deal of food, access to wage labour in the white commercial economy, and insufficient land. Many Natives had learned farming as farm labourers, but, in their circumstances, farming could hardly be more than a part-time activity.

Natives still fished, gathered, and hunted away from the reserves. Of these activities, fishing was the least obstructed by conflicting demands for land and resources. Gathering and hunting were increasingly squeezed. Yet Native women still picked cranberries in the bogs of Sea and Lulu islands, hunters still netted birds in marshes along the river, and families still dug clams on the beaches at Point Grey. Moving seasonally as they could through land they no longer controlled, Natives were everywhere and nowhere. But, as time went on, their off-the-reserve activities tended to focus on fewer work sites. In the 1870s, Tsawwassen men worked on the river as commercial fishermen; the women worked in the canneries. Cowichan still came to the spring oolichan and sturgeon fisheries, but more to the summer sockeye fishery organized around canneries near New Westminster. The lumber camps and sawmills around Burrard Inlet depended on Native labour. Traditional patterns of spatial mobility adjusted to these new employments.

Industrial work camps

Around the Lower Mainland after 1858, as from the beginning of European enterprise in Canada, work camps appeared at sites where local resources could be exploited and shipped to distant markets. In British Columbia during these years, many such work camps became industrial workplaces.

Some of the first were along the Fraser River. As early as 1864, independent entrepreneurs adopted methods employed by the HBC to salt-cure and barrel salmon and a few sturgeon. Little capital was required, nor was more required in the late 1860s when the first experiments began with canning. In the summer of 1871, a cannery operated on the left bank of the river just below New Westminster. Over the next decade, a dozen more were built, their locations shifting towards the river mouth as competition for fish increased (Figure 3.8). For a time, salting and canning coexisted usually in the same establishment, but canned salmon, a far less perishable product and one that reached the British market, accounted for 95 per cent of the value of fish exports from the Fraser by 1879. Cannery owners depended on commission agents in Victoria, who advanced cash for supplies and labour, insured, transported, and marketed the salmon (secured by a chattel mortgage of plant, boats, and equipment), and deducted all costs and fees before the cannery owner received any return for a year's catch. Because marketing took longer than the annual cycle of the fishery, prolonged indebtedness to commission agents was unavoidable for entrepreneurs of modest means operating far from markets.[35]

The cost of building and equipping a one-line cannery in the 1870s, around $5,000 for the building and considerably less for equipment, was less than half the annual cost of operating it. Canneries were labour-intensive workplaces that employed some 130 people per canning line. Before the fishing season, Chinese crews made cans from imported tin plate, and Native women made nets from flax twine. When fish were delivered to the wharf, they were butchered, washed, and cut into can-length pieces by hand. Cans were filled and soldered by hand, then lowered into cooking kettles, removed, tested for leaks, and cooked again. Eventually, they were lacquered, labelled, stored, and packed in forty-eight-can cases, all by hand: manual methods, but factory organization. In 1878, the inspector of fisheries noted that:

> Many ingenious devices, with labor-saving apparatus of divers kinds, are eagerly adopted as necessity suggests. It is of course only by an organized system of action and the minute subdivision of labour that the operations of the industry, from the cutting of the tin plates, the shaping, the soldering up to the final labelling of the cans, after the insertion and cooking of the contents, can be profitably or successfully carried on. It is pleasing to witness the order and regularity with which these various processes are accomplished.[36]

The most important of these 'ingenious devices,' a steam retort that pressure-cooked the salmon, was introduced in 1877. Gang knives that cut the fish to exact lengths at the push of a lever followed shortly thereafter.

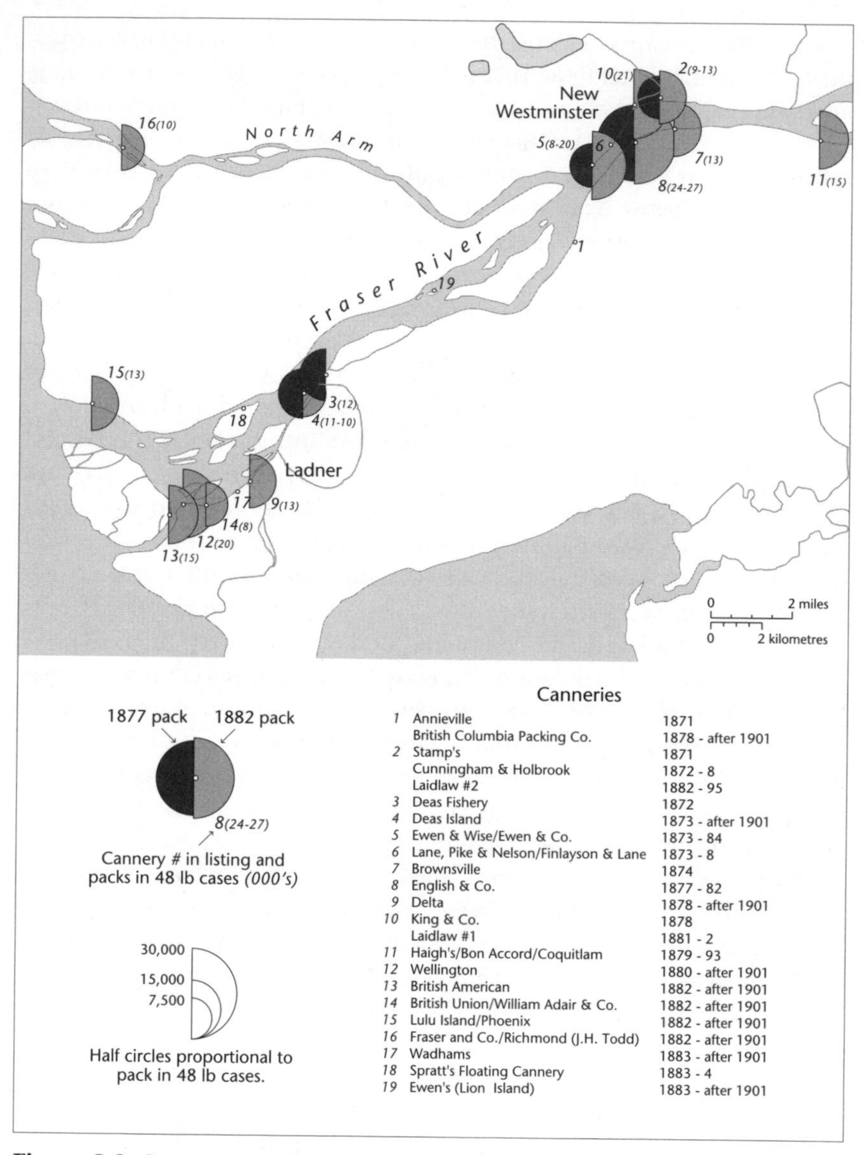

Figure 3.8 Canneries on the Fraser River, 1871-85

Only one species of salmon, the sockeye, was canned in the 1870s. Its large runs close to the surface, and its fairly uniform size (five to seven pounds), made it relatively easy to catch and process, while its red, oily flesh, though poor for drying, was favoured by the British market. In the Fraser's opaque waters, sockeye were taken in gill nets drifted behind small, flat-bottomed, two-man skiffs. In a good year, one such boat would catch 5,000 or more fish a season, which ran about thirty days beginning in early July. Because spoilage was rapid, fishing took place close to canneries until, in the late 1870s, steam tenders began to extend the fishermen's range. With tenders, they could operate from various points along the shore, taking their fish to a scow that the tender collected daily. With or without tenders, some twenty-five boats were required to serve each cannery line during the height of a run, and more were required as the run tapered off. Usually canneries owned the boats, which cost some forty dollars each.

In the 1870s, the canning industry on the lower Fraser depended on Native labour, not only Halkomelem-speakers but others, such as the Nlha7kápmx from the Fraser Canyon, who had never previously frequented the lower Fraser, or Lequiltok, who, fifty years before, had come to raid.[37] Native families, rather than individuals, canoed to the canneries each season, as they had previously gone to resource procurement sites; many stayed year-round at New Westminster. Under white foremen and alongside Chinese butchers, Native women did most cannery work, earning ten cents an hour. Older children must have worked as well, while younger children played, and babies were carried by their mothers. Men fished, earning a wage of $1.25 to $1.50 for a twelve-hour day. From the canners' point of view, such a cheap, reliable, and seasonally available labour force was indispensable, especially the women. Some canners hired more fishermen than they needed so that there would be Native women in their canneries. For the Natives, the sockeye fishery opened up a familiar resource where traditional Native technology could hardly exploit it, and provided a seasonal income approaching $100 per family; also, the timing of the fishery lay conveniently between the spring oolichan and sturgeon fisheries and the late summer and fall runs of what the canners derisively called 'dog' salmon: species that dry-cured easily and were the basis of the Native fall fishery.

The commercial fishery was a point of intersection of the world economy and the Native subsistent economy, of industrial work and time discipline and Native spirit worlds, and of peoples of drastically different cultures who, unless they spoke Chinook, usually could not talk to one another. For Native men, these disjunctions were less severe: they worked, unsupervised, in small boats, with the river and its fish. For Native women, it was quite another matter. They worked on a cannery line, subject to industrial discipline under the eye of a white foreman. Yet Halkomelem was the principal language in a cannery, plus other Native tongues, Chinook, Cantonese, and English. Native women prepared their families' food, taking sunburned and slightly spoiled fish to dry beside the tiny frame houses, apparently Native-built, in which they lived.[38] For women, men, and children, canning was a social occasion, as was the case whenever large groups of Natives briefly assembled. Then the sockeye run ended and, except at New Westminster, the Native peoples dispersed. Cannery buildings were left to a watchman.

The large sawmills built on Burrard Inlet in the 1860s provided, on the other hand, virtually year-round, mechanized, factory-organized work. British capital seeking to build a 'first class sawmill' arrived in British Columbia in 1859. 'The only question,' its manager Edward Stamp informed Governor Douglas, 'is where the establishment is to be fixed.'[39] His first choice was at the head of the Alberni Canal on the west coast of Vancouver Island, but within five years the mill there closed for want of accessible timber. Having raised another £100,000 in Britain, Stamp decided a new mill should be located in Burrard Inlet. He initially favoured a site on the government reserve at First Narrows, in present-day Stanley Park. But in the summer of 1865, he fixed on a site three kilometres to the east on the south shore of Burrard Inlet, where a large, steam-powered mill was built; after 1870, it was known as Hastings Mill. In 1865, a sizeable, water-powered sawmill (S.P. Moody and Company) was already in operation on the north side of the inlet near the mouth of Lynn Creek.[40]

These mills cut almost entirely for export, selling lumber around the Pacific Rim and spars in Europe. They were up to date mechanically; when Moody converted to steam in 1868, he equipped the new mill with 'the latest machinery available.' Visiting the mill in 1875, geologist George M. Dawson found 'a pair of large Circular saws, & a large gang saw, besides a small circular saw with long traversing table for cutting up the large planks, & others for cutting boards into lengths &c. Two planing machines, Mill driven by steam, but water power formerly used & still available, often employed to drive planers when other machinery Standing.'[41]

Attracting capital to Burrard Inlet were magnificent Douglas-fir and western red cedar forests located on gently sloping land close to tidewater and a sheltered, deep-sea port. With the creation of the Crown Colony, and improvements in oceanic shipping, these forests became accessible to the international economy. Yet capitalists wanted, and virtually got, their timber free. As Stamp explained to the colonial secretary: 'After a careful examination I am now satisfied that sufficient timber exists on Frasers River, Burrards Inlet, Hows Sound [*sic*], and the adjoining coast to justify me in a costly sawmill in that locality, I only now wait the government to grant me such concessions as are absolutely necessary to enable the company I represent to proceed with their undertaking.'[42] These concessions were a Crown grant of 243 acres purchased for one dollar (four shillings, two pence) an acre; the right to purchase another 1,200 acres at the same price; and 15,000 acres in leaseholds (most of Burrard peninsula) for an annual rent of one cent (half a pence) an acre.[43] By a conservative estimate, Stamp's leaseholds contained a billion board feet of prime timber. Moody received similar concessions on the north shore of Burrard Inlet.

The Native reaction to this can only be inferred. At Alberni, Stamp, who was also the justice of the peace, explained his sentence of a Native to four months of hard labour in Victoria as follows: 'Thefts have become so common here with the Indians; this step was absolutely necessary; I was told by the chief that I had stolen their land and they had a right to steal from us. Perhaps a good flogging would have done more good; but unfortunately I have not the necessary instrument of punishment by me; this defect I will remedy without loss of time.'[44] In Burrard Inlet, the surveyor of Stamp's proposed mill in the First Narrows reserve found 'the resident Indians ... very distrustful of my purpose and suspicious of encroachment on their premises.'[45] However, as the constable reported a few days later, 'they can at any time be removed. The ground does not belong to their tribe [the Squamish].'[46] He was right; they could be removed. The full apparatus of colonial power supported the timber leases. Over the next few years, fires destroyed a large part of the valuable timber on the north shore; Moody thought that Natives had set many of them.[47]

According to one of Homer Barnett's informants, Moody induced the Squamish to settle in Burrard Inlet. Certainly, in the early 1860s, some of their summer villages in the inlet became year-round residences as Squamish men took regular work on the docks or as general mill hands. Other Natives came from much farther away and, having left their families, lived in company bunkhouses. There were also Chinese in good number, eastern Canadians, Americans, Europeans of various nationalities, and a few Hawaiians. Here, as in the canneries and as earlier at Fort Langley, a multiracial, polyglot labour force was assembled. If there were a lingua franca, it was Chinook. Yet labour was scarce overall, and the mills required Native workers. Sproat, the Indian Reserve Commissioner, estimated in 1876 that $70,000 to $100,000 passed annually to Natives in Burrard Inlet, some in payment for fish, other foodstuffs, and hay brought by Natives to mills and logging camps.[48] A shift in the sawmills was twelve hours, the working week was six days, and pay for general labour was $.75 a day with room and board, or $1.25 without.

Such work was superimposed on the patterns and prejudices of vastly different lives. For many, as one white mill hand said, 'all there was to do was work, eat, and sleep.'[49] Many Natives in Moody's mill walked to work from their village a mile away. The Chinese lived in shacks east of Hastings Mill, segregated from the whites who lived to the west in the mill town of Granville. Apparently there was a Chinese bunkhouse in Moodyville and, as that settlement grew, a 'Frenchtown' and a 'Kanaka Road' (for Hawaiians). Racism or sheer cultural distance, usually both, kept people apart. Space was also gendered. The sawmills, bunkhouses, and docks were male places. The Chinese shacks were male, for the families of Chinese workers were in China. Houses became increasingly female; the men, for the most part, were away or asleep. On the other hand, the Saturday night dances at the Hastings Hotel were attended by white men and Native or mixed-blood women. White women stayed away. Over these little-studied patterns of life around the sawmills on Burrard Inlet in the 1860s and 1870s loomed the mills themselves, the bosses, and the long machine-and-clock-dominated hours of work. People who had grown up on the banks of the Squamish River within a fishing, hunting, and gathering economy, or, for that matter, in an agricultural village near Canton, or on a farm in eastern Canada, would appear to have entered another world.[50] However, we know next to nothing about the ways in which industrial discipline and more traditional forms of social organization interacted in such settings.

The companies also largely controlled logging. Loggers hired by a company or by a logging contractor felled and bucked the trees, and as many as twenty yoke of oxen hauled logs over corduroy skid roads, made of small logs laid across a trail. In the 1870s, a few operations experimented with steam-traction engines run on tracks made of logs chopped flat on one side. By such means, massive logs could be hauled two or three miles to tidewater, where they were made into booms and towed by steam tug to sawmills. The gently sloping banks of Burrard Inlet and English Bay were ideal for such operations. There were, for example, five logging camps at different times in present-day Stanley Park, each with a bunkhouse (and perhaps a cookhouse), stables for oxen, and a network of skid roads. Such operations were expensive; a principal skid road itself might cost almost $1,000.

There were some independent hand loggers, who usually worked in pairs, logged virtually at tidewater, and lived with Native women, 'bought' for fifty dollars, in isolated cabins around the inlet. Native people quickly learned from such loggers, and began hand logging themselves. In 1875, the Sechelt cut and boomed 1.25 million board feet of timber, which the mills purchased for three dollars a thousand and towed to Burrard Inlet. Sproat urged the provincial government either to allow Natives in non-agricultural coastal areas to take out timber leases, or to grant them good-sized reserves for the purpose of logging. The provincial government did neither, which meant that, except as loggers working for wages, they were excluded from commercial access to the forests.

Towards an Interpretation

In 1881, the census enumerator in the Lower Mainland[51] travelled through a human geography (Figure 3.9) that did not exist there twenty-five years earlier, though, of course, it existed in broadly similar form elsewhere. The region had suddenly become part of a British North Atlantic world, part of the ways it organized and controlled space. The traders at Fort Langley had not sought or been able to exert such control,

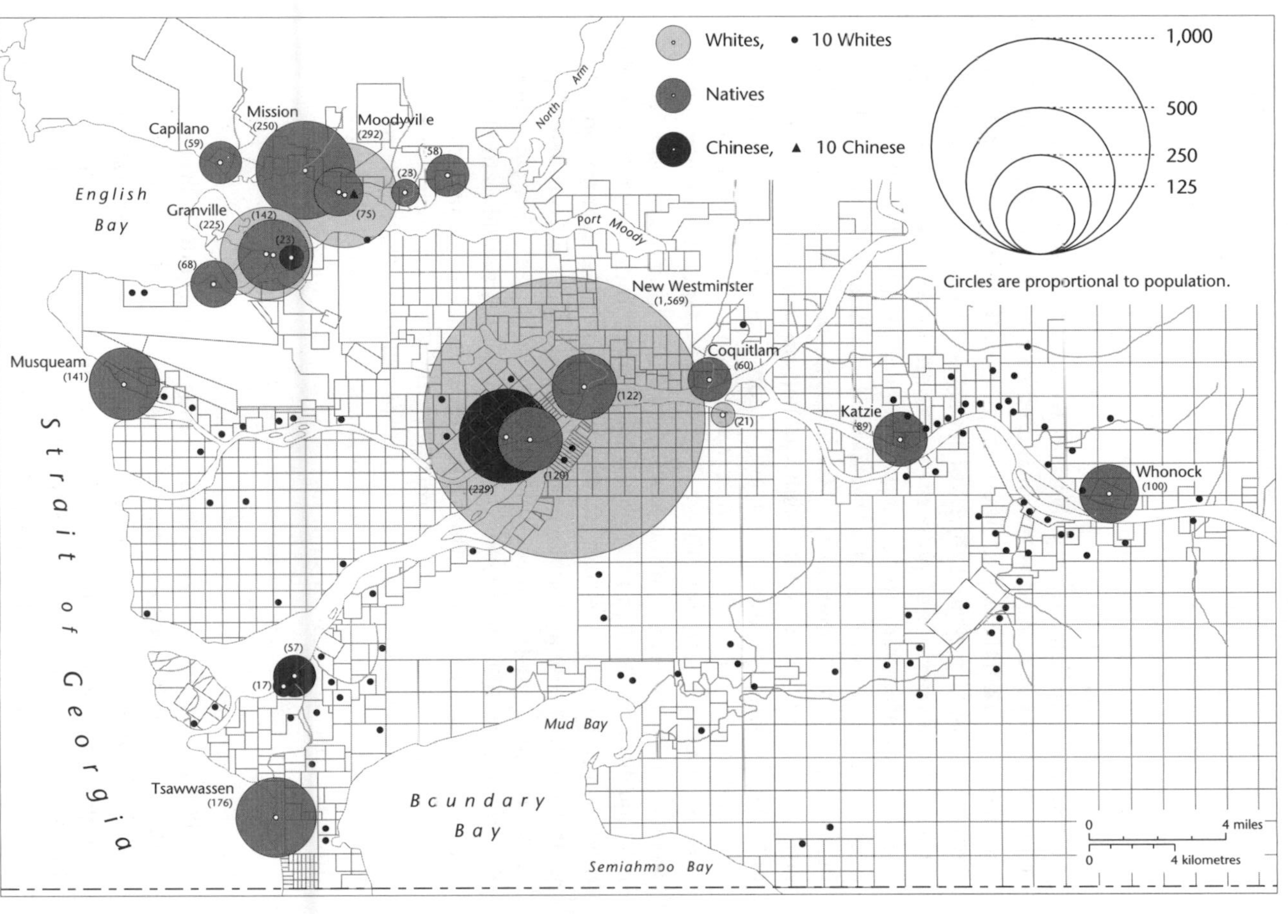

Figure 3.9 Population of the Lower Mainland, 1881

and when Natives dominated what became the Lower Mainland, they organized land and life in ways that, in most respects, were virtually the opposite of those that held sway in 1881.

A colonial regime had taken over. Although the tactics of colonial power operated across a broad front of interrelated activities and cultural assumptions, along the lower Fraser, as elsewhere, those that most affected indigenous livelihoods turned around the land system. Land policies were the explicit means by which the control of land was transferred from one group of people to another. Figures 3.5, 3.6, and 3.9 reveal, at once, a land system, a new geography of power, and something of the means of its enforcement.

These are maps of property. Natives were tucked away on reserves, while the land was being divided up and made available to others on various terms. Cadastral lines on these maps identify parcels of land that newcomers could pre-empt, own, or lease, and then occupy, work, or trade. This new regime of property rested on some of the immigrants' deepest aspirations. For some, landed property was a means to family-centred security, an opportunity, denied by land cost in Britain or increasingly, by the 1860s and 1870s, in Ontario, to acquire a farm and fashion a secure, independent livelihood. Behind such farms lay centuries of frugal, peasant craving for land, and deeply evocative discourses about the goodness of farm life that, in agrarian mythology, was self-reliant, close to nature, and family based.[52] For others, landed property was a speculation, but speculation was a basic right. The long history of English individualism was tied to the right of individuals to own and dispose of their own property as they saw fit. This was the popular assumption, and in most British thought about property rights, this was considered the most efficient, long-term means of allocating resources.[53] For yet others, the land was an industrial resource to be processed and sold as lumber or canned salmon. For them, the rights of industrial capital, the most aggressively expansionistic edge of the world economy, had also to be served by the land system. And they were. All these basic assumptions about property, deeply bedded in immigrant aspirations, required something like the land system that, after 1858, began to take shape in the lower Fraser Valley.

Supporting this introduced land system, and channelling the transactions and altercations it inevitably generated, were English civil and criminal law as interpreted by stipendiary magistrates, judges, and courts. Perhaps, as Tina Loo recently argued in *Making Law, Order, and Authority in British Columbia, 1821-1871,* the law acquired a particular salience in an immigrant society where the influence of custom was disrupted by migration.[54] With the law came policemen and jails. And with it, equally essential if further in the background, came military might. Edward

Bulwer Lytton, the colonial secretary when the gold rush broke and the colony of British Columbia was created, reminded Colonel Moody, commander of the Royal Engineers, that, as far as possible, civil societies should manage themselves. The Royal Engineers should lead by gentlemanly example. Nevertheless, internal civil stability required, Lytton averred, knowledge of a background military presence; as he put it, 'the unflinching aid of military discipline.' Externally, the colony could count on England's protection: 'wherever England extends her sceptre, there, as against the Foreign enemy, she pledges the defense of her sword.'[55] This was the language of imperialism and of sovereign power, backed by the most powerful navy in the world. Even further in the background, but underlying the reserves, the land system, and the whole colonial enterprise, were broad cultural assumptions about the global locations of civilization and savagery.[56] White British Columbians had no doubts about the location of either or about the benefits, for all concerned, of replacing the 'savage' ways they encountered with a form of European civilization.

The land system was a disciplinary appendage of this anatomy of power. Battles had not been necessary; shows of force and a few summary executions did much to establish the new realities. In a newly acquired territory where other forms of control were unavailable, the brutal, episodic, and public application of sovereign power established its authority, and fear bred compliance. Once the realities of sovereign power were demonstrated, other more disciplinary forms of power could begin to be put in place. Of these, the land system acquired a particular salience, a colonial instrument of what Michel Foucault has called biopower: control of the body.[57] It introduced exclusions that established where people could and could not go, and backed these exclusions with a decentred system of surveillance. Suddenly there were survey lines and fences on the land. There were owners who could identify trespassers, tell them to get off, and know that their commands would be backed, if need be, by the full apparatus of the state. Native people suddenly found that they could not go where they had; there were too many watchmen (property owners) backed by too much power. In a colonial regime, the emphasis of power had shifted towards the control of land and the management of movement thereon, an imposed spatial discipline with a profound capacity to modify Native life.

A regime of property backed by the colonial state provided means of and protection for development. Farmers could acquire land knowing their title was secure and the colony was safe for settlement. Townspeople could buy lots and live within the familiar guarantees of civil society. An immigrant, European society, especially its elite, could begin to put its world back together. But not, of course, entirely, if only because societies and their settings are not separate. Immigrants on pioneer farmsteads or in lumber camps lived in unfamiliar relationships with the land; all immigrants lived without a local past and amid a strange mix of peoples (see Chapter 9). Such mixing brought ideas of ethnicity and race to the fore, weakened somewhat the idea of class, and tended to turn what in other, more homogeneous settings were the unremarked details of everyday life into explicit and increasingly symbolic elements of difference. Of these, whiteness became the most generalized and powerful symbol and, as it did, racism was built into the landscape of settlement. The Lower Mainland was not a replica of any other place, yet its emerging human geography conveyed a complex of power that had come, broadly, out of the English-speaking North Atlantic world of the mid-late nineteenth century.

Native power over the Lower Mainland and, to a considerable extent, earlier Native lifeworlds had collapsed. Native settlements and spatial routines were radically different from those of a short generation before. Most Natives were ostensibly Roman Catholics, and at the church-run residential school at Mission, not far upriver from Langley, some Native children were taught English and meticulously disciplined so that 'savagery' would yield to civilization.[58] How much the Native cognitive world had changed is another question. Most Native people still spoke little or no English. Spirits still haunted Burrard Inlet near Deep Cove; Natives would not go there. For some, Christianity offered a new trail to a familiar land of shades and dancing ghosts. Yet changes in the Lower Mainland were such that Native cognition could not long survive unaltered.

By 1881, a new place, the Lower Mainland, had come into existence. The land had been restructured, and the way had been made for a railway, ever-more-modern sawmills and canneries, a largely British and eastern Canadian middle class, a city, and a metropolis. Native peoples, pushed to the margins, would turn increasingly to the heart of their problem, the land question, and, in so doing, run squarely into the geographical reality of a place remade by others.

4
The Fraser Canyon Encountered

On 19 June 1808, Simon Fraser, explorer/trader for the Montreal-based North West Company, noted in his journal that he and some men had reached the Native village of Nhomin on the west bank of what he thought was the Columbia River, just above its confluence with a large, clear tributary that Fraser named the Thompson.[1] At Nhomin, Fraser met some 400 people who, he thought, ate well and seemed long-lived. From there he was taken across the river to a camp where he found 'people ... sitting in rows to the number of twelve hundred.' He shook hands with all of them. The 'Great Chief' made a 'long harangue,' pointing to the sun, the four quarters of the world, and the explorer. An old, blind man, apparently the chief's father, was brought to Fraser to touch. Next day, the dash to the sea resumed, but they had not made many miles when a canoe capsized and broke up. Most men got ashore quickly, but one, D'Alaire, was carried three miles downstream where, exhausted and barely able to speak after dragging himself out of the river and up a cliff, Fraser found him. The precarious descent of one of the rawest rivers in North America by twenty-two tough, experienced employees of the North West Company and two Native translators/guides had lost only a few hours.

Some Nlha7kápmx, the people along this part of the Fraser River, described these events very differently. Long after Coyote had finished arranging things on earth, he reappeared on the river with Sun, Moon, Morning-Star, Diver, Arrow-armed Person, and Kokwe'la.[2] They came down from Shuswap country, landed at the junction of the two rivers, and many people saw them. Shortly after they left, Moon, who steered the canoe, disappeared with it under the water. The others came out of the river and sat on a rock. Arrow-armed Person fired lightning arrows, and Diver dived. Sun sat still and smoked. Coyote and the others danced. 'Coyote said, "Moon will never come up again with the canoe"; but Sun said, "Yes, in the evening he will appear." Just after sunset, Moon appeared holding the canoe, and came ashore. All of them embarked, and going down the river, were never seen again.'[3] This was Coyote's only appearance since the mythological age.

Here are two remarkably different accounts of the same event, both told not very long ago. Time seems telescoped in British Columbia; the place appears to rest on a vast ellipsis. In Europe, the equivalent of Coyote and his band are too far back in time to have any reality, and so, invented and abstracted, they appear as noble savages (Rousseau) or as members of traditional lifeworlds (Habermas). But in this new corner of the Europeans' New World, abstractions become realities, and the long story of emerging modernity, extending back through European millennia, is compressed into 100 years or so. The ethnographers who, at the end of the nineteenth century, began to study the Native societies of British Columbia, assumed this. Since then, most of our scholarship has become more local; British Columbia tends to be studied on its own or in relation to the development of Canada. But to do so, as the best of the ethnographers knew, is to diminish the monumental and relatively accessible encounter – here, not long ago – of nineteenth-century European culture with Coyote, Sun, Moon, Morning Star, and the others, an encounter that underlies the world we live in.

Thoughts such as these have led me to the Fraser Canyon. However difficult a route, the Fraser River was a huge source of food, and in the canyon, where fishing sites were abundant and excellent, it probably supported as concentrated and dense a non-agricultural population as anywhere in the world. Soon after Simon Fraser, these people began to participate directly or indirectly in the fur trade (Fort Kamloops, 1811; Fort Langley, 1827; Fort Yale, 1847) and in associated provisioning trades. In 1858, they were caught up in a gold rush that brought thousands of miners to the terraces on which they lived. Soon Royal Engineers were surveying townsites, the route of a turnpike road, and the first Native reserves. Settlers arrived – many of them single Chinese men, most others of various European backgrounds – and acquired land and water rights. Suddenly there were land laws and, behind them, a colonial administration. There were Anglican and Roman Catholic missionaries; then, in 1878, an Indian reserve commission to regulate the 'Native land question.' In 1881, the people of the canyon were enumerated in a federal census, and work was under way on a railway. Some thirty years later, there was another railway, a slide that virtually destroyed the salmon runs, and another commission to regulate the Indian land question. In short, the Fraser Canyon bore the concentrated brunt of much of what the nineteenth century threw at British Columbia. Were it possible to understand a little of what went on there, something of the encounter of Coyote and his people with an aggressively colonizing European civilization should begin to come into focus.

In this chapter, I consider several phases of this encounter over a span of more than a century. After a brief description of the canyon peoples of Simon Fraser's day, the astonishing meeting of Natives and miners in the canyon in the spring and summer of 1858 is discussed. Two years later, Anglican bishop George Hills and the Royal Engineers arrived, the one intent on laying the foundations for pure Christianity (the Anglican church), the others on building a wagon road. In 1878, Gilbert Malcolm Sproat, Indian Reserve Commissioner, worked his way through the canyon to adjust Native land claims. Each of these comings is considered. Finally, I treat the canyon that Native leaders described when they addressed another Indian reserve commission, the McKenna-McBride Commission, which came in 1914 to find a final solution to the land question. My objectives are to describe something of the sequence of colonization in the canyon and, much more tentatively, something of the strategies of Native resistance.

The Canyon in 1808

Simon Fraser noted that, south of present-day Lillooet, he left the territory of the Askettih (Stl'atl'imx or Lillooet) Nation and entered that of the Hakamaugh (Nlha7kápmx or Thompson); and that just north of what is now Yale, he left Nlha7kápmx territory and reached the first village of the Ackinroe (Stó:lō), though neither boundary, judging from his account, was sharp. By the time he reached the Stó:lō, Fraser had crossed what linguists would later identify as the boundary between Interior and Coast Salish language families, and entered what ethnologists would later term the Northwest Coast cultural region. The large, shed-roofed houses Fraser saw near Yale were new to him. Along the way, he stopped at several Native villages, most of which can be identified precisely, and was hospitably received. He saw a few European goods: one gun, which probably could not be fired, several kettles, some cloth, bits of blanket, some brass wire, and an iron sword. One person, a Tŝilhqot'in (Chilcotin), claimed to have seen white men on the coast. He also noted horses among the more northerly Nlha7kápmx, an introduction that preceded him by some fifty years, and evidence of smallpox among the more southerly Nlha7kápmx, a trace of the devastating epidemic of 1782 that may have killed more than half the population of the lower canyon (see Chapter 1).

It is impossible to know exactly where and in what number people lived in the canyon in 1808. Fraser saw only a fraction of the villages, and estimated the populations of only a few. More information about villages can be obtained from later ethnographic sources, government surveys, archeological records, and field investigations; such data, cross-checked, yield a map of early-nineteenth-century villages that may be fairly accurate (Figure 4.1). Apparently there were at least thirty villages

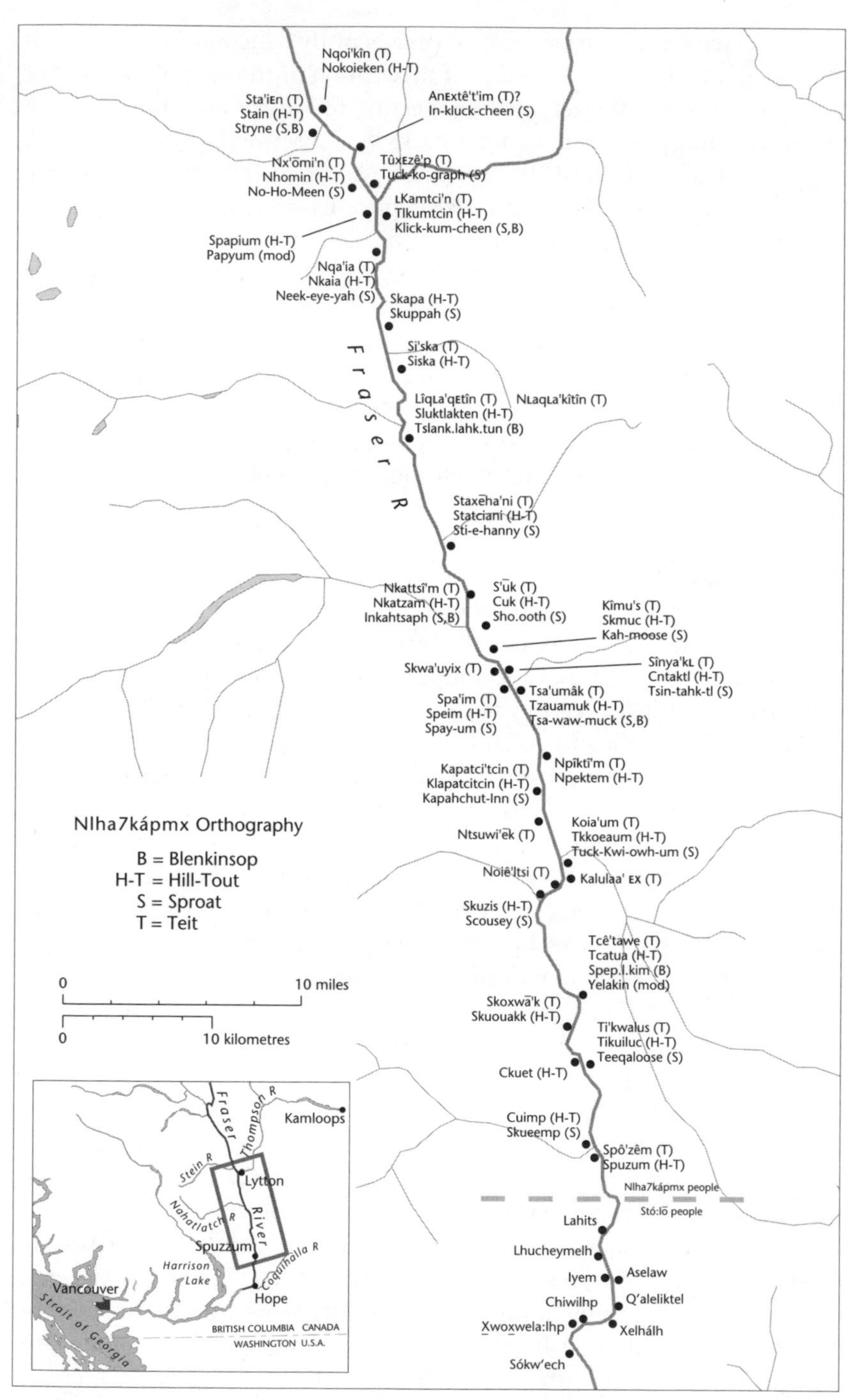

Figure 4.1 Winter villages in the Fraser Canyon, early nineteenth century

between Yale and Lytton, some large judging by the archeological record. At present, the only useful evidence of population is the 1830 census, compiled at Fort Langley (see Chapter 1, Figure 1.5). It identified 1,480 men between Whee y kum (Koia'um, just south of Boston Bar) and Teitton (Yale), or approximately 7,500 people along this thirty-five kilometre stretch of the river (Figure 4.2). Fifty years after the smallpox epidemic, the population had rebounded, whether or not to pre-smallpox levels. We know that the final ten kilometres of the canyon supported a large resident population, and also thousands of people from the lower Fraser and Strait of Georgia who fished there in August and September. There were equivalent fishing sites a little farther upriver in Nlha7kápmx territory; with a seasonally abundant food supply and the means of preserving it, the canyon supported a lot of people.

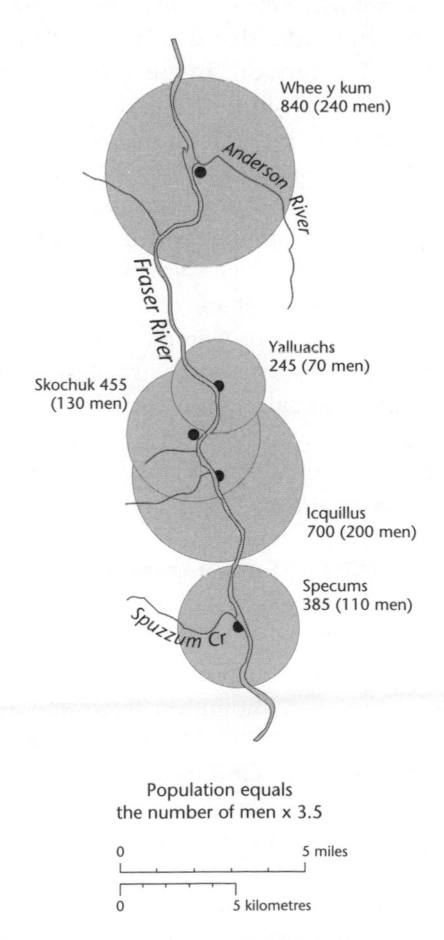

Figure 4.2 Population of the lower canyon in 1830 (after HBC census)

According to James Teit, the Scottish settler-ethnographer who knew the early-modern Nlha7kápmx far better than any other non-Native, the Fraser Canyon was not an important route of coastal-interior trade. Adjacent Nlha7kápmx and Stó:lō villages, Teit noted, 'traded considerably with each other, but very little of this trade passed on up the river.'[4] According to Teit, there was more direct coastal-interior trade at what is now Hope, terminus of a trail from the Similkameen, than along the Fraser. Among the canyon peoples themselves, luxury goods such as big horn sheep spoons, animal dentalia, and buffalo skin bags moved downriver; canoes, cedar bark, and processed salmon moved up.[5] But there was no great emporium such as the March oolichan fishery on the Nass River, or the summer salmon fishery at the mouth of the Bridge River, that drew traders to the Fraser from afar. The falls above Yale, which attracted thousands of people each summer, were but the accessible lower end of a chain of rapids and superb fishing sites that were not available to outsiders due to the terrain and the hostility of canyon Nlha7kápmx living close to their principal resource. Apparently the people who converged on the lower canyon came primarily to catch and dry fish, rather than to trade. There was local seasonal movement within the canyon, some of it into the mountains, some along the river to preferred fishing sites. The most southerly Nlha7kápmx, for example, tended to move north during the salmon runs to fishing sites in Black Canyon, just south of Hell's Gate, thereby pulling away from the peoples coming to the lower canyon from the lower Fraser and the Strait of Georgia; many people from around Boston Bar moved south to fisheries at or just above Hell's Gate. In sum, with little interregional trade along the Fraser and next to no through traffic, the peoples of the canyon lived not so much along a river as on a local body of water that seasonally yielded enormous quantities of food.

In Teit's view, the canyon Nlha7kápmx were far less mobile than the Halkomelem-speakers of the lower Fraser and southeastern Vancouver Island, most of whom lived within networks of kin and associated rights to resources that criss-crossed the Strait of Georgia and extended up the Fraser to the canyon (see Chapter 3). Teit accompanied his discussion of cosmology with a Nlha7kápmx map of the world (Figure 4.3).[6] It shows the junction of the Fraser and Thompson rivers and a few villages in a small territory surrounded by a lake from which, towards sunset, an underground trail leads to the land of souls and dancing ghosts. We know that some Nlha7kápmx had larger worldviews – some of them, Fraser reported, knew of the sea and of traders east of the Rockies – yet the map does seem to catch something of the fixity of canyon life. People lived within local, intimately known worlds,[7] in which the experience of one was, essentially, the experience of another, and personal stories intertwined with creation stories. It would be impossible to stand aside from

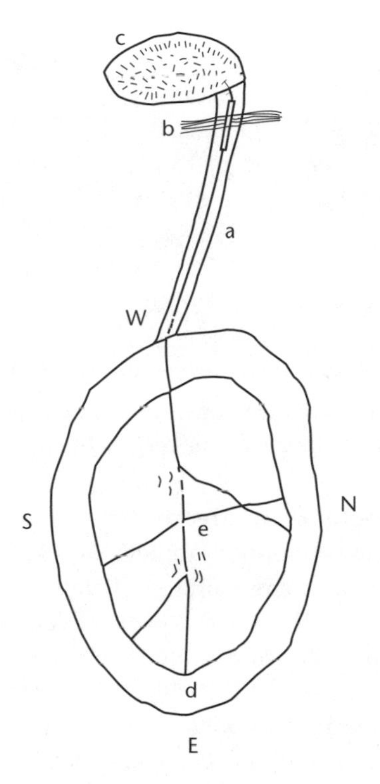

a) Trail leading from the earth to the land of the ghosts, with tracks of the souls
b) River and log on which the souls cross
c) Land of the ghosts, and dancing souls
d) Lake surrounding the earth
e) Earth, with rivers and villages

Figure 4.3 Nlha7kápmx sketch of the world

the enveloping experience of such a lifeworld; events would be interpretable only within a framework of lived experience and stories.[8] Robin Ridington makes this point in his impressive studies of the Beaver people,[9] and there is no reason to suggest that the canyon Nlha7kápmx lived otherwise.

The Summer of 1858

Some 25,000 to 30,000 miners, most from California, poured into British Columbia in 1858, and a good majority mined in or passed through the Fraser Canyon. Nothing remotely like this had happened there before. Except in the south, and there only briefly after 1848, the canyon had not been a route of the fur trade, and whites were rarely seen. Some white

Line drawing of Yale during the gold rush. The camera had not yet reached the Fraser, and even this sketch lagged a year behind the principal influx of miners.

goods, obtained directly or indirectly from Hudson's Bay Company (HBC) forts, had become common: muskets, iron knives, kettles, blankets, and clothing of European manufacture.[10] Potatoes, introduced from the forts, were grown in small gardens. Beaver were almost trapped out. Native life had incorporated these material changes, and a second severe epidemic (measles, in 1848)[11] in a still Native place. But the gold rush suddenly brought thousands of well-armed miners, often eager to work the very terraces on which the canyon Nlha7kápmx lived. For the Nlha7kápmx, this was an altogether unprecedented invasion. For the miners, it was part of a gold rush to a wilderness inhabited by 'savages,' beyond the reach of formal government. There were only three government officials in or near the canyon to oversee thousands of miners during the extraordinary summer of 1858: a revenue collector at Yale, another at Lytton, and a justice of the peace at Hills Bar, three kilometres south of Yale. The miners hardly took them seriously.[12] They managed themselves and their own dealings with Natives, organizing meetings, electing officers on individual bars, and applying and administering their own rules, as they had done in California and in camps throughout the west.[13] The Nlha7kápmx had to figure out how to cope with hordes of well-armed, aggressive strangers in their midst.

Up to a point, either group appears to have been useful to the other. To judge from their accounts, the miners turned to the Nlha7kápmx for guides, canoes, canoemen, porters, provisions, trade gold, and women; and the Nlha7kápmx turned to the miners for a variety of trade goods and, in a few cases at least, men.[14] There is some evidence that relations were fairly cordial at first, but as more and more miners arrived, some of them seasoned 'Indian fighters' from the American South who held that the only way to deal with 'Indians' was to exterminate them, relations rapidly deteriorated.[15] By August, miners and Natives were at war in the canyon. Some miners were killed, most canyon diggings were abandoned, and thousands of miners, bent on retaliation, collected near Yale. A party from the Thompson River fought its way through this miner-evacuated territory to Yale, burning rancheries (Native villages) and killing Indians whenever they could. The heaviest miner casualties, more than thirty killed by some estimates, may have occurred when miners camped for the night panicked in the dark and began firing at each other. Overall, the number of fatalities cannot be established. Years later, Edward Stout, a former miner, reminisced that about thirty-six whites were killed during the 'indian troubles' and 'a great many indians.'[16] H.F. Reinhart, another miner, said that a company of miners found several Indian camps and 'just killed everything, men, women, and children.'[17] Who knows precisely what happened? None of this is in focus. But it is clear that some miners were more than prepared to kill Indians indiscriminately, and that virtually all of them assumed that their security depended on their own vigilance, organization, and firepower.

It had been common practice from the early days of the fur trade along the Columbia River to organize as many men as possible in paramilitary discipline and formation when traders passed through hostile Native territory (see Chapter 2). Such practices continued, somewhat altered, along the Oregon Trail, then during the Indian Wars in Washington and Oregon, and wherever a mining rush encountered Native resistance. The Californian miners pouring into British Columbia did not have to invent a tactical response to perceived Native threats. To take one example, during the Yakima Wars in the summer of 1858, John Callbreath reached Fort Walla Walla, at the junction of the Columbia and Snake rivers, in a company of five from California. He waited until there were 250 men (and 500 mules and horses) to form a company, elect a captain, and march northward through the Okanagan to the Fraser.[18] Such companies bristled with firepower, supplied by the men. As 'Indian trouble' increased along the Fraser, the miners' response was the same: for a time, at least five companies, some apparently several hundred strong, ranged in the canyon.[19] These were formidable fighting forces, armed as the Natives were not. Some Native peoples still used bows and arrows, and the smooth-bore, muzzle-loading, flintlock muskets that others had obtained from the HBC frequently misfired, were ineffective in wet weather, required at least a minute to load (in a vertical position), and had an effective range of some eighty metres, less than that of a good bow. Most miners, on the other hand, carried Colt revolvers that fired five or six shots in quick succession, and also rifles with percussion locks (which rarely misfired even in wet weather), spiral barrels, and oblong bullets with an effective range of perhaps 300 metres.[20] Natives knew the lay of the land and could mount surprise attacks, but they lacked the technology and military organization to stop a well-led company on the march.

The miners argued about how to use their power. Some favoured a wholesale slaughter, but the majority view, apparently, was to use the threat of force to secure peace treaties. As many as ten such 'treaties' (contents unknown) were concluded in the canyon in August 1858. At the forks of the Fraser and Thompson rivers, where fifty years before Fraser said he had shaken 1,200 hands, H.M. Snyder, miner and captain of a company called the Pike Guards, told eleven chiefs and a large council of Natives gathered from above and below 'that this time we came for pease [*sic*], but if we had to come again ... we would not come by hundreds, but by thousands and drive them from the river forever. They ware much supprised & frightened to see so many men with guns & revolvers ...'[21] A treaty was agreed to. Like all the others that summer, it had no legal or official standing: it was not made by government officials with treaty-making authority, and it did not even represent all miners. Effectively, the treaty's contents hardly mattered. For the miners, a treaty was a device to gain time until the device was no longer needed. For Native people, for whom a treaty, agreed to after speech-making, was one means of terminating conflict, these treaties were probably perceived quite differently. Captain Snyder informed Douglas that, in his opinion, they 'will be held Sacred by the Indians.'

Native opinion, too, was divided. When confronted by a marauding company of miners, Natives tended to disappear into the mountains. A company bent on peace, and with an interpreter who managed to make contact with a Native, might draw them back.[22] Many Natives counselled war. At the forks at Lytton, according to one account, there were several days of fiery debate before Snyder arrived.[23] The Lytton war chief, Cuxcuxê'sqEt, urged war, as did the chief from Spences Bridge and several others. Some Okanagan and Shuswap promised aid. But the great chief, Cexpe'ntlEm (Spi'ntlam), known as a peacemaker after returning slaves and negotiating a peace with the Stl'atl'imx some years before, urged peace, and eventually his view prevailed. It was said that the war chief never forgave him. Quite possibly Spi'ntlam and the other chiefs thought they were dealing with Governor Douglas.[24]

After these treaties, an uneasy calm returned to the canyon, and the miners to their diggings. Natives passing camps of miners often showed a white flag, and miners, convinced that only fear deterred Natives from violence, grouped together as much as possible and maintained their guard.[25] There were intermittent incidents. Natives occasionally killed a miner here or there in retaliation for particular injuries,[26] and miners still took action into their own hands, as William Yates, HBC trader at Fort Hope, reported:

> One day a big crowd of miners came down here [Yale] hustling an indian along with them. This was in October 1858. Mr Allard [HBC trader at Fort Yale] used to interpret for the indians and so did I. An indian would sometimes pick up a boat capsized in the canyon and the miners would think that the indians capsized the boat and they would get hold of the indian and rush him down to us. They supposed the Hudsons Bay knew all about the indians and they would run them down to find out particulars. That afternoon a party of forty or fifty came down with an indian lugging him along. I was sitting in front of the store. We saw them coming and Mr Allard says "Come inside Mr Yates they are coming with another Indian again." I said "to hell with them they can't do any harm to me." In a few minutes they were right here. I knew the indian well. I did not know that he had been doing anything but the miners supposed he was. They rushed him right up and the indian grabbed me by the hand and would not let me go. I said "Let me go – let me go –" but he would not let me go. The miners said "You are a Hudsons Bay man?" I said Yes What kind of an indian is this - what kind of an indian is this, they yelled. I said I did not know - he was good as far as I knew. A party from the outside called me a liar and they dragged me and the indian off from the Hudson Bay store away into the crowd. Judge Perry [George Perrier, justice of the peace at Hills Bar] was there and he rushed in and Ned MacGowan and got me away from the party. I went over to Hills Bar that night and stopped all night with Judge Perry. The Judge took me over so as to stop the trouble.[27]

It is not clear what happened to the Native man.

In mid-September, less than three weeks after Snyder's company returned there, Governor Douglas visited Yale, and addressed the miners.[28] They were all welcome, he said, 'to our country' and to the protection of British laws, as long as they 'obey those Laws and pay the Queen's Dues like honest men.' The proposal to create a mainland colony was before parliament; provisionally, he would authorize the survey and allocation of town plots and twenty-acre farm lots. Laws would be administered 'with justice and impartiality,' and the miners, knowing 'the value of good Laws,' were exhorted 'to come out manfully in support of those Laws' and the civil officers. In fact, neither the law nor an adequate civil administration was yet in place. The miners introduced and managed – bar by bar, and with more or less attention – versions of Californian mining law regarding the number and size of claims, and the conditions by which they were held.[29] Elected committees of miners administered these rules and meted out punishments, which could include a miner forfeiting 'all his right, title and interest' in the bar. And, in some of the ways shown, they had managed their dealings with Native peoples, imposing, in a territory beyond the effective control of the HBC or the state, a set of paramilitary, western American practices that broke the back of Native resistance.

The Summer of 1860

In June and July 1860, George Hills, newly appointed Anglican bishop of British Columbia, and officers and men from a detachment of Royal Engineers were both in the canyon, the one on a reconnaissance of his new diocese, and the others to survey land and construct a wagon road. Hills and Colonel Moody, the commanding officer of the engineers, had travelled upriver to Yale together. They got along well, sharing privileged backgrounds, picturesque imaginations, and the conviction that the greatness of Britain and her empire rested not on commerce, nor even on technology and industry, but on religion, the true, pure Christianity of the Anglican church and prayer book. British Columbia was in its infancy, it was important to build well for the future, and this, above all, meant securing the place of the Anglican church. Progress, empire, and Anglicanism fit seamlessly in their minds. On the morning of June 12 in Yale, work officially began on the wagon road. In the evening, there was a tea to meet the bishop. Colonel Moody encouraged those present, apparently most of the permanent white inhabitants of Yale, to adhere to a religious life, and the chairman urged this diverse group 'to become a unified body and make the Church of England their religion.' Hills was moved. 'In the morning,' he wrote in his diary, 'the contract had been signed for making a road, to be the great road to the interior, perhaps to Canada & England. It was a great step in civilization & progress. Fitting was it to solemnize the occasion by expression of respect for religion & for advancing the cause of Christ's church.'[30]

The Fraser Canyon was not an obvious receptacle for this blend of engineering and the Church of England. As he advanced up the canyon, Hills claimed in one place that 'the path was nil, the projection for the foot not an inch. It seemed like the crawling of a fly upon the perpendicular wall.' In another, the trail was no more than 'a mere indentation for a naked Indian heel. A slip from this would precipitate a fall down into the abyss of the whirling torrent.' Although Hills's style was melodramatic, such were, approximately, the canyon's most rugged parts, which the Royal Engineers attempted to rework in engineering drawings and engineered solutions. By the end of June, one had made a sketch map of the east side of the canyon at the scale of four feet to the mile, with information about hydrology, relief, settlements (very minimally), existing trails, and the proposed route of the wagon road, together with general instructions about its construction, and comments about the suitability of the land for agriculture: 'splendid grazing country, soil in many places deep and loamy.'[31] Such a map was both a tool for the colonial appropriation and management of land, and an engineer's working drawing. A new form of order was being introduced to the canyon. It would surface more elegantly, and with more explicit imperial connections, in town plans (Figure 4.4); and more starkly in engineering drawings of the river (Figure 4.5), the clearest possible indications of the direction of change that the engineering mind would seek to impose on an abrupt and tangled landscape.

Anglicanism was perhaps an even more awkward transplant. England was not at hand, and Hills found almost no Anglicans among the several thousand people in the canyon. Everything about the mining landscapes seemed raw and new: terraces from which the top twelve feet of soil and gravel had already been removed, in some places by hydraulicing (water under pressure in hoses); flumes, some miles long and carried over gullies on flimsy trestles; and rough log huts scattered near the principal diggings. Along the trail were a few gardens, a few incipient farms, a few roadhouses where a roof for the night could be had and a place on the floor. Hills usually slept in a tent. Boston Bar, the principal new settlement of the middle canyon, comprised 'five houses, two stores, a liquor shop, a restaurant & a blacksmith's.' In Lytton, where there were several stores and restaurants, and where the Royal Engineers were 'laying out a town' on a treeless terrace, there was one Englishman. A varied collection of people moved along the canyon trail. The muleteers were mostly Mexicans. Natives, especially women, carried loads that Hills could hardly lift. Chinese charged tolls at rough bridges over some gullies. The miners were a diverse population: Canadians, French, Germans, Spanish, Irish, Australians, but principally Americans ('terrible swearers') and Chinese. A Chinese merchant in Lytton estimated there were 3,000 Chinese above Yale, and 2,000 more expected that summer. Native people, some of whom Hills conversed with in halting Chinook, were numerous. The canyon was hardly Anglican territory, but, at least to Hills, it seemed peaceable. Revolvers, he said, were no longer needed; everything was 'as quiet and orderly as possible.'[32]

Hills did what he could to prepare for an Anglican presence. He identified sites for churches and cemeteries and, at Hope, purchased eighty acres with a trout stream; a beautiful place, he thought, for a college or a bishop's residence. He talked to everyone he could, and enjoyed getting quickly to serious religious matters. He upbraided miners for swearing and working on Sunday. He encouraged a young Chinese miner, who spoke some English and said he prayed to Shung Ti, to hear and read of Jesus, and hoped that this conversation 'might be a commencement of holier thoughts to him and a streak of dawn to his people who are coming over in great multitudes.' He often urged professed Christians of whatever denomination to come to the Anglican church, there to 'learn and hold the pure truth as it is in Jesus.' Everything he learned of the missionary activities of Roman Catholic priests reaffirmed his conviction that they taught and practised error: teaching, for example, about the Virgin Mary, rather than about Jesus, and baptizing too quickly.

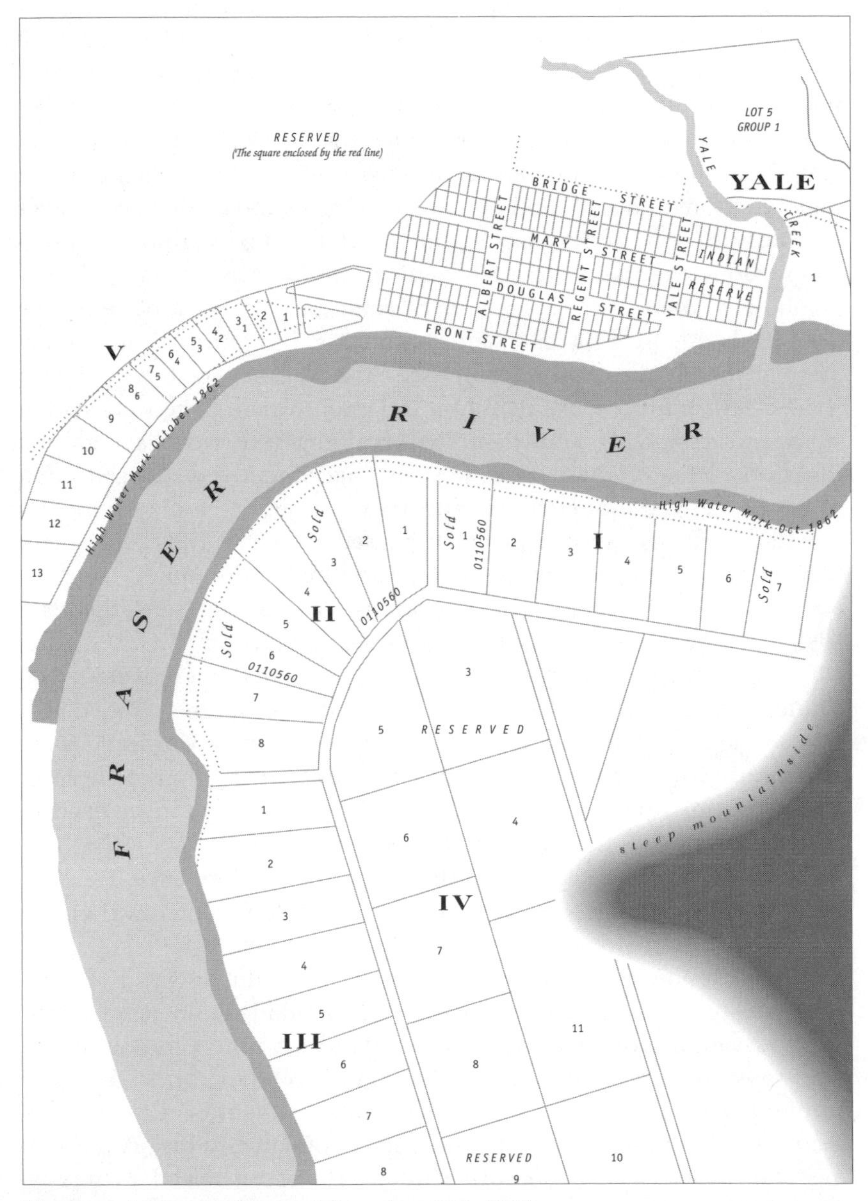

Figure 4.4 Plan of Yale, by J. Launders, R.E., 1862

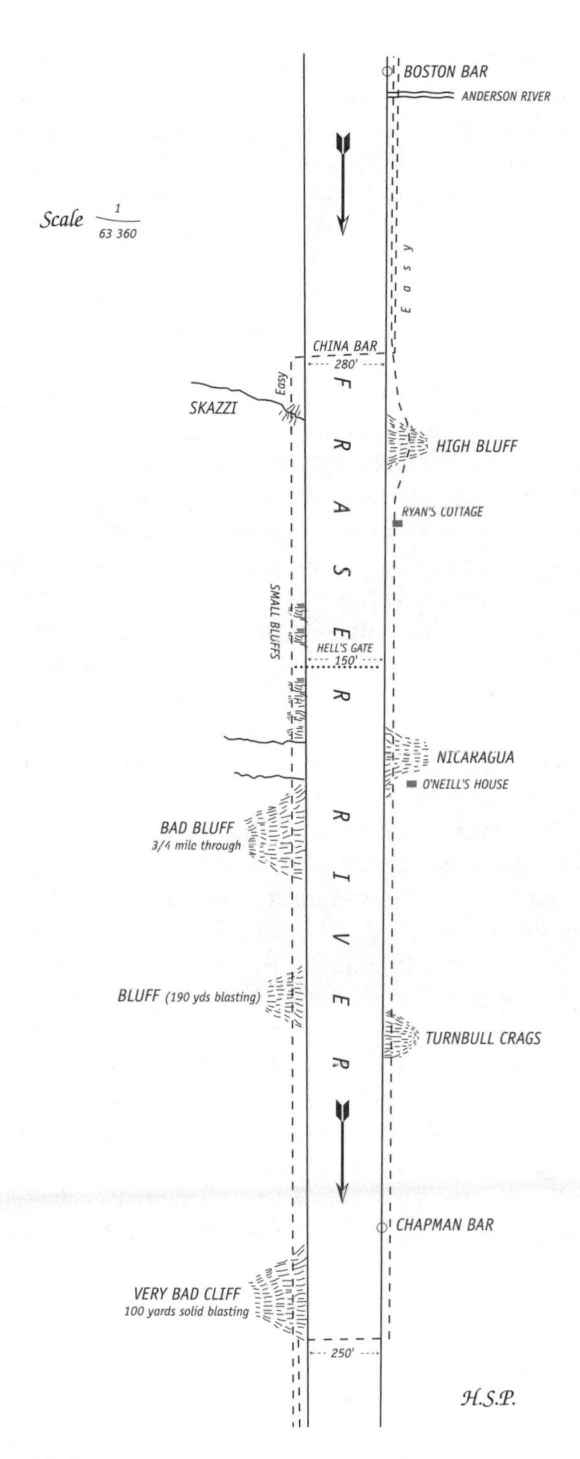

Figure 4.5 Engineering drawing of Fraser, 1860

Hills himself thought Native people were as precious as any others in the eyes of God (he was no racist), but were 'poor' because they lived in 'darkness' and 'sin.'[33] They did not know God and Jesus; they did not know the Word of God. He said of one of his encounters: 'I addressed them. Told them who I was, why I had come, showed them the Bible, told them it was the Word of God. We knew what it contained, they did not.' Here was the essence of Hills's missionary equation: Native ignorance, missionary knowledge, and with it the opportunity of salvation – the consummate assertion of the relationship between power and knowledge.[34] When Hills predicted and explained an impending eclipse of the sun, a great deal of Native discussion ensued. 'Of course we directed them from nature, up to nature's God and while showing our superior knowledge, pointed out the blessings of the knowledge of God which we also possessed.' Hills offered himself as one with special knowledge of the route away from darkness and sin, and towards light and eternal salvation – knowledge he would impart to those who followed his teaching and did his bidding. As Natives learned, they could become children of Jesus just as, Hills said, he was himself. 'One day we shall all dwell together in heaven and there will be only one language.' The Royal Engineers sought to transcend the canyon in one way, Hills in another.

Working with his newly acquired Chinook and an interpreter who knew Chinook and the local language, Hills explained the fundamentals of Christian faith. To a large assemblage of Natives just south of Boston Bar, he spoke, so he noted in his diary, of the love of God expressed in Jesus Christ, showed that the Gospel invitation was open to all, gave some particulars of the life of Jesus, and explained the spiritual nature of man. At Lillooet, he explained 'the death, resurrection and ascension of Christ,' and told his audience that they must accept 'the mercy of God in Christ.' How Hills got any of this into Chinook, essentially a trading pidgin, what sense his interpreter made of it, and how it was rendered in a Native language can hardly be imagined.[35] The problems of communication were overwhelming, and it seems impossible that what Hills thought he said and what his audiences thought they heard had much to do with each other. At Lillooet Hills was mortified to learn that *Saghalie Tayee Papa,* the Chinook for God (literally, the above chief father), was understood to be the Sun. Sun, of course, had been in the canoe with Coyote, Moon was his wife, and the Stars were their children.

The Summer of 1878

On May 18, 1878, Gilbert Malcolm Sproat, Indian Reserve Commissioner, and his party arrived at Spuzzum, the most southerly village of the Nlha7kápmx, near the south end of the Fraser Canyon. Sproat's intention

Gilbert Malcolm Sproat, Indian Reserve Commissioner, in camp at Spuzzum, May 1878.

was to adjust reserves in the canyon to Lytton, then along the Thompson River to Spences Bridge, then in the Nicola Valley. He had intended to start the field season earlier but, receiving no support from the provincial government, had been forced to become 'a record ransacker' in the land office in Victoria.[36] It was pointless to go into the field without knowing what land had been conceded where, when, and on what terms. Sproat's salary was paid by the federal government, and he shared the opinion, apparently held in Ottawa, that the Natives of British Columbia had prior title to land, and that their title could be circumvented by the quick, generous allocation of reserves.[37] The provincial government had no such views, and largely ignored Sproat's many requests for clarifications of its land policies. When Sproat arrived at Spuzzum, he believed, incorrectly it turned out, that his decisions would be final. The Natives awaited him eagerly. He had been importuned by the chiefs of the lower Fraser Valley to visit their settlements.[38] Natives were 'quiet and obedient to the law,' they said, but settlers had been permitted to acquire land they had hoped to get. Similar pleas emanated from many parts of the province. Sproat hoped to survey the lower valley before the end of the year, and he asked that the provincial government grant no land near the reserves in the meantime, a request it ignored.

At Spuzzum, Sproat and his assistant, George Blenkinsop, recorded 107 people where, Blenkinsop noted, 'a short time since' there had been 400.[39] As the commission toured the canyon, Blenkinsop continued the census, enumerating 1,622 people between Spuzzum and the Stein River (some eighty kilometres), less than a quarter the number that, fifty years before, the McDonald census recorded between Boston Bar and Yale (some thirty-five kilometres). Most of the older settlements were still inhabited (Figure 4.6), but populations were small: 285 at Klick.kum.cheen (Lytton); 106 at Tslank.lahk.tun (Kanaka Flat); 237 at Kwi.owh.um (near Boston Bar); 107 at Spuzz.um; and about 50 at most other sites. The Native population of the canyon may have been no more than a seventh or eighth of what it had been in 1830. In this case, the decline was not due to smallpox. The province-wide epidemic of 1862 had largely bypassed the canyon because missionaries and government officials had vaccinated most Natives in time. The decline noted in 1878 reflected, in proportions not yet known, the measles epidemic of 1848, tuberculosis, venereal diseases, a variety of unidentified and probably introduced diseases, and the effects of alcohol and warfare. Infant and child mortality rates were exceedingly high.[40] Cumulatively the effects were probably worse than those of any single smallpox epidemic. The Indian reserve commission was travelling through an ongoing demographic disaster.

Yet in 1878, the canyon's population was still overwhelmingly Native, though others, and the properties of others, were also there. Most newcomers were Chinese, single men who, Sproat found, seldom spoke either English or Chinook, and lived by mining and farming.[41] Many were

Boothroyds roadhouse on the Cariboo wagon road, c. 1867. A typical roadhouse on the only lengthy wagon road in the BC interior.

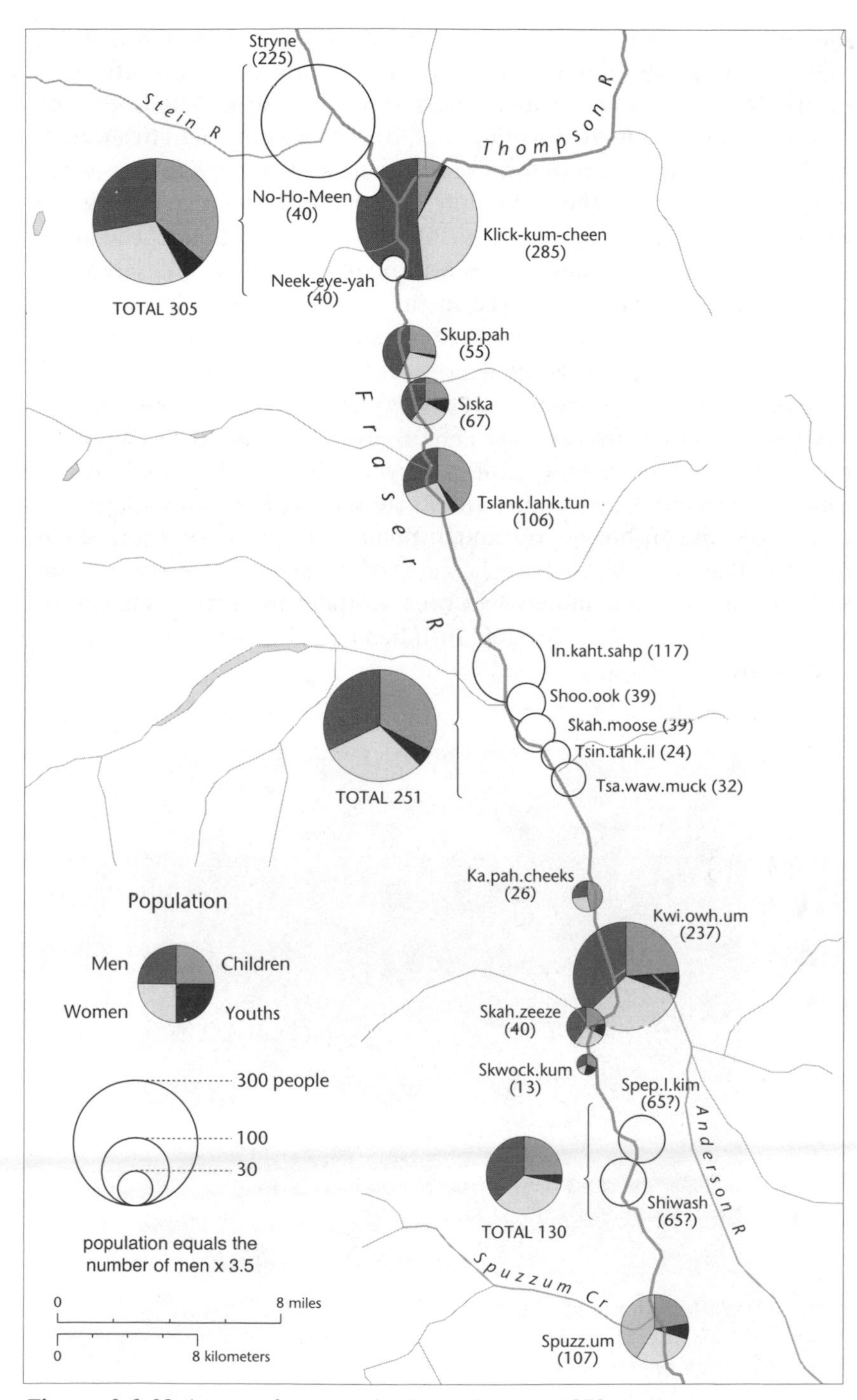

Figure 4.6 Native population in the Fraser Canyon, 1878

squatters; a few had pre-empted or purchased land and recorded water rights. Others, who still owned land in the canyon, had returned to China. The whites were a varied few, and not very fixed. The large-scale pattern of settlement is revealing. Boothroyds was named after a man who, in the 1860s, acquired a Crown grant and water rights to some ninety acres of good land – the only such land in the area – along the wagon road, where he operated a roadhouse and a small farm. The property remained in his name in 1878, though Boothroyd had left years before. The only white who lived in the area, W.A. Jamieson (and perhaps his family), had pre-empted 160 acres and worked as a section man on the wagon road. Across the river, workings abandoned by white and Chinese miners had been reoccupied by 'Chinamen ... [who] will not allow Indians to share the water.'[42] Otherwise, the Boothroyds people were Natives. At Kwi.owh.um, the only water that could be used for irrigation was recorded by a white, Tim Ryan, who, Sproat was told, 'makes bad fences: Indian horses go through them and Tim makes the Indians pay for trespass.'[43] On the large terrace across the river from Kwi.owh.um, Chinese miners had been working the gravels for almost twenty years (Figure 4.7). The gold rush had left a human remainder, part of the canyon in 1878.

Washing for gold near Yale. Taken some twenty-five years after the gold rush, the picture shows a small placer operation, the head of steam navigation on the lower Fraser, and the dramatic southern entrance to the Fraser Canyon.

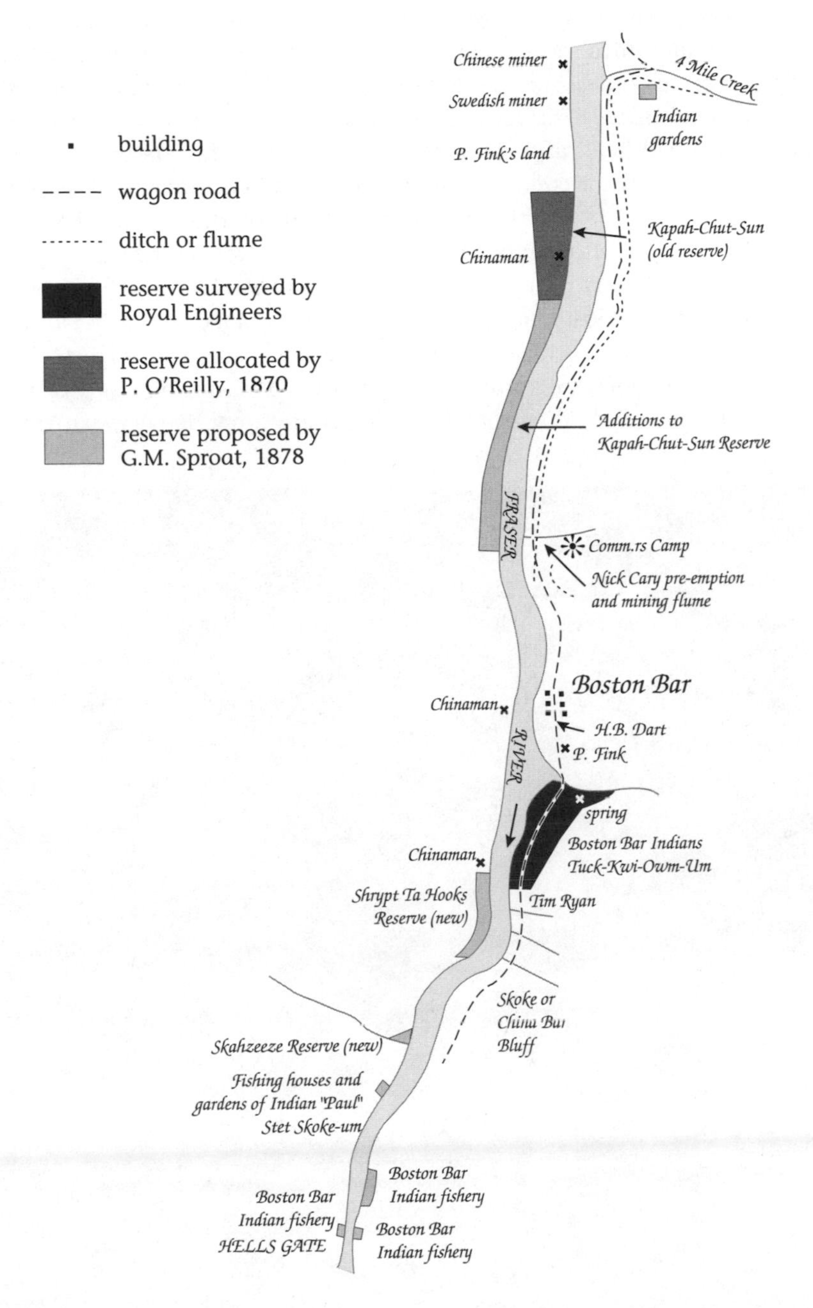

Figure 4.7 Country of the Boston Bar group of Indians (after G.M. Sproat, 1878)

Sproat was travelling through an extraordinary human landscape composed of many unconnected elements. There were still traditional Native pit houses and conical summer lodges, if not always with traditional coverings, and also, in 1878, Native log cabins. Native horses and a few cattle grazed on small fields and open range. There were Native potato patches here and there (the second superintendent of Indian Affairs sent packets of vegetable seeds, but, without water for irrigation, they were not planted). Some Native settlements had disappeared, obliterated by placer mining. Across the river from Kwi.owh.um, the surface of the Native cemetery stood almost three metres above the cobbled, recently worked surface of the land. Although offered a good price, the Natives had declined to let their ancestors be 'washed up.'[44] From one end of the canyon to the other, flumes and ditches, many now derelict, ran from

Road and telegraph in the Fraser Canyon.

small mountain streams to terraces along the river (Figure 4.7). All terraces that such water could reach bore the effects of placer mining; in 1878, some small operations remained, worked by Chinese. The few white farms usually were also roadhouses: a house built of squared logs or milled lumber with framed glass windows, pole- or timber-frame farm buildings covered with shake roofs, and fields still dotted with stumps, and surrounded by rough picket fences on either side of this cluster of buildings.[45] Through these patches of settlement in a depopulated valley ran the wagon road, seventeen feet wide, massively cribbed in places, blasted out of bedrock in others, by any standards an impressive feat of engineering. At the north end of the canyon, Lytton was a collection of shacks and log huts, an Anglican church with Gothic revival elements, and a few other frame buildings on the grid of streets the Royal Engineers had surveyed in 1860.

Sproat, however, was there to consider the land question.[46] He found a few reserves of winter villages, most only two or three acres, which the Royal Engineers had surveyed, and some larger reserves. These had been laid out quickly in 1870, just before British Columbia entered Confederation, by Peter O'Reilly, reserve commissioner, acting on the instructions of Joseph Trutch, chief commissioner of lands and works for the colony.

For twelve years, therefore, through a major gold rush, there were no Indian reserves through much of the canyon. When they were finally laid out, the best land was already taken, and the accessible water already recorded. Whatever his intentions, O'Reilly had to shoehorn reserves into a prior pattern of alienated land. He recorded no water rights. Against the rhetoric about Native agriculture was a simple canyon reality: in 1878, Natives did not have enough water to farm there. Twenty-seven water records were granted in the Lytton area between 1861 and 1877, none to Natives.[47] At Nhomin, where Simon Fraser met some 400 people, O'Reilly conceded a small reserve of bouldery land, three acres of which could be cultivated, on either side of Nhomin Creek. First water rights to Nhomin Creek were held by Thomas Earl, whose farm was immediately north, and second water rights by Ah Wah, whose farm was immediately south, of the reserve. They controlled the good land and virtually all the water that could be used for irrigation along a considerable stretch of the river.[48] Between Earl and Ah Wah, amid the boulders, lived thirty-five to forty Nlha7kápmx. In most of the canyon, Sproat thought he found satisfactory ways through the tangle of property and water rights. In the Lytton area he simply did not know what to do; there seemed to be no solution.

By 1878, there was a considerable British Columbian land policy: Crown grants, pre-emptions that were confirmed by certificates of improvement, mineral rights, water rights, grazing rights, as well as

Native reserves,[49] all of which Sproat had to negotiate as he moved through the canyon. Evidence of prior Native settlement, he assumed, overrode any non-Native claims, which should in these cases be revoked. Where there was uncertainty, the balance of doubt should favour the Natives. Otherwise, for Sproat, property was property, title was title. He defended equally a Native who had pre-empted land before it became illegal to do so, a Chinese miner who had become naturalized and had acquired Crown land, and absentee owners, though he was dubious about some who showed no signs of returning, as well as settlers. Sproat believed in a regime of property and law.[50]

Whatever their opinions on particular matters, so did almost all white British Columbians. A concept of property that was less European than English was an implicit part of the province's white political culture. In this tradition, it was enough to inquire what gave one good title to property; there was no need, as on the continent, to delve into the philosophical bonds between person and property, or to worry about intrinsically satisfying work. Rather, the justification for property was extrinsic to the individual: private property was 'an effective means to the end of efficiently exploiting the resources of the natural world, in comparison with any other system of rights and duties.'[51] It promoted a working, thrifty population, laying the basis for a good life for many, and providing some assurance of subsistence for all. This was its sufficient justification in a tradition that dominated English common law, and that white British Columbians, including Sproat, took for granted. Sproat held that the reserves should be subdivided into lots so that Natives might become acquainted with the advantages of private property.[52]

By 1878, a new regime of control, centred on private property, the law, and government administration – of which the Indian reserve commission was a striking symbol – was in the canyon, but the range of its jurisdiction and its capacity to enforce were far from clear. So much had happened so quickly over such a large area that neither the law nor the means of enforcement could keep pace with the rate and shifting geography of change. Sproat knew this, but kept raising awkward, fundamental questions: Could mineral claims be held within Indian reserves? Did laws of trespass apply where fence districts had not been designated? Could reserves be conceded within land set aside in the railway belt? The government did not want such questions, the honest answer to which, usually, was that it did not yet have a policy. Sproat thought some of the policies it *did* have were absurd, and he said so. When the federal government considered curtailing Native net fisheries in the canyon to protect commercial fisheries at the mouth of the Fraser, Sproat responded that the land question in the canyon was trivial compared to the salmon question. In muddy waters, salmon could only be taken with nets. 'The

Government of England twenty-five years ago might as well have prohibited the cultivation of potatoes by the Irish.'[53]

Native peoples, too, peppered Sproat with questions: Could they hunt on Crown land? (Yes, but only in season.) Were the canneries at the river mouth going to take all the salmon? (No, as long as the spawning beds were protected.) Other questions were more difficult to answer. What were the boundaries between 'church' law and 'Queen's' law, especially in matters of divorce and child custody? Could an Indian work hard and acquire private property? Could Indians hire a teacher for their children? A white doctor for an Indian hospital? Some requests were poignant cries for help in changing, unknown circumstances. 'One old chief with whom the Missionaries had been able to do nothing for 20 years told me that he was going to be a Jesus Christ man now that his land questions were settled, and as proof he forthwith put away the ugliest of his three wives and she followed me for 100 miles to make repeated inquiries as to the share of the Chief's land to which she was entitled.'[54] A Spuzzum woman had raised her grandson after his mother died. Then the child's father, an American black, returned, demanded his son, and told the grandmother that if she did not give up the boy, he would tell the authorities and she would go to prison. The grandmother could not evaluate this terrifying threat.

How are we to understand all this? Certainly the internalized lifeworlds of the Native canyon, within which people had ordered their understandings, had been fragmented and colonized to some considerable degree.[55] The cast-off wife and the grandmother who was threatened with prison could no longer evaluate their circumstances entirely from within their experience. Totally unfamiliar systems of power were in the canyon, and now seem to have been recognized as such. Sproat, rather than Coyote and his issue, was approached to tell an old woman in Spuzzum whether or not she was going to jail. In effect, Native knowledge had been radically decentred; it no longer fully explained the canyon and its events, as not long since it had. In 1878, the complex of introduced power depended less directly on guns and firepower than on property rights defined by law and defended by courts and jails. With this power, the reserve commission, which sought to identify patches of land held for Natives and demarcate them from all the rest, was completely complicit. Property rights were binding. Sproat respected them, so did the government and the courts, and so, however begrudgingly, did Native people as they came to understand what whites considered offenses against their property, and the penalties they imposed. In effect, Sproat was an agent of a powerful disciplinary regime – centred on land and backed by law, and ultimately by violence – that determined where people could and could not go: this was the most intrusive system of disciplinary power in the canyon in 1878. Neither Indian agents nor residential schools were yet in place. Although Anglican and Roman Catholic missionaries were established at either end of the canyon, Natives themselves were active participants in the missionary process. The land system, on the other hand, was imposed, and with it came a pervasive transfer of local power as Native mobility and access to resources within traditional territories were curtailed.

And yet, in 1878 this system was still being worked out, and the Nlha7kápmx, to judge from the questions they put to Sproat, were doing what they could to understand the new complex of power in the canyon and their place within it. In general, they seem to have accepted the Queen's authority while assuming that it left a good deal of latitude for them. Their most decisive attempt to find their own distinctive place within an introduced system of power came a year later. On July 17, 1879, seventy-one years after Simon Fraser, another gathering of 1,200 Nlha7kápmx encamped at Lytton with tents, flags, and 1,500 horses. This time, they had come to elect representatives of the whole tribe and lay plans for its government. Sproat and other government officials had been invited, but only Sproat came. As he approached a large building put up for the occasion – boarded sides, a canvas roof decorated with greenery, and 'a pendant crown made of boughs' above a platform at one end – a cannon, acquired from somewhere, fired a twelve-gun salute. Sproat made a speech, then retired to be available as needed as legal adviser. A head chief and thirteen councillors were elected for three years, subject to the Queen's pleasure. Then, after two weeks of discussion, several proposals emerged. The tribe would build a school at Lytton and hire a teacher of arithmetic and reading, paying for both from a school tax. It would hire a white doctor, paying him from a medical tax. There would be fines for drunkenness, potlatching, gambling, and animal trespass; villages would be 'made to look well.' The duration of fish traps and hunting seasons would be regulated, useless dogs would be killed, and women would not work in the fields while men idled. No one would be jailed; punishments would be fines or confiscations. Everyone was to respect the council's decisions and help enforce them.[56]

The list probably bears the hand of the former Anglican missionary in Lytton, J.B. Good – though by 1879 his influence among the Nlha7kápmx had waned, and he was living in Yale – and, indirectly, of the Indian Act of 1876. But it also seems to reflect a people trying, with assistance, to find a legal means, within the terms of white law, of gaining some control over new circumstances. While deferring to the Queen, the Indian Act, and a measure of white protocol, the Nlha7kápmx were apparently manoeuvring to secure their own place and define their own authority in their changing world. Sproat was enthusiastic about the prospects for Native self-government,[57] but the proposals produced such howls of indignation from newspaper editors, settlers, and the provincial government that Ottawa would not support them, and they came to naught.[58]

The Canyon in November 1914

During a week in November 1914, the Royal Commission on Indian Affairs for the Province of British Columbia, the McKenna-McBride Commission, visited the principal settlements of the Fraser Canyon from Lytton to Yale. The commission had been created in 1912, a federal and provincial response to increasingly organized Native protests over land.[59] Its role was to make a 'final adjustment' of Native lands; to do so, the commission could alter reserves, but could not open the question of title; this, the Natives were told, would be decided in the courts. At each stop, the local chief, and usually several other Native people, addressed the commission; their remarks and the ensuing discussion were translated for the commissioners and recorded verbatim.

By this time, there were two railways in the canyon: the Canadian Northern, just built, and the Canadian Pacific Railway (CPR), then some thirty years old. The old Cariboo Wagon Road had been damaged by railway construction, and was impassable south of Boston Bar. In a sense, the river itself had disappeared; it had never been a transportation route, and in 1914, after a slide at Hell's Gate during the construction of the Canadian Northern, most of its fish were destroyed. Small railway stations had replaced roadhouses, and a divisional point on the CPR (North Bend) had become the principal white settlement in the middle canyon. The commission travelled by rail through territory that, in many ways, was well incorporated within a transcontinental nation-state. As part of the railway belt, a twenty-mile strip on either side of the CPR, most land was administered from Ottawa and, topography permitting, was laid out in a broad grid of ranges and townships (Figure 4.8). Parts of the canyon had been mapped by G.M. Dawson for the Geological Survey of Canada. Post offices operated by the Dominion of Canada served small non-Native populations, including some Chinese. But, as in 1879, Natives were the majority of the canyon's people. Government authority over them rested locally in an Indian agent responsible for the Lytton agency, which then included, besides the Fraser River Nlha7kápmx, a ribbon of river peoples from Halkomelem-speakers below Hope to Shuswap-speakers above Lillooet.[60] Most of the canyon Nlha7kápmx were baptized Anglicans; those in the south were Roman Catholics. Denominational residential schools for Native children were supported by ecclesiastical and government funds.

The McKenna-McBride hearings in the Fraser Canyon brought together two vastly unequal parties: senior officials of a federal nation-state and of

BRITISH COLUMBIA

Plan of N.E. 1/4 Township 10, Range 26, West of the Sixth Meridian

FIRST EDITION

SCALE 20 CHAINS TO AN INCH

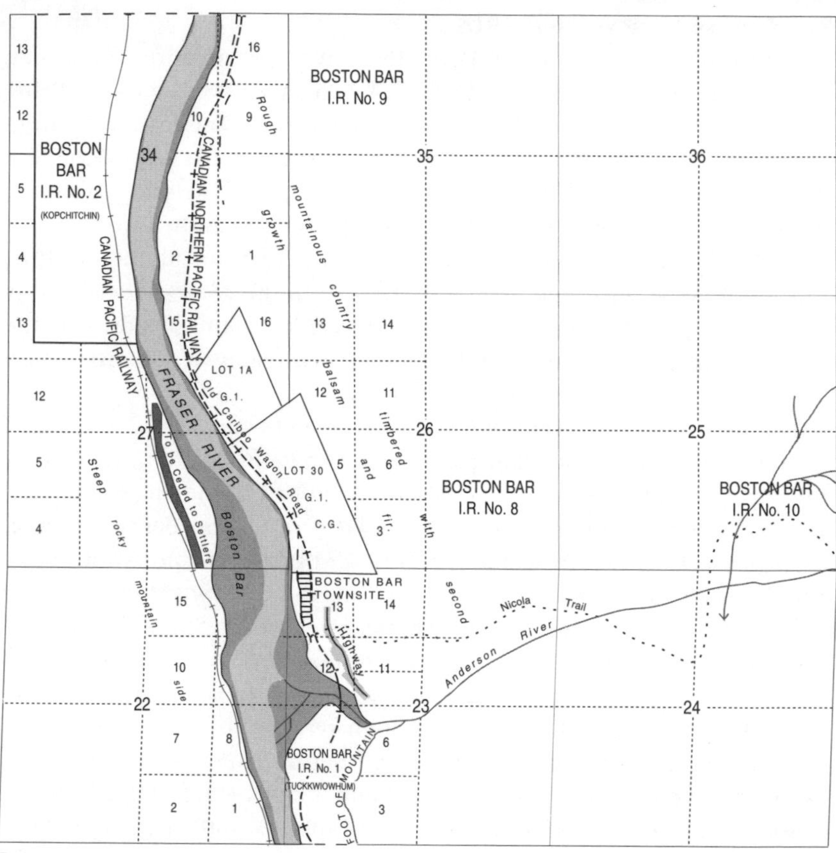

Portion to be retained by C.P.R. coloured Red
Additional R.w. required for double track coloured Blue
Portions to be ceded to Settlers coloured Green

PHOTO-ZINCOGRAPHED AT THE SURVEYOR GENERAL'S OFFICE, OTTAWA, CANADA.

Compiled from official surveys by
A.W.Johnson D.L.S. 16th November, 1904
P.Melhuish D.L.S. 20th November, 1912
A.E.Hunter D.L.S. 8th December, 1913

Department of the Interior, Ottawa, 6th November, 1914.

Approved and Confirmed.

E.Deville
Surveyor General.

Note: Distances are in chains. Bearings are reckoned from the astronomical meridian through the centre of the township. Areas in acres are marked on all lands surveyed, except lands that have been patented and are taken to the banks of the Fraser River. Legal subdivision numbers are shown thus.......8.

Figure 4.8 Plan of N.E. Township 10, Range 26, West of the Sixth Meridian

the British empire, and people denied elementary rights of citizenship and treated, childlike, as wards of that state. The commissioners, representatives of British Columbia, Canada, and the Crown, embraced an optimistic rhetoric of progress and development against which lands for Native people, a population thought doomed to dwindle and disappear, appeared as distractions to be minimized as much as possible. They took for granted the superiority of white ways, and easily stereotyped Natives as lazy, lying, and inferior. With the assistance of Indian agents and residential schools, they believed Natives might become more like whites.[61] The commissioners held most of the cards: theirs was the power to grant, withhold, or – as unfolded eventually, in spite of promises to the contrary – withdraw land. Awkward questions were shelved, either by referring them to the Indian agent or by declaring them beyond the commission's terms of reference. Such rulings were final. In this unequal setting, Native speakers, in common with colonized peoples worldwide, offered up a complex mixture of compliance and resistance.

The commissioners had no doubts about their own authority. They carried a commission, signed by the governor general of Canada, and could, if need be, cite higher authority. When a chief claimed that the 'Lord Almighty' gave whites and Indians free use of the mountainsides, a commissioner replied that if the chief really understood his Bible, he would know that 'God placed men in authority – laws are therefore made for the benefit of us all and they must be obeyed by us all.'[62] And the commissioners had a clear conception of 'good Indians': those who cultivated land, sent their children to a residential school, and obeyed the Indian agent. They had not come to listen, but to establish whether they were dealing with 'good Indians' and, therefore, whether each chief and his band were entitled to more land. Goodness was established quantitatively; in the Fraser Canyon, as in the French asylums and reformatories that Michel Foucault studied, discipline became 'a political economy of detail':[63]

Q. How many people are there in the 3 families [on Reserve 5a]

A. About 10

Q. Any children

A. Yes.

Q. How many.

A. Four.

Q. Are they of school age

A. Yes, some of them are.

Q. Do any of them go to school

A. Yes, some of them go to school at Mission.

Q. How many go to school

A. There are 2 going to school at Mission, and 2 at Lytton.

Q. How many acres have the Indians under cultivation on that Reserve.

A. I don't know how many acres – I don't know anything at all about acres.

Q. Would half or quarter of the Reserve be under cultivation.

A. Perhaps about half.[64]

Note the chief's reluctance to accede to this discipline of numbers, this measured goodness.

Nor were the commissioners troubled by, or probably even aware of, the contradictions in their demands, contradictions which, because they did not have to be explained, only served to emphasize the reality of colonial power.[65] In the same breath, the commissioners enjoined Natives 'to help themselves and obey the instructions of the Indian agent,' self-reliance and submission apparently going hand in hand. They believed in individual liberty while participating in a colonial process that denied it. They believed in economic development, the market, and Native agriculture, while examining a reserve system that provided insufficient arable land, water, and market access for commercial farming. Native efforts to overcome these difficulties were approved, but hardly supported. Consider the testimony of Henry Mack at Lytton:

Q. What do you do with the potatoes you grow on this land.

A. We cant take them anywhere to sell, so we use them all ourselves.

Q. You dont sell any because you cant get across the river

A. That is about right; we havent got a road, and we cant go

Q. You have a cable over the river, have you

A. We have strung a cable across the river about one mile below our Reserve, and we had to use a ripeur to cut our lumber out and build a little scow for ourselves to bring the produce across the river.

Q. Did the Indian Agent or the Government give you any money towards building this cable and scow

A. No; not a cent ...

> Q. [Questions about possible locations of a bridge:] When these Indians have gone to such trouble and expense, you are entitled to some help, but none of the Commissioners know how to build a bridge, but we will ask Mr. Graham [the Indian agent] to look into this matter.[66]

The Indian agent had no power in this matter; there would be no bridge.

For their part, Natives employed various rhetorical tactics of resistance, some of which may have discomfited the commissioners without shaking their authority. They adopted the white language of property to request compensation for property violations, requests the commissioners turned over to the Indian agent. They laced their comments with irony. Consider the words of Peter Hohohaush, sub-chief of a reserve near Lytton:

> I have not very much to say, as I am well satisfied with the present conditions. I am very pleased to meet you gentlemen, and know that you have come here to settle all our troubles. You see that our country here is very rocky and mountainous, and though we are all very poor we still keep on living here on our Reserves, because God has put us here in this part ... because God ordained that we should live here, and we still continue to do so, even though we are poor. On the small reserve that I am on, my children have got only about 3 acres of land that is fit for cultivation, and yet my children and myself work this little piece of land, and we dont grumble ... I am pleased to think that you people are here to look after our interests.[67]

Hohohaush, of course, was not 'well satisfied' with three arable acres and poverty. At Boston Bar, Patrick wanted to know on whose authority the commissioners came, and when shown the governor general's commission, he exclaimed:

> I understand now, and am glad to have seen that. It is as though Christ himself has come, when the Duke of Connaught sent you here to investigate our conditions. I am very glad to have you here, because you have come today. I have been very sorry for a long time, and today I see you. I am delighted to have you here, so now I shall be satisfied. I shall now endeavour to speak to you, just as if I were speaking to God Almighty. So that now, my conditions will be improved, and I will never have any cause to be sorry in the future.[68]

From Patrick, who did not cooperate with the commission, this was dangerous irony. Even the many melancholy references to patches of unproductive land, the failure of the salmon fishery, and poverty should be read as indictments of the whites as much as descriptions of canyon life.[69]

Beyond this interplay of power and resistance was the canyon itself, somewhat revealed by the hearings. There was still some agriculture: potato patches, chickens, tiny gardens (cabbages, turnips, and carrots), a few horses and cattle, but not enough water and not enough agricultural land. Some men worked in railway construction gangs, some families went to Chilliwack each season to pick hops, many had once worked in the canneries at the mouth of the Fraser, but no longer. There was not much work, not much agriculture, and, in 1914, the fishery was threatened. After the slide caused by construction of the Canadian Northern near Hell's Gate, Natives were not allowed to fish. They were angry. As a chief told the commission, 'Whose fault was it that I hadn't sufficient food to eat this year? Who was the cause of our poverty? It was not my fault that today we are poor. I was stopped from providing myself with food. No one should be stopped from providing themselves with food. When they came to stop me they told me that if I did not obey I would be put in gaol.' A commissioner replied that slides had many causes, and that fish must be protected. 'The reason of this slide was caused by white men,' said the chief. 'We are not here to discuss that,' replied the commissioner. There was poverty bordering on starvation and, on top of it, mangled reserves. 'I have some trouble with the C.P.R.,' said a man at Boston Bar. 'They want to take my land – that is, the land I have been living on for some years. They told me I would have to leave there because it belonged to them. The C.P.R. has moved their fence right up to my house, and they have taken in the principal dwelling part.'[70]

The chiefs were protesting against poverty and, even more, against the regulations within which they now lived and over which they had no control. The Indian agent was detested. Beyond the reserves were a host of laws (especially fish, game, and land laws), policemen, and jails. Children were to attend school, and parents were to send them back if they ran away. In effect, the Natives of the canyon lived as wards within the regulative environment of the modern nation-state. As regulation settled around them, constraining their lives more and more, Native protest appears to have become more generalized and abstract. Gone were plans for Native schools, hospitals, and a measure of Native self-government. Native demands had become broader and more territorial. The whole Nlha7kápmx people had always lived within four posts, a large area from Spuzzum to Lillooet and including the Thompson Valley to Kamloops, and the Nicola Valley. 'Christ ordained that we should live with this area, and we dont want things changed until Christ returns.'[71] Patrick at Boston Bar put the case as clearly as anyone:

> God Almighty put me here, and gave us the birds and animals for our use; and he made these birds and animals for our food. He made all the things on the earth. He made this so that we would have sufficient to live on, and that we need never be in need nor want; and when he had made all the things of the world, he went back from here, and went back to his own home in heaven; and before God left he never meant to have any gaols or policemen to restrict us. So today we don't want any gaols or any policemen, because the policemen are always restricting us from going and using the things we claim as our own. They wont allow us to shoot, or anything else, and here everything is going to waste. The trees in our forest, we are not allowed to use them without permission. And I don't want to be stopped from fishing salmon in the River. God made those for our use, and it is from salmon that I make my living. Therefore, I wish everything to be set free.[72]

The Queen, however, gave reserve land and promised, the chiefs claimed, that no white men would trespass on it. But they do 'come in and take up our land, and tell us we have no right to it. They take the water and everything.'[73]

From Simon Fraser to this in 100 years. Coyote and his band had been absorbed, ostensibly at least, in a Christian cosmology. But the peoples of the canyon remained, albeit depleted. The Nlha7kápmx had not become Europeans; their old lifeworld was violated, but not entirely destroyed. Power over the canyon resided elsewhere. Arguments about power turned into arguments over land. An incoming white society appropriated most of the land; indigenous peoples were crimped by reserves and regulations, the 'narrow world strewn with prohibitions' that Frantz Fanon described in *The Wretched of the Earth*.[74] Figure 4.8 suggests the changed geographical reality.

The sequence of change appears to have been approximately this: However much introduced diseases and goods altered canyon life during the fur trade years, the canyon remained Nlha7kápmx territory until the spring of 1858. Then it was invaded by gold miners, an invasion that, overall, the Nlha7kápmx could not repel. The miners maintained their position by force, and broke the back of Native resistance in the canyon during the summer of 1858. Following shortly in their wake was a much more comprehensive and subtle panoply of occupying powers vested in governments; backed, if need be, by police or troops; and tied to a pervasive European discourse about the location, worldwide, of racial/cultural superiority and inferiority. All whites in the canyon – government officials, missionaries, miners, and settlers – subscribed to this discourse in some form. Associated with it were assumptions about the superiority of

European land use, based on a regime of private property. This regime of property, one of the corollaries of which was the creation of Native reserves, quickly became the most pervasive form of white disciplinary power in the canyon. Even so, it took time to work out. In the late 1870s, the Nlha7kápmx could still assume that considerable powers were left to them to establish their own legally sanctioned place within the Queen's authority. Thirty-five years later, with two railways cutting through the canyon's reserves, experience with Indian agents and residential schools, years of farming without enough land or water, and the collapse of the salmon fishery, it had become clear just how minuscule this place was. Native protest became more generalized, invoking Christ, God Almighty, and broad claims to tribal lands, some of which probably went back to the treaties the Nlha7kápmx thought they had negotiated with Snyder, or Douglas, in August 1858.

With railways on either side of the river, new property lines and fences on the land, and new settlements and peoples at various points, the canyon itself was a changed place. The Nlha7kápmx lived within this changed geography, which for them was a geography of exclusions. They had lost control of most of the canyon's land and resources. In the late 1870s, with an Indian reserve commission coming to regulate the land question, and the new Indian Act appearing to allow a measure of local government, there seemed a window of opportunity. As it turned out, the window was closed. It remained closed for well over 100 years, and only now may be opening a little. We shall see. The angry chorus of settler and editorial opinion that greeted the modest Nlha7kápmx plan for local government in 1879 can still be heard, long and loud. If the window does not open, is there any reason to expect the Nlha7kápmx – who still have a land problem, but are far better equipped to confront colonialism than were their ancestors – to live quietly within a colonial regime?

5
A Population Geography of British Columbia in 1881

with Robert Galois

Hinged between a largely Native past and a largely non-Native future, the British Columbia census of 1881 is the first approximately comprehensive report of the population of a huge segment of the North American Cordillera.[1] It is a record of very different peoples who came together during the century following the first Spanish and British contacts with the Northwest Coast. For all these peoples, old ways of life and their settings were no longer quite at hand. Social spaces were changing. Natives and immigrants found themselves in new settlements composed of different peoples in new social configurations. Sudden deletions from former lifeways, coupled with encounters with strange peoples in unfamiliar settings, affected the way people lived and thought of themselves. In effect, society and space were recalibrating each other,[2] and something like a larger British Columbian society – the society recorded in the census of 1881 – was beginning to emerge.

The aggregate census of 1881 was published in 1882, and the nominal manuscript census – that is, the enumerators' handwritten lists giving each person's name, age, sex, place of birth, ethnic origin, religion, marital status, and occupation, as well as information about housing and school attendance – became available (on microfilm) 100 years later.[3] The nominal census is the far more detailed and telling document, but it is not easily interpreted. It is an under-enumeration – particularly, we suspect, of Native and Chinese peoples, and of geographically isolated populations – but it is impossible to ascertain by how much. It was an instrument of the growing regulatory power of the modern nation-state, and a reflection of the cultural myopia and the racial and gendered assumptions of the white Canadian society that devised and administered it. The 1881 census provides almost no information, therefore, about women's work, and is less explicit about Natives and Chinese than about whites. Basically, the nominal census is a very circumscribed document: it identifies people by name, age, and sex; describes where they came from; and records their principal occupation in the commercial economy.

Yet the 1881 census does provide some information about almost all people in the province, and by cross-checking census listings against other records, most of these people can be located fairly precisely.[4] As this is done, intricate population geographies hidden within the broad regional categories of the published census begin to be discerned, and as they are teased out and fitted to the personal data, elements of British Columbian society begin to come into focus. So manipulated, the nominal census of 1881 is a revealing body of data; however deficient and warped, it is the basic social survey of British Columbia in the late nineteenth century.

The published census gives a total of 49,459 people, and the nominal census rolls record 50,387 people in British Columbia in 1881. Some Native groups were not enumerated, and we use a variety of other sources to estimate a total population in 1881 of just over 53,000 people,[5] distributed as shown in Figure 5.1. The population density was exceedingly low: about one person per eighteen square kilometres, probably lower than it had been for centuries.[6] In the interior, most people lived along the Fraser River and its tributaries, or along the Skeena. The largest coastal concentration was around the Strait of Georgia, but there were sizeable populations along the west coast of Vancouver Island and near the mouth of the Skeena. Just over three-fifths of the people in the province had been born there; the provincial ratio of males to females was 3:2.

In the categories of the census, more than half the population was 'Indian' (Native), and some 4,200 were 'Chinese.' Almost all the others (over 19,000 people) were identified by a European nationality, but most of them would have said that they were 'whites' (Table 5.1). In the first part of this chapter, we use these categories, on which, as we worked it out, this essay became a reflection, and consider some of the demographic, occupational, and spatial characteristics they represent. We begin with the whites, who largely constructed the social categories and whose influence already dominated the province. Then we look at three regions: the north coast (lower Skeena and Nass), where Native peoples outnumbered whites by 15:1; the southwestern interior, where Natives remained a bare majority; and the south coast (bordering the Strait of Georgia), where most of the population was non-Native, and the urban, agricultural, and industrial development of a new province was already concentrated. In conclusion, we return to questions about the categories we have adopted in this analysis. This leads to a discussion of the nature of social power in a vast, thinly occupied territory that recently had been added to the Dominion of Canada, was beginning to be influenced by industrial capital, and was variously intersected by culture, race, class, and gender.

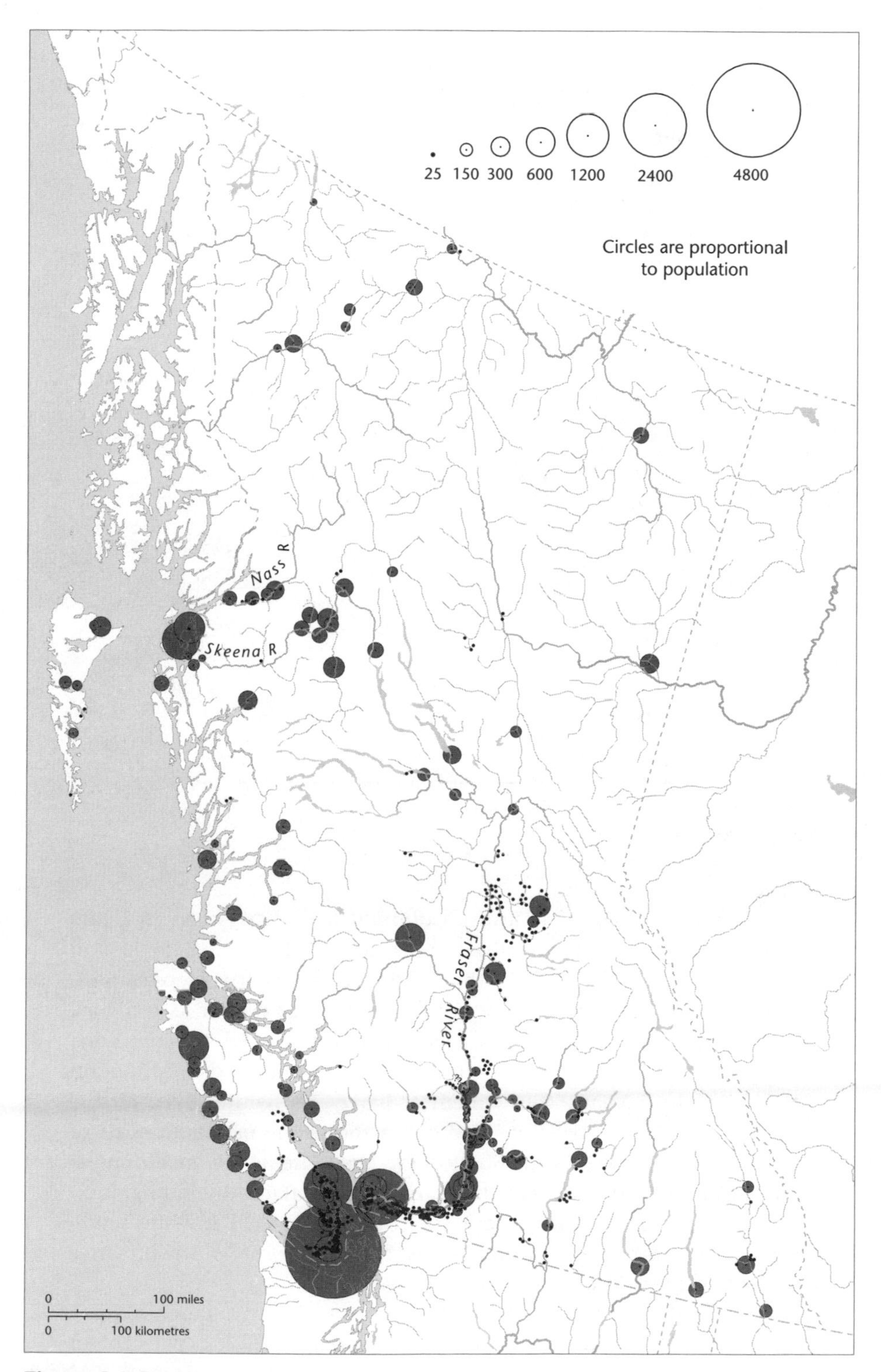

Figure 5.1 Population of British Columbia, 1881

Table 5.1

Population in 1881 (uncorrected nominal returns)	
'Indians'	
Native rolls	26,299
Non-Native rolls	550
Subtotal	26,849
'Chinese'	4,195
'Whites'	
Born in BC	6,954
MB/ON	1,765
PQ	385
Maritimes	777
US	2,367
Eng./Wales	3,147
Scotland	1,337
Ireland	1,248
N.W. Europe	737
Other	352
Subtotal	19,069
'Africans'	274
Total population	50,387

Three Peoples

Whites

The distribution of whites in British Columbia in 1881 is shown in Figure 5.2. Seventy per cent of them lived on or near the Strait of Georgia, and more than a quarter in Victoria, the province's capital and deep-sea port. In the interior, most lived along the Fraser River or one of its principal tributaries. Beyond the Fraser drainage, there were few whites anywhere: some 200 in the Okanagan Valley, fewer than 100 in the Rocky Mountain Trench, 200 in Cassiar, 50 in Omenica. Barely 100 whites lived on the west coast of Vancouver Island and along the whole mainland coast of British Columbia north of the Strait of Georgia. The pre-colonial population geography of the fur trade had largely been effaced by immigration and economic diversification between 1848 and 1881. Yet white settlement had not expanded far from the southwestern corner of the province and the few lines of transportation to mining areas.

Just over a third of the whites had been born in British Columbia. Some 30 per cent were born in Britain (mostly in England), 15.5 per cent in

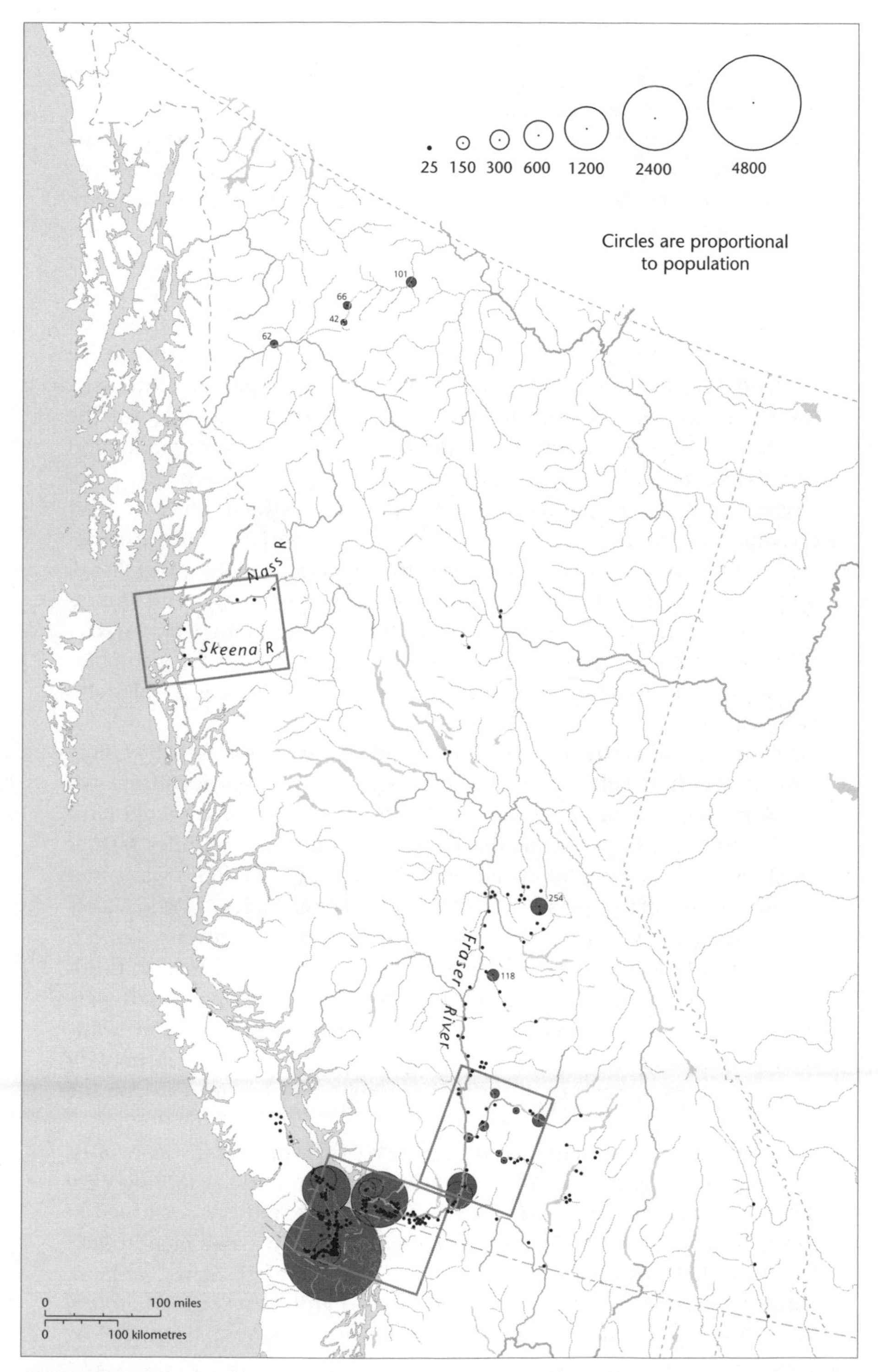

Figure 5.2 White population of British Columbia, 1881

eastern Canada, 12.5 per cent in the United States, and 4 per cent in northwestern Europe. Males outnumbered females by almost 2:1. There were fewer elderly overall (about 3 per cent of whites were 60 or over) than in the societies they had left. The great majority were Protestants: mostly Anglicans, Presbyterians (or Church of Scotland), and Methodists of some stripe, but a few were Baptists, Lutherans, and Congregationalists. Almost 19 per cent of whites were Roman Catholics.

Forty per cent lived in three towns. In Victoria, where there had been a sizeable white population longer than anywhere else in the province, 41 per cent of whites were BC-born, and their sex ratio was fairly balanced at 1.26:1. Most of the non-BC-born had come from Britain, primarily England, and relatively few from eastern Canada. In New Westminster, the percentage of BC-born and the sex ratio both closely reflected the provincial averages; relative to Victoria, New Westminster's population was drawn much more from eastern Canada, and much less from England. In both towns, there was far more occupational diversity than elsewhere in the province, a reflection of their varied administrative, commercial, and industrial functions. In Nanaimo, on the other hand, wage work was dominated by collieries, and there was only a small middle class. White Nanaimo was not far from being gender balanced – 1.29:1 – and primarily comprised working-class English or Scottish families, a product of company-organized emigration[7] of young couples and their families.

In farming areas, where the common unit of production was the family farm, gender imbalances diminished rapidly with the passage of time. On the Saanich Peninsula just north of Victoria, which had attracted farm settlers in the 1850s, and in the Cowichan Valley a few miles farther north, males only marginally outnumbered females. The ratio was about 3:2 in the farming populations of the lower Fraser Valley. In the Nicola and Okanagan valleys in the southern interior, the ratio was over 2:1; there, a third (34.5 per cent) of the wives or partners of white male heads of household were Native women.[8] In all these areas, most men were farmers (or, in the Nicola and Okanagan valleys, ranchers), but a few were farm labourers and others were artisans, shopkeepers, teachers, or clerics. The infrastructure of settled farming communities was coming into existence.

As elsewhere in western North America, the work camps associated with railway construction, placer mining, logging, and sawmilling were different demographic worlds. Most whites in the railway construction camps in the Fraser and Thompson canyons were unmarried men in their twenties or thirties who had been born in the United States, Ireland, Ontario, or continental Europe. There were hardly any English among them. The populations in the gold camps were equally male, but older and from different backgrounds. In the Cassiar, near the British Columbia-Yukon border, there were some two hundred white men and two white women; around Barkerville in the Cariboo, the sex ratio among whites was 6:1. Cassiar miners were mostly Americans or Irish; their median age was over forty. In the longer-established mining areas in the Cariboo, white miners were primarily middle-aged eastern Canadians or Britons. In the logging and sawmill camps around Burrard Inlet, the white workforce was characteristically younger, unmarried, and of exceedingly diverse backgrounds.

Elements of fur trade society persisted here and there. Many men at the Hudson's Bay Company's (HBC) northern posts were offspring of British Columbia- or Manitoba-born French Canadian men and local Native women. Almost all the women at the posts were Natives and Roman Catholics; their children were raised in their mother's religion and enumerated in the non-Native rolls. Many former HBC officers remained prominent; the commissioner of the B.C. census of 1881, Joseph McKay, was a former fur trader, as was at least one of his enumerators.[9]

Chinese

The distribution of Chinese in the 1880s is shown on Figure 5.3. In the placer mining districts of the Cassiar and Cariboo, the Chinese remained after most whites had left, making up the bulk of the population. Most Chinese scattered as miners along the Fraser and Thompson rivers, and the few in south-central and southeastern British Columbia were also placer miners; here as elsewhere, they worked low-paying gravels long after the gold rushes had passed. The large concentrations of Chinese in the lower Fraser Canyon and on the Thompson River were navvies building the Canadian Pacific Railway (CPR). Chinese also worked in salmon canneries at the mouths of the Fraser, Skeena, and Nass rivers, as sawmill hands in Burrard Inlet, as coal miners at Nanaimo, and as market gardeners near Victoria. They constituted some 10 per cent of the populations of Victoria and New Westminster.

Virtually all the Chinese came from Guangdong Province at the mouth of the Pearl River in south China, and were sharply differentiated by clan and/or county affiliations.[10] This, however, cannot be established from the census, which lists most Chinese by their first name and usually gives their origin as 'Chinese.' Neither the enumerators nor most British Columbians sought to explore the category; the census gives us only gender, age, and occupation to go on.

Among Chinese, the male to female ratio in British Columbia was 28:1. Of 283 Chinese in the Cassiar, 4 were female; of 260 Chinese in and near Barkerville, 12 were female.[11] Very few Chinese men were married to, or living with, Native women. The Chinese railway construction camps in

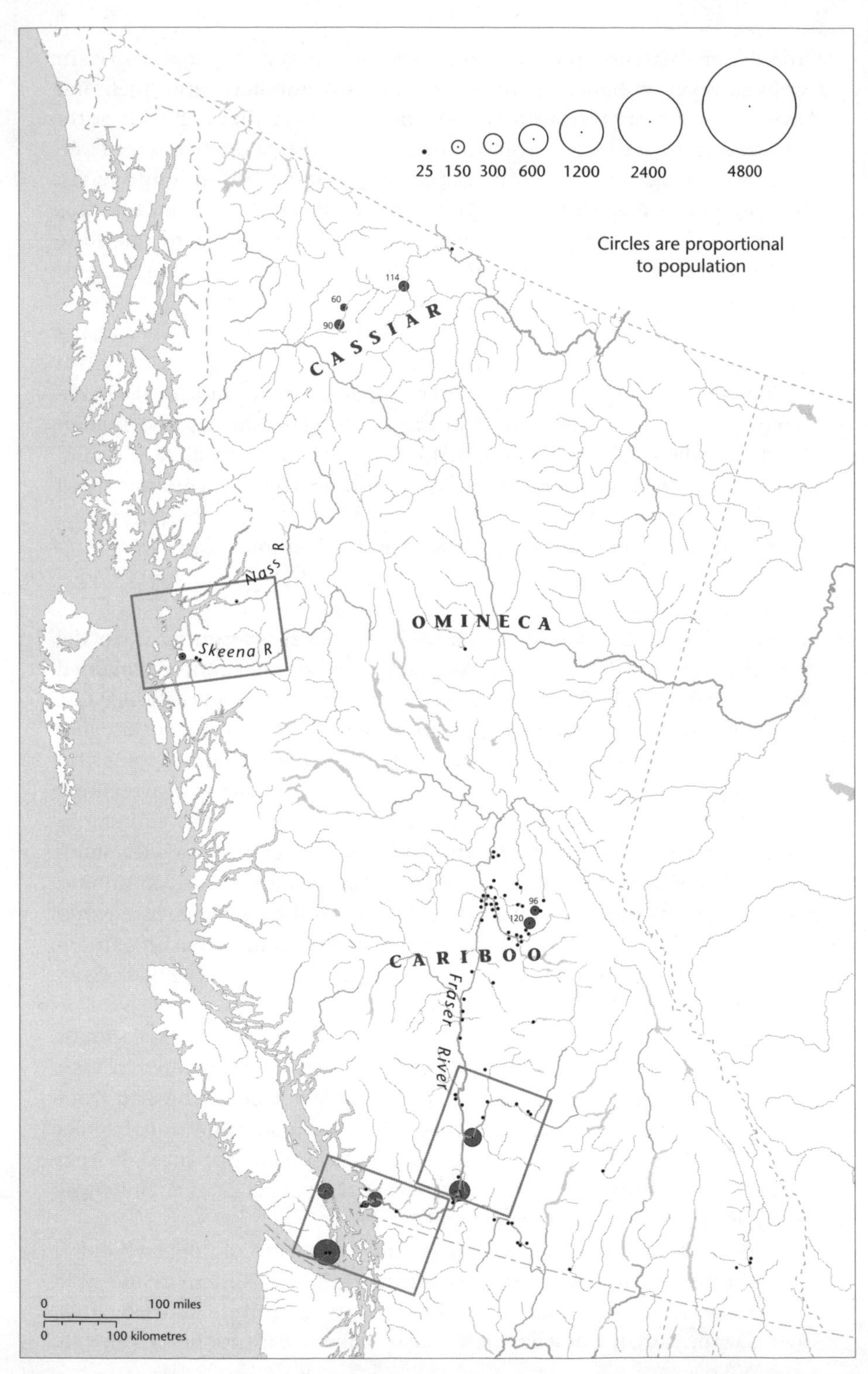

Figure 5.3 Chinese population of British Columbia, 1881

the Fraser and Thompson canyons were concentrations of men. In the colliery town of Nanaimo, there were 278 Chinese men and 3 Chinese women, and there was a similar imbalance at the canneries. Even at the Chinese market gardens near Victoria, there were neither family farms nor women. In New Westminster and Victoria, the demographic imbalance was not quite so severe: in New Westminster, there were 206 Chinese males and 23 females (13 women); in Victoria, 526 males and 66 females (51 women). Shop and restaurant keepers were somewhat more likely to have wives in British Columbia than fishermen, cooks, or labourers. Many Chinese, brought to British Columbia as labourers, were perched at isolated worksites.

Apart from a very few cooks, washermen, and clerks – or, in Barkerville, shopkeepers and gamblers – all Chinese men in the placer camps were listed as miners. The age of Chinese placer miners ranged from lads in their teens to elderly men in their sixties, but the median age was higher (as high as 40) in the older camps, an indication that the workforce was not turning over rapidly. Of the 275 Chinese in Nanaimo, 237 were mine workers, and their median age just under 30. Twenty-four were cooks, many living in white, middle-class households.

Most Chinese in Victoria and New Westminster were listed in service occupations such as cooks and laundrymen, as labourers, or as workers in resource industries. There were also clerks and proprietors of various kinds living in Chinatown, providing services for the Chinese. As in Nanaimo, most cooks lived in white households. The median age of the Chinese in Victoria and New Westminster, as in Nanaimo, was lower than in the mining camps.

Usually the Chinese lived apart from other people. Sometimes Chinese and white placer miners worked in the same operations, but more often they did not. The same was true of railway construction workers; most workplaces were racially segregated. There was more mixing in the sawmill camps in Burrard Inlet, but even there, places of residence tended to segregate along racial lines. Most urban Chinese lived in Chinatowns.[12] There was some overlap, of course, with other peoples. The three sons of Won Lin Ling, a restaurant keeper in New Westminster, were born in British Columbia and raised as Anglicans; at least one son, a bookkeeper, knew English well. A Chinese woman in Victoria lived with several Indian women. There were Chinese cooks, as we have seen, in middle-class urban households. In the Okanagan, a few ranchers also employed Chinese cooks; in the lower Fraser Valley, farmers commonly hired seasonal Chinese workers. Chinese proprietors of shops and restaurants served English-speaking customers; they and a good many other Chinese in British Columbia learned some English. However, most Chinese in British Columbia lived and worked with other Chinese. In

Chinatowns or work camps, they comprised a male society apart. The census records no domestic partnerships of Chinese men and white women, and few with Native women.

Indians

Census takers enumerated or estimated 26,849 Natives in British Columbia in 1881, including 550, most of them women living with non-Native men, in the non-Native returns. As several groups were omitted, primarily north of Quesnel, and others were underestimated, we estimate that some 29,000 Native people lived in the province in 1881 (Table 5.2).

Table 5.2

Native population, 1881

Language group*	Nominal rolls total	%	Revised total (authors)	%
Tsimshian	4,402	16.8	4,427	15.8
Haida	829	3.1	829	2.9
Bella Coola	631	2.6	631	2.4
Northern Wakashan	835	3.3	835	3.1
Kwakwaka'wakw	2,281	8.4	2,281	7.9
Nuu-chah-nulth (page list)	3,610	13.3	3,610	12.5
Coast Salish				
Mainland	3,384	12.5	3,446	11.9
Island	2,198	8.1	2,198	7.6
Interior Salish	5,747	21.2	5,747	19.8
Athapaskan	1,578	5.8	3,346	11.5
Kootenay	804	2.9	804	2.7
Total	26,299		28,154	
Natives on non-Native rolls	550	2.0	550	14.9
Total	26,849		28,704	

*Data aggregated by language groups to facilitate comparison with other estimates.

A third of these people lived in a narrow band extending from southeastern Vancouver Island through the Lower Mainland and up the Fraser River to Lillooet (Figure 5.4). Another 20 per cent lived on the west coast of Vancouver Island (Nuu-chah-nulth) or on the north coast of Vancouver Island and the adjacent mainland (Kwakwaka'wakw). About

10 per cent lived on the north coast in the vicinity of the lower Skeena and Nass rivers (Coast Tsimshian and Nisga'a); and about 10 per cent elsewhere on the coast. Excluding the ribbon of people along the Fraser south of Lillooet, barely a quarter of the Native population lived in the province's vast interior. In the northern interior, where the biological carrying capacity was low and salmon runs were absent or unreliable, the population density was less than one person per 150 square kilometres.

In general, this distribution reflected the persistence of pre-contact settlement patterns that, in turn, reflected the regional availability of food. In detail, however, a century of contact had brought about significant changes. As Native numbers fell from the impact of diseases – compounded by alcohol and, probably, by heightened intra-Native warfare associated with new wealth and firearms – some groups disappeared and others merged in an effort to maintain a measure of cultural and demographic viability.[13] For example, a HBC census compiled around 1840 lists 6,607 Haida in thirteen tribes;[14] in 1881, there were 829 Haida in eight tribes. In southeastern British Columbia, where the smallpox epidemic of 1862-3 was particularly devastating, large areas were almost completely depopulated.[15] While the overall Native population declined, the developing white economy drew Natives to new economic opportunities: to fur trade posts where they might control, and profit from, the flow of furs; to Victoria, where a variety of commercial opportunities attracted a transient Native population drawn from most coastal peoples; to seasonal work in the salmon canneries; or to more year-round work in the sawmills and logging camps around Burrard Inlet where, in 1881, there was a much larger resident Native population than before the sawmills arrived. Missionaries of all denominations sought to counteract such attractions, sometimes by sequestering Native converts in model Christian villages where they would be isolated from nefarious white influences.[16]

Native age/sex data in the 1881 census are fragmentary and difficult to interpret. In the province, as a whole, the Native population was evenly balanced (50.4 per cent males, 49.6 per cent females), though, as some 400 Native women lived with non-Native men, there were fewer women of reproductive age in Native society than these percentages suggest. The population pyramids for the Nisga'a, Kwakwa̱ka̱'wakw, and Shuswap (Figure 5.5) indicate that different Native groups had different demographic histories, though the effects of the smallpox epidemic of 1862-3 seem to have been pervasive. Among the Kwakwa̱ka̱'wakw, the decade and a half following the construction of Fort Rupert in 1849 stands out as a period of dramatic population decline associated, probably, with a series of wars and the effects of the ready availability of alcohol, as well as the smallpox epidemic.[17]

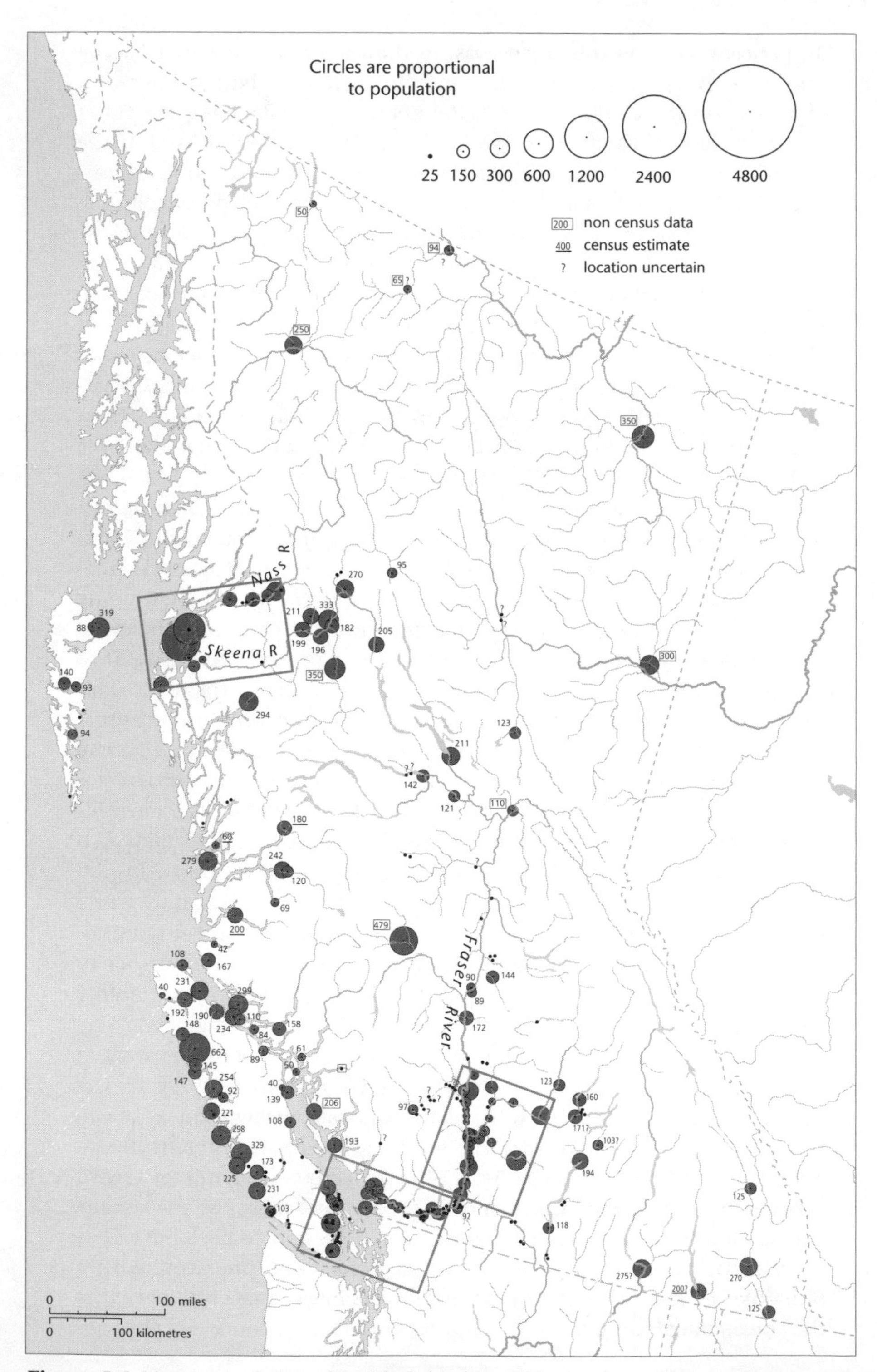

Figure 5.4 Native population of British Columbia, 1881

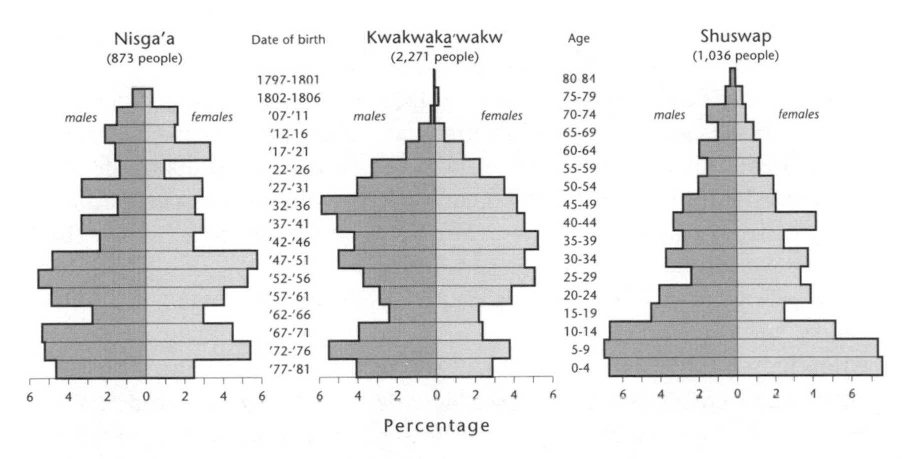

Figure 5.5 Native population pyramids

By 1881, nearly two-thirds of the Native population was at least nominally Christian. Almost all Native Christians in the interior, apart from an Anglican population around Lytton, were Roman Catholics. Anglicans and Methodists dominated the north coast and had footholds on the central coast. On the south coast, the large majority of Natives were Catholics, but there were Protestant enclaves in Burrard Inlet, Nanaimo, Chilliwack, and Yale. Native religions, like Native seasonal rounds, survived best where whites were fewest and Native populations most isolated. Where non-Native settlement was significant, Natives' access to their traditional resources was restricted, and they often had little choice but to take up new occupations, while pursuing more elements of former economies than the census indicates.

Three Regions

Whites, Chinese, and Natives met in British Columbia. However immiscible most contemporaries thought them to be, British Columbia society comprised them all. Still, patterns of coexistence and interaction differed greatly from place to place.

The Lower Skeena and Nass

In this area, the census recorded 2,893 Natives, 92 whites, and 101 Chinese, distributed as shown in Figure 5.6. The whites came predominantly from Britain and eastern Canada; all but 16 were male. Hardly any were agricultural settlers. They had come, rather, to work in the fur trade (Port Simpson), salmon canning (Aberdeen, Inverness, Croasdaile's), missions (Metlakatla, Port Simpson, Greenville, Kincolith), a sawmill (Georgetown), or the Skeena River trade (Port Essington). With them came elaborate external connections: cannery owners and fur traders were connected through

Victoria to Britain and the world economy; missionaries shared the rhetoric and international evangelical strategies of their missionary societies.[18] Most whites were British subjects backed by Dominion and provincial governments, and, if need be, by British imperial power. At the same time, the whites were heavily engaged with, and in a sense dependent upon, the surrounding Tsimshian and Nisga'a peoples. The Chinese, all male cannery workers, lived seasonally at the canneries before returning south to the Chinatowns of Victoria or New Westminster.

The Native population had apparently declined by half since the HBC census of 1842, and its distribution had been greatly influenced by the white presence. Port Simpson, Port Essington, Metlakatla, Kincolith, and Greenville were all post-contact settlements.[19] Each represented a Native response to one or more components of the contact process: the fur trade, missionary activity, and salmon canning. Many Natives had adjusted their seasonal round to take advantage of employment or trading opportunities in Victoria or in American settlements on Puget Sound, to fish commercially for a cannery, or, in the case of women, to work on a cannery line.[20]

Missionaries, promoters of a sedentary ideal, sought to discourage these movements, but with limited success. Traditional seasonal patterns of resource procurement persisted. Even at Metlakatla, where William Duncan, the Anglican missionary, had championed a variety of European trades and was planning a salmon cannery, the occupation of most

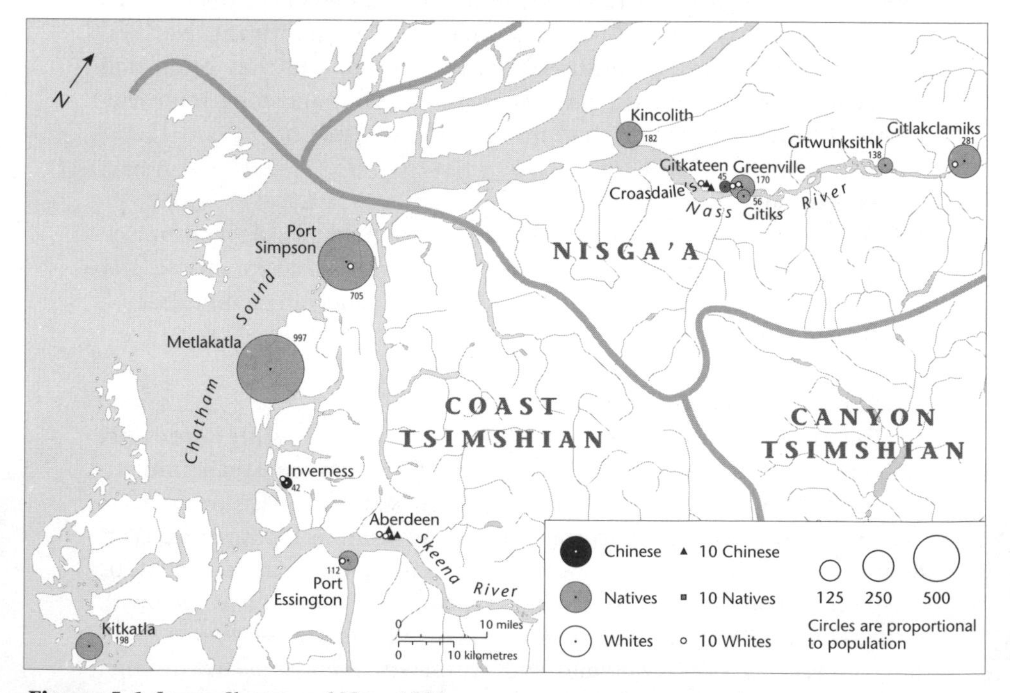

Figure 5.6 Lower Skeena and Nass, 1881

Native men, according to the census, was 'hunter' or 'fisherman.'[21] Although most Tsimshian and Nisga'a were now ostensibly Anglicans or Methodists, and some of their children attended denominational schools, Native names and languages persisted. Nor, yet, were there reserves or Indian agents; in their absence, the Native system of regulating access to land and resources largely continued to operate. Where white claims of property interfered with this system, Native opposition arose.[22]

The Southwestern Plateau

In the area shown in Figure 5.6, there were, in 1881, approximately 3,500 Natives, 2,000 whites, and 1,000 Chinese. There had been resident fur traders in this area for almost seventy years (at Kamloops), a major gold rush in 1858, the beginnings of commercial ranching shortly thereafter, and the construction of parts of two major transportation systems: a wagon road built through the Fraser and Thompson canyons in 1862, and the Canadian Pacific Railway, under construction during the summer of 1881. These intrusions had been superimposed on what, at contact, had been some of the densest fishing, hunting, and gathering populations in the world.[23]

Natives lived approximately where they had fifty years earlier, though many settlements were abandoned and most others were much reduced in size. In one short stretch of the Fraser River between Boston Bar and Spuzzum (Figure 5.7), for which there was a census in 1830, the depopulation ratio over fifty years was, apparently, almost 6:1. As this area bore the brunt of the first gold rush, and as some of its people resettled in the Nicola Valley, the population loss may have been exceptional.[24] However, Natives were still the regional majority in 1881. All, according to the census, were Anglicans or Roman Catholics. Most lived in small log houses; a few still wintered in traditional pit houses. J.B. Good, the Anglican missionary at Lytton who enumerated most of the Natives, listed the men in the canyon as 'farmers,' 'labourers,' or 'packers,' while noting that 'Indians engage in all kinds of occupations'.[25] Although most lived on reserves, they still relied on fishing, hunting, and gathering supplemented at most villages by garden patches (without water rights)[26] and a few chickens, cattle, and horses.

Occupationally flexible and geographically mobile, Natives provided intermittent or seasonal labour for the white economy as packers, railway construction workers, farm labourers, commercial fishermen, and cannery workers. Some Native women lived with white ranchers, a very few with miners; such liaisons were usually arranged when the woman was in her early teens, and brought together in single households not only vastly different cultures and individuals who initially could hardly converse, but also, potentially, the combined authorities of age, patriarchy, and race.[27]

The majority of the Chinese shown in Figure 5.7 were railway construction workers, most recently hired in San Francisco or Hong Kong.[28] They spoke little or no English, lived in construction camps with other Cantonese-speaking workers, and ate food prepared by Cantonese cooks. Here and there along the Fraser and Thompson rivers were Chinese miners or farmers, not all of whom were Cantonese, who had been in British Columbia for years, and who had usually pre-empted or purchased land and secured water and mineral rights. Most spoke a little English and Chinook; a very few of these more established Chinese lived with Native women.[29] In Yale there were several Chinese shop or boardinghouse keepers, an interpreter, bookkeepers, and a few tradesmen.

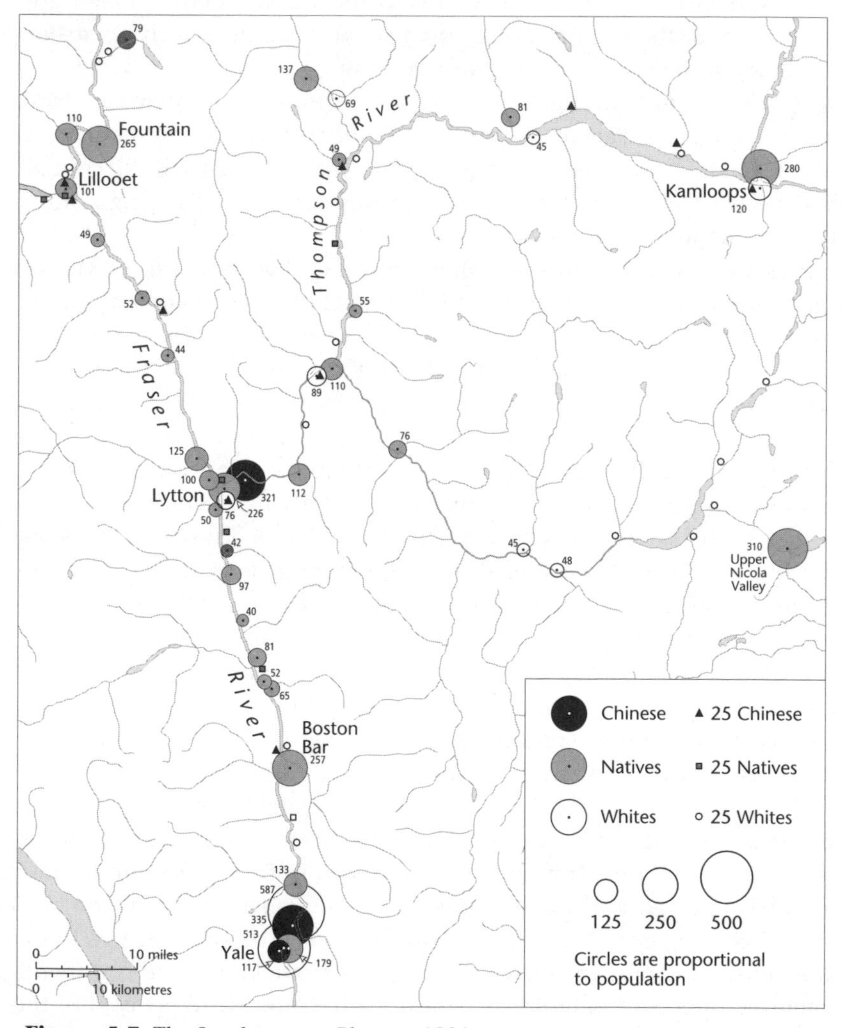

Figure 5.7 The Southwestern Plateau, 1881

Most whites in the area had also been drawn by the railway: many as construction workers living in Yale or in camps nearby, others as proprietors of small businesses in Yale or Kamloops, or as tradesmen or artisans there; a few as the salaried engineers, surveyors, managers, and foremen employed by the CPR. Some men had brought families with them. There was also an older white population – a few miners, more farmers or ranchers, some shopkeepers or tradesmen – who lived either at mining sites along the rivers or on patches of farm- or ranchland. They had preempted much of the choice land before reserves were set aside for Natives, and also controlled most accessible irrigation water. Although few, they were influential – settlers with the ear of government. In the Nicola Valley, where there was no placer mining and only two Chinese, white and Native ranchers competed for range land.[30] Many white men in the Nicola Valley lived with Native women.[31]

In 1881, the southwestern plateau contained a mix of peoples, many from afar; a regime of property that opened up the land for settlement and defined Native lands as small reserves; and a railway under construction (steam technology and the transcontinental state). Natives still frequented many traditional resource procurement sites, but, as the intrusions into their world were backed by laws, courts, constables, and jails – ultimately, by sovereign power – such movements were increasingly curtailed.

Strait of Georgia

In 1881, the Strait of Georgia region contained about 40 per cent of the provincial population, a little over 20,000 people, two-thirds of whom lived on Vancouver Island (Figure 5.8). Three-quarters of the regional population were non-Native, of which 10 per cent were Chinese. This distribution reflected aboriginal patterns of settlement, now much disturbed; the early colonization of Vancouver Island, guided by the HBC; and the rapid demographic and economic developments initiated by the gold rushes. The region included the three towns in British Columbia in 1881, most of the province's cultivated land, and most of its industrial work camps, with the exception of placer operations.

An urban system, linked by scheduled steamship runs carrying information, passengers, and freight, had come into being. It focused on Victoria (seat of government, maritime port of entry, and centre of a variety of manufactures), and included New Westminster (river-mouth port, local market centre, and cannery town) and the colliery town of Nanaimo. With some 6,000 people in Victoria, 2,000 in New Westminster, and 1,700 in Nanaimo, these three towns contained 18 per cent of the population of British Columbia, and almost 40 per cent of the non-Natives.

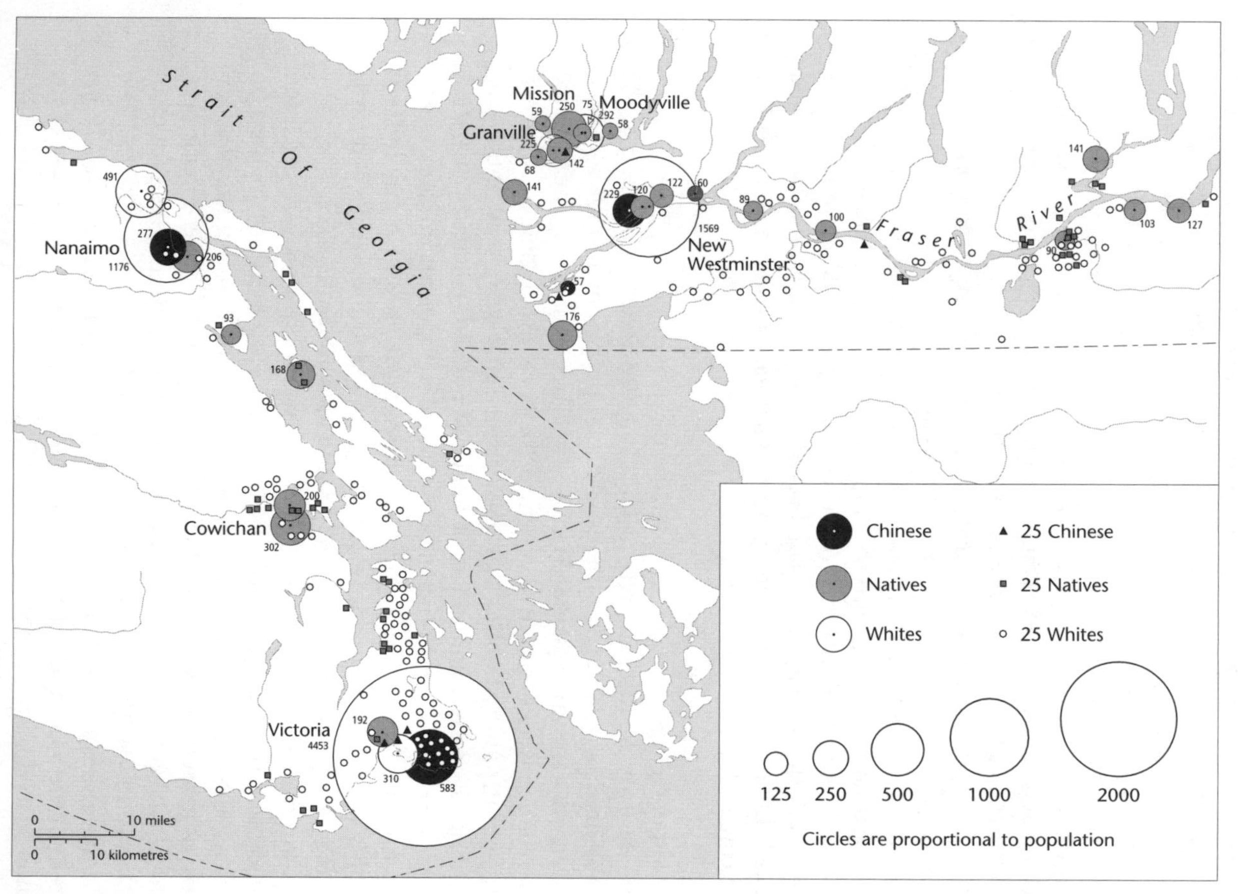

Figure 5.8 The Georgia Strait region, 1881

Like other towns in early Canada, they were complex social and cultural transplantations in which whites could find many landmarks of a familiar world. In appearance and socio-economic organization, they were very recognizable late-nineteenth-century products of the North Atlantic world. Victoria was the most English, containing the largest middle class of the three; Nanaimo was a Protestant, non-conformist colliery town of British background, while the population of New Westminster was somewhat more eastern Canadian and American. Resemblances, however, were only approximate. Low land costs created lower population densities than in British cities. Immigration juxtaposed whites of very different regional and national backgrounds and, on the Pacific, raised the issue of race. Chinatown was part of urban life, and there were Chinese cooks and servants in prosperous white households. An abstract image of the 'Oriental' gave way to the familiar sight of pigtailed Chinese men, and to lurid white visions of filth, opium dens, and prostitution in Chinatowns.[32] There were also Natives. In Nanaimo, most Natives lived on a reserve just south of town; in New Westminster, they lived in shacks along the river close to the canneries, near, but separate from, the Chinese; in Victoria, they lived at the edge of the central business district, often close to Chinatown. All these Natives participated, more or less, in the white economy as cannery workers, general labourers, dock workers, deckhands, prostitutes, many having travelled hundreds of kilometres to find seasonal work. Victoria drew Natives from all the main coastal peoples; Southern Thompson people from the Fraser Canyon worked in the canneries at New Westminster.[33] In white eyes, neither the Chinese nor the Natives were part of society. But they were there, parts of the population of each town.

The patches of agricultural settlement around the Strait of Georgia were essentially white. Farm families depended on mixed farming and the emerging infrastructure of settled rural communities. As much as anything, religion and place of origin, coupled with isolation, differentiated these communities from each other; different migration chains had fetched up in different patches of land. For example, Chilliwack, near the head of the lower Fraser Valley, was settled primarily by Ontario Methodists; Langley, downriver, was more Presbyterian; Ladner, at the river mouth, was largely Anglican; the Cowichan Valley was English and Anglican.[34] Except, perhaps, near Victoria, the costs of clearing, dyking, and draining land were high, and markets for agricultural products were weak. In these circumstances, pioneer farms might yield a living, but hardly wealth. When they could be afforded and were available, Chinese or Native labourers did some of the heaviest development work (clearing or ditching), and such labour might be employed briefly at harvest time. But, excepting the Chinese market gardens near Victoria, Chinese did not live in these countrysides; they came from the towns as their labour was required. Natives, who did live there, were on small reserves, usually associated with traditional village sites, and created when an alien regime of property opened most land to white settlers. They farmed, though not as assiduously as the Indian agents and missionaries wished. This was partly because reserves were small and often ill-suited to agriculture, partly because traditional subsistent economies still generated a lot of food, and partly because more cash could be earned by wage labour. Essentially, Natives were being marginalized in the process of creating white countrysides.[35]

The resource camps were polyglot and multiracial. Inside work in the canneries was performed by Chinese men, Native women, and a few white boys, all, usually, under the eyes of white foremen. Fishing was done in small boats by Native men. Although different races came together in the canneries, they lived apart: the Chinese in bunkhouses, the Natives in shacks they had built, the whites in houses or small bunkhouses – all distinct social spaces.[36] The same was broadly true of the logging and sawmill camps around Burrard Inlet. Chinese millhands, for example, lived east of the mill at Granville (soon to become Vancouver), whites west, and the Natives, some of them, on reserves.[37] In Nanaimo, too, where whites, Chinese, and Natives worked in the mines (though rarely together at the coal face), they lived apart.

Wage labour impinged in various ways on traditional Native rounds. The Squamish had moved from the head of Howe Sound to live on Burrard Inlet where, though they still hunted and fished, they had become accustomed to wage work.[38] The commercial salmon fishery, which was seasonal, fitted less disruptively into traditional Native strategies of resource procurement. Sockeye, the principal commercial species, was taken in early summer, overlapping little with runs of the varieties the Native fisheries favoured. Few Natives appear to have held steady jobs, month after month, in the same place. The Cowichan, who lived amid the considerable white settlement on southeastern Vancouver Island, worked for wages in coal mines, sawmills, logging camps, and fish canneries, and on white farms, while cultivating fields of their own. The local Indian agent estimated that in 1881 their earnings at the Fraser River canneries would exceed '$15,000 in wages.'[39] White settlement and such employment restricted but did not eliminate traditional hunting and fishing, though these activities were are not recorded in the census. The Cowichan had always gone to the Fraser to fish; in 1881, they also went there to work for the canneries.

More generally, however, the human geography of the Strait of Georgia region had been remade in approximately European terms. It had become a place of towns, 'pioneer' countrysides, and industrial work camps, all broadly controlled by the infrastructure of the state and the cultural assumptions of its English-speaking inhabitants.

The Nature of Social Power

The census of 1881 petered out in the north, and so did the hold of the state. With few settlements and almost no roads in a huge, mountainous area, the logistics of regulation were overwhelming, even though regulation did fan outward from the province's southwestern corner, and a rudimentary core-periphery spatial economy was being constructed on top of pre-existing Native economies. For the most part, life was local, or was connected to distant societies. At anything like the scale of the province, British Columbians could not begin to know each other or the vast territory in which they lived. The province had not yet become a single society in the sense that it was uniformly regulated within its political borders.[40]

The census's attempt to describe the provincial population, the work of a white, middle-, or upper-middle-class minority, probably reflected the values of most white settlers fairly well. Its categories, broadly, were theirs. The census did not use the category 'whites,' though it is implicit in the enumeration of Natives and non-Natives in separate rolls, because the people who would have been so identified wanted more finely drawn information about themselves. But they used 'white' colloquially to distinguish themselves from those they identified as Indians or Chinese. Following the census and this usage we, too, have employed these socially constructed categories. What, now, have we to say about them?

We can say that in the British Columbia of 1881, these categories provide shorthand representations of deep-seated social differences. People identified as 'whites,' 'Chinese,' or 'Indians' lived in different places within quite different demographic, occupational, and cultural arrangements. In this sense, the categories reflect social realities. A more difficult question is whether they emerged as after the fact descriptions, or whether, in effect, they constituted the society they described. Our tentative answer is that they did both. Pejorative white identifications of Chinese and Indians certainly underlay Chinatowns and reserves.[41] Backed by legislative and coercive power, white prejudices pushed people into defined spaces, whether or not they wanted to be there. Had Natives been treated as people, rather than as Indians, there would not have been reserves. But although the categories themselves were active participants in the province's social organization, it is also clear that people of very different backgrounds and lifeworlds had converged in British Columbia. To a considerable extent, the categories reflected the crude attempts of people who fundamentally did not know or begin to understand each other to identify very different, very unfamiliar cultural groups. Simple categories labelled the 'otherness' that permeated British Columbia in 1881, and also tended to impose closures, sealing off people, already different enough, from each other.

Closure became a strategy of racism. Whites brought the category and pejorative connotations of 'Oriental,' and intensified and sharpened them in British Columbia where the 'Orient' was only one ocean away, and the cultural security of an immigrant, British society was not established. The real or imagined characteristics of Chinese workers and settlements became a handy, disparaging yardstick of difference. In the sympathetic white view, Natives were children capable of instruction, but hardly white children. At the same time, many Natives judged the Chinese harshly (a judgment the Chinese probably reciprocated and extended to whites),[42] and the Native response to whites ranged from admiration to hatred.[43] The essential difference, of course, between white and non-white racism was that the former was backed by the power of government and capital.

In our view, then, there were deep social and cultural cleavages in British Columbia in 1881 that corresponded, broadly, to the boundaries between 'white,' 'Chinese,' and 'Indian.' These categories provided simple racial ways of identifying the extraordinary, late-nineteenth-century convergence in a vast, little-populated territory of three broadly different historical experiences: one indigenous, one European, one Asian. In a sense, all British Columbians in 1881 had been detached from their pasts; their futures, therefore, were insecure. There was also a huge resource base that was suddenly accessible to the international economy. In the ensuing scramble for position, white legislative and coercive power, coupled with a simple categorization of people, eliminated much of the competition.

For the most part, questions of class, ethnicity, and gender in British Columbia need to be approached within these even broader cultural/racial divides. Speaking different languages, living within different lifeworlds, objects of different racial discourses, and usually living apart, Native, Chinese, and white workers could not quickly identify common class interests. Even white workers, employed in very different, geographically scattered activities, could not think provincially in class terms. More locally they could, as in the colliery town of Nanaimo, where, by 1881, there had already been several strikes.[44] But, even in Nanaimo, different languages and lifeways narrowed and muted working-class identity. In the British Columbia of 1881, class identity was most developed among the elite: the small group of white, Protestant men, most of whom knew each other, who dominated the government, the courts, the churches, and the commercial economy. Having access to the levers of power in a newly organized political space; living atop the pyramid of race, class, and gender; and facing, in a sense, a scattered, disaggregated opposition, the elite found British Columbia exceedingly agreeable.[45]

Local cultural identities also appear to have blurred across cultural/racial categories. Within cultural groups, local identities remained; therefore, a census prepared by whites explored the background of white society, and provided much less information about others. In the census, the Chinese were simply Chinese. In some white agricultural settlements, the great majority of settlers shared common ethnic and religious backgrounds. However, the nominal census also reveals many cross-ethnic marriages; often migration had mixed up people of different ethnic backgrounds, scattering them through different settlements. As elsewhere, many details of former lives and social structures were lost.[46] As elsewhere, juxtapositions of different ethnic backgrounds probably tended to diminish real differences in lifeways, increasing the symbolic content of ethnicity – to the point that, in proportion to their sense of racial threat, whites identified themselves racially.

The census sheds little light on how the preponderance of men in immigrant populations and the shortage of external employment for women affected the social construction of gender. Clearly, gender was constructed differently in different settings. The isolated, largely male work camps of British Columbia intensified the growing, gendered dichotomy between home and work in industrializing societies, and probably encouraged images of tough, competitive men and of pious, pure, and domestic women.[47] For the men who worked in them, rough workplaces in wilderness corners of British Columbia evoked images, associated with women, of home and civility elsewhere.[48] White women, a demographic minority within a commercial economy oriented overwhelmingly to men, almost always lived in towns or on farms. White gender relations in the older rural areas and in the middle-class parts of town probably largely reproduced those in the societies from which people came. Working-class white women, for whom there was virtually no wage work, may have been more confined to the house than their counterparts in industrial societies elsewhere.[49] On pioneer farms, women worked in the fields; the subsistent nature of these operations probably retarded the gendered separation of work associated with competitive market economies.[50] Native women faced a variety of new opportunities, ranging from cannery work to lives with non-Native men, the implications of which cannot be judged from the census.

More generally, as this chapter has sought to show, early British Columbian society cannot be understood apart from the different human geographies in which people lived. Resource camps, farms, and towns were very different settlements. Within each, different peoples worked out different daily and seasonal paths, and lived in different social spaces.[51] Even in Victoria, the oldest, largest, and most English town in the province, there was a well-developed Chinatown. Nearby, most (if not all) the Native languages of coastal British Columbia could be heard. In some ways, Victoria was a transplanted English town; in other ways, it was not. The different social geographies in Victoria or, for that matter, the collection of buildings and social spaces at a salmon cannery – that is, the settings in which people were working out their changing lives – reflected and constituted assumptions about race, class and gender.

However different these lives, they were not unrelated. Natives had been reduced to the status of legal minors by the Indian Act; most were at least nominally Christians; and almost all experienced the authorities of a priest, an Indian agent, or a white employer. The Chinese who worked in the canneries, collieries, and railways were an imported, male labour force, a needed but unwelcome appendage to the larger society. The whites responded to the different peoples around, not only by employing them, but also by reconceptualizing themselves: fixing on their whiteness, intensifying their racism, abstracting their ethnicity. In this sense, there was a larger British Columbian society, even in 1881.

Considered as a whole, this society bore little resemblance to any in Britain or eastern North America.[52] The distinctive preconditions of its formation seem fairly clear: a numerous Native population, but not so numerous or so powerful that it could not be quickly marginalized; a great deal of land with vastly different, widely scattered resources and limited agricultural potential; the late-nineteenth-century immigration of predominantly English-speaking settlers and of workers from Asia; some industrial capital; and the disciplinary strategies, controlled by whites, of the modern state. The closest equivalents of these conditions were probably found in the American west coast, New Zealand, and Australia, other segments of the Pacific Rim where gold rushes had provided the impetus for immigrant settlement. But even these comparisons are very approximate. British Columbian society has to be taken on its own terms, and in that endeavour, the nominal census of 1881, the first tolerably comprehensive social survey we have, is an obvious starting point.

6
The Struggle with Distance

The world economy began to emerge in the sixteenth century, slowly expanded into the corners of the world that were least accessible to Europe, and, more than 200 years after the first Spanish galleons crossed the Pacific from Acapulco to trade Mexican silver for Chinese spices and silks, reached the Northwest Coast of North America. After the Spanish and British encounters in the 1770s, and the beginning of the trade in sea otter pelts in the 1780s, the process of incorporating this coast and the cordilleran massif beyond it into the world economy accelerated slowly, then with a rush after 1850. The costs and delays of transportation and communication decreased, items other than sea otter pelts became 'resources,' and more corners of land became accessible. In the process, distances shrank; the territory that became British Columbia was repositioned and restructured.

From their earliest encounters, Europeans had begun to remake this territory in their own terms: mapping it, renaming it, claiming possession of it, bringing it within reach of the European imagination. They created a cartographic and conceptual outline of what, for them, was a new land, placing its coast and principal rivers on their maps, identifying the land as wilderness and its peoples as savages. These abstractions were agents of European colonialism, as many general analyses of what has come to be called 'colonial discourse' have convincingly shown.[1] Complementing them were changes in transportation and communication that, in effect, actualized the immigrant presence on the ground. As the high costs and inconveniences of distance were reduced, more elements of the outside world could enter this distant place, reaching more corners of previously inaccessible land. With enormous cost and effort, distances were diminished, and thresholds of exclusion reduced. The conquest of distance, partial as it was, was at once a central motor of colonization, enabling an immigrant society to impose its ways; and of modernization, facilitating the spatial economies, disciplinary tactics, and many of the assumptions of advanced industrial societies.

In the years from early contact to about 1850, external connections were dominated by pre-industrial technologies: sailing ships at sea, canoes and pack horses inland. Over the next forty years, modern distance-diminishing technologies – particularly steamers, telegraphs, and railways – ushered in a period of sharp time-space compression. Whereas return letters between Victoria and London could easily take a year and a half before 1850, in 1890 they took about a month, and telegraph messages a few days. As much as in any area of recent European expansion, the principal towns of British Columbia had become integrated components of the larger, modernizing world. It was another matter, however, to extend this degree of connectivity across the length and breadth of British Columbia. Rather, a few corridors of modern transportation and communication were constructed, and from them a host of more local strategies, many improvised on the spot, reached into some of the spaces between. All these developments opened up new economic opportunities, and imposed new powers on peoples and land. None, as Harold Innis understood years ago,[2] was politically or culturally innocent. A territory and its peoples were being reconfigured within a set of assumptions and practices that immigrants brought to British Columbia, and that conformed to their sense of its future.

External Distance

For people of European background, the Northwest Coast of North America at the end of the eighteenth century was as inaccessible as any mid-latitude coast on earth. Juan Perez, sailing north from Spanish Mexico in a small ship in 1774, took several months to reach the Queen Charlotte Islands. A year later, Bodega y Quadra needed four months to reach a landfall just south of Cape Flattery at the entrance to the Strait of Juan de Fuca. For travellers from Europe and eastern North America, this isolation was compounded. The English trader James Colnett reached Nootka in early July 1887 after a voyage from England of almost eight months; news that the Spanish had arrested him there, in early July 1889, reached London via Mexico City and Madrid in late January 1790 (Figure 6.1). Captain Vancouver, sailing around the Cape of Good Hope and then eastward to Australia and Tahiti, was off Cape Flattery thirteen months after leaving England. John Jacob Astor's ship *Tonquin,* outbound from New York on September 6, 1810, was at the mouth of the Columbia in late March. For maritime fur traders sailing from Boston or Salem or, by the 1820's Hudson's Bay Company (HBC) ships sailing from London, a voyage in much under 200 days was considered fast. Even in 1860, J.D. Pemberton, surveyor general of Vancouver Island and British Columbia, estimated that the 17,000-mile trip from London - 'the longest that can be taken from England to any known port rounding either cape' – took almost five months.[3]

The transcontinental connection was no easier. After the merger of the HBC and the North West Company in 1821, the land-based fur trade was connected by canoe, pack horse, and open riverboat to York Factory on Hudson Bay. Express brigades carried letters and accounts from the lower Columbia via Athabasca Pass to York Factory in three months, and from the upper Fraser country (New Caledonia) via the Peace River in two. In early July, when the ice was off the bay, they met the supply ship from London; by mid-July the brigades were on their way back. In this way, despatches written in London in March or April reached the lower Columbia at the end of October (Figure 6.1). Replies would leave the lower Columbia, headed east, late the following March.

Such connections sufficed, however, to bring the Northwest Coast and adjacent Cordillera within range of the three most mobile components of European life: its imagination, its commercial capital, and, from time to time along the coast, its warships. Accounts of this distant place, beginning with Cook's at Nootka Sound, were published in Europe.

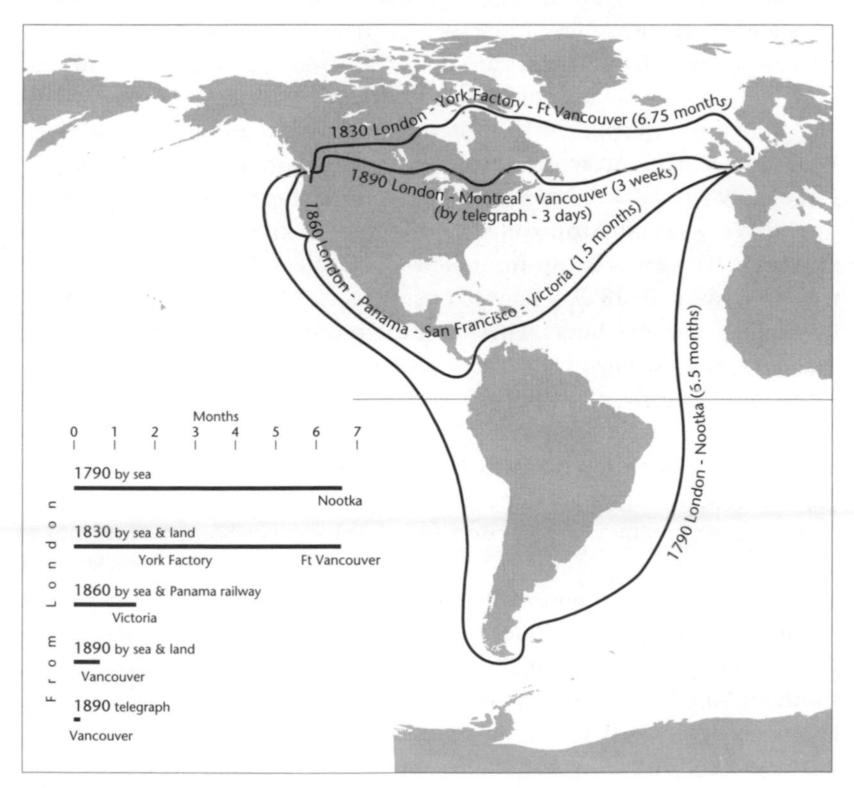

Figure 6.1 London to Northwest Coast, 1789-1890

Much territory was 'explored,' mapped, and renamed. The northwestern corner of North America was no longer a blank in the European global imagination. Information about it entered the European consciousness, strengthening Europeans' sense of their own superiority as it defined the 'otherness' of the rest of the world, and in this way bore, indirectly, on the values that colonial administrators and settlers would later bring to British Columbia. Commercial capital sought valuable, light-weight goods, at first finding only furs, but by the 1840s along the coast, where transportation costs were lowest, testing other exports: salted and barrelled salmon, lumber, flour, even cranberries and isinglass.[4] Detached from most other institutions of European society, companies operated largely on their own in the Cordillera (see Chapter 2). Settlers and the state's administrative apparatus lagged behind, fended off by distance. A European military presence – the Spanish garrison at Nootka, Vancouver's voyages, the Royal Navy sloop *Racoon* at Fort Astoria in 1813, and so on – touched the coast, but not the interior.[5]

Then, just before mid-century, the California gold rush provided the impetus for a series of drastic time-space compressions that allowed the outside world to engage British Columbia much more comprehensively. In the early 1850s, American clipper ships with improved navigation to take advantage of winds and currents[6] cut average sailing time from New York to San Francisco to about 130 days, the fastest sailings to ninety days. The American government instituted regular postal service between New York and San Francisco in 1849; express steamers took the mail to Panama, where relays of horses took it across the isthmus – 'the Golgotha of the West,' Pemberton called it – to meet express steamers for San Francisco. The express trip from New York to San Francisco took about thirty-five days. In 1855, a railway opened across the isthmus, making the fifty-mile trip in five hours. Thereafter the more valuable freight as well as mail and gold travelled via Panama rather than around the Horn; charges for maritime freight between New York and San Francisco fell from $60 a ton in 1850 to $7.50 in 1858.[7] An American mail steamer linked San Francisco to Portland, and from there, by the mid-1850s, a stage ran to Puget Sound and then aboard a HBC ship to Victoria. By 1858, American mail steamers from San Francisco sailed into Puget Sound, stopping at Victoria.[8] In 1860, Pemberton calculated it this way: London to New York to Aspinwall (eastern end of Panama railway), sixteen to twenty days; Panama to San Francisco, about fourteen days; San Francisco to Vancouver Island, four to five days; total travelling time from London, England, to southern Vancouver Island, allowing for slight delays at New York and San Francisco, about forty-five days (Figure 6.1). The trip could be made even more quickly by taking the train from New York to St. Louis, and the express stage (twenty-two days) from there to San Francisco.[9]

A transcontinental telegraph reached San Francisco in 1861, and four years later was connected through the principal towns of Oregon and Washington to New Westminster, the fledgling port at the mouth of the Fraser River. A local newspaper editor thought it 'a wondrous fact' that 'an infant city established only six years before ... was to be linked with the electric systems of Asia, Europe, and North Africa.'[10] These links had not yet been made, but the anticipated power of the telegraph had already provoked competing schemes to lay a trans-Atlantic cable, and to build northward from San Francisco to Bering Strait and across Siberia to Europe. An American senator, urging his government to support the latter, sensed new geopolitical opportunities: 'We hold the ball of the earth in our hands and wind upon it a network of living and thinking wire, till the whole is held together and bound with the same wishes, projects, and interests.' The telegraph would enable the United States 'to suppress rebellion at home' (the Civil War was in progress) and 'extend her great commercial and scientific power over the earth.'[11] Controlled by the Western Union Company, the overland telegraph was rushed ahead: a line between New Westminster and Quesnel on the upper Fraser built in three months in the summer of 1865, 400 more miles the next summer to just beyond Kispiox on the Skeena (9,246 poles and fifteen relay stations).[12] There, with the successful laying of a trans-Atlantic cable, the project stopped.

Although the telegraph was expensive and slow for an electronic medium,[13] its arrival at New Westminster and the completion of the trans-Atlantic cable a year later repositioned British Columbia. Although cost reduced personal communications to rare, brief announcements, the telegraph was an admirable carrier of commercial intelligence (its principal use) and news (for newspapers). Merchants could now obtain virtually current information about distant markets. An account of the assassination of Lincoln in Washington, DC, the first news story received by telegraph in New Westminster, was in the *British Columbian* five days after the event. By the end of 1866, the turn-around time for express communications between British Columbia and London was less than a week.

The railway was not that much slower. The Union Pacific Railroad was completed to San Francisco in 1869; coupled with steamer connections, the trip between London and Victoria suddenly took less than a month. The Canadian Pacific Railway (CPR), completed to Port Moody at the head of Burrard Inlet in November 1885, and moved a few miles west to Vancouver and opened to passenger traffic before the end of 1886, reduced this time even more. The distance between Vancouver and Montreal was now calculated in hours (137); through passenger trains ran six days a week. Even in the mountains, they maintained an average speed of thirty-five miles per hour. Fares were high, averaging about three cents a mile for regular second-class passengers, and half as much for immigrants;[14] and freight rates were much higher than by sea; but the railway opened up possibilities for transcontinental travel and trade that had not previously existed. Rail integrated British Columbia in a new transcontinental state, marking the final nineteenth-century stage of an extraordinary sequence of time-space compressions.

The nineteenth-century assault on time and space was most dramatic at the margins of the world system. In a few years, British Columbia's external connections had been transformed: by 1890, telegraphs carried compact, high-value information in and out of the province within hours; mail arrived from eastern Canada in about a week, from Britain in two weeks, and from China and Japan within a month, the CPR having contracted to provide monthly mail service between Halifax and Hong Kong in twenty-eight and a half days.[15] Bulk freight moved far more readily than ever before. These changes expanded British Columbia's connections with the world economy, situated it squarely within the circuitry of a global empire, and underlay the introduction of government and the emergence of settler society.

The founding of the Vancouver Island colony coincided with improved communications with London following the California gold rush. British Columbia became a province of Canada on the (promised) overland strength of telegraph and railway. As shipping costs declined, industrial fish canning, sawmilling, and coal mining began on the coast; by 1890, the first hard-rock mines were shipping high-grade silver ore from the Kootenays (see Chapter 7). Cattle ranching, an extensive land use on low-value land at the very edge of the world economy, took over much of the dry belt (see Chapter 8). Immigrants were attracted by prospects that apparently could be reached without undue risk or loss of contact with home. Their arrival accelerated the colonial appropriation of land. Yet, as the distribution of immigrant population suggests (see Figures 5.2 and 5.3 in Chapter 5), there were sharp geographical variations within British Columbia in the extent of connection with the outside world. The few towns on southeastern Vancouver Island and in the lower Fraser Valley and, by 1890, stations along the main line of the CPR were the primary points of connection beyond which, more or less rapidly, the outside world dropped away.

Internal Distance

As late as 1870, only a few elements of modern transportation were superimposed on a huge, otherwise-organized land (Figure 6.2). There were a great many Native trails, many no longer used as Native populations declined, many unknown to whites. There were also the brigade trails of HBC days, most of them Native routes adapted to pack-horse use.[16] There were miners' trails around the gold rush camps, a wagon road from the head of navigation on the lower Fraser to the principal Cariboo diggings, and a trail, in good part impassable by 1870, across southern British Columbia to diggings in the Rocky Mountain Trench.[17] A telegraph ran up the Fraser River to Quesnel; the line to Kispiox was not maintained (Wet'suwet'en had used some of the wire to hang a suspension bridge over the Bulkley). There were small steamers on a few rivers and, in 1870, some twenty-five post offices. This changed little during the 1870s. In the 1880s, the CPR and another telegraph line arrived, but they were lines without thickness; in themselves, neither line had the capacity to occupy a territory.

In British Columbia, outliers of civilization seemed suspended in wilderness. This was Governor Seymour's feeling in the summer of 1864 as he accompanied a punitive expedition against the Chilcotin people into parts of the Coast Range 'almost unknown to whitemen.' His party seemed out of communication with 'the civilized parts of the colony.' 'Thus isolated in the bush our fate became a matter of speculation throughout the Colony and the most painful rumours circulated.'[18] In 1870 the editor of the *Cariboo Sentinel* in Barkerville, still the largest settlement in the interior, complained in a somewhat similar vein. The telegraph line had been too long out of operation; the government was repairing it too slowly. There was no postal service for six months a year, and service only twice a month in summer.[19] Such were the problems of connection in a vast, recently resettled, mountainous land. When the railway arrived, it suddenly became physically easier (though not cheaper) to reach Montreal from a point along the line than to reach the railway from many places only a few miles away.

Modern distance-diminishing technologies were imposed very incompletely, and with great difficulty, on this vast, angular land. Yet, because the white control of the land required such technologies, the effort to introduce them was enormous. The most aggressive impetus, by far, came from capital as it identified resources, and sought to connect them to markets. The state did what it could to encourage capital, extend its own territorial reach, and, after a time, service a growing settler population. Settlers themselves built trails and roads here and there, but, by and large, relied on a communicative grid imposed by capital and government. The main channels of this grid were railways, steamer runs, and, eventually, a few roads, whereas the interstices tended to be reached by more vernacular, western North American methods.

In the southern interior, and eventually in much of the central interior as well, networks of transportation and communication developed around railways. As the American environmental historian William Cronon recently put it, railways were 'artificial corridors' that replaced

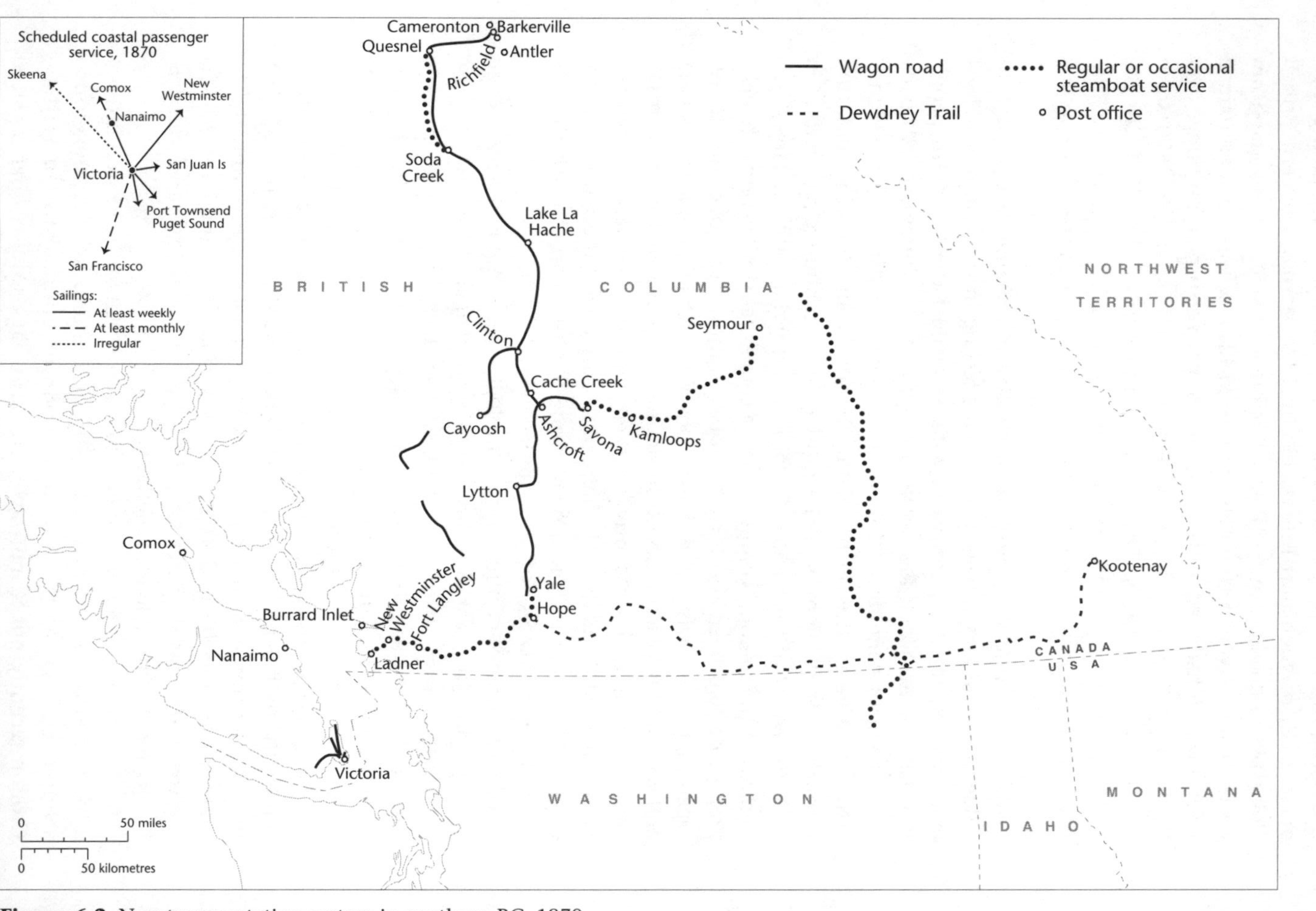

Figure 6.2 New transportation system in southern BC, 1870

the complexities of the surface of the earth with lines of machined steel, and the irregularities of topography with engineered grades. Operating on precise schedules, they emphasized clock time, and they substantially nullified three age-old constraints on land transportation: night, inclement weather, and seasonal climates. Their artificiality gave them their power, allowing steam engines to haul by day or night, summer or winter, in a great variety of terrains.[20] But they were expensive to build, especially in mountainous terrain, and lacked lateral extent. In British Columbia, railways rarely ran through what Europeans would have called countryside. Rather, these lines of late nineteenth-century technology wound along rivers, through canyons and forests, and around mountainsides.

In the southern interior, transcontinental railways – the CPR in the north, and the Northern Pacific and, from 1893, the Great Northern south of the border – bounded the transportation system (Figure 6.3).[21] The Great Northern was built expressly to drain Canadian trade southward, and the principal mining activity in British Columbia at the end of the nineteenth century lay between it and the CPR. Vying for this trade, both rail companies built feeder lines into the north-south-tending valleys between them. At huge expense over a period of some twenty years, and against the grain of the topography, the CPR also opened the Kettle Valley Line across southern BC, completing it in 1916 when the principal mining excitements in southern BC were over. Two new transcontinental lines, crossing the Rockies well north of the CPR, opened as World War I began: the Grand Trunk Pacific, built by British capital to exacting standards, and intended to provide a rapid and economical link between Britain and the Orient; and the Canadian Northern, built with eastern Canadian capital, and intended to encourage local development. The provincial government built ineffectively northward from Squamish, at the head of Howe Sound near Vancouver, intending but failing to reach the Grand Trunk. Figure 6.4 shows the railways in British Columbia in 1917 (excluding logging railways), when their construction stopped until well after World War II. There were four east-west lines and many spur lines, some 3,000 miles of track in total, many of them enormously costly: the heart of the inland transportation system and a far larger investment than the provincial economy warranted.

River and lake steamboats filled some gaps in the railway system with a flexible, inexpensive technology that had evolved in the interior waterways of North America[22] (Figures 6.3 and 6.4). Small steamboats could operate in two feet of water, and could nose ashore almost anywhere. On lakes, they could make fifteen miles per hour or more. Although engines had to be imported, hulls and superstructures could be constructed locally, making it far easier and less costly to put a steamboat on a lake or navigable river than to build a railway along it.

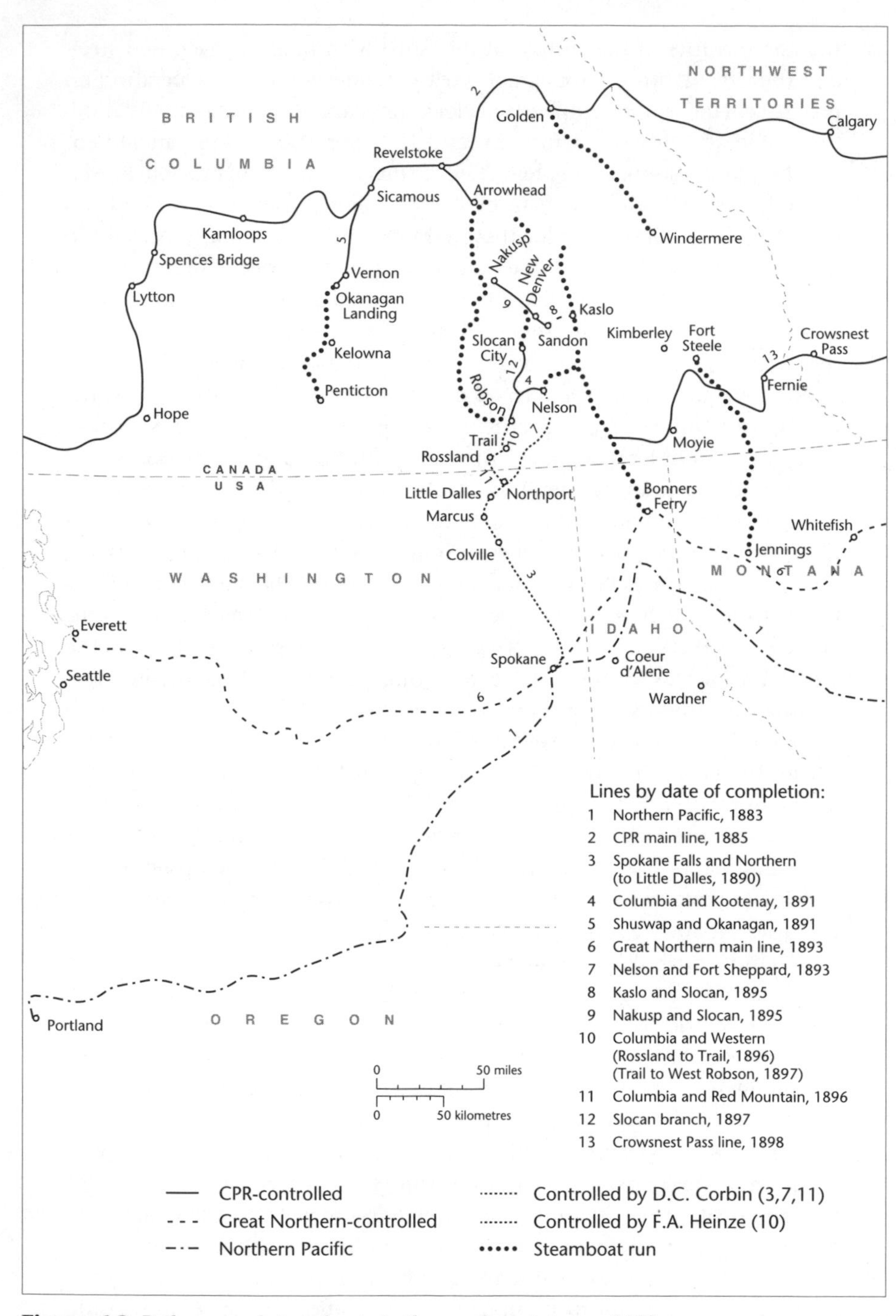

Figure 6.3 Railways and steamboats in the southern interior, 1898

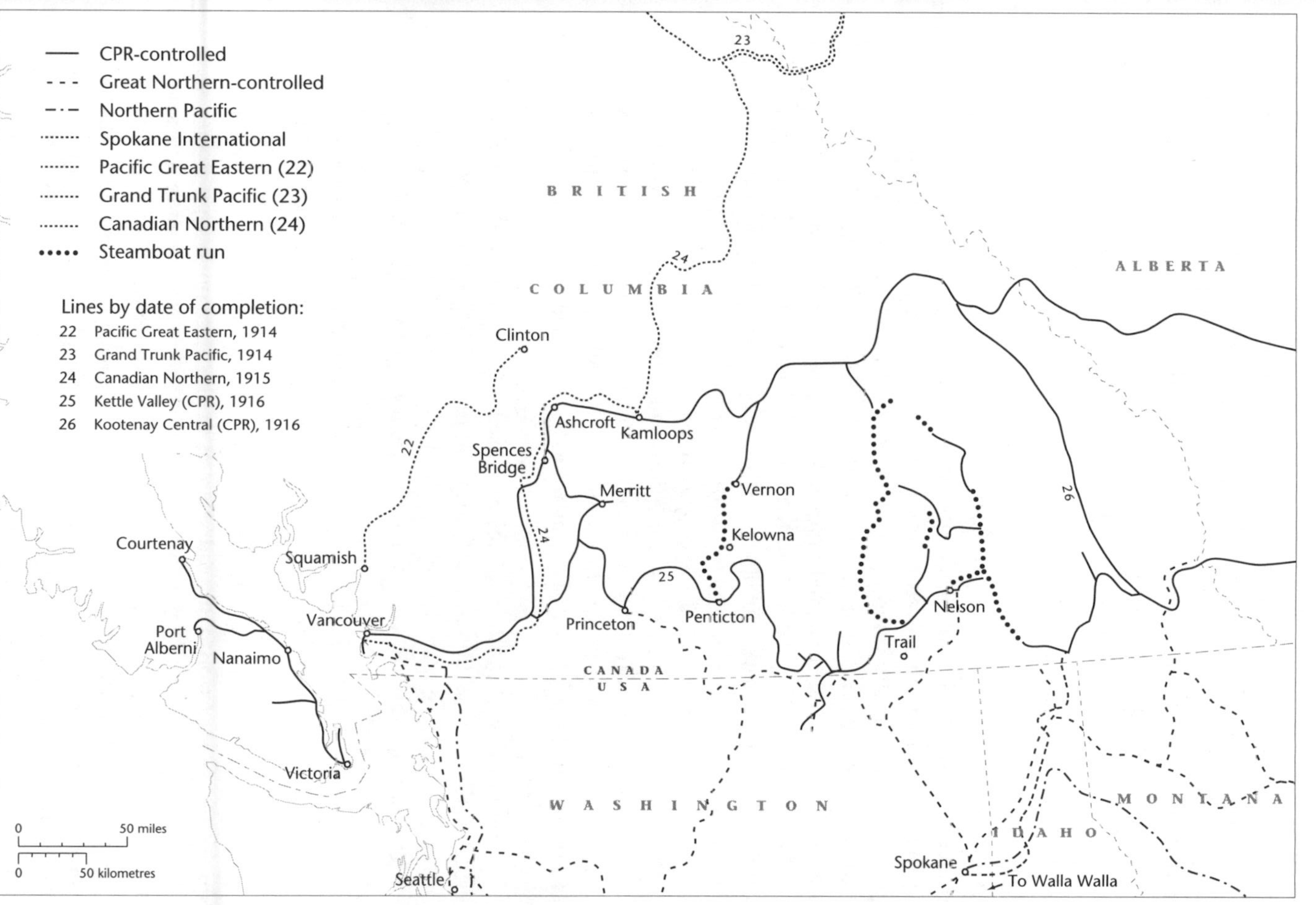

Figure 6.4 Railways and steamboats in southern BC, 1917

In most larger valleys of southern British Columbia, steamboats provided the first steam power, and some remained links in railway systems as late as World War II, transporting freight cars, passengers, and local freight. Due to trans-shipment costs, they rarely competed for long with railways over the same routes, and were discontinued as the railway network expanded.

Roads, the only other public carriers of inland passengers and freight, were nowhere numerous, and most of BC was not served by them. Only in the drier, less heavily forested, and less mountainous parts of the interior, where road construction was relatively easy, was there something like a network of roads in 1900 (Figure 6.5). There were no roads along the coast north of Georgia Strait, no roads north of Barkerville, no roads in the Coast Mountains; even in the Kootenay mining regions, the most populous parts of the interior, there were no through roads. Surviving parts of the Cariboo Wagon Road – built in 1862-5, and originally eighteen feet wide, cambered, well graded, and bridged – were still the best roads in the province. As the government let only small, intermittent contracts for road work, the characteristic road in British Columbia was an unsurfaced dirt track twelve to fourteen feet wide. Yet express and freight companies operated stages and freight wagons on the principal roads in the dry belt, especially north from the CPR mainline at Ashcroft to the Cariboo (Figure 6.5). For years, there were twice weekly stages between Ashcroft and Barkerville, a distance of 280 miles, and roadhouses, most built in gold rush days, at intervals of fifteen to twenty miles along the way.

As the number of motor vehicles increased – from 200 registrations in British Columbia in 1906 to nearly 100,000 in 1930 – the need grew for a different, greatly expanded road system. Automobile traffic required wider roads, less abrupt curves, gentler grades, and stronger bridges. In the 1920s, the provincial Department of Public Works borrowed several million dollars a year to finance the capital costs of road construction, appointed an engineer, and hired a road crew in each road district. By 1930, the province had replaced most wagon bridges, opened a road through the Fraser Canyon (the first road link between coast and interior since CPR construction destroyed sections of the Cariboo Wagon Road), and had three roads through passes in the Rockies (Figure 6.6). These dusty, washboarded, dirt or gravel roads were often virtually impassable in spring and fall; the new road in the Fraser Canyon was two feet narrower than its predecessor. The system had expanded, but remained meagre. In 1930, there was only one road from the interior to the coast. The road trip within Canada from Vancouver to Calgary, while possible, was circuitous and slow, as were most provincial roads. The far easier route east was south, then through adjacent American states. The east-west

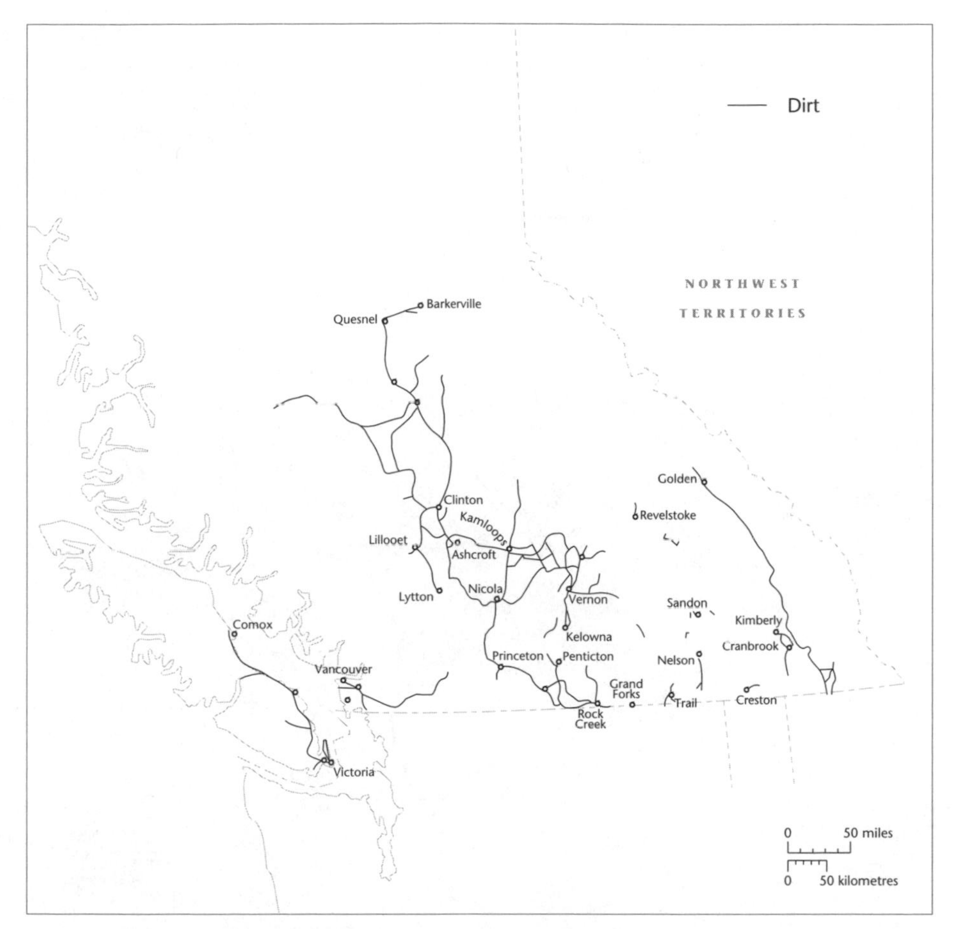

Figure 6.5 Principal roads, 1903

roads between vallcys in the southern interior were switchbacked and so narrow that meeting vehicles often had to back up. Most of British Columbia remained roadless.

Such a road network was a weak complement to a system of inland transportation still based primarily on railways and steamboats. An average of only forty-five cars a day negotiated the new road through the Fraser Canyon during the six months following its opening in 1927. In 1930, there was no stage (bus) service between Vancouver and the interior, and commercial trucking had barely begun. Motor-touring Vancouverites drove south, to the paved roads of Washington State. In the 1930s, several small BC trucking companies were most successful where, as in the Cariboo, there was little competition from railways. They also began to connect Vancouver with the interior, providing more

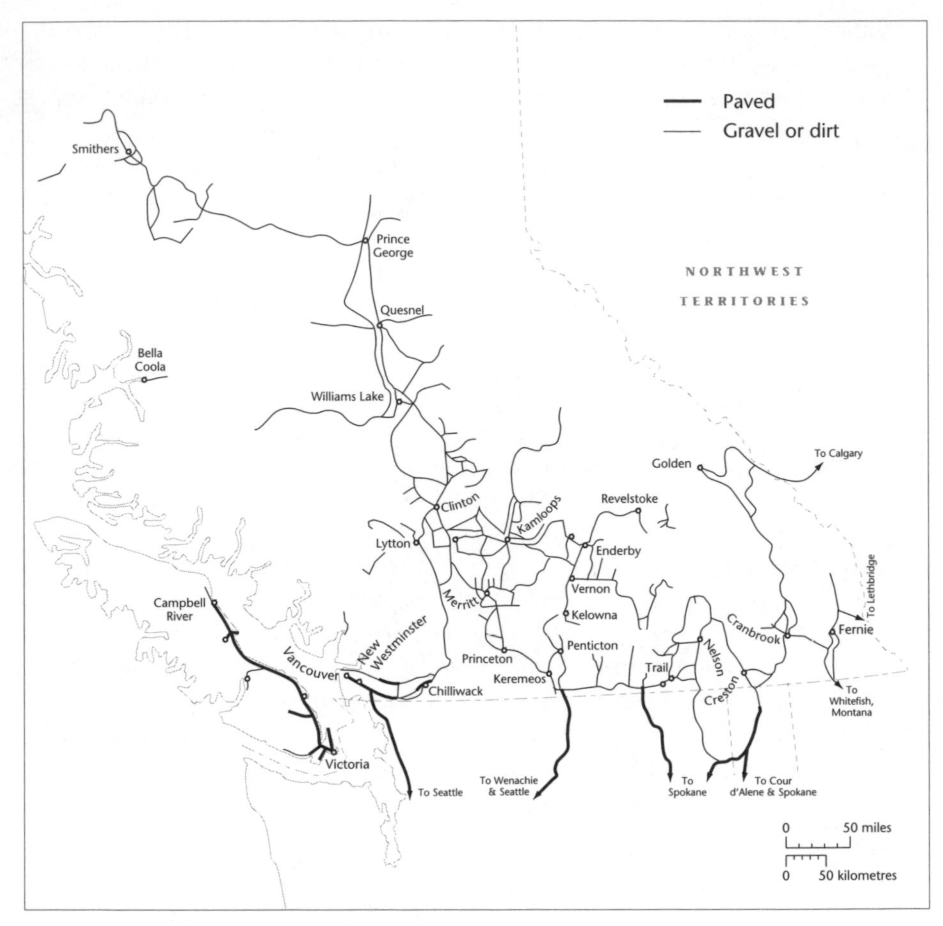

Figure 6.6 Principal roads, 1930

flexible through- and way-haulage than the railways, but at higher cost and subject to the vagaries of weather and road. Trucks were often stuck or over the bank; driving them was a frontier adventure.[23] Buses, too, began to provide interregional service but, like general trucking, competed weakly with the railway until the roads improved.

Coastal waters accepted modern technologies of transportation far more easily. The HBC put its first steamer, the *Beaver*, into coastal service in 1836, thereby taking the fur trade into inlets where sailing ships had not ventured. Throughout the nineteenth century, most coastal steamers were wood- or coal-burning side- or sternwheelers; by World War I, steel hulls and propellers had largely taken over, some steamers were converted to oil, and turbine engines were being used in passenger ships. The Grand Trunk's new passenger liners, operating between Prince Rupert,

Vancouver, and Seattle, were licensed to carry 1,500 passengers at top speeds of eighteen knots. A few years later, the CPR operated nineteen ships along this coast, a diversified modern fleet for an investment of $10,000,000. Overall, the coastal fleet was a motley of vessels of different sizes and capabilities that linked the principal towns and camps along a fjorded coast from Alaska to Puget Sound for a small fraction of the cost of overland transportation.

Scheduled passenger and freight sailings along the coast in 1890, 1901, and 1921 are shown in Figure 6.7. The cartograms show an expanding system increasingly focused on Vancouver, and suggest something of the services different companies provided. Union Steamships relied on small, multipurpose freighters that supplied the logging camps, canneries, mines, and few farms scattered along the inside passage between Vancouver Island and the mainland; they also made weekly runs farther north to Bella Coola, Rivers Inlet, and the Skeena. Like the riverboats, Union ships would put in to isolated settlements on demand.[24] The Canadian Pacific Navigation Company made longer, less flexible runs to the north coast and Alaska, controlled most of the passenger traffic across southern Georgia Strait between Vancouver, Victoria, and Nanaimo, and provided weekly or monthly service to the west coast of Vancouver Island from Victoria. The Grand Trunk, by 1921 part of the Canadian National system, provided fast runs between Prince Rupert, Vancouver, Victoria, and Seattle, and a more local service, analogous to Union Steamships', out of Prince Rupert.

These different transportation systems all carried the public mail, the principal form of long-distance communication throughout these years. Before 1858, the mail was handled by the HBC, and later, during the gold rushes, by American express companies; as gold rush business declined, the colonial and then the Dominion government took over postal services. A post office, a crucial commercial and personal link with the outside world, became part of any new, fairly permanent settlement. Figure 6.8, which shows the distribution of post offices in 1890, gives a fair summary of the distribution of immigrant settlement: a good many post offices on southeastern Vancouver Island and in the lower Fraser Valley, some along the route to the Cariboo, some along the CPR, some in the new ranching or mixed farming settlements south of the CPR, and few anywhere else.[25] As immigrant settlement expanded, post offices became more numerous. Figure 6.9 shows their distribution in 1915 in the Kootenays, then the most populous part of the interior. Almost wherever there were settlers, there was a post office nearby, a measure both of a high degree of access to the outside world and of local limitations on personal mobility and mail deliveries. The (usually) short, regular visit to the post office became part of everyday life.

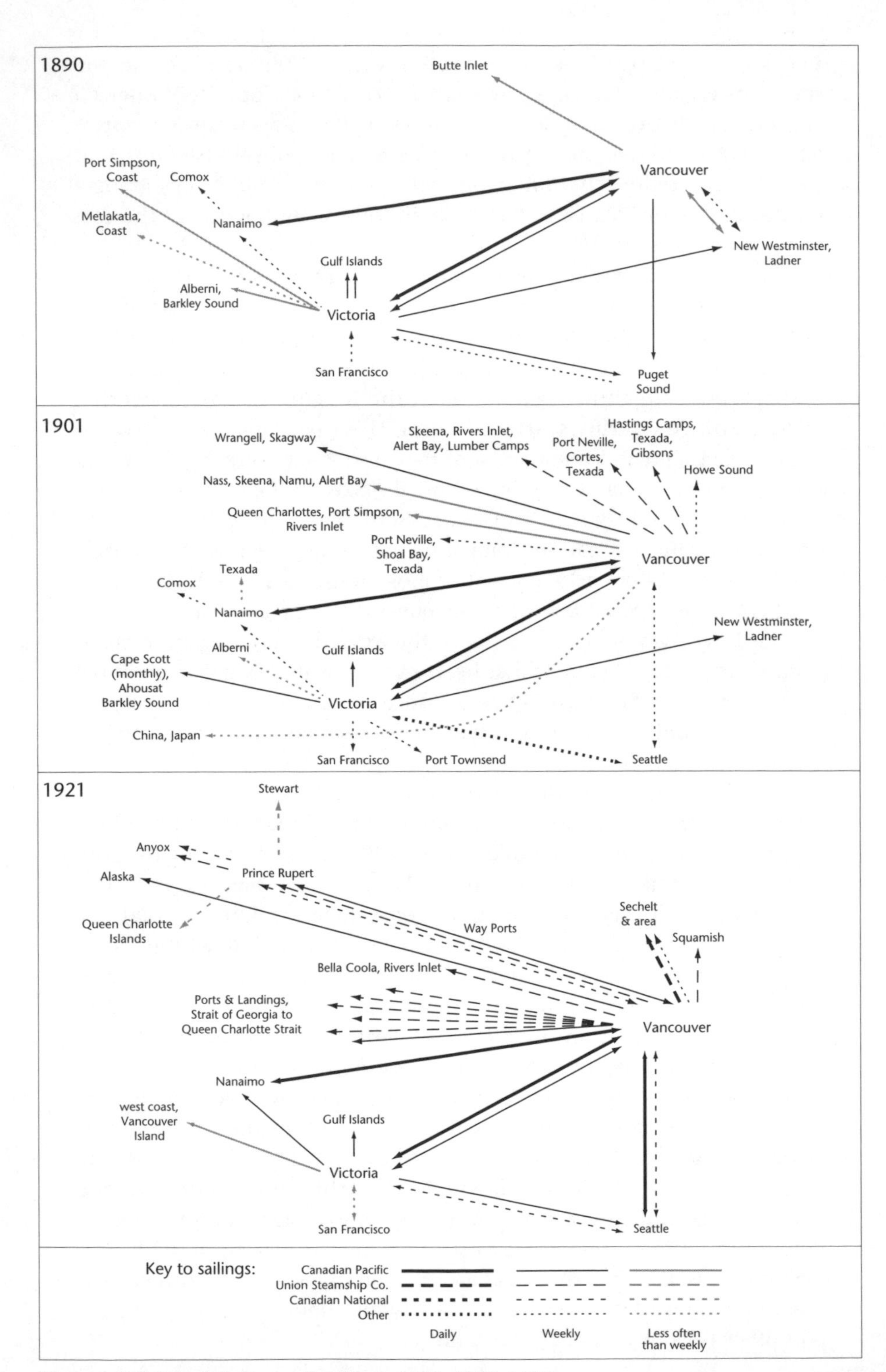

Figure 6.7 Scheduled coastal sailings, 1890, 1901, 1921

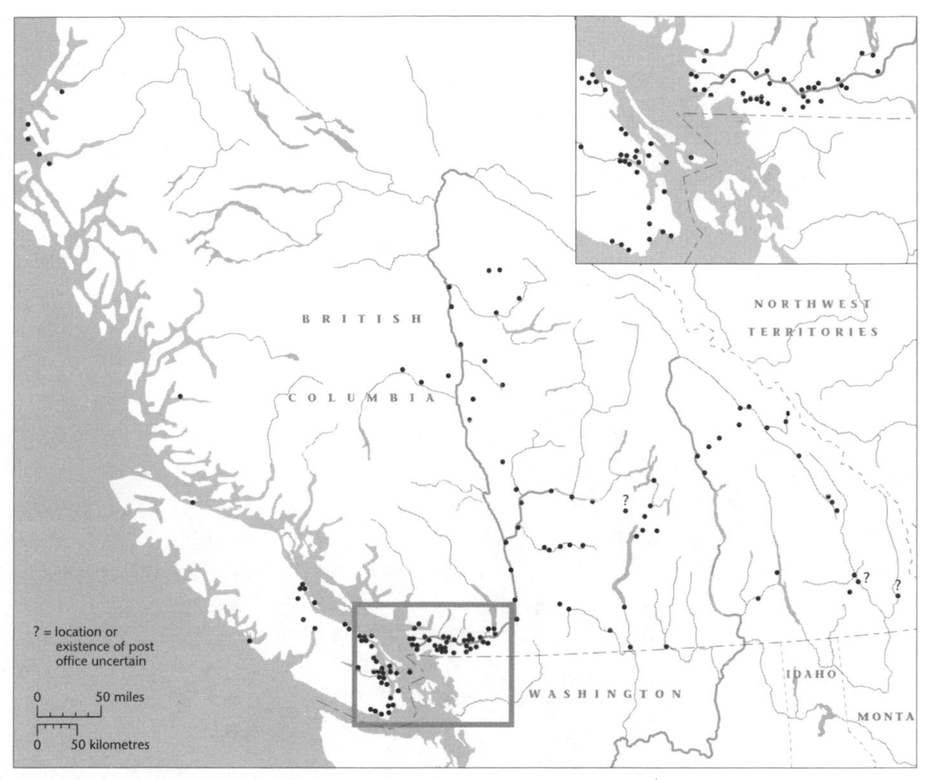

Figure 6.8 Post offices, 1890

Telephones, first used in the 1880s, had far more to do with local than long-distance communication. The Anglican missionary William Duncan connected the store and sawmill at Metlakatla by telephone, and CPR contractors kept in touch with their foremen by telephone; at the turn of the century, farmers and storekeepers near Kamloops contrived short telephone connections along barbed wire fences. Before 1900, a number of local telephone companies operated local exchanges, many merging in 1904 to form the BC Telephone Company.[26] There were 20,000 telephones in the province by 1911, most in Vancouver. The different regional exchanges were beginning to link up, and it was possible, using American lines, to call from Vancouver to Ottawa. By 1939, there were long-distance connections between all sizeable settlements in BC, all Canadian provinces, and (just beginning) with Britain, the Philippines, and Japan. Northern parts of the province were beginning to be reached by radio-telephone. The cost of long-distance calls was high, however, and like the telegraph they were used primarily for commercial purposes; for individuals, long-distance calls were brief, expensive, and often somewhat alarming. Radio, which was becoming popular in the 1920s, was poorly received in interior valleys. Local stations were weak – in 1930, the

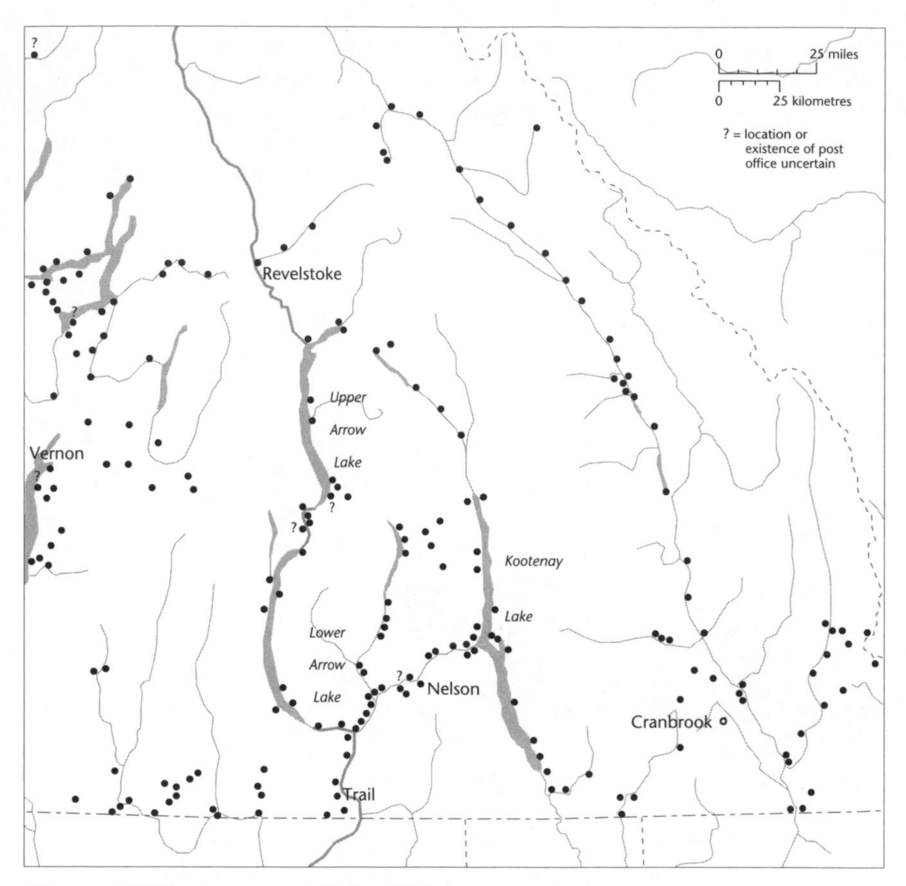

Figure 6.9 Kootenay post offices, 1915

total broadcasting power in the province was under 1,400 watts – and the stations that could be picked up were usually American.[27]

Telegraph, railway, road, steamer, and mail service comprised the main elements of the new communicative environment that reconfigured British Columbia before World War II. By any measure, their introduction was an impressive achievement: an enormous investment of capital, labour, and lives to reshape spatial relations and facilitate modernity. Yet in themselves they were an outline without much capacity to reach beyond a few narrow, introduced corridors of modern connectivity. Steamers connected points along the coast, but behind that coast steamer whistles quickly faded into tangled forests and mountainsides. Along most of the three thousand miles of railway, the situation was much the same. Essentially there were not enough roads, not the intricate miles of local tracks that in any older agricultural society had once taken carts and wagons, and later would be improved to take automobiles and trucks.

The interior of British Columbia had essentially one road in 1870, and though the road system had expanded greatly, it was still minimal seventy years later. Without prior roads, new corridors of transportation would not, automatically, have any lateral effect. And yet the resources identified by immigrants in British Columbia lay in the spaces beyond the transportation corridors, often high on mountains or tucked away in inaccessible valleys. Here was a more local challenge of distance. While strategies to overcome it differed in each resource industry, they usually depended on methods recently worked out in similar settings in the United States, combined with much practical individual ingenuity. There was always the same essential challenge: to connect isolated resources, tucked in corners of the province, to one of the corridors of modern transportation.

Martin Allerdale Grainger's novel *Woodsmen of the West*, set in an isolated coastal logging camp before World War I, is, in some ways, a British Columbian parable that turns around just this problem. The Union steamer *Cassiar* brings a tenderfoot English logger, Mart, from Vancouver to Port Browning, near the mouth of Coola (Knight) Inlet, 175 miles north of Vancouver. His destination, however, is Carter's logging camp, a small, thoroughly marginal operation seventy miles beyond Port Browning, up Coola Inlet. Much of the novel deals with this tenuous connection: a succession of tiny, makeshift steamers (the best of them a 'god-forsaken looking tub'), their propellers or rudders dropping off, their boilers bursting, their rotten planks leaking. There are night runs up dark channels. There are groundings and sinkings. Then, because the camp is eventually steamerless, the connection to Port Browning becomes Mart's solitary, seventy-mile row in an open, leaking, eighteen-foot boat – in winter. At Carter's operation, camp and donkey engine are on rafts, the 'donk' is 'jumped' from raft to shore, winched up-slope, its cable hauled a thousand feet up. Jack screws 'coax' logs to the sea. A four-hundred-foot boom secures logs. Everything is bent to 'getting out logs.' Carter, as driven as Captain Ahab, identifies with the machine that moves his logs: 'I and the donk.' The parable turns on the drive to master nature and distance beyond the transportation corridors, at the very edge of the world economy.

In the mountains of southeastern British Columbia, the Kootenays, Grainger's tale could be told around prospecting and mining. Prospecting took place almost anywhere, but 'proving up' a prospect required a horse trail, built by hand usually with enormous labour across difficult terrain. Mining would not begin until there was a railway or steamboat nearby – the impetus for the expansion of both in the Kootenays. The mines, however, were perched in the mountains and at first, when only the highest grade ore was shipped, the gap between them and steam power in the valleys was filled by pack trains or by rawhiding (using horses to pull ore wrapped in raw hides down mountain trails in winter). More developed mines required better connections: usually an overhead tram comprising towers, cables, and ore buckets built by an American contractor familiar with such systems; or a short, switchbacked wagon road. Where the tram/wagon road met the railway/steamer run, there was a mill, another link in the transportation system. At the mill, the ore was gravity fed and concentrated, then loaded into box cars (see Chapter 7).

In the coastal forest, the focus was on moving logs. When logs were hauled by oxen over greased, corduroy roads, operations could not take place more than two or three miles from tidewater. With logging railways, logging could move well up valleys, while the donkey engine and high-lead operations allowed loggers to go some distance up the valley sides (Figure 6.10). The reach of a donkey engine could be doubled or tripled by cold decking: winching the donkey itself to the end of its cable, and building a platform (cold deck) from which its cable could reach another 1,000 feet. Local solutions were numerous. In some operations, flumes transported shake bolts and, in the interior, logs. Some loggers used steam tractors or cog railways on steep slopes. By the late 1920s, bulldozers were building logging roads, and trucks were hauling logs; this combination would soon take logging far beyond the range of the logging railways and, beginning in the 1930s, would close them down.[28]

The salmon fishery, too, expanded its reach: from a gill-net river fishery using flat-bottomed skiffs or Native canoes, and targeting sockeye, to a much more wide-ranging, predominantly deep-sea fishery using gas-powered fishing boats, tenders, and various nets and trolls, and targeting all varieties of salmon.[29]

Farming, on the other hand, required roads, both on and off the farm. Off-farm roads in the transportation corridors were usually short, perhaps no more than a few hundred yards from a farm on a post-glacial terrace to a steamer landing on a lake. Where patches of farmland were broad enough to permit some density of farms, as in the lower Fraser Valley or the Peace River, networks of rural roads emerged, though this was uncommon in British Columbia because agricultural land was so limited (see Chapter 8). Many farms were also connected to the uplands behind them. In the dry belt, creeks were dammed, and flumes, ditches, or wire-bound wooden pipes brought irrigation water, occasionally from dams as much as thirty or forty miles away. Cowboys and shepherds drove cattle or sheep from bottomland winter pastures to high summer ranges, in the process occupying these ranges for particular ranches.

These local struggles with distance embodied much of the creative, practical ingenuity in early modern British Columbia, and created much

Figure 6.10 Logging roads near Menzies Bay, after R.D. Turner

Dry belt wagon road near Ashcroft, c. 1890. Easily built and maintained in the dry belt, such roads provided freight connections beyond the CPR.

of the texture of its changing human geography. Allowing the province's primary resource economies to expand well beyond the transportation corridors, they put flesh on a few bones and, by enabling newcomers to occupy ever more land and use it to their purposes, considerably filled in the modern map of British Columbia. As new media of transportation and communication reached into more and more land, the geographical transformation was huge; by the beginning of World War II, as much as a quarter of British Columbia may have been effectively reoccupied.

Distance and Power

Here and there, these developments drew on Native precedent, but for the most part they did not. Immigrants considered Native ways irrelevant, treated British Columbia as a tabula rasa, and constructed their own systems of transportation and communication essentially from scratch. These systems were among their principal achievements, the framework on which the province's changing human geography was hung. As such they were enormously powerful, for they shaped many of the spaces in which British Columbians lived and, in so doing, many of their social relations.

The relationship between empire and the media of transportation and communication has been widely explored, in this country first, and perhaps most suggestively, by Harold Innis in his studies of the CPR, the fur trade, and the bias of communications. Railways, steamers, and telegraphs were admirable tools of imperialism, incorporating into empires the territories won by the overwhelming superiority of European firearms.[30] As much as troops on the ground, a nineteenth-century empire depended on the capacity of interlocking networks of rail, steamship, wire, and mail to overcome distance. As space collapsed, territory awaited the powerful, and the rhetoric of expansion became more and more self-evident. Strong states, it was held, would inevitably expand, and should absorb weaker, less civilized societies.[31] The question was not of the right to expand, which was taken for granted, but of which strong state would expand the most – the impetus, for example, for the rush of European states to carve up Africa. Geopolitical thinking flourished in this climate. A telegraph line connecting Washington, DC, and Moscow was a vision of American commercial and cultural empire. The Trans-Siberian Railway was an alarming instrument of Russian power in the Pacific; the British geographer Halford Mackinder thought that railways had tilted the balance of world power landward, and would shift global power towards the state (Russia) that occupied the great Eurasian heartland of the world.[32] British Columbia was not detached from such geopolitical thinking. The CPR, for example, consolidated a transcontinental state, and enabled central Canada to reach quickly outward, as it did by both railway and telegraph when putting down the second Métis rebellion (the second Riel Rebellion) on the Prairies. The CPR was also a link between Britain and Asia; together with the empress ships that sailed out of Vancouver and that, by prior agreement, the admiralty could commandeer at any time and convert to troop carriers, it provided an alternative route to India should the Suez Canal be blocked.[33] The Grand Trunk Pacific, built with millions of British pounds, was the final, imperial northwest passage in the railway age.

Within British Columbia, imperial visions merged with the realities of colonialism. As distance diminished, newcomers were able to possess the 'wilderness' more comprehensively. Edward Said has suggested that the construction of the Suez Canal 'destroyed the Orient's distance, its cloistered intimacy away from the West,' and that, unsheltered, the West could now possess it. 'After de Lesseps no one could speak of the Orient as belonging to another world ... There was only "our" world ... '[34] So too in British Columbia as distances were undermined. Claiming political control of a territory was an act of imperialism, coming to know it was often another, but using it was far more intrusive than either. Improvements in transportation and communication enabled the world economy to use British Columbia's space not through Native intermediaries, as during the fur trade, but by distributing Western technologies, labour, and settlers across the land. They allowed the state greatly to expand its reach, providing the channels by which it collected information, distributed regulation, and imposed order. Although it would not be quickly possible to extend the state uniformly over British Columbia's territory – a characteristic, according to sociologist Anthony Giddens, of modern societies – the thrust, facilitated by the decline of distance, was in this direction. From a Native perspective, white territorial claims, place names on maps, and exploration and survey parties were being followed by a far more tangible form of colonialism: white workers, settlers, and their machines using Native land for their own purposes. As long as Natives had been able to hunt, fish, and gather in their former territories, the small reserves the reserve commissioners laid out for them had little meaning; however, the implications of reserves, and the exclusions they entailed, became ever more apparent as non-Natives occupied and used the surrounding land. A logging operation in a mountain valley previously used for seasonal hunting marked a huge transformation of land use and power. For those experiencing it, colonialism was enacted locally, on the ground.

Viewed in this light, the systems of transportation and communication that spread into British Columbia were the capillaries of colonial appropriation. They allowed non-Natives into the land, not as explorers, visitors, or passers-through, but as users and settlers. Coupled with a regime of property rights validated by the state, they effected a vast transfer of

Canyon Creek bridge, Kettle Valley Line. Especially in the mountains, the railway was a line without lateral extent.

local power from indigenous peoples to immigrants. They did so not as the result of any one event, but incrementally, as a flume was built here, a corduroy road laid out there, a donkey engine brought into the bush. This pervasive geographical expansion, superimposed on a depopulated land and backed by the immigrants' cultural confidence, technological superiority, and force of arms, was itself a diffused form of power that prized open more and more nooks and crannies of an alien land, and civilized them in terms a modern immigrant population could understand. French social philosopher Michel Foucault has insisted upon the relationship between social power and the configuration of space, but whereas Foucault's examples turn around prisons, asylums, and reformatories, in British Columbia the prime example is the land itself, reconfigured into new patterns of appropriation and social control.[35] Colonialism and colonization were about the control of land; land use itself defined new rights, exclusions, and patterns of dominance; and strategies for the effective control of land operationalized colonial rhetorics and discourses. In British Columbia, immigrants were preoccupied with the challenges and opportunities of a remote land into which global imbalances of power and the British empire had incongruously brought them; as they reduced the problems of distance and gained access to the land, immigrants relegated the former population ever more to the sidelines. A Foucauldian analysis of the decentred strategies of disciplinary power is shifted in such settings, becoming more preoccupied with land and the disciplinary power associated with reaching and possessing it.

Closer to the British Columbian mark, in some ways, is the work of two other French philosophers, Gilles Deleuze and Félix Guattari, on what they call the 'desiring machine' of capitalism,[36] or what the geographer David Harvey calls, with some of the same meanings, capitalism's 'spatial fix.'[37] Harvey argues that capitalism required new space both for profits and to quell social unrest within established capitalist societies. As capital travels – in British Columbia, along routes largely constructed for itself – it 'is perpetually deconstructing ... social power by reshaping its geographical bases.'[38] Deleuze and Guattari treat capitalism as a surface of desire that transcends individuals and, machinelike, stamps its own rules across the land. For them, capitalism had to deterritorialize societies that were otherwise constructed, in the process decoding their social rules, and then re-territorialize land and recode the social rules to fit its own requirements. Only then could it function. The desiring machine consumed otherness and regurgitated its products in spaces remade around its own assumptions about markets, money, property, and objectively known nature.[39] Such analyses are obviously relevant to the changes explored in this chapter, with the qualification, in my view, that capitalism was only one source of a reterritorialization that was as much grounded in cultural assumptions that were pervasive in an immigrant society as in the spatial logic of capital.

There is yet another side of the colonial question: the extent to which new systems of transportation and communication were themselves agents of Native cultural change. This is a matter awaiting exploration, but it is worth bearing in mind Jean and John Comaroff's conclusion, with respect to Protestant missions in South Africa, that colonized peoples often 'reject the message of the colonizers, and yet are powerfully and profoundly affected by its media.' The very meeting of different ways, they suggest, had the capacity to redefine 'the taken-for-granted surfaces' of everyday worlds. In the missionaries' implicit assumptions, rather than their explicit evangelical narratives, lay the 'hegemonic forms' that shaped 'colonial subjects.'[40] If a steamboat or a railway were less conventionally articulate than a missionary, they perhaps took as much for granted: clock time, linear distance, rational empiricism, a revised geographical relationship with space and with other peoples, an instant relativity that situated the local in the world. A railway that ran past a Native village was more than an intrusive symbol of white power; it redefined the 'surfaces' of life in that place, making local people more self-conscious, situating them within a global, rationalized civilization, taking away their local integrity. A talking wire, the telegraph, initially perceived as another form of white spirit power, eventually led to a wholly other way of thinking about the world.[41] Such connections remain to be examined, but it can hardly be doubted either that new media of transportation and communication powerfully imbalanced white-Native interactions or that they were themselves powerful colonizers of Native consciousness.

From the newcomers' perspective, most of this was invisible. The land was wilderness awaiting development. The few legacies of a Native past were irrelevant to an immigrant future; British Columbia was a beginning. In terms of the media of transportation and communication, this meant not only that systems were constructed *de novo*, but also that they were constructed without interference from the past. Liberated from the past, they faced an open, untrammelled relationship with the future, a relationship affected by the terrain through which they would pass, but not by prior human geographies. Immigrant British Columbians knew this. The location of their future was still very much up in the air, an uncertainty that was the source of the strident boosterism with which they promoted this or that settlement. Transportation schemes frequently underpinned such boosterism, also for obvious reasons. Transportation would provide the links with other places; in good part, settlements would grow in proportion to the strength of such links; and a railway or other form of modern transportation was often the difference between an

Solutions to local problems of distance in the primary resource industries.
Top: North Pacific Canners' tender towing sailboats on the Skeena River.
Bottom: Timber yarding, Shawnigan Lake Lumber Co., c. 1917.

efficient connection and none at all. The transportation system, in short, was seen to have enormous power, not to complement or supplement, but to create; and there was abundant evidence at hand that it did.

Victoria, the first town, grew out of the HBC's main Pacific depot, moved from the lower Columbia River to southern Vancouver Island in

1843, less in anticipation of the border settlement three years later than, as Richard Mackie has recently shown, to secure an accessible harbour for the company's growing Pacific trade.[42] New Westminster emerged during the gold rush as a classic gateway town, a river-mouth, steamboat port on the main route to the diggings. Vancouver, which superseded New Westminster, was a creation of the railway, and its spectacular growth to metropolitan dominance reflected its location at the junction of the main corridors of transportation affecting the province: railway routes east, coastwise steamer traffic, and deep-sea shipping.[43] At no other point in a network dominated by a few channels was there anything like equivalent access to goods and information. By the time Prince Rupert became the Pacific port for the Grand Trunk Pacific, the pattern of urban dominance was already set; Prince Rupert could not begin to compete with the many linkage advantages, both within the city and beyond, that already had accrued to Vancouver. And small, railway-dominated towns emerged at divisional points, to a railway approximately what roadhouses were to a wagon road.

Another category of towns, all of them small in early British Columbia, emerged at points where local resources and access to distant markets were available. Nanaimo, the first, was a colliery town on the coast, accessible to shipping. Across Georgia Strait and later, Britannia was a company town beside a concentrating mill, at the junction of two transportation systems: a tram bringing copper ore to the mill from mountainside mines, and ships loading concentrates. At Hedley in the Similkameen Valley, and at many other small hard-rock mining towns, the pattern was essentially the same. The closer the town to the resource base on which it depended, the more ephemeral it was likely to be. Phoenix, atop a copper mine in Boundary Country, became an open pit; Anyox, another copper town on the coast north of Prince Rupert, closed down with its mine. Sandon, a silver-lead town in the Kootenays, faded away as its small mines closed; Kaslo, on the other hand, a gateway to the Sandon mines via a narrow-gauge railway from Kootenay Lake, survived. Small developments that provided short-term employment remained as camps: perhaps an adit, rock dump, a few mine buildings, and bunkhouse accommodation for men high on a mountain. A logging railway might produce a sawmill town, like Chemainus, but logging alone produced camps, though the distinction between camp and small town was often blurred. The camps of the salmon fishery were seasonally occupied canneries, located close to the resource and accessible to steamers; at the mouth of the Fraser, enough canneries bunched together to create the small town of Steveston. In the few places with dispersed farming populations, as in the lower Fraser Valley, the Okanagan, and the Peace River, small towns emerged as rural service centres. Some towns combined several of these functions. All these different towns and camps were at advantageous locations in a new matrix of transportation and communication, which was a necessary condition for their existence.

Regional economies and land uses were also being reworked as distances declined and the reach of the international market expanded. Here, as elsewhere, the market's influence was to commodify land and specialize land use. Trees began to be calculated in board feet, salmon in the number of twenty-four-can packs. Clearcuts were products both of techniques of logging and hauling, and of the market's unrestricted access to forests. Various forest tenures gave clear title, the Natives were on reserves, and, apart from their discounted, largely inaudible voices, there was no interference from past or current populations with other agendas. The equation seemed greatly simplified: wilderness and market bound, as it were, by logging railways and donkey engines. Provincial land policies that allocated land for specialized purposes, such as forestry, mining, agriculture, provided institutional support for an international market economy that depended on the division of land and the functional integration of economic space as much as on the division of labour. In older societies, regional specializations tended to be imposed slowly in the face of a good deal of resistance from prior, more regionally self-sufficient economies. In British Columbia, however, such specializations were the abrupt accompaniment of the virtually simultaneous arrival of settlers, low-cost transportation, and the market. Ranching, logging, or mining quickly dominated particular regions; at various scales, heartland-hinterland relationships were quickly introduced. Economic specialization tended to create ecological simplifications, such as agriculture or, later, tree plantations. In these restructurings was a whole new geographical order of things – Deleuze and Guattari's reterritorialization. Compared to what had gone before, a thick layer of difference was imposed across the land.[44]

In short, introduced systems of transportation and communication incorporated British Columbia within the modernizing world, and created patterns of settlement and land use that bore many characteristic stamps of modernity. But modernity is itself a collection of shifting relationships, and relocation adjusted the complex of modern ways that reached British Columbia from the east. These adjustments were bound up with the particular flows of goods, people, and information into and within the province.

Most immigrant British Columbians could remain closely in touch with the places they had left. Letters and all manner of printed materials followed them, keeping them in close contact with distant families, prevailing opinion in home societies, and world news. Letters were particularly awaited and protracted correspondences, lifelines between distant

Settlements and transport. *Top*: Early 'shacks' at Prince Rupert, terminus of the Grand Trunk Pacific, c. 1912. A townsite created by a railway. *Bottom*: Pilot Bay smelter, Kootenay Lake. A silver-lead smelter with steamboat and railway access to the outside world.

worlds, were common. Newspapers and magazines were sent from home, and books not locally available were ordered. Mail order catalogues displayed current fashions and consumer goods, some of which were usually available in even the smallest dry goods stores. Few immigrants came to British Columbia to escape the modern world, and those few hardly could, for a modern communicative environment was at hand with a vast capacity to distribute information. At the same time, immigrant and home societies communicated with each other out of different contexts, which over the years diminished their capacity for mutual understanding. Daisy Phillips, prim, brave, and as unprepared as the British army officer-turned-orchardist she had recently married, lived surrounded by forest on a terrace clearing in the Windermere Valley in southeastern British Columbia, and corresponded with a mother and sister in a four-storey Georgian town house on High Street in Windsor, England. She knew their world but could not reproduce it, and they could only imagine hers. A Chinese coal miner living in the spare male accommodation of Nanaimo's Chinatown received a scribe-written letter from his wife in a peasant village near Canton: husband and wife living in vastly different settings thousands of miles apart. A pioneer woman learned about the latest domestic science at a local meeting of the Women's Institute, and returned to a log cabin with a water barrel in a corner. A colonial secretary, writing from Downing Street, communicated a theoretical experience of empire to officials in British Columbia, who somehow had to accommodate such theory to their sense of local realities. Texts, in short, travel more readily than contexts, and to the extent that both are required for communication, British Columbians were on their own. Most fundamentally, perhaps, British Columbia reproduced neither space nor time as they were commonly understood in Europe.

Colonization appeared to have simplified space. This was partly because immigrants considered that they had left the past behind, an assumption encouraged by their deeply implicit assumptions about the location of civilization, savagery, and plummeting Native numbers. To take the past out of space was to eliminate most of its human texture, an unimaginable subtraction even in a rapidly urbanizing, industrializing Britain, the heart of the modern world, but an obvious fact of immigrant life, apparently, in British Columbia. Moreover, immigrant activities tended to be spatially segregated by the uneven distribution of resources, and the specializing tendencies of the international market. One region was dominated by the equipment, work routines, logistics, and, after a time, the subculture of logging; another was similarly dominated by mining; another by ranching. Regions changed as resources were depleted and technologies and markets evolved; they variously overlapped, but large stretches of land tended to be dominated by a few particular strategies of resource extraction. The economy of British Columbia as a whole depended on a few resource industries, each with its characteristic, much-repeated human geography. Vancouver's metropolitan dominance was another form of spatial specialization, in this case around flows of goods and information. Simplified space was also partly the creation of people who wanted to avoid complexity, and relocated it when they could: by legislating reserves for Natives or by the constant pressure of racism that largely created Chinatowns and Japtowns.[45] As Edward Said has pointed out, people who are themselves dislocated and threatened by the unknown and the previously distant tend to fall back on their own basic texts; in the case of British Columbia, immigrants drew on beliefs about the superiority of European civilization and the inferior otherness of the rest of the world.[46] Essentially, a relocated, simplified version of loosely 'British' culture sought to contain the unfamiliar complexities of its new situation.

This textual agenda and associated spatial strategies, coupled with the denial of a local past, and the territorial specializations inherent in international market economies and supportive government policies, encouraged new, simplified constructions of space. Men worked in camps, enclaves of capital and labour largely abstracted from social contexts (other than ethnicity, itself an abstraction) and relocated in wilderness. Because there were often no other media, the lines of industrial transportation became those of social interaction. Men in mountainside bunkhouses rode the ore tramways to nights out in the bars below. Men leaving the coastal logging camps or canneries caught the steamer to Vancouver; there was nowhere else to go. The drab toil of a work camp, the bright lights of a city; the tough maleness of a work camp, the softer, civilized femaleness of home: simple spatial dichotomies within simple constructions of space. Much of the interior dry belt was quickly known as cattle country and recognized as such in provincial land policy, but the very speed of such homogeneous regional identifications is a measure of the lack of perceived alternatives. Even in Vancouver, rows of California bungalows emerged on the west side of the city, their occupants white, English-speaking, middle-class people who lived, as much as possible, within networks linking others of their kind in Vancouver and to home societies in eastern Canada or Britain. Modernizing British Columbia denied many of the novel elements of complexity within it.

And the province appears to have jumbled time: displacing it, destroying its linearity, mixing elements from the past like raisins in a pudding. There was little continuous British Columbian time, rather, essentially, a present and its future. The European past was relevant but distant; it contained the history of most people who came to British Columbia, but not of the place where they lived. Yet artefacts from this geographically displaced past crept in. Settlers built log cabins, dwellings not seen in western Europe south of Scandinavia since the medieval forests were cleared. Packhorse trails and railways intersected. Wherever transportation costs were high, local labour and pre-industrial technologies were viable alternatives to imported manufactures, as when Hawaiians pit-sawed lumber at Fort Langley, and the fort blacksmith made tools that, in Britain at the time, were factory-produced. In such ways, immigrants lived with introduced anachronisms. One, perhaps, was the ethnographers' quest for traditional

Native culture. I suspect that this was neither disinterested curiosity nor colonial appropriation, but a quest for the original uncivilized Europe. In this light, British Columbia appeared to contain the beginning and the current end of Europe, together with a few intervening artefacts.

Finally, the elimination of distance has been a primary tactic of power in modernizing British Columbia. Distance at first fended off the outside world, while the progressive conquest of distance allowed ever more of that outside world in. The conquest permitted government to extend its influence through most of the province, giving what initially was an abstract geopolitical space, British Columbia, concrete political meaning. It enabled capital to reach out to ever more land, exploit the land's resources, and then connect them to the world economy. It enabled immigrants to settle, knowing that they would be in touch with home and with many familiar ways. From a Native perspective, it ushered in a barrage of land appropriation and cultural change that could be resisted in various ways, but hardly stopped. The assault on distance was too pervasive, too central to the agendas of colonialism and modernity. A road might be blockaded here or there, but to hold off the changed relationship with space that was being forged in the modern world, and the new land uses and human geographies that accompanied it, was another matter altogether.

7
Industry and the Good Life around Idaho Peak

This essay was researched and written in the late 1970s and early 1980s, was published in the Canadian Historical Review *in 1985 (66, 3:325-43), and is reprinted here with permission. However, I must comment on my assertions that the Slocan Lake was not mapped before 1890 (endnote 4), and that no one had lived near Idaho Peak until the miners arrived.*

The Slocan Lake had largely dropped out of the consciousness of newcomers in the late 1860s, 1870s, and early 1880s when few if any Native people lived around it. There were no people to attract missionaries or traders. In the 1840s, when the valley was still inhabited and there were souls to save, the lake figured on a remarkable map of the northern Cordillera and plateau by Father Pierre-Jean De Smet, S.J.[1]

My proposition that no Native people had ever lived near Idaho Peak is absurd, and grows out of the common assumption, with which I grew up, that a mining rush had been superimposed on wilderness. James Teit, early ethnographer of the Interior Salish peoples, was better informed and wiser. Between 1904 and 1909, he interviewed elders of the Sinixt (Lake) people (whose ancestors had lived in the Columbia Valley between Revelstoke and the border, in the Slocan Valley, and around parts of Kootenay Lake), and drew up a list of twenty of their former winter village sites. Seven were in the Slocan Valley:

> 12. *SnkEmi'p ('base, root, or bottom,' with reference to the head of the lake). At upper end of Slocan Lake.*
> 13. *TakElexaitcEkst ('trout Ascend'? from ai'tcEkst, a variety of large trout). On Slocan Lake, below No. 12.*
> 14. *Sihwi'lEx. On the lower part of Slocan Lake.*
> 15. *Ka'tntca'k. On Slocan River, below the lake.*
> 16. *Nkweio'xten. On Slocan River, below No. 15.*
> 17. *SkEtu'kElôx. On Slocan River, below No. 16.*

> 18. *SntEkEli't.ku. Near the junction of Slocan and Kootenai Rivers. This was a noted salmon-fishing place. Salmon ran up the Slocan River, but could not ascend the Kootenai because of the great Bonnington Falls. Salmon were formerly plentiful throughout the Slocan district, and many people lived at all the villages.*[2]

Teit estimated that the Lake tribe 'must have numbered 2,000 or more. A conservative estimate of their 20 village communities in British Columbia, allowing an average of 50 person to each, would give 1,000; but this is probably a very low estimate, as some winter camps were credited with a population of from 100 to 200 people.' When Teit visited them, there were not many more than 300 people, almost all living on the Colville Reservation in Washington State:

> *According to all accounts, the decrease in the population of these tribes [the Okanagan and Sanpoil, the latter including the Lake] had been much greater, and began at an earlier date, than among the Shuswap and Thompson. About 1800 the Colville and Lake were decimated by smallpox, which reached the Sanpoil, but spared the Okanagan. About 1832 all the tribes were decimated by an epidemic, probably smallpox. The Okanagan suffered almost as severely as the others. It appears that the Shuswap and Thompson escaped all the epidemics until 1857 and 1862. The indians ascribe the great decrease in their numbers to these epidemics and, to a less extent, to other diseases brought by whites at a later date.*[3]

Pending a full analysis, which has not yet been made, I would revise this only slightly. The smallpox epidemic 'about 1800' was probably the epidemic of 1782; that of 1832 was probably measles in 1848. Smallpox in 1862, reaching an unvaccinated population, was probably the final straw. So much for age-old wilderness. The miners, like so many others in British Columbia, dropped into extraordinary demographic circumstances that they did not begin to understand.

Now, the original essay.

Capital and labour began to penetrate the recesses of Canadian space early in the sixteenth century and, in various forms, have continued to do so ever since. Settlements, most of them ephemeral, have suddenly appeared in the wilderness, their locations dependent on transportation technology and resource availability, their economies tied to distant markets, their populations migratory and largely male, and their rhythms of work and leisure bound to technologies of resource procurement. When modern British Columbia was being settled, the well-established pattern continued: first in association with the fur trades, then with the gold rushes, and, in the last decades of the nineteenth century, with fishing, logging, and hard-rock mining. All these activities relocated capital and labour close to new resources, far from markets, and, often, where no one had ever lived before.

In British Columbia, the late-nineteenth-century influx of capital and labour, accompanied by a pre-tested industrial technology, fuelled by largely unregulated speculation, and cushioned neither by agriculture nor the past, had a particular intensity. Camps, probably the most common form of settlement in the province, burst into existence, generated other settlements by their momentum, and then flickered and died, leaving a residue of people, settlements, and derelict landscapes. Such, generally, is the story of the Slocan Valley in the Kootenay district of southeastern British Columbia. In 1890, the valley was virtually unknown. Five years later, it was served by spur lines of two transcontinental railways, and by 1910, when a forest fire burned out many railway trestles and mine buildings, the Slocan Valley was already a quiet backwater in the wake of a mining boom. In the twenty years since the first discoveries, some 28 million ounces of silver and 200 million pounds of lead, with a gross value of nearly $30 million, had been shipped from the Slocan (Figure 7.1).

Lying between the deep valleys of Silverton Creek to the south and Carpenter Creek to the north, Idaho Peak rises 5,700 feet above Slocan Lake (Figure 7.2). In 1890, it was unnamed and almost unseen;[4] probably no Indians had ever lived nearby.[5] Prospectors were in the region, however, and in September 1891, a party ranging west from Kootenay Lake discovered high grade silver-lead ore on a ridge above Carpenter Creek.[6]

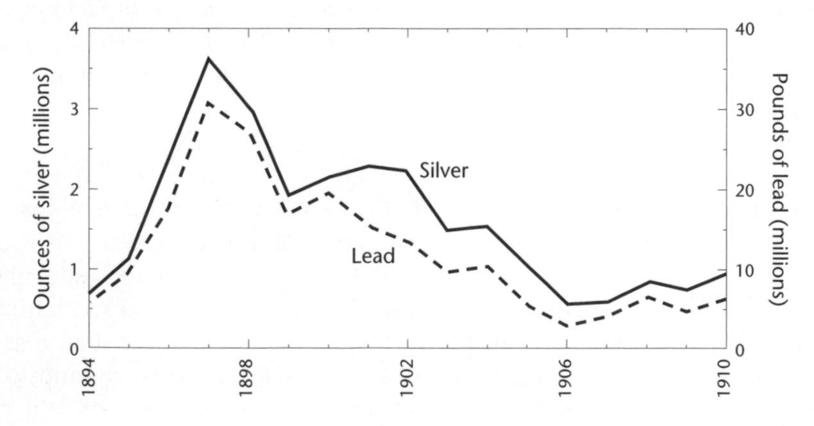

Figure 7.1 Silver and lead production in the Slocan, 1894-1910

Outcrops of such ore were fairly easily located, especially above the tree line, and initial development required little capital. News of discovery drew a rush of prospectors. Some 140 claims on or near Idaho Peak were recorded in the fall of 1891, and more than 3,000 were recorded in the Slocan Valley over the next five years, a patchwork tangle of claims superimposed on steep mountainsides. Most of the men who staked these claims were Americans, representatives of a cordilleran hard-rock mining complex that had evolved out of the Californian placer fields of the 1850s, through the Nevada Comstock of the 1860s and 1870s, and such base-metal camps as Eureka, Nevada, Leadville, Colorado, Butte, Montana, and the Coeur d'Alene, Idaho, in the 1880s.[7] The silver and lead discoveries in 1884-5 in the Coeur d'Alene, less than 200 miles away as the crow flies (Figure 7.3), were the Slocan's immediate antecedents. Ore bodies in the Coeur d'Alene were larger and lower grade than those in the Slocan, but the terrain was much the same, and with the Slocan discoveries a relevant mining system was at hand to create another base-metal camp in another wilderness valley. Coeur d'Alene square sets became the common timbering in Slocan mines; equipment designed in Chicago soon operated in Slocan mills; American vaudeville companies performed deep in the Selkirk Mountains in American union halls; and American miners exploded giant powder in kerosene tins to celebrate the fourth of July more boisterously than the first. On Slocan Lake, the delta townsites of New Denver and Silverton, their names from Colorado, backed into Idaho Peak.

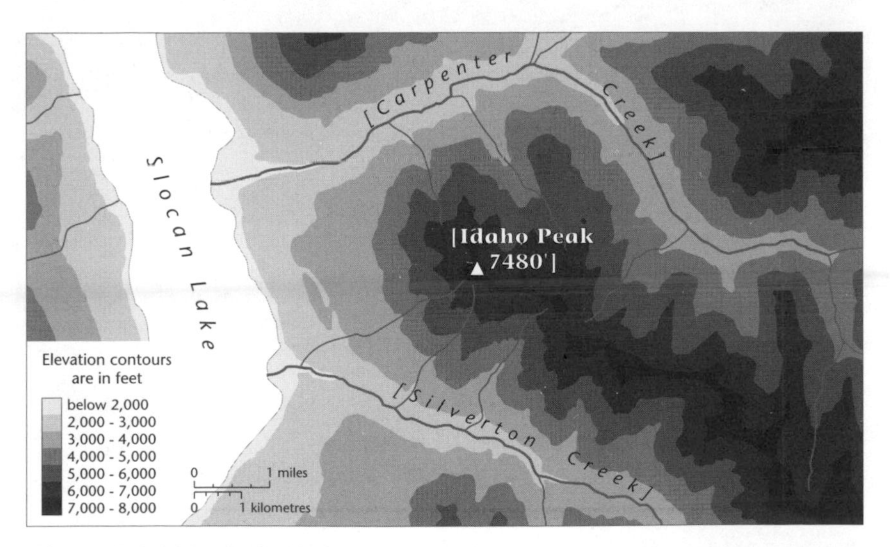

Figure 7.2 Idaho Peak, 1890

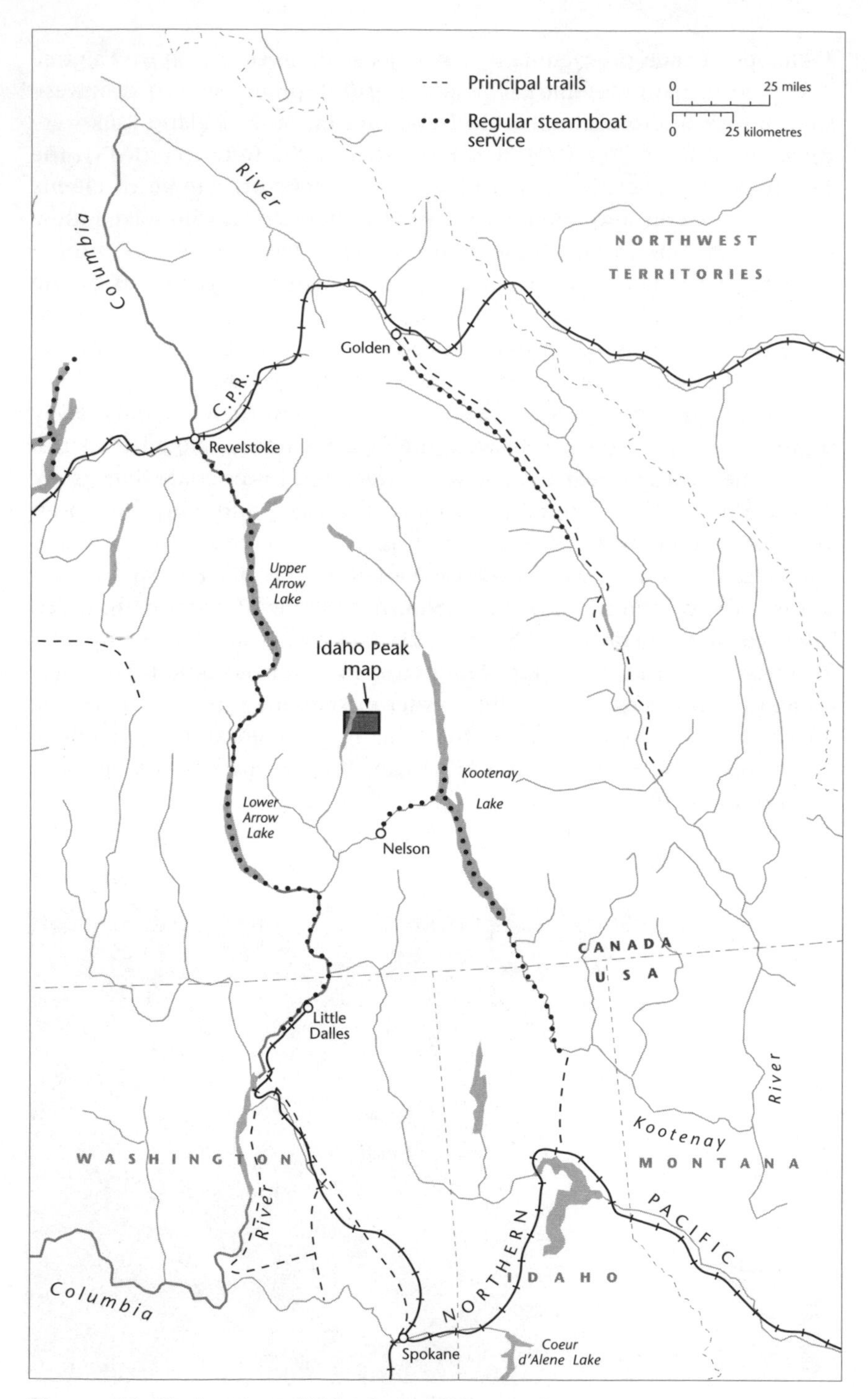

Figure 7.3 The location of Idaho Peak, 1890

The first workings were tiny – pick-and-shovel operations at high elevations – their rich, hand-picked ores[8] worked during three or four snow-free months and backpacked down preliminary trails. As surface showings gave out, adits went underground, the mouth of each marked by a dump, a new scar of loose rock on a mountainside. Eventually a large mine might have six or eight adits aligned up the slope and connected underground by shafts and stopes. Mountainside trails were soon widened to handle horse and mule trains in summer, rawhide trains in winter. A horse carried two 125-pound ore sacks, a mule three, but one horse could haul twelve to fifteen sacks wrapped in a raw hide, hair out, and two or three skinners could just handle a rawhide train of twenty horses – simple, gravity-dependent transportation for rich ores from high mines. Some mines put in wagon and sleigh roads. Before the end of the century, the large shippers depended on aerial tramways as much as two miles long, on which ore buckets descended from mine to mill and railway, often through the char of recent fires that, sometimes, prospectors had deliberately set.[9] The summer air was hazy with smoke.[10] Every winter and spring, avalanches pouring down newly bare slopes took some buildings and men with them.

From Idaho Peak, pack-horse trails were soon cut to reach sternwheelers on the Kootenay and Arrow lakes. Railways followed before the end of 1895: the Kaslo and Slocan, a narrow-gauge line from Kootenay Lake chartered and built by Vancouver businessmen with a federal cash subsidy and provincial land grant, and soon bought by the Great Northern;[11] and a Canadian Pacific Railway (CPR) spur line from the Arrow Lakes

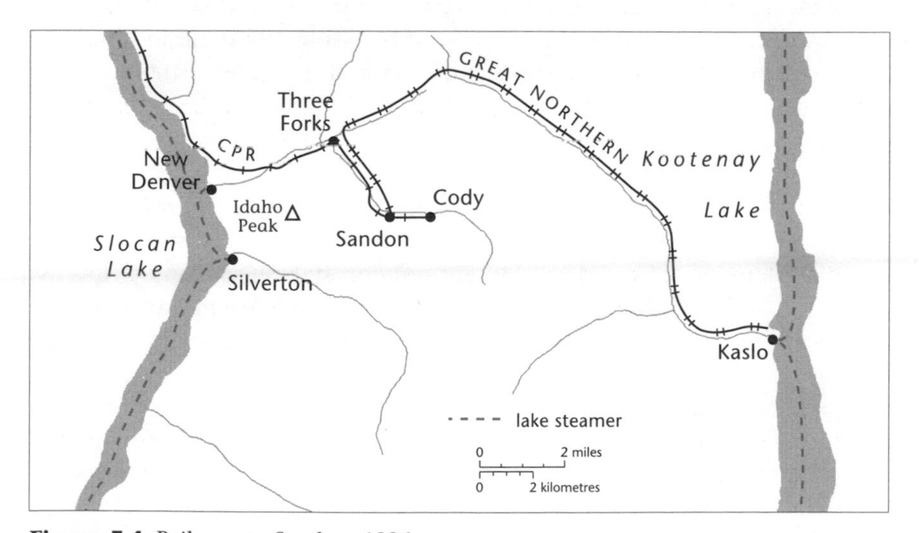

Figure 7.4 Railways to Sandon, 1896

(Figure 7.4). As soon as the railways were laid, concentrating mills could be built just above the tracks. They received ore from tramways on their up-slope side, passed it by gravity feed through the mill, and discharged concentrates into a railway car at the bottom. In a gulch near the head of Carpenter Creek, in the heart of the mineralized zone, the railways also developed the townsite of Sandon from a collection of cabins amid the stumps in the summer of 1895 to a town of some 2,000 people by 1897. Its main street, virtually its only possible street in a valley deep in the mountains, was adorned by bay windows, elaborate cornices, electric streetlights, and plank sidewalks. In 1897, more than 100 new buildings, costing almost $190,000,[12] were added to a mining town that was barely three years old. On the other side of Idaho Peak on the delta at the mouth of Silverton Creek, a smaller, less promoted, but essentially similar town (Silverton) served mines that could not be reached by the railways to Sandon.

New Denver, at the mouth of Carpenter Creek, developed as a small service centre for the mining region. Hotels, a bank, stores, and offices clustered near the wharf, the point of sternwheeler contact with the outside world. The townsite was laid out in a rectangular grid of street and small lots; with houses, picket fences, and gardens, its townscape was soon residential. Before long, a local-improvement committee supervised the planting of trees along the streets. On meagre benches behind New Denver and Silverton, a few men began to farm, intending to supply the local mines.

Thus, a human geography was suddenly imposed on Idaho Peak. A cordilleran mining boom set the primary patterns, but by the end of 1897 the most frantic boom years were over; the economy was becoming a little more diversified. People lived around the same mountain in different settlements and with different experiences and memories. The next section describes life in these settlements before World War 1, starting high on the mountain and working down.

The snow left high elevations in June or July, and returned three or four months later. At first, prospectors seized these months, camping in the 'hills.' Many were 'wildcatters,' intent only on staking as many claims as possible, and then finding a broker to buy them for a few hundred dollars apiece.[13] Others began some development work on their claims – cutting trails, 'proving' the 'ledge' – until driven off the mountain by snow. A man could lengthen his alpine working season by building a cabin, and cabins soon appeared, rudimentary, cross-notched, log structures perched on the mountainside. Later, companies built bunkhouses. Located with an eye to the avalanche hazard and as close as possible to the adit mouth, the larger bunkhouses were frame buildings for as many as forty to fifty men. Accommodation was minimal: a dormitory room or two lined with wooden bunks, each for two men (who supplied their own blankets and cut spruce boughs or grass for mattresses), a dining room,[14] poor reading light, and often no running water. By 1910, many companies provided wash and drying rooms. Miners paid one dollar a day for bunk and meals, and owners obtained year-round labour.

This high, mountainside world was male; there was no accommodation for women at the mines. Most of the miners were in their twenties or thirties; 45 per cent of the men treated in the Sandon Miners' Hospital from 1902 through 1904 were under thirty, but some were over fifty, a few over sixty.[15] In the early 1890s, most men came from the United States, but probably not more than one-third of them were native-born Americans. Many were Cornishmen (cousin Jacks), expert miners driven from closing Cornish mines, and many others were Irish. There were Scandinavians, Germans, and Italians; and perhaps 10 per cent of the miners who came into the Slocan from the United States had been born in eastern Canada.[16] As the years passed, this Canadian component of the work force increased. The commission appointed in 1899 by the federal government to investigate the charge that mine owners had imported alien labour during a strike concluded that about half the Slocan miners were British subjects;[17] a few years later, the majority was definitely eastern Canadian, mostly Nova Scotians and Prince Edward Islanders. In 1909-10, the number of Italians and Scandinavians increased sharply. Orientals were kept out. Should Chinese workers appear, white miners were more than ready 'to drive all the Chinks off the hill.' They struck mines that employed Chinese cooks. Acting like 'a real white man' and 'thinking white' were common expressions of approbation.[18]

Most miners worked for a company and under a foreman. Only prospectors, miners developing their own claims, and, from about 1905, a growing number of lessees of largely worked-out mines were self-employed. The working day was ten hours (at the rock face) until 1899, and eight hours thereafter.[19] When employed, miners worked seven days a week. Christmas and the 24th of May were the only holidays in the early years, later July 1st and Labour Day as well. But work was irregular. Mines opened and closed, men were taken on and laid off, and miners usually wanted to work seven days a week when they had work. Overall, 200 days was perhaps an average work year.[20] The work itself was rapidly mechanizing and, in the process, diminishing the skills of the expert miner,[21] though the small, rich ore-bodies in the Slocan were some protection against this change. As late as 1910, few mines around Idaho Peak were electrified or mechanically ventilated, and single and double jack drilling (with irons and sledge) were still fairly common. Steam hoists and pumps were less necessary where veins could be reached by horizontal adits and tunnels, along which ore cars could be pushed or hauled, and water drained. Yet power drills were increasingly used; with them, dust levels and the frequency of miners' consumption (silicosis) rose. A few miners quit when the new drills came in.[22] Underground work was always dangerous, especially as the new technology increased the depth and speed of operation and brought electricity into wet workplaces. Throughout the Cordillera, about one miner in eighty was killed underground each year.[23] In the Slocan, far more miners were crippled by accidents or rheumatism,[24] or were killed above ground by snowslides. These risks were known and accepted, part of a working life.

After a day's shift, there was rarely time or energy for the long, steep hike to town. Unless they could ride the ore buckets to the valley bottom and back, few bunkhouse men would attend the union meeting in Sandon on Wednesday night. In deep snow and with the threat of avalanches, miners might not get off the mountain for two or three months. Then a night in town was an escape, usually into the bars and brothels. Some miners attended vaudeville shows in the union hall in Sandon.[25] From time to time, the union held a dance. On Christmas Eve the mountain emptied, weather permitting, as men came down to Sandon; on the 24th of May, the 1st of July, and Labour Day in one or other of the Slocan towns, there would be horse and foot races, rock-drilling contests, baseball games, and a dance. Special trains brought the miners, and a lot of money would change hands, some of it going to professional athletes who competed incognito. These were big days in lives of work. Occasionally a letter came back to the union secretary from the bright light of a distant city: 'We were out last night all over the place and i tell you it makes a man feel bad to think he is living away his life in a lonely way like what we do up there.'[26]

Because jobs in the cordilleran hard-rock mines came and went, mining life was highly mobile. After weeks or months of daily work, a miner would quit or be laid off and come down to recuperate in Sandon or Silverton, living for a time in one of the miners' hotels. Unemployed men might hang around the Slocan, and then, if not taken on locally, head out looking for work in cordilleran mining camps from Alaska to New Mexico. Some wrote back to the union secretary in Sandon.[27] From Silverton: 'I am leaving Silverton today I dont know where I am going yet I may go up that way but I am not sure ... I will write you about it from wherever I go.' From Kaslo: 'I am going to the Cour dalenes Idaho and if I cant find anything there to stop fore I might take in Monte Cristo work. On way to Arisona.' From Seattle: 'I guess I can get along until spring when I Intend to go north or somewheres I havent made up my mind yet where it will be.' From Atlin in northwestern BC: 'I expected one time that i would be back in sandon this winter But not likely now as I am doing beeter than their.' From Tonopah, Nevada: 'I met a number of the Slocan boys here.' If they found work in a camp with a local of the same union, the Western Federation of Miners, they would write to Sandon for a transfer card; Figure 7.5 shows the location of these requests between 1902 and 1904 from miners who had recently worked near Sandon. Most came from Kootenay camps nearby, but many from far away as miners searching for work moved through a third of a continent.

Miners lived for a time on Idaho Peak because they had work there; few looked forward to bunkhouse life. Men from different backgrounds were thrown together in confined spaces; except at the evening meal, someone was always asleep. There was not much to do except work, sleep, play cards, and, sometimes, talk:

> They had a Bunkhouse here about the size of a piano box. Stowed in it were about 25 men.
>
> They put up a new dining room and kitchen and fixed up the old dining room for a bunkhouse. But even then there is no convenience to write home about. Old R.J. McPhee is a hard Shell. Hell, but he is mean. We have a cracker-jack of a cook and he puts up fine grub. When you say they feed you well you say it all. We are liable to be all frozen up some night. We have nothing but green jackpine for wood and an old stove that the Company picked up on some ash pile. Just now as I write the air is blue with the fellows swearing at the stove and fire ... Oh Hell. I will have to stop. John Holey has the floor on one side preaching Socialism and there are two Scots from Cape Breton hitting the Gaelic.[28]

There was pride, especially before the mines were mechanized, in being a good miner, and disdain for inexperienced newcomers, but men usually hoped to get into something else and a lot of them dreamed of marrying and settling down.

It would not be easy. Slocan miners earned $3.50 through the 1890s, then $3.95 after the compromise settlement of the strike of 1899, and soon $3.50 again for the remaining years before World War I – wages that were half again as high as those in the eastern coal mines.[29] In 1913, a conciliation board rejected union demands for a fifty cent raise on the ground that the $3.50 wage enabled a miner to support a family.[30] But it hardly did. If a man worked 200 days a year, he earned $700. Bunkhouse or hotel cost $1 a day. After the expenses of room, board, and travel, there was little more than $300 left, and some of this would go for clothing and, probably, were he married, for life insurance. Little could be sent to a family in Nova Scotia or Sweden. To bring a family into the Slocan was to face the uncertainty of employment and the high cost of living in

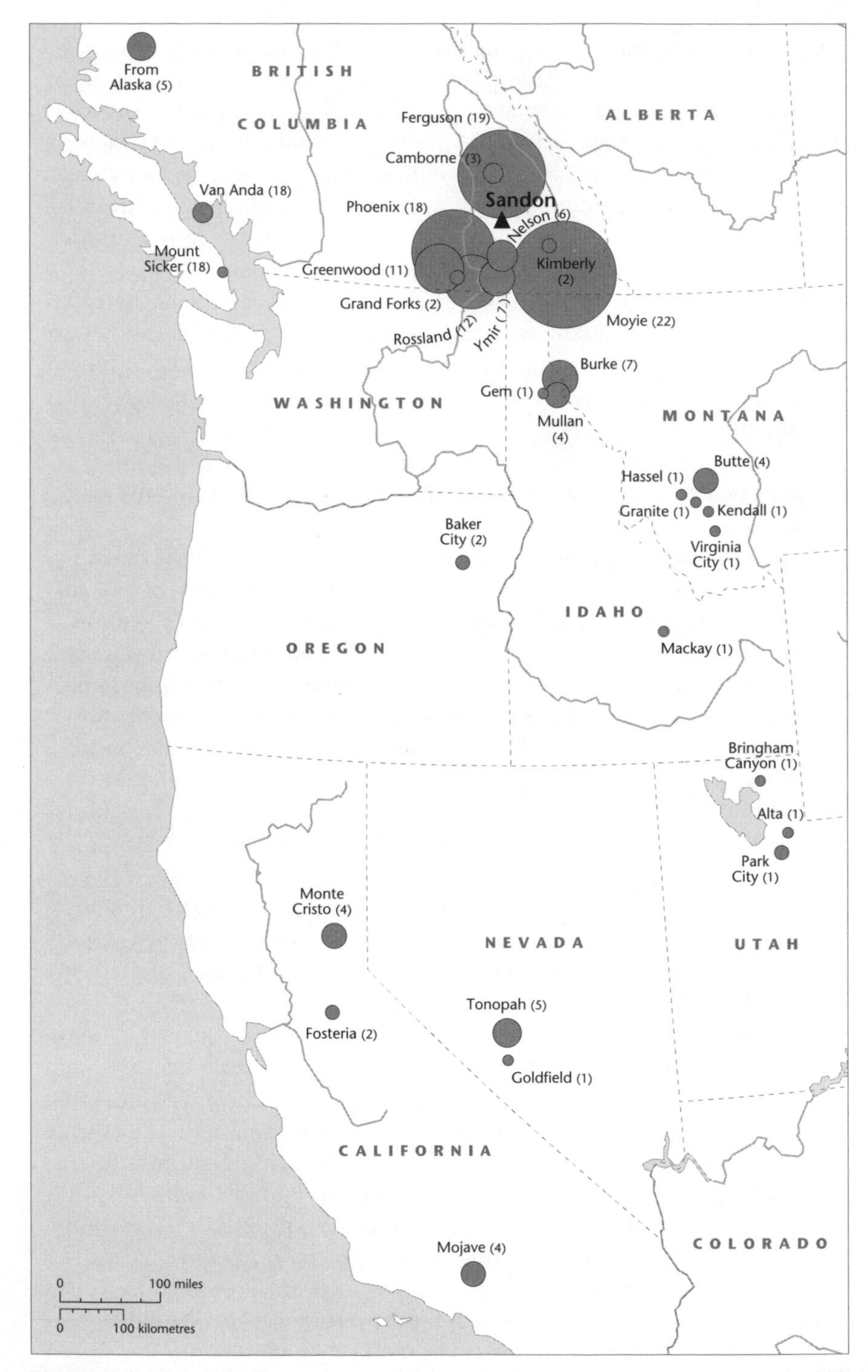

Figure 7.5 Location of requests for transfer cards from the Sandon Local, WFM, 1902-4

a mining camp. To marry in the West, a miner needed some savings so that he could set up his wife and children in some western town while he worked in different camps, or he could work at a large mine where he could expect steady employment and a life underground. Claiming a cost of living twice that in southern Ontario and 25 per cent higher than in the American camps, the union argued that a family of three needed $1,000 per annum.[31] Indeed, hard-rock mining in the western camps and married life were barely compatible. Probably no more than one-fifth of the miners in the Slocan before World War I were married, and most of these married men sent money to families elsewhere. Once a man was embarked on a life in the western hard-rock mines, potential wives were hard to meet, and marriage was an expense that could scarcely be borne. Some miners spent next to nothing, though in the arduous, lonely life of the camps, temptations to spend were enormous – bars and brothels compensated for absent families. After years of underground work, many miners had few more personal effects than a young Prince Edward Islander, killed on Idaho Peak in 1902, who left $11.80, a suit of clothes, two Bibles, a bundle of laundry, and a pocket book.[32] Unless extraordinarily frugal and robust, they would likely end their working lives with paltry savings and broken health. Such men would drift to a skid row in a western city, live on a tiny union collection in a cheap room in the dry belt where the air was thought to alleviate miners' consumption,[33] or perhaps spend their last years in a shack somewhere at the foot of Idaho Peak.

The early concentrating mills in the valleys below the mines were small[34] and employed a small fraction of the men in the mines above. They created a cluster of buildings – the mill itself, a company office, a blacksmith shop, a stable, perhaps a house for a manager and his family, and perhaps a bunkhouse – but none of the early mills around Idaho Peak was itself large enough to generate a town. Rather, townsites served many mills and mines. In 1894, the tent town of Three Forks was the temporary railhead; by the end of 1895, it had been eclipsed by Sandon, three miles farther up Carpenter Creek.

The following illustrations show part of Sandon in 1897 at the peak of the boom. The three-year-old town provided accommodation, retailing, and services for almost 4,000 people in the upper valley of Carpenter Creek. By mid-June 1897, there were seventeen hotels, some fifty stores and shops (including three jewellers, two millinery shops, and a news agency), eight offices (law, medicine, assay, insurance, and brokerage), a sawmill, a sash and door factory, a brewery, and two newspapers.[35] The Methodist church arrived later that year. In 1900, Sandon burned to the ground and was rebuilt, more modestly and with more order, along a main street over a wooden flume carrying Carpenter Creek.

The main street of Sandon, c. 1897. An instant town following a western American model.

Rebuilding Sandon after the fire, 1900. In front of the new commercial blocks, the flume for Carpenter Creek, the top of which became the main street; immediately behind the blocks, the CPR; middle-distance centre, a concentrating mill.

Sandon was predominantly but not exclusively male. A few miners and most of the shopkeepers brought families with them; there were also the women in the red-light district at the edge of town. Socially Sandon was stratified and differentiated, comprising owners and managers, a middle class, and workers. Among the working men, miners were the largest and most identifiable group. Some of them visited Sandon irregularly from the bunkhouse world above. Many others lived in Sandon in cheap hotels or boarding houses where a dollar a day provided room, board, and two glasses of whisky. A few lived with their families in tiny houses. Their bosses, the owners and managers in Sandon, usually stayed in the Reco Hotel, Sandon's best, surrounded by a measure of end-of-the-century pomp. They belonged, while it lasted, to the Sandon Club, which provided billiards, stuffed chairs, plush carpets, a selection of fine cigars, and 'the best newspapers and magazines in the English-speaking world' for a membership of seventy-five.[36] The middle class, 'citizens' in their own eyes,[37] tended to be church-going, house-and-family-centred people. After the first years when most were American, they came out of the main currents of migration that were settling British Columbia at the end of the nineteenth century: eastern Canadians from Ontario and the Maritimes, English, Scots, and Irish, only a few Americans, and a few others from the continent. They brought families and came to stay. During the long strike over the eight-hour day in 1899-1900, when most miners left to find other jobs and some owners were promoting their mines in Spokane or New York, the merchants and hotel keepers remained and suffered, tied to their inventories. Later, when Sandon was clearly declining, they trickled away, usually to another Kootenay town or to the coast.[38] The boundaries between these groups were not rigid, but nor were they easily crossed. Only a few prospectors at the beginning of the Slocan rush struck it rich. Miners did not easily get out of mining, not, at least, in the Slocan valley.[39] Some merchants who grub-staked prospectors became owners of small mining properties, and some mine owners also were land speculators and hotelmen.[40] Some owners made and lost two or three fortunes. For those who stayed, mobility was generally downward; Sandon, like other fading mining towns, contained its share of those who had not sold and lived on belief in the camp's future.

But in its heyday, Sandon was a focus of speculative mining capital and was tied by networks of brokerage and deals of every sort to money markets in Spokane, Denver, and New York, and later in Vancouver, eastern Canada, and England. For the most part, the mines around Sandon attracted relatively small-scale speculative capital bent on quick returns. Mines were highgraded (stripped of their best ore) with as little development work as possible; it was only after about 1905 that some companies began expensive, and usually unprofitable, long-term development. The larger the company, the less likely its head office and president would be in Sandon. None of the mansions built by profits from the surrounding mines was there. Whether resident or not, owners and managers were well aware of their own interests. Facing labour strife and, in their eyes, unwarranted government legislation, in April 1899 they organized a Silver Lead Mines Association of BC, based in Sandon, open only to mine owners and managers and dedicated to the promotion of mining, which, in their view, meant the protection of mining capital.[41] With other mining associations, they petitioned against the Inspection of Metaliferous Mines Act of 1899, the Master and Servant Amendment Act, and the Eight Hour Law, all of which they considered to interfere with freedom in the workplace.[42] They considered the Western Federation of Miners a federation of 'Dynamiters and Murderers,' and received reports from detective agencies employed by American Mine Owners' Associations to infiltrate this union. They received lists of all men who had worked in American camps during labour 'riots.'[43] Presumably they also employed the agent of the Thiel Detective Service Co. of St. Louis, Missouri, who for several months towards the end of the long eight-hour strike was in several Kootenay mining towns, including Sandon and Silverton.[44] The union was an enemy to be broken. 'The principle of freedom of contract' was held to be 'the birthright of every British subject'; mine owners bound themselves 'to use every legal effort to obtain legislation rescinding the present Eight Hour Law, and maintaining the right of free labour.'[45]

Three doors from the Reco Hotel, along the main street built over Carpenter Creek, was the Union Hall of Local 81 of the Western Federation of Miners (WFM). Organized in Butte, Montana, in 1892, and perhaps the most militant union in the United States,[46] the WFM had over 200 locals in western mining camps by 1901, five of them in the Slocan. The Sandon local was organized in March 1899, and in June it struck the mines to uphold the $3.50 wage in the face of the owners' offer of $3.00 for the eight-hour day. For nine months, until a compromise settlement was reached, it ran a well-managed, law-abiding strike (the royal commissioner sent by Ottawa to investigate the charge that the owners were importing alien labour found the camp as calm 'as the old, settled parts of Ontario'[47]) in an atmosphere charged by recent violence in American camps[48] and by the conflicting ideologies of union and owners. Union leaders advocated public ownership and embraced a millennial vision of the 'co-operative commonwealth.' With the churches – indeed, church and union were not nearly as different, except in clientele, as they thought themselves to be – they sounded another note in the materialistic environment of a mining camp.[49] But after the eight-hour strike, with prices low and production falling, the union had little economic leverage. Radical economic change was a distant goal, and it became, essentially, a beneficent organization working to improve miners' working conditions and self-respect. It tried to give lonely men some social support: the regular Wednesday night meeting, the shows in the 320-seat union hall, the dances, the friendship of a union secretary.[50] It buried the dead, sought out distant relatives to return effects, fought compensation cases, and tended the union graves in the Sandon cemetery. It organized collections for invalid miners and their dependents. In 1899 it established a cooperative miners' hospital in Sandon, rebuilt it after the fire of 1900, and maintained it for the next thirty years largely on the miners' hospital dues of one dollar a month.[51] Throughout, the WFM tried to emphasize that union membership embodied a commitment to a principle of fellowship, and encouraged members to consider recruits in this light: '... he would not wish to join here if he saw a passable show of holding his job. He evidently dont show himself possessed of that principle which should be contained in a good union man, and for the benefit of our organization such men should be kept out.'[52]

But the principle of fellowship was hard to maintain among men from different backgrounds moving from camp to camp, united primarily by the terms and conditions of work, and, perhaps, infiltrated by company spies. The union tried to screen its members: 'thiss Richard Olson has gust come out from the old country a short time ago i think He as allright and thiss Gorge McDonald is the fellow thay call Black Gorge the fidlar and those two Campbell are yong felloes not long out from N.S. i think thay are all right ...'[53] Stressing the brotherhood of labour, the WFM tried to break down barriers of ethnicity and language, but always had difficulty attracting non-English-speaking labourers, a difficulty the companies exploited.[54] If miners had some sense of collective identity as miners and as members of a working class, the bond between the 'boys,' as they called themselves, and the cooperative commonwealth was an abstract, conceptual step that few would take. Their dreams had less to do with social reconstruction than with self-interest, and even a union assessment to support an injured miner could elicit sharp reactions:

> i was very much supries to note another assesment as I was under the Impreshing that two asesment a year Was all that thare Was a Loud in any one year ... I cannot aford to Put up so Much money for all the Benefit I am geting out of it so I think our Leaders should look in to this Bee faure it is to late fore in the nex year thars is going to be More Truble in the W.F.M. than thare has Ever Ben sen it oregnation and thare is another thing Wich To draw you atention to is the agetaters in are Ranks tha should be surpres More then wat tha are at the Present.[55]

By 1910 the boom was long over, and Sandon was a quiet mining camp of about 400 people. Three-quarters of its workforce were miners, and everyone depended directly or indirectly on the miners. Although zinc ore, of which there was a good deal in the Slocan, was beginning to be marketable, most of the mines around Sandon were worked out and closed. Several long adits intended to tap veins at depth had failed. The Kaslo and Slocan Railway was burned out by a forest fire and not rebuilt. The Sandon Club had long since closed. Briefly the focus of North American mining excitement in the mid-1890s, Sandon was fading away fifteen years later. Revived during World War I, it was a ghost town by the 1930s.

The fate of New Denver, a village on Slocan Lake at the mouth of Carpenter Creek, was somewhat different. One of the portals to the mineralized belt, New Denver was a service centre for the mines, not a mining camp. In 1900, there were only about twenty miners among the 500 or so people living there.[56] Although, later, the percentage was a little higher, for the most part New Denver provided employment for tradesmen, shop and hotel keepers, clerks, agents, and casual labourers. Yet its economic base was only one more step removed from the mines than Sandon's. Orchard promotions near New Denver after 1905 produced a flurry of excitement, but few orchards. Tiny logging and sawmill operations around Slocan Lake served a local market. Before World War I, there was no alternative export economy; New Denver's service economy boomed with the mines, then limped along. The residential attraction of land beside a mountain-rimmed lake was balanced by the underlying weakness of the economy.

Like Sandon, New Denver participated in the flow and ebb of a mining rush, but more people stuck. Ministers, bankers, CPR agents, mining promoters and engineers, and miners were particularly likely to come and go; but many people settled down, raised their families, and lived out their lives: 41 of the 114 people listed in the 1910 directory had been there in 1901, 12 had been there in 1894, and 36 would remain in 1921.[57] Although most of the first arrivals were Americans, as in Sandon the population was soon predominantly eastern Canadian and British; by 1910 people in New Denver of American birth were rare.[58] The common unit of settlement was the nuclear family; demographically the population was fairly balanced. Many New Denverites had come to or with relatives, and as time passed and people married, families became increasingly interconnected. Many children growing up in New Denver before 1914 had an aunt or uncle there. They knew everyone in town and considered many people old-timers. New Denver had assumed a past and, considering that past, a considerable residential stability.

Figure 7.6 shows the distribution of households in New Denver just before the beginning of World War I.[59] Superimposed on the ambitious

New Denver on Slocan Lake, 1900. New Denver was a portal to the mining district; Sandon, on the other side of Idaho Peak, was in a mountain gulch, and most of the mines were in the 'hills'

cadastral plan of the early 1890s was a scattered village. The main street, launched optimistically in 1893 with the elaborate New Market Hotel and the Bank of Montreal, had not developed much beyond an unostentatious block of frame commercial buildings. Some streets were lined with trees and sidewalks, gardens were usually fenced and tended, houses were painted, and porches were embellished with bits of gingerbread. Although the rough pioneer landscape was already some years behind, there was no visible wealth; the most impressive houses were frame two-storey buildings, gable end and porch to the street, a common end-of-the-century style throughout western North America. Most people just got by, the economic gradient was neither very steep nor very long, and no one in New Denver employed more than three or four other New Denverites. Nor was there much residential segregation; the village was not large enough. People of different ethnic backgrounds were scattered through a population that was predominantly British in origin. A French Canadian was married to a Swede; another Swede ran the St. James Hotel. A German with an American wife owned the butcher shop and looked after an elderly, broke Brazilian. An Italian household that spoke Italian, played bocci, and, at first, stayed well away from the English-speaking provided board for recent immigrants who worked in the mines. A family of Chinese launderers worked hard and kept as low a profile as possible, but their boy went to the public school. Beyond the predominant Anglo-Saxon population, there was no ethnic critical mass to resist assimilation.

The nearest city, Nelson, was a day away by lake steamer and train. Most New Denverites did not make this trip from one year to the next.

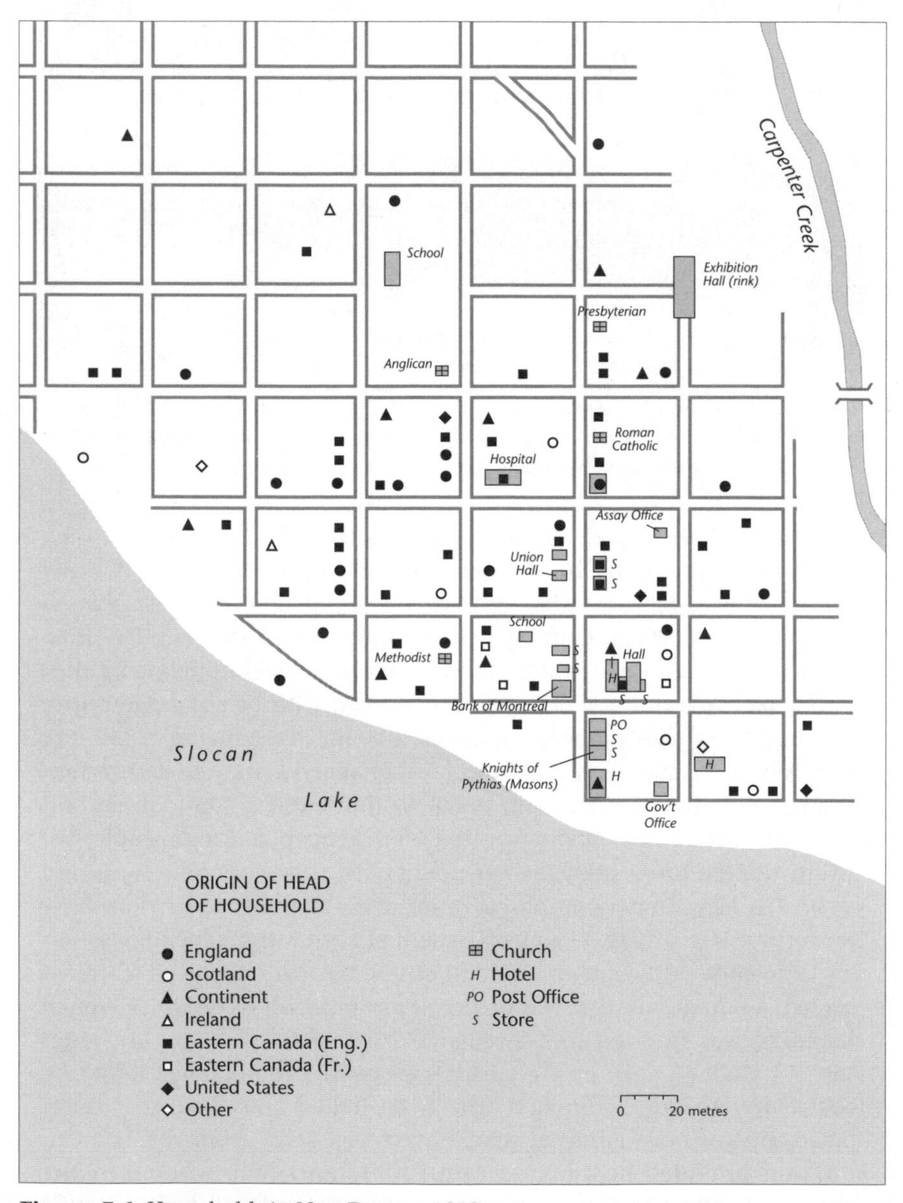

Figure 7.6 Households in New Denver, 1913

The village had an elementary school, post office, hospital, and basic stores. Small congregations of Anglicans, Methodists, Presbyterians, and Roman Catholics created their Sunday schools and social activities. Merchants belonged to the board of trade and the Masons, whereas working men tended to join the Knights of Pythias. A New Denver Brass Band, organized in 1895, usually had about twenty members.[60] The New Denver Improvement Society built sidewalks, planted trees, and laid out a trail to the glacier across Slocan Lake. There was a rifle and a launch club (there were some twenty small inboard launches on Slocan Lake), and baseball, football, and hockey teams. A skating rink was built with a small grant from the provincial government for an agricultural hall, and a gazebo bandstand stood near the lake.

Some of the people who lived in New Denver were outside the community. The black American madame of a brothel tucked away near Carpenter Creek was not acceptable on two counts. Nor, although prejudice was less than among the miners, were Chinese or, for a time, Italians. The French Canadian drayman, Swedish hotelman, and German butcher, however, were well accepted. Orangeism came to New Denver with the Ontarians, but quickly faded; at most there was some implicit bias towards Anglo-Saxon Protestants, the bulk of the population.

Within this group and some distance beyond it, the social gradient was diffuse. As individual backgrounds were not collectively known, social standing was not associated with family name. Nor, as business flagged after 1900, was it closely defined by the economy. No one in New Denver was making much money. Yet the bank manager was a person of some eminence, as were some of the owners or managers of small mines. Merchants and miners perceived their social standing less differently than in Sandon because more of the miners in New Denver were family men and because, after the boom years, the incomes of both were low. The prominence of the doctor and of the ministers in their respective congregations was institutionally defined. Personality influenced social standing in inverse proportion to the weakness of tradition and economy. Some people were liked, others were not. Some participated in the community, others did not. The druggist, who came from Ontario, was a stalwart of the Presbyterian church, a member of the Masons and Knights of Pythias, president of the launch club, active in the rifle club and the New Denver Improvement Society, and, for a term, a Liberal member of the provincial legislature. The little money he made went to the Presbyterian church. No more prosperous but another leading citizen was the Scottish dry-goods merchant, who was secretary of the Masons for thirty years, an elder of the Presbyterian church, and a justice of the peace.

Surviving in the background of life in New Denver was an English code of gentlemanly behaviour. Of the three private tennis courts in the village, one belonged to the bank manager and the others to English families with a little English money. Such people held tennis parties and took young people on climbs to the glaciers. The keenest alpinist in the Slocan, an Englishman with a good public school education, lived on a benchland farm a mile north of New Denver, grew alpine flowers in his rock garden, and exchanged seeds with Kew Garden in London. On a bench south of New Denver, another Englishman, son of a Wiltshire industrialist, cleared a farm, planted an orchard, and built the largest house on the flanks of Idaho Peak. A Fabian socialist, he ran as an independent in the provincial election of 1909, advocating a closed Sunday, a tax on undeveloped mining properties (after Henry George), and the nationalization of forests. Such views had no local constituency; they annoyed miners (who wanted Sunday work), mining promoters (who opposed any mining taxation), and merchants (who suspected socialist schemes), and he received few votes.[61]

New Denver and Sandon voted very differently. In 1904, when Sandon gave sixty votes to a socialist and fifty-one votes to Liberal and Conservative candidates combined, New Denver had only four socialist votes against fifty-two for the conventional parties.[62] They were different places, the one a mining camp, the other, essentially, a residential village. All adults in New Denver lived with memories of other places, but New Denver itself had many attractions. A house and considerable garden were available far more cheaply than in a British or Canadian city, home for a family. There was a community of known people, if not the people of one's youth, many familiar institutions of life, and magnificent scenery. Some New Denverites worked endlessly to try to make a reasonable living in a place with a weak and declining economic base. Others did little enough, relying, perhaps, on some money from elsewhere and on odd jobs, just enough to get along. From the vantage point of the hotels and rooming houses in Sandon or the bunkhouses on the mountainsides above, it was another world, and the maudlin comments it sometimes elicited touched a sensitive nerve: 'the scene at New Denver is of the greatest charm ... It is hard to tear away from the place, and go back to bare rocks, rushing water, and burnt black stumps ... New Denver is one of those rare spots created by nature, and endowed with all that is good for ideal home making.'[63] Developed by the mines, New Denver was also a haven from them, indeed from the industrial system. As the mines closed, New Denver lingered on, a place to live but not to prosper. In 1910, it had almost as many people as Sandon, and when Sandon was a ghost town, there were still families and gardens in New Denver.

Much of what happened around Idaho Peak had been anticipated, not only in the American Cordillera, but long before when European capital and labour first penetrated North American middle latitudes. The sixteenth-century Basque whaling stations on the Labrador Coast, the shore installations of the migratory dry fisheries in the seventeenth and eighteenth centuries, and the fur posts on Hudson Bay and in the hinterland of the St. Lawrence, like the mines on Idaho Peak, were temporary, male workplaces in wilderness.[64] All were connected by lines of credit to distant sources of capital, and by ties of family and culture to distant sources of labour. All were dominated by specialized economies and techniques, and by the transportation problem. All were vulnerable to international fluctuations in price and to local depletion of stocks. Often there was no alternative employment. When whales were hunted out off bleak shores, fur bearers trapped out from areas of granite and muskeg, pine cut from sandy soils, or mines worked out on Idaho Peak, workplaces were abandoned. Perhaps there were regional, if not local, multipliers. Staple trades would encourage urban growth, initially nearer the source of capital than the resource, but eventually at points of regional accumulation. The closer the nucleation to the resource, the more vulnerable it would be.[65] Sandon was too close to the mines and too dependent on them to survive when they closed. New Denver soon had no region to serve, and lapsed into a residential village.

But the lifelines from the mines ran to cities farther away, as had those of the earliest fisheries. Staple trades brought out people who, here and there, spied alternative economic opportunities – and almost inevitably struggled to make commercial connections in new settings far from markets. Such was the case of the Acadians around the Bay of Fundy, where tidal marshes provided an agricultural alternative to both fur trade and fishery; or of habitants along the lower St. Lawrence, who raised crops and livestock that, for many years, shipping costs excluded from external markets. These settings admitted families and discouraged commerce as, eventually, did New Denver.[66]

Staple trades, as Harold Innis insisted, were the initial, and long the most vigorous, motors of the Canadian economy.[67] In all of them, specialized strategies of resource extraction were abruptly superimposed on uninhabited or sparsely inhabited land. Because the strategies were different in each staple trade, each created characteristic spatial patterns, settlements, and landscapes; but all removed the buffers of tradition and custom that in older societies tended to moderate the relationship between capital and labour. In these trades, wages were free labour's common return from the resources of a new land. Men worked under a foreman in isolated workplaces where tasks were specialized and standardized.[68] Social relations were sharply, often brutally, hierarchical. Labour was detached from its social context; only at the end of the nineteenth century would unions attempt to interpose between employer and employee. Long before the mechanized factory, the staple trades separated place of work from place of residence – not by a walk through the brick streets of an industrial city, but often by a seasonal migration of hundreds or thousands of miles.[69] In the western hard-rock mines, the separation was such that place of residence, and with it family and home, often disappeared, and life became a bachelor journey through a succession of mining camps.[70]

The weak commercial economies that developed around the edge, as it were, of staple trades in settings where people could live but not participate vigorously in an export economy often outlived their staple-trade progenitors. In the long run, these economies, which Innis hardly considered, nurtured much of the early Canadian population. The societies associated with them were relatively detached from local and external capital, and also, in new settings, from traditional, landed power. If the staple trades abstracted capital, specialized technique, and labour from former contexts, these societies abstracted the sentiment of the family and relatively subsistent economies. They tended to turn around their own internal momentum, and their social range was not very great. For all the boosterism of the early years, by 1910 New Denver was quickly slipping into a truncated, early-twentieth-century version of this pattern. In an earlier Canada, such economies depended on mixed farming, but Idaho Peak, like most of British Columbia, barely permitted this option. Although some people in New Denver depended directly on the mines, most lived on the modest trade of a declining service economy, on institutional employment (school, post office, hospital, churches), and on odd jobs – just enough employment to open a niche somewhat apart from a staple trade. With neither space nor time to expand, this niche was filled by a village that soon exported most of its young. Over the years, lives were being reassembled in Canada in settlements somewhat like those around Idaho Peak. The community of memory and custom that underlay societies where people had lived together for many generations was absent. Rather, the process of migration had extracted relatively mobile components of such communities – particularly individuals and nuclear families – and new settlements had juxtaposed people of different background in, often, highly specialized work environments.

In the mines, as in all staple trades, technique tended to override culture. From outside, the men were miners; even from inside, common work, a measure of common interest, and friendship soon cut across cultural backgrounds, if not as quickly or as completely as the union would have wished. Although men of similar ethnicity congregated when they could, sometimes providing most of the labour at a given mine, little of the larger culture from which they had come was at hand. Ethnicity as an implicit way of life was being succeeded by work.

Languages other than English (or various dialects of English) would survive for a time if there were enough men to speak them. National days would be boisterously observed, and a man's sense of his own ethnicity would tend to become explicit. But the context of life was not established by ethnicity: men worked in the mines, slept in company-built bunkhouses, ate food prepared by a cook, cursed bosses, and drifted through much of a continent looking for jobs. In such circumstances, ethnicity became increasingly symbolic, an identification rather than a way of life, and eventually expressed by a few essential markers – to the point, around Idaho Peak, where 'whiteness,' a concept that overrode all the local texture of ethnicity, could become the essential criterion of acceptability.

In places like New Denver, where families settled down, there was more opportunity for cultural replication, but even there, different backgrounds were not reproduced and assimilation was rapid. Detached minorities had no cultural support. English-speaking people of British background, the majority, came from many different regional traditions in the British Isles and eastern North America, none of which could be sustained in a small, new settlement dependent on a different economic base and composed of diverse people. Everyone left a good deal behind; details, but never the whole composition, of former cultures survived (see Chapter 9). In New Denver, as elsewhere, selection reflected the requirements and limitations of the economy and the prevailing background of immigrants. Had there been time for generations to pass and relatively contiguous space for expansion, as often there had been in eastern North America, the new mixture could well have expanded into a regional, North American culture.

Around Idaho Peak, there was neither time nor space. Settlement began in 1891, soon ran out of resources, and had nowhere nearby to go. On a continental scale, it was insignificant. But Idaho Peak was a patch of New World wilderness that, like many another, was suddenly penetrated by capital and labour, and it has something to say about the process. It reveals the characteristic stamp of cordilleran mining camps and, more broadly, of staple trades in wilderness. It provides examples of the sequestered economies that often emerged, somewhat inadvertently, in their train. These two basic constituents of the economic geography of early Canada were frames within which a good deal of the country's demographic, social, and ethnic character evolved. In the East they were often separated. Around Idaho Peak they converged, creating the close juxtapositions of different backgrounds and experiences that so complicate regional and class definition in British Columbia, and impart such shrillness to the province's political debate. Idaho Peak concentrated two basic New World economies, within one or the other of which a great many early Canadians assembled the detached elements of Old World lives. More than fifty years ago, Innis identified part of the pattern, and I suspect that his essential ideas about early Canada are more expandable than the last generation of Canadian studies has conceded.

8
Farming and Rural Life
with David Demeritt

Except for a little tobacco grown on the Queen Charlotte Islands, agriculture was not a pre-contact relationship with nature in British Columbia. In the interior, where dry uplands were burned regularly to encourage edible roots and berries, and in places along the coast where camas bulbs (*Camassia quamash*) and *wapato* (Indian potato, *Sagittaria latifolia*) were dug, Native life took on some proto-agricultural characteristics, but it was never associated with owned, fenced land and the reduced ecological diversity of cropped fields. Later, missionaries and government officials tried, with varying degrees of success, to fix Natives in year-round settlements, and turn Native economies from fishing, hunting, and gathering – what, derisively, John Locke called living off the 'spontaneous hand of nature' – to farming.[1] Farming, they thought, would 'improve' nature and replace idleness with regular work. Europeanized landscapes comprising small log barns, fences, cropped and irrigated fields, and, here and there, orchards appeared on some reserves.

For the most part, however, farming was an immigrant activity in British Columbia. It placed a new regime of property on the land, as well as families that intended to stay. Much more than an economy, it was a way of life centred, usually, on the nuclear family and the idea of family-centred independence. In a new place, it appeared to present an opportunity, denied elsewhere, to get ahead, and a context for social reproduction. Publicly and privately, agriculture introduced a vision of the future that was anchored to long pasts in distant places; as vision, it embodied some of an immigrant society's most essential values. It also introduced assumptions about nature and the ordering of space and time that most immigrants took for granted, but that were relatively new in British Columbia. As a result, farm landscapes were expressions of introduced cultural and ecological arrangements, and were drastic departures from indigenous pasts. In a sense agriculture was a culmination of processes of imperialism and colonialism that began with the first explorers, continued through the fur trade years, and reached a conclusion when ordinary people came into the province, took up land, made it into farms, and considered them home.

Compared to prior Native land uses, these farms focused labour on small amounts of land. Gathering plants was much less labour intensive than planting, weeding, and harvesting them, but required much more land. Whereas Native peoples moved themselves from one ecosystem to another as resources became seasonally available, farmers operating from relatively fixed locations exchanged commodities in a market economy and, within their plots of land, allocated land uses in response, roughly, to the relative costs of land, labour, and capital. The result, compared to Native practice, was intensive, specialized land use that reduced biological diversity and increased particular outputs. Essentially, farming traded the larger grains, sweeter fruits, and higher yields of domesticated plants for the work of cultivating them. Such cultivation, together with the restricted grazing of animals, led to problems of soil erosion and exhaustion that were counteracted by manually circulating nutrients (fertilizers) that had once circulated much more slowly. Accompanying this system of land use was a host of ecological invaders from song birds to weeds, some introduced as reminders of former homes, others arriving inadvertently.

Agriculture, then, was a social and economic introduction with complex ecological and cultural subtexts tied to colonialism and to the creation of an immigrant society. It had been practised since the early days of the continental fur trade, then had expanded when Vancouver Island (1849) and mainland British Columbia (1858) became colonies, and a regime of private property was instituted, land policies were worked out, and Natives who had survived the epidemics were isolated on reserves. By 1891, there were almost 4,500 farmers and a total of almost 8,000 people in the province whom the census considered to be employed in agriculture (among a total population of just under 100,000). Most of this farming population was on southern Vancouver Island or in the lower Fraser Valley (Figure 8.1).

This was small-scale, family farming that, in relation to then current agricultural practices in much of North America, was still relatively unspecialized, in good part because farmers were uncertain about what should be raised where. Climates and soils were little tested for agriculture, the limits of the agricultural ecumene were unknown, and in every agricultural district settlers experimented with crops and livestock. There was equal uncertainty about markets. Those in gold and the railway construction camps had declined, but the transportation system was evolving rapidly. The Canadian Pacific Railway (CPR) mainline was built, a spur line was under construction to Okanagan Lake, and sternwheelers plied some interior rivers and lakes. In these circumstances, farmers'

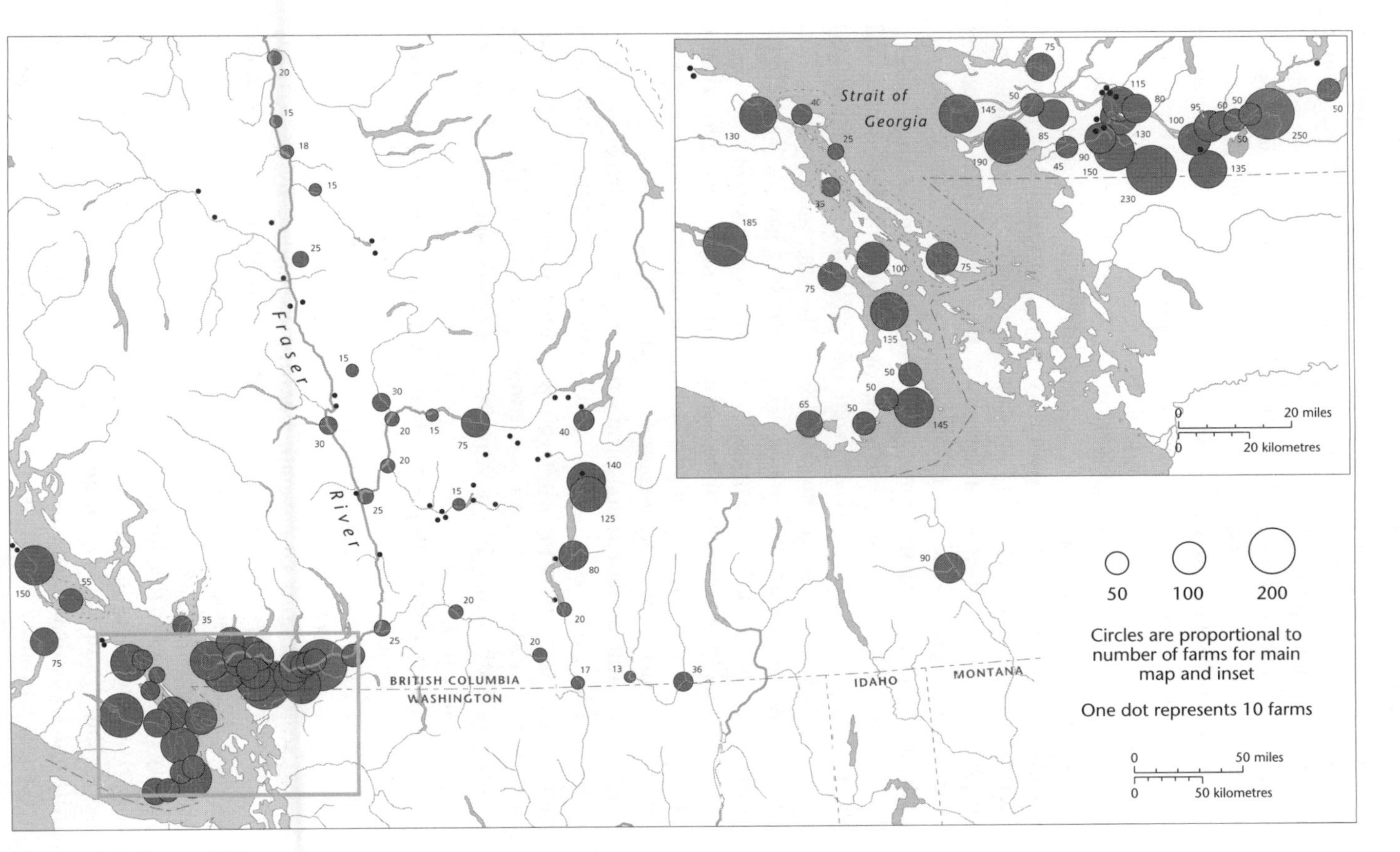

Figure 8.1 Farms, 1891

market connections and, consequently, the location of commercial agriculture were in flux. Away from southeastern Vancouver Island and the adjacent Lower Mainland, farmers could only guess what markets might become available and at what cost.

Such uncertainties, coupled with the subsistence needs of farm households and the labour requirement of pioneering, tended to produce a highly diversified, mixed agriculture. It was based on cereals (principally wheat, barley, and oats), roots (principally potatoes and turnips), hay, livestock (principally cattle, and also horses, sheep, and swine), and a variety of fruits, vegetables, and poultry. In 1891, cattle ranching in the interior dry belt and, to a limited degree, dairy farming and market gardening near the towns around Georgia Strait were the only sharp specializations. Elsewhere, diversity was characteristic, though regional emphases varied. Wheat was relatively little cultivated on Vancouver Island and in parts of the lower Fraser Valley where the climate was wet and the cost of clearing high; much more was cultivated in the northern Okanagan Valley where land costs were lower, the rainfall moderate, and the railway within reach. Orchards were being planted near Kelowna and in the lower Fraser Valley in the early 1890s. Dairying was emphasized on the low pastures near Chilliwack, 100 kilometres east of Vancouver, where the only cheese factory in the province was located. But overall, in a province of great physiographic variety, agriculture was remarkably unspecialized. There was no export staple; specialization, such as it was, reflected the most blatant constraints of environment or distance.[2]

The basic unit of agricultural production was the family farm. As on other frontiers, settlers with no capital could not establish such farms even though they could pre-empt 160 acres for a few dollars. The cost of clearing the coastal rainforest was some $300 an acre, the wage of a Chinese or Native worker for a year. Farmers who could not afford such wages usually had to take seasonal off-the-farm work. In these circumstances, farms developed slowly and many were abandoned. In the interior, costs of clearing were much lower, but techniques of irrigating and farming in semi-arid environments had to be mastered, often by settlers without previous farming experience. There, too, failures and abandonments were common. Yet, overall, clearings expanded. By 1891, many pioneer log cabins had been replaced by frame farmhouses set amid planted, fenced fields. Often there were neighbours within walking distance, a general store, church, and post office – the rudiments of a civil society connected to the outside world.

Everywhere farming replaced local ecologies, consciously as forests were cleared and fields planted, unconsciously as blights and weeds (introduced with imported seeds or in the sweepings from box cars) appeared, spreading exotics beyond the fields. Farming had introduced simplified plant communities together with their associated insects, blights, and weeds. Wild animals that broke fences or preyed on domestic livestock became 'pests' to be shot or poisoned. Farmers complained of coyotes, wolves, bears, cougars, and, in the interior, wild horses.[3] A sympathetic government placed bounties on these animals.

The Changing Context: 1891-1941

Between 1891 and 1941, the population of British Columbia increased from just over 98,000 to almost 820,000, largely through immigration. Most immigrants were of British background: eastern Canadians whose roots were usually Irish or Scottish, and immigrants directly from the British Isles, the majority English. The eastern Canadians usually came from small towns or farms, but the majority of the English were from cities, and a good many of them were educated, middle-class people, part of the great diaspora of their kind in the late days of empire when much of the world seemed at hand, and children of even one family might fetch up on several continents. There were also immigrants from the United States and western Europe, a few – their numbers checked by immigration policies – from China and Japan, and a few others from eastern Europe. Immigration and population growth fuelled boosterism, land speculation, and the expanding urban system shown in Figure 8.2.

During these years, the transportation system evolved primarily to serve the export economy, real or imagined (see Chapter 6). By 1917, when railway construction stopped in the province until well after World War II, there were three transcontinental railways and a variety of local lines, usually to mining districts. Complementing the railways were steamboats on many interior waters and an array of coastal shipping. The road system developed more hesitantly. Vancouver was linked by road to the interior only in 1927. In 1941, there was still no more than a skeletal provincial road system, and only the lower Fraser Valley had a considerable density of roads. Intercity trucking was just beginning.

These developments affected the relative location of agriculture. Provincially, the location of markets was becoming more defined and the means of reaching them faster and less costly. By some combination of road, steamboat, and rail, farmers in many parts of the province could hope to reach export markets. As the friction of distance diminished, interregional competition and the spatial and regional division of labour and land use increased. Moreover, as the market expanded, a new ecology emerged in which, as the American historian William Cronon has remarked, 'species thrived more by price than by direct ecological adaptation.'[4] The city-dominated market, rather than local environmental conditions, would increasingly determine what grew where, and in British

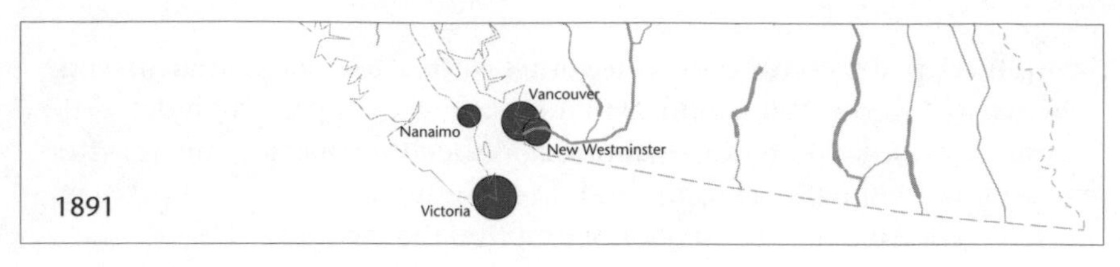

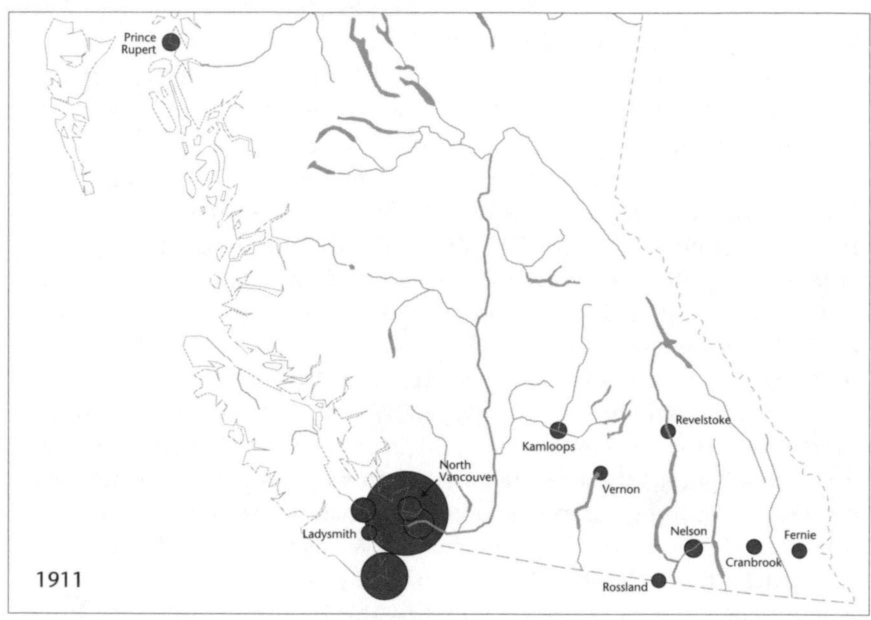

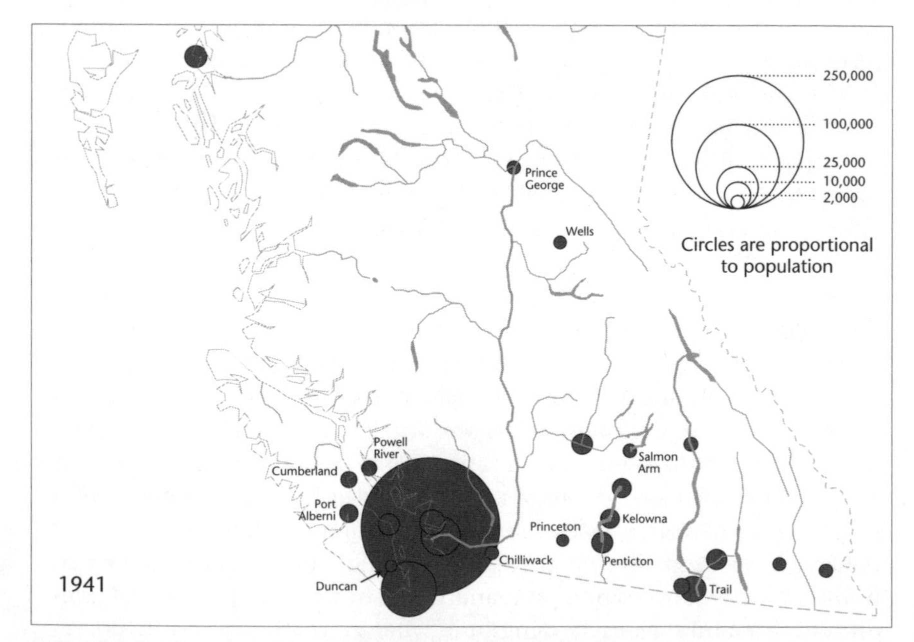

Figure 8.2 The expanding urban system, 1891-1941

Columbia no activity was more sensitive to this new ecological pressure than agriculture.

A similar pressure towards land-use specialization was exerted by changing farm input costs. As capital costs rose, farmers were forced to make decisions about the type of equipment they would need, decisions that affected the type of agriculture they would pursue. Expensive, specialized equipment and specialized land use went hand in hand. Moreover, those who could afford such equipment could achieve economies of scale and sell profitably at lower prices than those who could not. Increasingly, farmers on small farms would find themselves in a cost-price squeeze created by rising capital costs and the declining real value of agricultural products.[5] In the long term, the solutions were either to acquire enough land and capital equipment to reduce unit costs, or to quit farming.

In spite of these pressures, agriculture remained less dependent on wage labour organized through the market mechanism than on families and their internal divisions of labour. Some farmers employed hired hands, many more hired seasonal labour, and a few large operations depended almost exclusively on wage labour; but in 1941, as in 1891, the patriarchal family farm was the basic unit of agricultural production. In this, agriculture was unlike the other major resource industries in British Columbia. As farm work became more mechanized, it usually became more male, and women's work more domestic. The outside (market) economy was becoming male, the inside economy female.[6] Where market connections were weak, the reallocation of family labour was usually delayed.

In a sense, the family farm survived because, by combining long hours of work and an internal division of labour, it was still a competitive unit of production in most branches of agriculture. As it were, the family exploited itself, sometimes, simply because people were trapped, but also, often, because of the social attraction of land and the vision of family-centred independence associated with it.[7] In the background were the age-old craving, whether of tradespeople in towns or of peasants in countrysides, for as much family-centred independence as possible, and the decline of this opportunity with industrialization. At the same time, agrarian discourses that celebrated the social and moral virtues of rural life and family farming were in the air, influencing ordinary people and permeating society to its highest levels. In 1919, the federal minister of the interior argued that 'the basic class [is] the agricultural class,' and made land available for soldier-settlers.[8] Immigrants seeking a measure of independence and security for their families, and long accustomed to think that the ownership of farmland was the safest means to do so, pre-empted land and took up farming.

As ideology, agrarianism was closely allied to the idea of progress, material and moral. It was associated with social control: rural people made satisfied (and thus compliant) citizens. It was grounded in a (primarily American) vision of freedom based on a society of independent producers, the backbone of republican virtue. It was part of a middle- and upper-middle-class English view of nature rooted in the Romantic poets, John Ruskin, the picturesque landscape, and a broad reaction against urban, industrial life.[9] Different agrarian strands mixed in various ways, but, in general, all were culturally and racially specific. They opened little space for non-Europeans, Natives among them, and for those whose vision of rural life excluded the family farm.

By the end of the nineteenth century, agrarianism was increasingly allied with science and supported by government. In British Columbia, the federal government operated experimental farms, and the provincial government hired district agricultural experts to advise farmers. Ministries of agriculture published scientific reports and advice on many specialized agricultural topics. In some areas, the government assisted with the basic costs – for draining, dyking, and irrigation – of bringing land into production. When issues of public health or of plant or animal disease were involved, government inspectors began visiting farms and abattoirs. Government legislation facilitated marketing. Women's work, many thought, should be seen as 'domestic science' subject to 'the rule of reason' and the demands of efficiency. Such was the message that Alice Ravenhill, a former lecturer of hygiene at King's College for Women in London, brought to Women's Institutes throughout the province, and to the bulletins she wrote for the provincial Department of Agriculture.[10] Although male and female work were increasingly separate, the same standards of scientific efficiency should apply. Each required experts and government assistance – both science and a more regulative and managerial relationship between government and countryside.

Indeed, the relative location of rural society, as much as of rural economy, was changing rapidly. Train, steamboat, or automobile linked farm and town. The circulation of magazines, mail order catalogues, and newspapers; the introduction of telephones and then of rural electrification accompanied by radios and domestic appliances; and the expansion of public schools with standardized curricula all tended to create an information field in which the distinction between urban and rural counted for less and less.[11] Yet these changes did not occur overnight, and some of them came slowly to British Columbia where an increasingly modern information field was superimposed on immigrants from many backgrounds, great distances, strikingly different and little-known physical environments, and the atavistic tendencies inherent in pioneering.

Semi-Subsistent Family Farming

Throughout the period from 1891 to 1941, the family farm, weakly connected to the market, remained the common unit of agricultural production in British Columbia. The factors that produced such farms in 1891 – a vision of agriculture as a secure, independent, and felicitous way of life; the demands of pioneering; the subsistence needs of farm families; environmental uncertainty coupled with insufficient land; and unreliable or expensive access to markets – remained in play. In 1941 as in 1891, most farms were fairly minimal operations dogged by poverty and the need to make some accommodation between farm and off-the-farm work.

Encouraged by government publicity and programs, the exuberant promotions of railway and land companies, and settlers' own cravings for land, farming expanded to and somewhat beyond the limits of the agricultural ecumene. The limits imposed by growing season, aridity, or excess moisture only slowly became known. As the process of experimentation went on, settlers often took up land where there were neither local markets nor established external connections. The old problems of transportation remained. The costs of pioneering were substantial; unless settlers came with capital, some off-the-farm work usually had to be found. In such circumstances farms developed slowly, sales of farm produce were few, and purchases were kept to a minimum. Farming was a struggle that many quickly abandoned. Others worked out their lives only to find, when finally they had created farms, that they were too small to finance modern farm machinery, and too isolated and unspecialized to compete with larger, more advantageously located operations. Ruins of family farms on unlikely edges of land, their ecologies considerably rearranged, are scattered across British Columbia.

On these farms, weak markets and the demands of pioneering tended to fend off the specialization of labour and land use. Farmhouses and barns were usually settler-built log structures. As much as possible, dwellings and equipment were made, repaired, and patched on the farm. A kitchen garden, a dairy cow or two, poultry, and probably a few pigs, all of which the woman commonly tended, were essential components. When wage work took the husband away, his wife and children ran the entire farm. New agricultural equipment was barely afforded and slowly introduced. In many areas farms were not electrified nor was there modern plumbing until well after World War II. Yet many a wife was exposed through the Women's Institute to current ideas of domestic science. Such contradictions abounded as people of many different backgrounds created small, mixed, twentieth-century farms that hardly supported the families that worked them.

Daisy and her husband Jack Phillips arrived in the Windermere valley from Windsor, England, in 1912, drawn, along with many other middle and upper class English people, by the clever, distorted promotions of the Columbia Valley Irrigation Company. Jack purchased twenty-eight acres of forested land at 3200 feet and set about establishing an orchard; Daisy tried to create a middle class English home. Neither was at all prepared for what they were trying to do. Jack had been an army officer, and Daisy, who previously had lived with servants, had never done a washing, sewn, or cooked. They worked and they learned, setting out an apple orchard (where apple trees could not survive), and furnishing a house with belongings from England. Without servants or appliances, and driven by middle class English standards, Daisy was caught in an endless round of housework. The two dressed for dinner, set the table with bone china and silver, and then scrubbed the pots. The Windermere Valley absorbed their limited capital, and their few sales – a few dozen eggs, a few heads of lettuce, a little alfalfa – were inconsequential. They were creating a subsistence farm. Then the First World War came, Jack was called up in December, 1914, and was killed in France the following April. Daisy, who never returned to the Windermere Valley, remembered her short time there as the golden years of her life.[12]

Nan Capewell, from a working-class family in Derby, England, emigrated to Vancouver just before the depression of 1913, eventually found work in the Grand Trunk Pacific Hotel in Prince Rupert, quit, and with five dollars to her name got a hotel job in Aldermere, a new settlement on the railway in the Bulkley Valley. There she met Joe Bourgon, a French Canadian farmer and livery man, and eventually, hesitantly, married him. This was no love match. Joe needed a farm wife, and Nan, who was thirty-four, poor, and alone, was drawn to the security of a marriage and a farm. The two moved to Joe's farm – a shack in a clearing – and lived there for the next thirty-seven years. Joe threw himself into the farm; he spent nothing on household furnishings and considered his wife mad when she planted flowers in the garden plot he had fenced. Nan, who had been a seamstress in England, became, approximately, the variously-skilled farm wife Joe had sought. Their children were English-speaking and Roman Catholic. The farm itself produced much of what they ate and money was exceedingly scarce, but eventually, by the standards of the Bulkley Valley, the Bourgons were prosperous. After a time Joe could afford a seed drill, a binder, a thresher (with neighbours), and a hired hand; he sold milk (to Prince Rupert), grain, and hay, sawed a little lumber on his own small mill, and cut railway ties in winter. Nan boarded the teacher to acquire a little of her own money. They had become pillars of a small rural community. Joe was president of the Farmers' Institute, Nan a stalwart of the Women's Community Club. When the University of British Columbia held extension classes in the Bulkley Valley, Nan helped with the arrangements.[13]

Stephen Farina, from a farm village in [what became] Czechoslovakia, worked for a time in the coal mines at Fernie, and in 1905, with his wife Susan and baby boy took up a homestead of 160 acres south of Kamloops. Many of their neighbours were also Czechs, who also came via the coal towns of the Kootenays. The federal government promoted such homesteading – in the federal railway belt – envisaging wheat farms, but on this high, dry, rolling land homesteads were much resented by the cattlemen, whose ranges they took. The Farinas, like other homesteaders, coped with drought, unseasonal frosts, grasshoppers, and poverty; lived as much as possible off the farm (preserving food, including wild Saskatoon berries, through much of the summer); and delivered a little grain to the elevator of the Maple Leaf Milling Company in Kamloops. In 1922 Stephen died, leaving Susan and eight children, the oldest a boy (Andrew) of eighteen. The family, now English-speaking, stayed, struggling to survive by selling a little wheat and experimenting with turkeys and mink. In 1940 Andrew finally bought a tractor; in the same year one of his sisters, Caroline, won the gold medal for graduating nurses at the Royal Inland Hospital in Kamloops. By the early 1960s when rural electrification reached the Farina farm, most homesteads were unoccupied, and the area had largely reverted to ranching.[14]

These, in their ways, are the success stories. The soldier-settlers who, in 1920, trekked 135 miles beyond the railway at Grande Prairie, Alberta, to homestead near Sunset Prairie in the Peace River Block, were on their own, completely inexperienced, in the northern bush, far from markets and supplies, schools, and medical attention. Half of them, miraculously, were still there ten years later when C.A. Dawson, a sociologist from McGill, studied the 'pioneer fringe' in the Peace River Valley.[15] By that time, the railway was being built into the Peace River Block; many one-room rural schools, financed by the provincial government, had opened; and wheat was becoming an export staple on farms near Dawson Creek, Rolla, and Pouce Coupe (Figure 8.3). Dawson was looking for success – he shared, with a veneer of scientific detachment, the widespread belief in the region's agricultural future – but often encountered failure. Women, he thought, suffered more than men from pioneering, because of their particular isolation, the double burden of farm and domestic work, and the lack of medical attention. A woman on an isolated homestead reported that she and her husband had come, with high hopes, seven years before, but now their capital was gone, only a little land was cleared, and a creek drowned much of their crop each spring: 'If things keep on this way I do not know what we will do. I don't do anything but visit neighbours once in a while. We are too busy with the struggle to make a living, and the children keep you at home. There is church service at the school three miles away, but we have left the farm only once to go there in the past twelve months.'[16]

The ruins of British Columbia's marginal farms have such tales to tell. Struggling units of production, they were also settings in which immigrant lives were changing, and different cultures were finding their way with each other and with the modern, western Canadian world. Lives had been drastically relocated. Former homes were far away; the context of life had changed. Daisy Phillips focused her Englishness on the inside

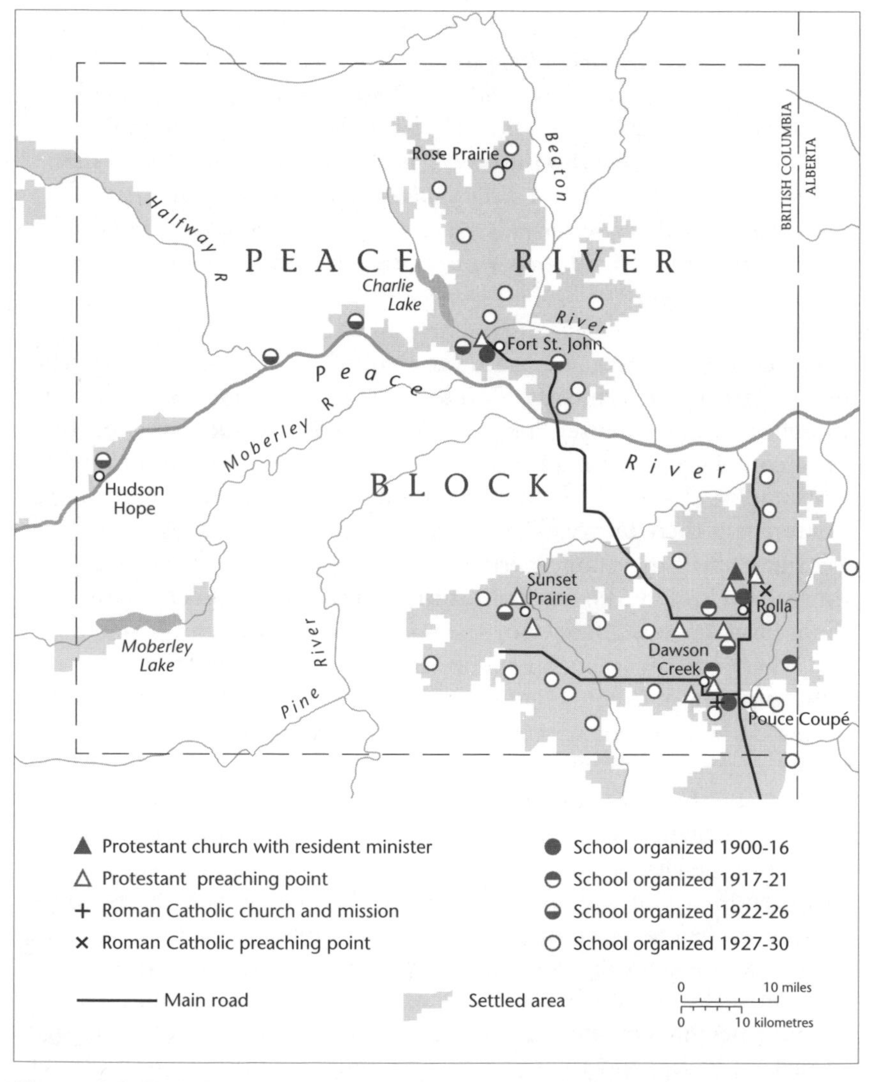

Figure 8.3 Schools and churches in the Peace River Block (after C.A. Dawson)

of her house, but the larger world she had known was not at hand: the English birds and forest flowers, the vesper bell announcing evening prayer. Nan Bourgon wanted flowers in her garden – her grandfather, a gardener, had filled the Capewells' window boxes in Derby with flowers – but she lived with a French Canadian husband on a pioneer farm in the Bulkley Valley (see Chapter 9 for further details of Nan Bourgon's life). The hills south of Kamloops reminded the Farinas of their Czech homelands, but no ancient peasant village was tucked into these hills, nor a lord's estate. Susan Farina spun wool as she had been taught in her native land, while her daughter studied nursing. Past and present, thousands of miles apart, coexisted on such farms.

In the literature on agriculture, these farms are hard to locate: they are not examples of specialized, twentieth-century capitalist agriculture, they are not peasant holdings, and they are only somewhat like pioneer farms in eastern North America in the nineteenth century. They grew out of a particular, twentieth-century convergence of immigrants and the land they took to be wilderness in the byways of British Columbia – a convergence that often made it almost impossible to adopt the economies of scale and the specialized divisions of labour and land use of competitive modern agriculture, yet admitted many ideas and strategies of twentieth-century society and many legacies of pasts elsewhere.

Few of these marginal farms ever became successful commercial operations. The young rarely stayed, and farms were sold or abandoned, leaving behind, often, decaying buildings and landscapes full of alien species. Except in the Peace River, which became the far northwestern extension of prairie wheat farming, the commercial specializations that did emerge – principally orcharding in the Okanagan and Similkameen valleys, cattle ranching in much of the dry interior, and dairying and market gardening near the towns – usually had quite different origins.

Orcharding

Orcharding in the Okanagan and Similkameen valleys developed out of the speculative British Columbia land market before World War I. Limited liability companies, usually launched by local entrepreneurs and financed in Britain, bought up dry benchlands, installed irrigation works, subdivided the land into orchard lots (usually of ten to twenty acres), and promoted them in eastern Canada, Britain, and, in some cases, India.[17] The first such schemes were at Peachland (1899), Summerland (1900), and Kelowna (1904). In a typical real estate promotion, an area just north of Kelowna known as Dry Valley was renamed Glenmore, subdivided as shown in Figure 8.4, and marketed as suburban orchard lots. According to the land company, the climate was benign and healthy, orcharding easy and profitable, and sport and society at hand. Irrigated land sold for

$200 to $300 an acre. Development costs were high, particularly for storage dams and miles of flumes, concrete canals, siphons, and ditches, but as promotions brought settlers who paid well for land, there were profits to be made.[18] Similar schemes spread to the Kootenays, where, in 1912, one of them drew Daisy and Jack Phillips. Many of these promotions were failures, their mismanagement, miscalculations, and, in some cases, fraudulent operations somewhat hidden by World War I; but a good many settlers stuck, and in the Okanagan and Similkameen valleys, they established a specialized, almost entirely export-oriented agricultural economy, the first in the province.

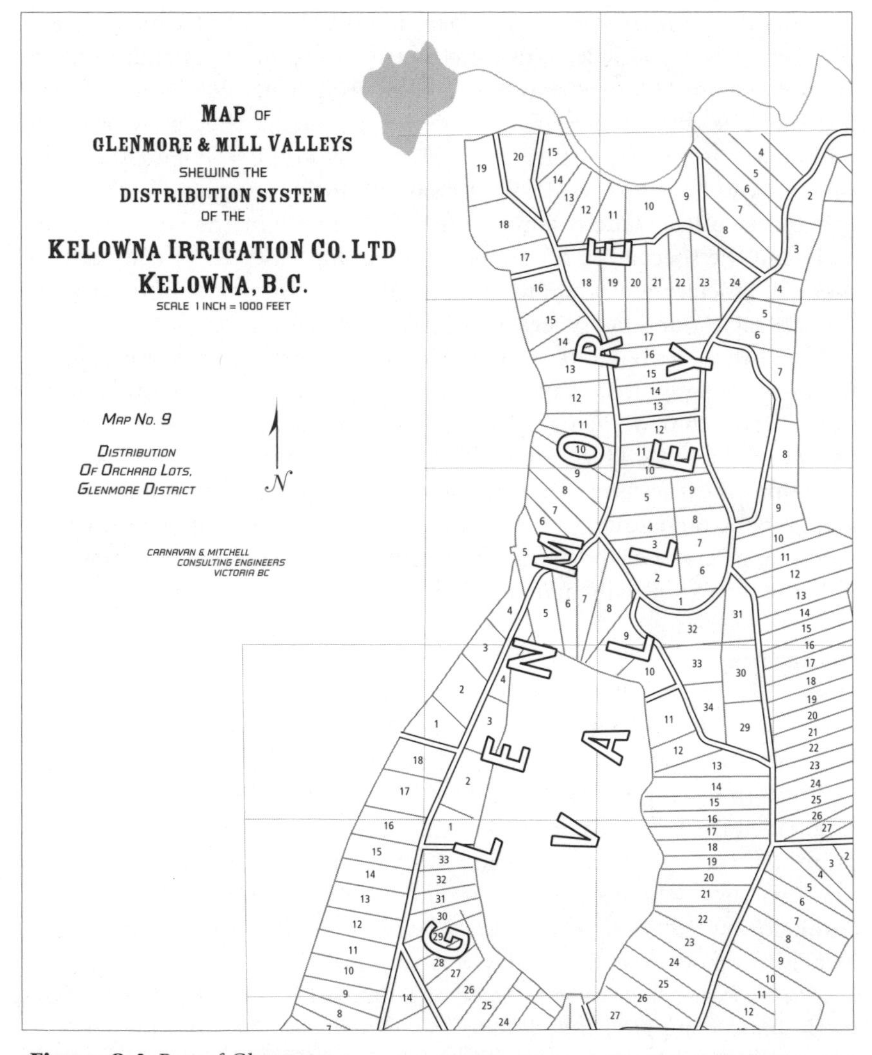

Figure 8.4 Part of Glenmore

For all the claims of the land companies, no one really knew how to develop successful benchland orchards.[19] No information was at hand about what soils and slopes were most suitable, what varieties should be grown, how best to irrigate, whether to cultivate the spaces between trees, or how to deal with many of the insect pests that, sooner or later, descended on the orchards. This all needed to be learned, mostly by trial and error, mostly by the settlers themselves. Some land companies hired 'experts,' but they too were learning. The district horticulturalists (provincial) and the experimental farm at Summerland (federal) considerably facilitated the process; from the latter, eventually, came discoveries of serious trace element deficiencies in Okanagan soils (boron principally, but also manganese, zinc, and magnesium) and the development, in 1936, of an early, heavy-bearing apple (the Spartan) suited to the Okanagan environment. Understandings and skills were acquired, and orcharding took hold. By the early 1920s, the Okanagan and Similkameen valleys produced some three million boxes of apples a year, by the mid-1930s, some five million. Most of the varieties of apples planted during the early era had been replaced by McIntosh and Delicious, selected for their yields per tree and marketability. The whole operation rested on rearranged local ecologies and an increasingly engineered nature. Irrigation enabled fruit to be grown in an arid environment that was unsuited to some of its predators in more humid climates. Fertilizers engineered the quality of soils; even apple genes were reworked to suit the Okanagan environment.

As problems associated with production were overcome, those associated with marketing loomed larger. Growers produced for distant, potentially highly competitive, luxury markets, principally in Britain and on the Canadian prairies. Access to the Prairie market was protected by a Canadian tariff of thirty cents a box on American apples, and, except in Manitoba, by relatively higher shipping costs from eastern Canada. The reputation of British Columbian apples, coupled with preferential colonial tariffs, gave fruit growers in British Columbia access to the British market. But between the growers and these distant consumers lay packing houses, brokers, a railway, jobbers, and retailers that took most of the fruit's value. The first cooperatively owned packing houses opened before World War I and soon became common; during the late 1920s and 1930s, most of them introduced cold storage, enabling them to release fruit more evenly. Grower control of selling was more difficult to achieve. The Okanagan Fruit Union (1908), the Okanagan United Growers (1913), and the Associated Growers of British Columbia (1923) all failed as cooperative marketing agencies because they did not represent all growers. If they withheld fruit to raise its price, independent growers sold and profited (the free-rider problem). In 1931, the Supreme Court of Canada declared *ultra vires* provincial legislation to centralize grower control of marketing ('one desk selling') if requested by 75 per cent of growers. In the ensuing marketing chaos, and as the Depression deepened and orchards matured, some orchardists refused to pick their fruit – 'a cent a pound or on the ground' – and the great majority demanded one desk selling. It was achieved in 1939 with the creation of BC Tree Fruits Ltd., a company owned by the grower-controlled Tree Fruits Board. Henceforth, BC Tree Fruits hired its own brokers and marketed virtually the entire Okanagan-Similkameen fruit crop. As far as possible, the relationship between many small producers and distant markets had been collectivized.[20]

During these years, the small, labour-intensive orchard was the main unit of production. Capital costs, other than for land, were low, even after tractors became fairly common in the 1930s. Most orchard work was manual, and was performed by some combination of family and seasonal labour hired for thinning and picking. Yet this was highly specialized farming, part of a competitive, international spatial economy. The family orchard survived because there were few economies of scale in fruit production, and because it was not left to its own devices. With the collapse of the irrigation companies during or just after World War I, water management passed, with government aid, to grower-controlled irrigation districts. For all the starts and stops, marketing became collectively organized. Increasingly informed scientific advice, paid for by dominion and provincial governments, was at hand. Government officials inspected orchards for codling moths and other pests, and regulated the grading of fruit. Tariffs protected the Prairie and British markets. So supported, specialized, export-oriented family orcharding was established in the Okanagan and Similkameen valleys. In a little-known and arid land at the northern climatic margin of fruit cultivation, the ecology of orcharding had been a difficult introduction, and the marketing of fruit, once grown, had been a particular challenge from an eccentric location. There was not much margin; orcharding in British Columbia was a precarious specialization of the international economy. In the Kootenays, where the fruit harvest was two weeks later than in the Okanagan and Similkameen, and where the scattered distribution of orcharding made the collective defence of individual orchardists virtually impossible, most commercial orchards failed.

Ranching

Nineteenth-century cattle ranching in British Columbia was more established than orcharding, more grounded in western North American experience, and more influenced by local markets. By the 1890s, most ranchers were of British or eastern Canadian background, but ranching

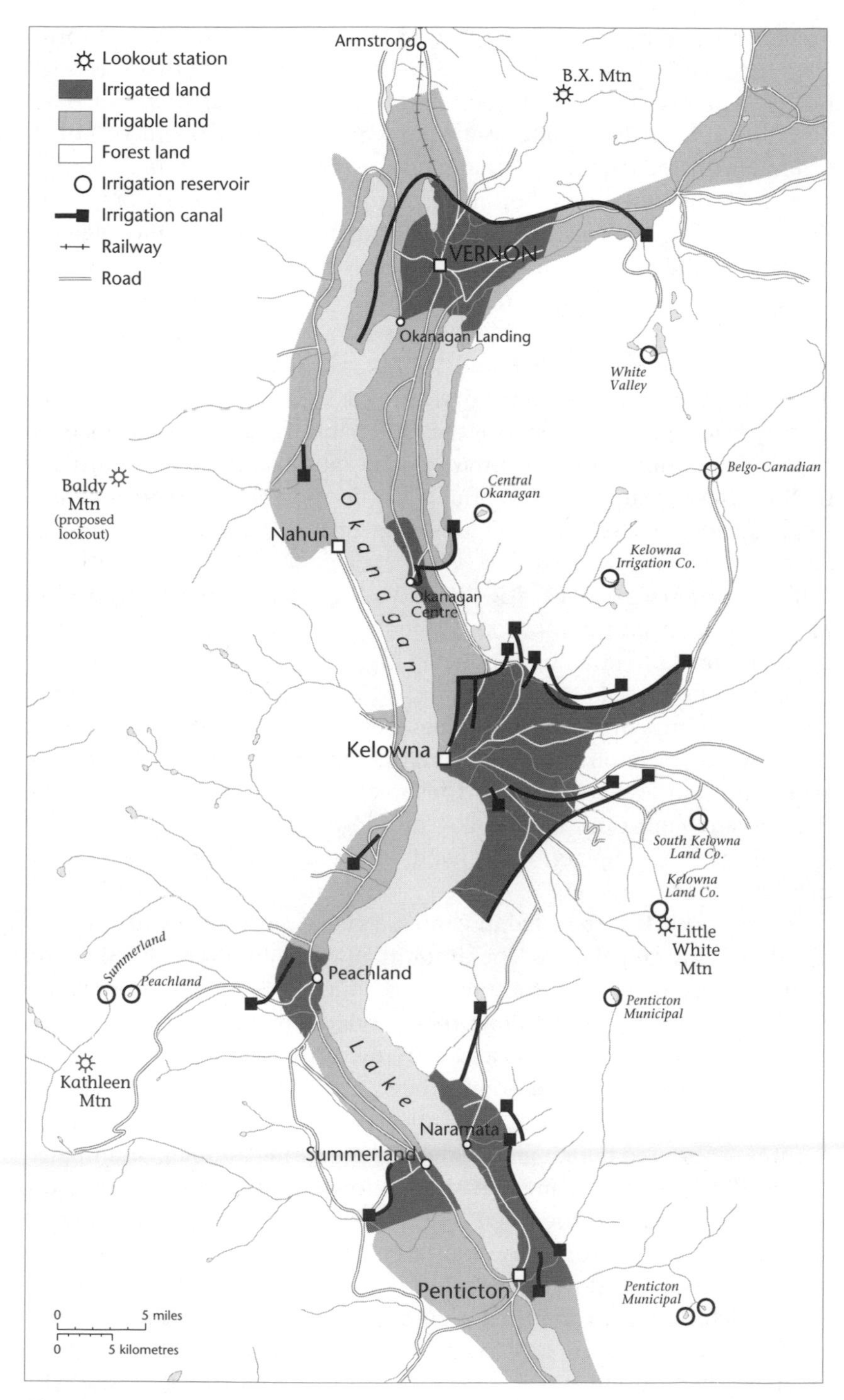

Figure 8.5 The irrigated Okanagan, 1913 (after map of lookout system, Okanagan Lake Watershed, Vernon Forest District)

itself had come from the south during the Cariboo gold rush. A northward extension of a western North American cattle culture that was originally Hispanic, it arrived just after Native populations had been decimated by smallpox, and at a time when the government of British Columbia offered land for purchase or lease for next to nothing.[21] Settlers soon took the best valley bottom meadows and bunch grass ranges. In the early 1880s, markets for beef in CPR construction camps provided the impetus for the buy-outs and consolidations that would produce some of the great ranches of British Columbia.[22] After the railway was completed, the coastal cities were accessible markets for cattle. Although land developers began converting ranchland to orchards in the Okanagan, and the government tried to introduce dry farming in other areas (such as the railway belt south of Kamloops), the older land use persisted across most of the dry interior of south-central British Columbia. Immigrants arriving in the fifteen years before World War I found that, apart from small patches here and there, the rangelands of British Columbia were already alienated.

In the summer of 1949, T.R. Weir, a geographer at the University of Manitoba, mapped the location of ranches with more than twenty-five cattle (Figure 8.6).[23] Had he conducted his survey some forty years before, the distribution would have been much the same. There were not a lot of ranches in a huge area. The largest ranches, and most of the beef cattle in the province, were on the bunch grass ranges in the Nicola, Thompson, and Fraser valleys. Away from these valleys, and particularly in the Cariboo and Chilcotin, natural hay meadows, which were usually small floodplains or swamps on the upland, also supported cattle, as, in summer, did forested upland.

Because cattle had to be fed in winter, a viable ranch included both hay meadows and rangelands. The amount of available hay, the size and quality of the range, and the number of stock were closely interrelated; ranchers needed to have enough hay to tide their stock over the winter, and then to balance numbers and carrying capacity as they moved stock from range to range. In the south, they raised hay in irrigated meadows in the valley bottoms, and fed cattle there for two or three winter months. They used bunch grass ranges in the spring and fall, and higher, timbered ranges in summer. In the Chilcotin and Cariboo, where the winters were long and the forest often too dense for grazing, they put up large quantities of natural hay, and often pastured their stock in summer on natural hay meadows. Strategies varied, but a typical ranch in the main ranching areas comprised a ranchstead and irrigated meadow in a valley bottom, and grazing land on grassy hillsides and in forested uplands. The bottomlands were the key to such landscapes. Those who owned them could control a valley because, without hay for the winter,

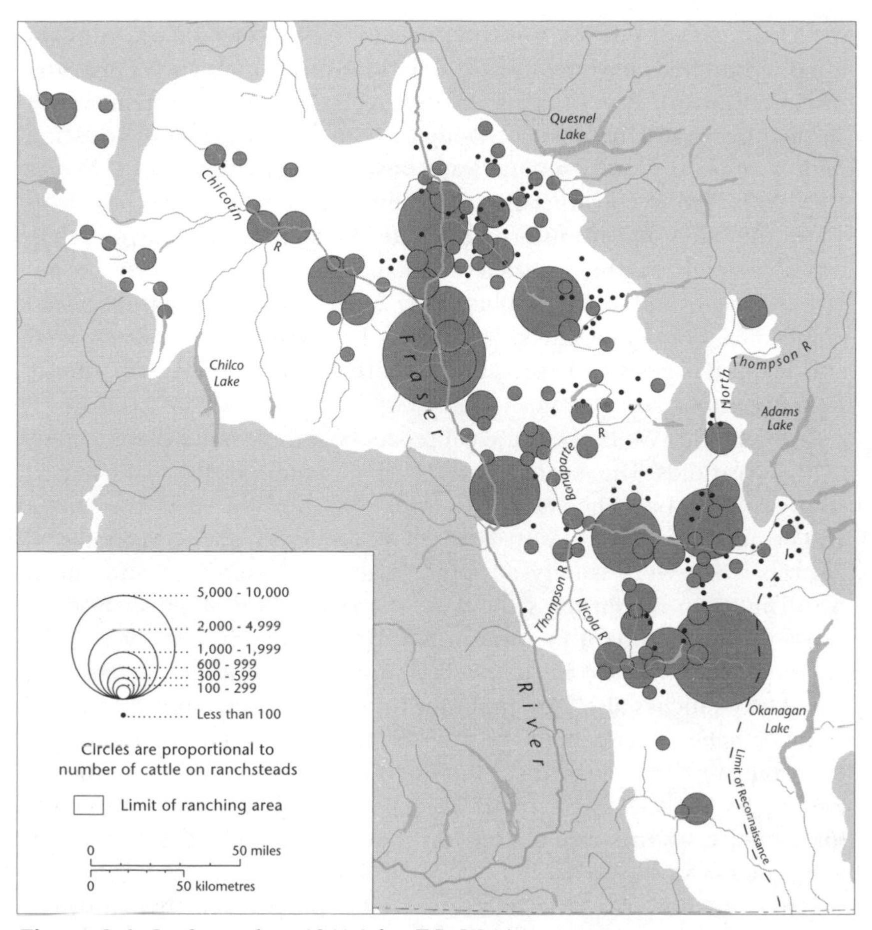

Figure 8.6 Cattle ranches, 1941 (after T.R. Weir)

the upland was worthless for cattle. Yet winter feeding also allowed more animals onto the valley sides than ever before. With small herds, the bunch grass was eaten once and left to recover; larger herds grazed more heavily and, eventually, bunch grass would give way to sage, a woody, less palatable plant.[24] The process was gradual and difficult to reverse as economically stressed ranchers worked their land harder, and damaged land increased economic stress.

The smallest ranches depended on family labour and controlled only a few hundred acres. A ranchstead on such a holding might comprise several small log buildings – house, root cellar, hay shed, and barn (for calves, a few horses, a milk cow or two, and chickens) – and simple corrals located at the edge of a small, natural hay meadow or amid a few acres cleared for hay fields.[25] The largest ranches, such as that owned by the Douglas Lake Cattle Company, owned, leased, or held grazing permits for hundreds of thousands of acres of prime bunch grass range and timbered upland. They were run by managers, overseen by foremen, and worked by wage labourers. At Douglas Lake, the cooks and irrigation men were usually Chinese – railway construction workers let off by the CPR, employed to construct and maintain irrigation works for hay fields – and the riders and teamsters were Natives and whites.[26] Such a ranch was a complex, multiracial society. Thousands of tons of hay were put up each year, and some 10,000 cattle were moved through seasonal ranges. The home ranchstead at Douglas Lake (Figure 8.7), which Weir also mapped, suggests the scale and something of the social structure of such operations.

Before World War II, the principal products of these ranches were grass-fed two year olds. The means by which they were produced had changed relatively little over the years. Herefords were introduced in the 1880s, and because they calved easily, fattened well on grass, and withstood cold winters, they were widely adopted, often in a Hereford-Shorthorn (Durham) cross. About the same time, the production of winter feed for cattle became standard in western North America; over the years, the largest ranches invested in the latest equipment for cutting and stacking hay. Many ranches also grew grain for horses and, increasingly, to finish cattle. Ranchers increasingly sought expert advice about cattle diseases. But, compared to orcharding, ranching drew far more on accumulated lore, far less on scientific expertise. The product was less vulnerable environmentally, and its production was much more grounded in western North American experience.

Marketing, however, reflected international prices, even though before World War II almost all beef produced in British Columbia was consumed within the province. The per capita consumption of beef was rising at a time when railways and refrigeration, which increased the spatial range of competition, and the growing importance of processed meats, which combined factory methods and modern merchandising, both tended to depress prices.[27] Across the continent in the 1920s and 1930s, the relative value of beef was falling.[28] In the early days, ranchers drove their cattle to market; later they sold at the ranchgate or railway to buyers who, for a time, represented butchers in Victoria or Vancouver, and then companies like T.P. Burns and Swift Canadian. Although the BC Stockbreeders' Association organized annual bull sales in Kamloops after 1919, without a central stockyard it could not control, nor did the larger ranchers wish it to control, the sale of beef.[29] As a result, ranchers with very imperfect market knowledge and few opportunities to sell were in a weak position to bargain with buyers from an oligarchic meat packing industry.

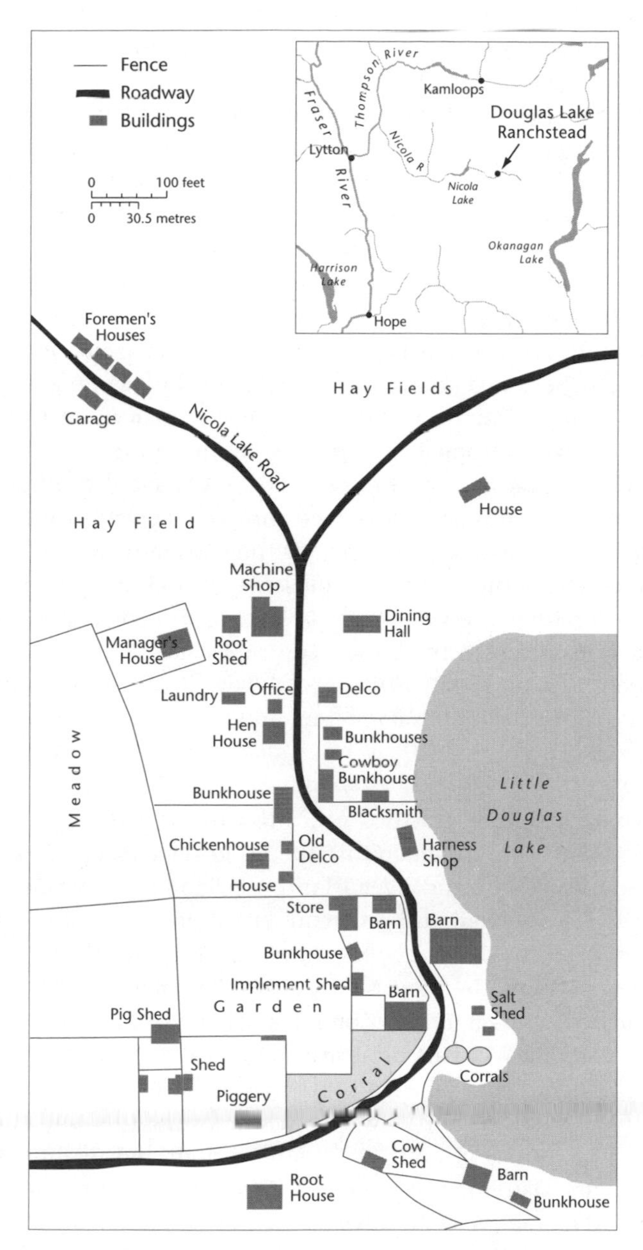

Figure 8.7 Home ranchstead, Douglas Lake (after T.R. Weir)

Such marketing pressures affected ranching practices. In general, the rangelands of British Columbia had been incorporated within a modified British system of property law, along an outer margin of an increasingly global agricultural economy. The rights of private property, the ambitions of immigrant families, and the specializing pressures of the international economy dominated land use. An exceedingly low density settler society – dependent on a range cattle industry based, in turn, on low land values – was scattered across the dry belt in precisely bounded, owned locations. Barbed wire and property lines blocked the movement of grazing animals and people, and influenced plant distributions and range quality. Ignorance, the pressures of debt or shareholders, family needs, or simple short-term profit taking created overgrazed, degraded pasture. In the 1920s and 1930s, ranchers used arsenic to battle plagues of grasshoppers, whereas the more durable solution was better range management to improve the stressed ranges that, apparently, had led to the outbreaks.[30]

Native peoples, most of whom lived on reserves, no longer burned the range to control shrubs and encourage the plants they once had gathered. Many of the deer and other animals they formerly hunted had been replaced by cattle occupying much the same ecological niche, but cattle were owned and wildlife were not. Native peoples could not hunt the herds that now occupied the range. The replacement of deer by cattle, and the protection of the latter by property law, dispossessed Native communities as effectively as did survey lines and fences.

Dairying

Dairying continued to be practised near most towns and cities. It became the predominant form of agriculture in the lower Fraser Valley and on much of southeastern Vancouver Island; dairying was common in the Okanagan and Kootenays, and was represented, in some form, wherever agriculture was practised. An age-old part of northern European agriculture, dairying was probably the most telling single barometer of the changing pressures on agriculture in British Columbia before World War II.

In 1891, dairying was part of a farm way of life, producing essential foods for the family and perhaps some income, primarily from the sale of fluid milk. In summer, butter was made on most farms, and cheese on a few; small quantities of both, of variable colour and quality, reached local merchants. Dairying was women's work, milking one of the chores of the day. Yet even in 1891, such ways were threatened by the large quantities of butter and cheese, standardized products of creameries or cheese factories, imported from eastern Canada. The provincial Department of Agriculture, convinced that British Columbia needed such facilities, advocated travelling dairy schools to instruct rural residents in the art of dairying.[31]

The new 'art' would be more specialized, capital intensive, market oriented, and male than the old. Farms that once had produced some dairy products became dairy farms. Government regulations and inspections, inspired by concern over public health, became more intrusive.[32] The quality of dairy cattle improved (and their cost increased), and governments disseminated the latest ideas, mostly from American land-grant colleges like Cornell or the University of Wisconsin, about feeding methods and productivity. Silos, which provided air-tight storage for chopped grass and corn, were shown to produce a high-protein feed that kept cattle fresh through the winter, but silos were expensive. They and other capital costs – for land, larger barns for larger herds, pure-bred cattle, and milking machines – made dairy farming an increasingly costly industry to enter. In 1927, the average value of dairy farms in Ladner, at the mouth of the Fraser River, was well over $24,000; in the Okanagan, the value was well over $15,000.[33] Specialization had driven up input costs, and the increases in productivity that followed from these investments tended to depress prices, a cost-price squeeze that, over the years, weeded out the small producers. As farmers specialized in dairying and invested accordingly, dairying became male work.[34]

Associated with these changes were expanding markets and improved connections to them. The major provincial market for fluid milk was in Vancouver. By 1910, when an electric railway reached Chilliwack, most dairy farmers in the lower Fraser Valley could reach the public through one of the many retail dairies that operated out of the city. Closer at hand were creameries, cheese factories, and condensed milk factories, though these manufacturers paid less well for milk than the Vancouver fluid market. There was always competition from imports; butter and cheese imported from eastern Canada or New Zealand depressed local prices for fluid milk as well as for butter and cheese. Against these international pressures were the facts that milk was perishable and that, even after the introduction of silos, production fluctuated seasonally. In these exchanges, the connection between individual farmers, the food they produced, and the people who ate it melted away. Milk became a standardized, interchangeable commodity, like the money that paid for it.

As the individual dairy farmer, like the orchardist, was at the mercy of a market in which farm produce was an increasingly abstract commodity manipulated by distant profit takers, collective action seemed to offer a means of controlling that market and of returning a larger share of the consumer price to producers. But cooperative marketing forced dairy farmers to engage fundamental questions: the merits of free and regulated markets, the balance between majority and minority rights, and, in Canada, the spheres of federal and provincial authority. Cooperative creameries and cheese factories were relatively easily established (Figure 8.8); they produced a more competitive product by shifting production away from farms. The cooperatives, however, could not control the market; if some creameries withheld summer surpluses to keep up prices, others sold to take advantage. The creation, in 1913, of the Fraser Valley Milk Producers' Association (FVMPA), a cooperative of dairy farmers, was a far more ambitious undertaking.[35] It sought to control marketing by gaining the support of virtually all the dairy farmers in the Fraser Valley, taking over creameries and dairies, and reorganizing milk delivery. By 1924, the FVMPA had purchased several creameries and retail dairies, and operated two condensed milk factories. However, it controlled neither all milk production in the valley nor all retail dairies, and the FVMPA's attempts to keep up fluid milk prices (by manufacturing milk) provided opportunities for independent producers. There were price wars, breakaways, and intense feelings. From the vantage point of loyal members of the FVMPA, who believed in the principle of cooperation, the independents were scabs; however, the independents, those who were more than opportunists, believed the FVMPA propped up inefficient farmers and forced conformity. Yet experience had convinced most dairy farmers that chaos attended the unregulated market, and, in 1929, the provincial government introduced legislation that would make collective marketing mandatory for all if the great majority of dairy farmers favoured it.[36] The ensuing period of stability ended in 1932 when the judicial committee of the Privy Council in London declared the legislation *ultra vires* because it impinged on federal powers. The matter was not resolved in 1940. The FVMPA represented most dairy farmers in the Fraser Valley, but had not succeeded in controlling the market. The attempt to do so had put dairy farmers face to face with some of the more intractable issues this century.

In the face of market integration, rising input costs, and growing specialization, dairying remained a family operation.[37] Officials of the FVMPA thought that 'The future prosperity of the farmer depends largely on himself. He will continue to produce as an individual but he must market cooperatively.'[38] The few very large dairies – such as the 200-acre Wells farm in Sardis (near Chilliwack in the lower Fraser Valley), which required seven farm hands, and a housekeeper to feed them, to milk 100 Ayrshire cows[39] – were not more efficient and did not yield a higher rate of profit than much smaller farms. Beyond a certain herd size, capital costs per cow did not fall; rather, farmers had to provide another set of milking and other facilities. Moreover, members of farm families often worked for longer hours for less return than hired hands. Nor did such a farm, which often was inherited, have to earn an average profit on investment.

For these reasons, family dairies with perhaps ten or a dozen cows on thirty or forty acres were common, especially in the lower Fraser Valley. Although small, they were highly specialized operations. Through trade journals and associations, dairy farmers were linked across the province and beyond, an identifiable, self-conscious group of (virtually) family businesses within an integrated economy. Such, at least, was the direction of change, though even at the end of the 1930s, the transition was far from complete. There were still many farmers who combined a few dairy cows with other farm activities or off-the-farm work, as did the Bourgons in the Bulkley Valley. There were still many women milking cows. Even in the Chilliwack area in the 1920s, only some 62 per cent of the gross receipts of dairy farms came from the sale of dairy products; in the West Kootenays at the same time, the figure was under 30 per cent.[40]

Market Gardening and Small Fruits

Most of these small, labour-intensive farms were located close to an urban market, principally Vancouver, or where attractive land and a railway were both at hand. They ranged from large, capital-intensive greenhouses and hop farms dependent on hired labour to small plots worked by single Chinese. This was the most racially diverse sector of British Columbian agriculture. As early as 1913, Chinese cultivated almost 3,000 acres of market gardens near Vancouver. In the interior, they were known for potatoes (Ashcroft), onions (Vernon), and celery (Armstrong). Most of the berry farmers at Maple Ridge, east of Vancouver, were Japanese. Prosperous white farmers relied on Natives or Chinese for cheap, seasonal labour.[41]

For the Chinese and Japanese, market gardens and berry farms, like laundries and restaurants, were accessible niches within a hostile society. Although some farmers' cooperatives tried to prevent their members from selling land to 'Asiatics,'[42] Japanese and Chinese purchases of private land were legal. Nor were there unions or professional associations to exclude them. Entry costs were relatively low; little land was needed, and labour could develop it. With few Chinese women in British Columbia, labour on many Chinese market gardens was organized in hierarchical male households composed of the landowner plus, often, relatives or neighbours from his home village or local region. Such units of work were indirectly controlled by distant relatives: a man who did not work hard or who disobeyed his superior would disgrace his family in China.[43] Larger operations may have depended on more impersonal labour relations contracted through a Chinese employment broker (a 'China boss'). The Japanese berry farms, on the other hand, were family operations supplemented, often, by a sponsored immigrant who, in return for sponsorship, worked long, unpaid hours. News of disobedience would get back to the village of origin and, again, bring shame to a family.[44] White farmers complained that such arrangements amounted to near slavery and gave Japanese farmers an unfair competitive advantage.[45] Cultural differences coupled with racist immigration policies juxtaposed very different ways of organizing work.

Produce from Chinese market gardens in the lower Fraser Valley went to Chinese vegetable wholesalers in Vancouver, and from them to the Chinese peddlers and corner stores that operated throughout the city – efficient, racially and linguistically internalized marketing that infuriated white competitors. Chinese peddlers, each with up to 200 pounds of produce in baskets suspended from a pole, were common sights in early Vancouver, as, later, were the black vegetable trucks that replaced them. Chinese market gardens, impeccable green rows in black earth, began at the outskirts of the city. Japanese berry growers, who produced strawberries and raspberries for markets in Vancouver and on the Prairies, as well as for local jam factories, faced much the same marketing problems as many other British Columbian farmers, and also tried to solve them collectively. Japanese initiative organized the Maple Ridge cooperative in 1927. In 1934, its manager shipped fifty tons of strawberries to England, hoping to create a market that would put small-fruit growers in a stronger position when negotiating with jam factories.[46]

Organized very differently, the large hop farms near Chilliwack in the lower Fraser Valley depended on cheap, seasonal, Native labour recruited in the Fraser Canyon or at the canneries at the mouth of the Fraser. In 1912, one hop farm owner, who previously owned a tea plantation in Ceylon, employed sixty-five women and men from the canyon (most of them Nlha7kápmx), and sixty-three from the canneries (some of them Tsimshian from the lower Skeena). A hired CPR car took his pickers from the cannery town of Steveston to New Westminster, where they were switched to a baggage car for the rest of the trip to Chilliwack.[47] He ran a second plantation, and the people who worked it were a seasonal proletariat.

Farming in 1941

In a sense, 1941 marks the end of an era. The census for that year recorded 26,394 farms, almost the same number as a decade earlier, and four times the number in 1891. Farming had spread into almost all the arable nooks and crannies of the province, though the earlier concentration in the lower Fraser Valley remained. The farm population was aging. Farmers' median age was just over fifty, and only a quarter were under forty. The young were drifting away from farming, a drift accelerated by the war. Aside from a few parts of the Peace River district, agricultural pioneers were no longer pre-empting 'wilderness' and replacing it with farmsteads, fields, and fences. The geographical limits of commercial agriculture were well known – tested by years of experience and the scientific studies of entomologists, agricultural economists, and district horticulturists – and the agricultural frontier had closed. The era of agriculture, such as it was in British Columbia, was passing.

By 1941, agriculture was no longer central to the idea of British Columbia, a change that had been a long time in coming. As early as 1918, the Canadian Commission for Conservation had admitted that less than 5 per cent of British Columbia was arable.[48] In fact, the creation of the British Columbia Forest Branch in 1912 was partly driven by the realization that the forest industry, not agricultural settlement, was the leading motor of economic growth in the province, and that forestry required its own ministry, run according to the precepts of forest science. Despite such countercurrents, however, the assumptions of agrarianism pervaded government policy through the 1920s. They underwrote soldier-settler schemes in the arid interior and on the cutover around Comox on Vancouver Island, as well as land surveys to set off pre-emptions from Crown land to be leased exclusively for logging or mining. But by 1941, after the dust bowl on the Prairies, the sad migration of the Okies, and the wide recognition of (and public debate about) endemic rural poverty, most Canadians did not see their future in the countryside. After World War II, there was some muted talk about another program of soldier settlement for returning veterans, but it was clear that many assumptions of agrarianism had lost their hold, and that the future of British Columbia and of Canada more generally lay elsewhere: in cities, industrial development, and the modern world. Agriculture had become one among many industries, and a relatively minor one at that.

In 1941, successful commercial farms in British Columbia were specialized operations raising a specific product, or a narrow range of products, for sale in a competitive market. They had become, in effect, rural family businesses. Particular types of commercial farms were concentrated where ecological advantages, coupled with favourable land and transportation costs, allowed specific agricultural products to be produced and marketed more cheaply than elsewhere. This spatial division of labour became ever more pronounced as improvements in transportation and communication linked most farms to world prices. It produced a sharply differentiated, regionally specialized agriculture: beef cattle on the interior grasslands, orchards in the Okanagan, wheat in the Peace River, and market gardening and dairying close to towns or with quick rail access to them. The Okanagan became an orcharding region because, with irrigation, it could supply apples to Prairie farmers and English townsfolk more cheaply than other locations. Orchardists tried to manipulate and reorganize local ecologies so as to produce a commodity, apples, at the lowest price. The same logic organized other agricultural productions. Joe and Nan Bourgon produced more and more fluid milk for the Prince Rupert market because it brought the most profit. Joe Bourgon cut fewer railway ties in winter, staying home to attend to the cows and feeding them the hay, oats, and potatoes that he could have used as winter forage for beef cattle and pigs.

Despite their visible differences, different types of farms and farming regions were being organized by the same logic of the market.

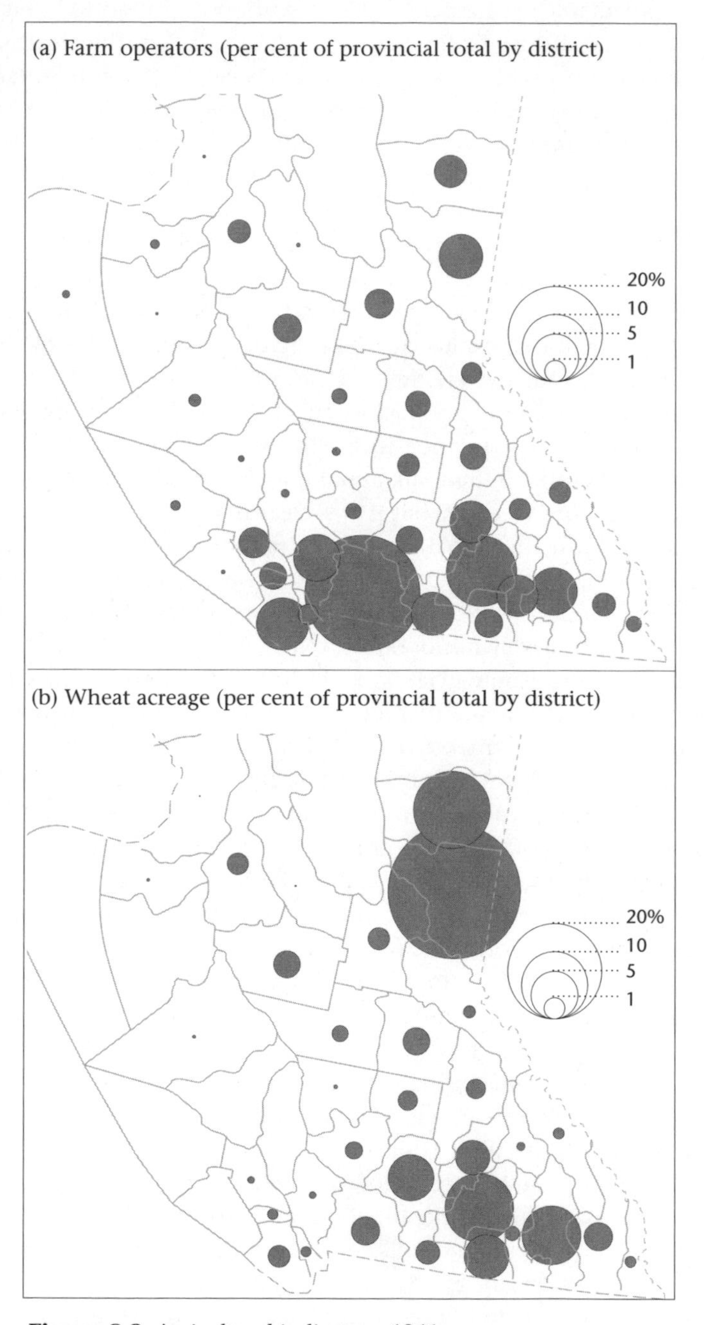

Figure 8.8 Agricultural indicators, 1941

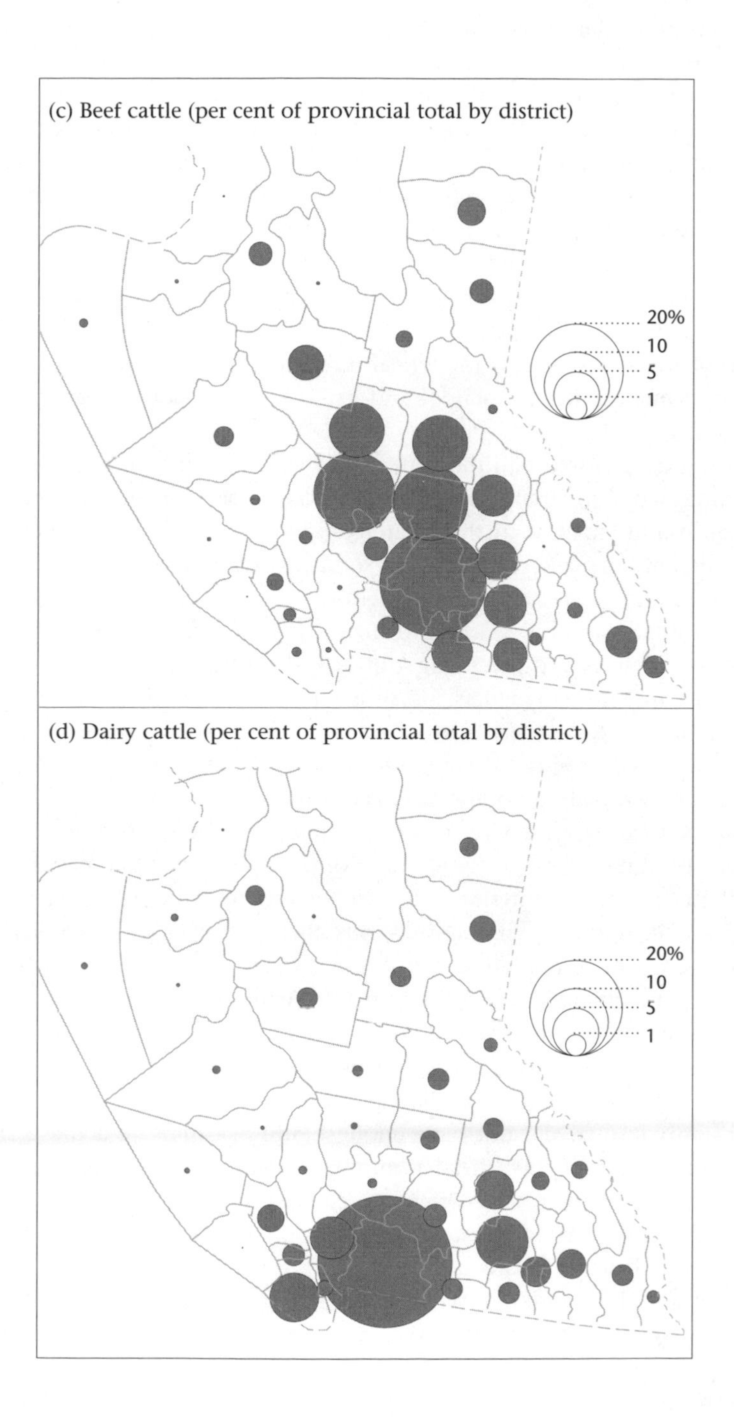
(c) Beef cattle (per cent of provincial total by district)
20%
10
5
1
(d) Dairy cattle (per cent of provincial total by district)
20%
10
5
1

This logic regionalized agricultural landscapes, work routines, skills, and, to some degree, rural cultures. An irrigated orchard in the Okanagan and a wheat farm in the Peace River area were, in detail, very different operations; each generated a somewhat different regional way of life. In the case of cattle ranching, these differences were supported by the accoutrements (for example, the clothing and vocabulary) of a western North American cattle complex of Hispanic origin. Yet such regional cultural differentiation, based on the spatial division of labour in the international market rather than on the past and on geographical isolation, as in traditional agrarian societies, existed within the same regulative state and, increasingly, within a similar information field. Children of ranchers in the Cariboo, orchardists in the Okanagan, and wheat farmers in the Peace River area followed the same curricula at school and listened to the same programs on the radio.

Far more deep-seated cultural differences in the countryside stemmed from immigrants' different backgrounds. Doukhobors in the Kootenays, like English and Japanese in the Okanagan, were orchardists, but they all spoke different languages, ate different foods, constructed different images of nature and home, and thought of themselves as different people. Market gardeners near Vancouver spoke Cantonese and lived apart. Natives, secluded on reserves and practising a little agriculture, were at least nominally Christian, but many elders still spoke little or no English. The market had not obliterated different cultural pasts in a predominantly immigrant society. Moreover, the racist categories that white people assumed, and deployed in their legislation and law, kept different peoples apart: Natives on reserves; Chinese in market gardens, but not in the countryside more generally; Japanese, after the confiscation of their property early in 1942, in detention camps in the interior. A reverse government strategy for dealing with difference – forced assimilation – was also employed, as when Native children were sent to residential schools and required to speak English, or when the government allowed the Sun Life Assurance Company to foreclose its mortgage on land the Doukhobors held communally. The market, alone, does not account for the British Columbia countryside in 1941.

Moreover, specialized commercial agriculture was not always attainable. A great many farmers did not have enough land or capital to achieve the economies of scale of specialized farming, or live within a large enough agricultural district to create efficient procedures for marketing. For them, the mixed, semi-subsistent farm – a base to support and employ a family, and from which to seek part-time wage work off the farm – was the only realistic option. It produced a living. Even during the Depression the family ate and was sheltered. In 1941, the majority of farms in British Columbia did not have a car, truck, or tractor. Most farmhouses were not electrified or served by running water. In terms of the market, most such farms were failures. But they were places where children were raised and lives lived, where dreams were played out, and in some cases, as with the Doukhobors, where radical social experiments were tried. They were places where non-English-speaking immigrants acquired a toehold in a new country, contributing themselves and their experiences to the larger society.

In sum, farming and rural life in British Columbia in 1941 reflected a number of fascinating intersections. The specializing pressures of capital-intensive agriculture connected to the international market were felt almost everywhere, and were variously responded to in pockets of agricultural land at the northern cordilleran end of the North American agricultural frontier. Specialized commercial farms and more diversified semi-subsistent ones embodied somewhat different ecological strategies, but both were superimposed on far more diverse local ecologies that, in various ways, farmers tried to suppress. The homogenizing cultural pressures of modern information fields, reinforced by the greatly increased scope of government, reached into the countryside to encounter very different cultures assembled from distant corners of the world. Immigrant cultures had largely displaced, but had not eliminated, Native peoples and their ways. The English language was the predominant, but far from the only, language of the countryside, and a rather ill-defined British Canadian culture was the standard of cultural assimilation. But homes elsewhere still figured strongly. Chinese youths working in market gardens near Vancouver knew that their conduct reflected on the honour of their families in villages near Canton; Nan Bourgon tended as best she could her English garden in the Bulkley Valley, while Daisy Phillips, to turn the equation around, endured the London blitz by dreaming of her short-lived home years before on an impossible farm in the Windermere Valley. The pockets of agricultural land tucked amid the mountains in British Columbia had culled a selection of strategies and dreams from the larger, twentieth-century world, and next to nothing from the Native societies that, not long before, had used these lands as their own.

Agriculture was a strategy of successful colonialism. It offered newcomers a fresh start in a new setting, a means of taking up land and making it their own. In 1891, the province was still exceedingly sparsely resettled; fifty years later, almost all land with any agricultural potential was taken, a massive appropriation that denied Native people access to familiar places and emphasized the smallness of their reserves. Agricultural settlers had come to stay, and the farms and families they created were both their achievements and the confinements of those they had largely displaced. Farming had created new cultural landscapes, neither more nor less artificial than Native cultural landscapes, but organized very differently, and had placed newcomers on the land to manage their own creations.

9
Making an Immigrant Society

Born in Ware, England, Topaz Edgeworth grew up in a wealthy industrial family, surrounded by servants, connections in high places, Methodist piety, and Victorian respectability. She remembered when the Duke of Wellington died – the Edgeworth family went into mourning – and admired Gladstone's principles and integrity all her adult life. She went to Mrs. Porter's School for Young Ladies at Brighton, to receive an 'English reflection of a classical education.' After her mother and stepmother died, and eventually, at a ripe age, her father as well, Topaz, unmarried and fifty, moved with her elder sister Annie and niece Rachel to Vancouver, where three of her nephews already lived. The three women and a somewhat corrupt Chinese cook named Yow (he went to jail for stealing from a subsequent employer) moved into a large house in the West End, the elite residential area in the city, when they arrived in the late 1890s. They soon settled in, aware that there seemed to be 'more mixing-up of people here than in Ware' – Yow, Americans with unusual table manners, and others – but secure in their position near the top of the social hierarchy. The three women's 'at home days' – tea and talk – were always well attended. Topaz joined the Minerva Club, a select group of ten literary ladies who met in West End homes to discuss Browning or an Elizabethan poet. She adored the royal family and wrote regularly to the Queen. The replies from the Queen's Lady in Waiting were published in a local paper. When the war came, Topaz organized the knitting of scarves for the troops. Late in her life, and to her boundless delight, she had a private audience with the Queen. At her death, 100 years old, she was still very much the voluble Topaz from Ware who had come to Vancouver fifty years before.[1]

Nan Bourgon (née Capewell) grew up in a Methodist working-class family in Derby, England. Taught by her grandmother, she became a seamstress, and was eventually employed by a titled family to make school outfits for the children. She moved into a life that alternated between a country estate on the edge of what remained of Sherwood Forest and a town house in London, lived within the ordered hierarchy of the servants' quarters, and was taught never to laugh or show the slightest emotion when Milord or Milady or any of their family or friends were about. Such, for a number of years, was her world. In 1911, Nan Capewell visited the Emigration Office in London, came back with literature on various colonies, and wrote to a sister in Vancouver. When she decided to leave, Milady was gracious: she presented Nan with a prayer book and offered to give her references.

In Vancouver, Nan worked as a dressmaker and as a waitress; then, caught by the depression of 1913, she got a job in the Grand Trunk Pacific Café opening in Prince Rupert. She went north by steamer and worked in the café for three months, then quit to escape a manager's unwelcome advances. She took the second Grand Trunk Pacific train out of Prince Rupert, winding up some 400 kilometres to the east in Aldermere in the Bulkley Valley, with five dollars to her name. There Nan found work for the local entrepreneur as the cleaning woman in his small hotel. From time to time, Joe Bourgon, a local farmer and livery man, asked her to ride in his buggy. Although he was French Canadian and Roman Catholic, she became known as Joe Bourgon's girl, and eventually, though not with much enthusiasm, she married him. Joe wanted a farmwife, and Nan, poor and thirty-four years old, sought a measure of security.

It was not an easy marriage. Their cultural backgrounds were exceedingly different, and they clashed over many details of house and garden. Once the priest, suspicious of Nan's Protestantism, threatened to take her children away. She left her husband shortly after their first child arrived, going to her sister in Seattle. But there was no work there, and when Joe sent her money for the trip back, she returned. Nan and Joe got by, coping with and needing each other, but hardly close. Joe was a good, practical farmer, and after a time his farm was one of the more successful in the valley, a family operation that shipped fluid milk by train to Prince Rupert. Joe became president of the Farmers' Institute; Nan was an occasional midwife and an organizer of community social activities. Eventually the Bourgons were among the valley's most respected citizens.[2]

At seventeen years of age, Leong May-ying, a beautiful young woman living in a rural village near Canton, was told that she would become the second wife, the concubine, of Chan Sam, a peasant from another village in Guangdong Province, who was then living in Gum San (Gold Mountain or North America). He had paid a high bride price, and the matter was settled. May-ying could go or commit suicide. She went, entered Canada in 1924 (the year after the Chinese Exclusion Act) on a falsified passport, was met by Chan Sam in Vancouver, and found herself working as a waitress in the Peking Tea House to pay off the money he had borrowed for her bride price, passage, and passport. The tea house took her wages, Chan Sam took her tips. Four years later, they and their two daughters returned to China to live for a year in her husband's village with his first wife. When May-ying was again well pregnant, she and

Chan Sam left the two daughters with the first wife, their official mother, and returned to Canada so the expected son would have a Canadian passport.

At the beginning of the Depression, May-ying was the more employable. She worked in tea houses in Vancouver and Nanaimo while relations with the frequently idle Chan Sam deteriorated. Eventually she prevailed on him to pay another visit to his first wife in China; her earnings paid for his passage, and, instalment by instalment, for the house, the largest in the village, that he would build there. She worked in the tea houses, gambled after hours, and, increasingly, drank and turned to prostitution. Her daughter Hing (the son was female) grew up in rooming houses and hotel rooms at the edge of her mother's world and within her mother's determination to be a traditional parent of an obedient child. May-ying regularly beat her daughter, who then, sobbing, would kneel and repeat 'I will be obedient. I admit I was naughty. I will be a good girl.' When Sam returned, he and May-ying soon separated. Her drinking, gambling, and prostitution increased. Hing went to the government school and to a Chinese school after hours. Covered with eczema, she was the best student in either class.

May-ying's separation from Sam was followed by a long, intermittent relationship with a professional gambler, as quick witted as May-ying herself, with bouts of drinking, and incessant gambling, increasingly on credit. As a young woman, Hing was allowed no social contact with boys; eventually she left, and her mother, try as she would, did not choose her husband. With the gambler out of the picture, May-ying came to live for a time with Hing's young family, but the arrangement did not work: too much drinking and lying, too many dark memories, and too much generational tension between mother and daughter. May-ying returned to cheap rooms in cheap hotels. Her grandchildren, when they saw her, remarked on how Chinese she was. Eventually she was killed in a car accident, a frail Chinese woman in broken health who spoke no English and had never wished to.[3]

After the mid-1880s, the majority of British Columbians were immigrants, most coming directly or indirectly from the British Isles, but others from continental Europe, and a considerable number from across the Pacific. The Native population, a small fraction of what it had been before outsiders and their diseases arrived, was declining rapidly. In 1891, Native people accounted for a little more than a quarter of the provincial total; in 1921, they were 4 per cent. In short order, a largely immigrant society had been put in place and largely immigrant human geographies created. British Columbia, a territory invented by British diplomacy, had acquired a new social and geographical reality. This new society was, itself, a late product of and an active participant in the processes of colonialism, yet such was the extent of its domination that most immigrant British Columbians were oblivious to the impact of their society on the peoples they had largely displaced.

What sort of society was this? Most British Columbians would have said that it was a modern society, part of the British empire, part of the Dominion of Canada, part of the reach of European civilization and progress. They would have struggled to be more analytical, and their analytical problem remains. This was not a modern society that had evolved *in situ*, as in Europe. Nor was it a colonial society, where a small European elite and its troops and retainers presided over a large indigenous population, the situation considered in almost all the recent literature on the strategies and tactics of colonialism and resistance.[4] Nor, even, was it much like the immigrant societies that had emerged in eastern, pre-industrial North America, where agriculture was the predominant activity, and forests yielded to the dispersed labour of axe and plough. Models of social change derived from such circumstances do not fit British Columbia very well, and the province as a whole remains rather uncharted social space.

To understand this society in some comprehensive way is to come to terms, I think, with its largely immigrant character. It was hugely influenced, of course, by industrial capitalism and the tactics of social control of the modern nation-state. But cutting across these dimensions of modern life were the basic facts of immigration: most British Columbians or their recent ancestors had left one setting, usually their home, for another; and in this new place, they encountered a different land inhabited by a different mix of peoples. A society was being composed out of extreme displacements and disaggregations: a severely disrupted indigenous population, and a largely immigrant population detached from the circumstances of former lives, juxtaposed to unfamiliar peoples and ways, and perched amid some of the most dramatic terrain in the world. People no longer lived in anything like the full societies they had come from, but commonly in small fractions of those societies assembled where resources and transportation combined to offer some economic opportunity. A certain astonishment was in the air, a quality that some of the province's best writers have caught.[5]

It is not easy to translate astonishment into analysis, especially when the main models of social change in modernizing societies have been framed in somewhat different circumstances. I doubt that British Columbians understand their society very well, a malaise of modernity perhaps, but probably accentuated here by recent immigration and the radically reworked land associated with it. Put somewhat abstractly, immigrants and capital had abruptly de-territorialized the prior inhabitants of British Columbia and had re-territorialized themselves.[6] The creation of an immigrant society in a reconfigured geographical space was a culminating colonial process, and in this final chapter I offer some thoughts about the formation and shape of such a society.

I start with the simple proposition, increasingly taken for granted by social theorists, that societies and the places they occupy are part and parcel of each other.[7] The one is not the stage on which the other evolves. Nor are societies made by their settings, as environmental determinists once thought, or settings the simple effects of human activity. The two are interrelated, each affecting the other in complex, ongoing interaction. It follows that to take people out of one setting and relocate them in another, radically different, is to change their social relations. It follows that different types of settlement in British Columbia express different types of social relations. The same society cannot be in different settings.

Three other propositions follow. First, immigrants reestablish elements, but never the sum, of former ways. If for no other reason than that already given, a society and its geographical context in all their complexity are untransferable. Immigrants live within lean replications of the world they have left behind. Second, they also live within a host of new experiences related to the novel setting (for them) to which they have come, the places they have constructed therein, and the unfamiliar people who are suddenly at hand. Third, both these deletions and these encounters are sources of social change.

These simple propositions may begin to provide a framework for analysis. One might say that the dialectic between the intertwined processes by which, on the one hand, a tradition is simplified and, on the other, it is introduced to new dimensions of complexity largely shapes the character of an immigrant society. One might then inquire by what particular means a tradition is simplified, and what form such simplification might characteristically take.[8] One might inquire whether there is a pattern to the ways in which a relocated fragment of a former society deals with the other fragments it encounters, and how different fragments begin to borrow from each other. Something of the shape of an immigrant society might begin to be discerned out of such an analysis. This, at least, is a line of attack, one that I am inclined to follow.

Deletions

A long tradition that includes the early-nineteenth-century English political economist Edward Gibbon Wakefield and the late-nineteenth-century American frontier historian Frederick Jackson Turner has held that when Europeans moved overseas into the depopulated middle latitudes, they encountered new environments that stimulated social change.[9] For both Wakefield and Turner, cheap land was the decisive ingredient of these new environments. Wakefield thought that it destroyed social bonds and created a rabble, Turner that it loosened the bonds of tyranny and provided context for American democracy. The one sought to seal the frontier and raise the price of land, the other lamented the frontier's passing, but both agreed about the social importance of a sudden change in land values. A rapid decrease in the value of land, relative to labour, had upset European property relations and the grid of custom and inheritance surrounding them. The result, they thought, was that segments of European social hierarchies could not reestablish themselves, a failure they either applauded or deprecated. For both Wakefield and Turner, a new environment put selective pressures on European ways, tending to accept some and reject others. The motor of social change was a new environment, particularly its new terms of access to land.

A very different approach to thinking about immigrant societies was suggested more than thirty years ago by the American political scientist Louis Hartz.[10] Hartz argued that only fragments, rather than the sum of European societies, migrated overseas, and that in these new settings the ethos of the fragment, suddenly detached from the constraints of a larger social formation, became the ethos of a whole society. The United States, Hartz held, was a liberal bourgeois fragment of Europe, New France a feudal fragment. Compared to their progenitors, Hartz thought immigrant societies had been drastically simplified, a process of social change he associated with the selective migration of elements of European society. Hartz, a political scientist interested in political ideas, was struck by how much of the European political debate was virtually absent in the United States, and believed he had identified the cause.

The point of agreement in these otherwise very different analyses is the common assumption that immigrant societies had pared back the complex social worlds from which they had sprung. I argued some years ago that this was an important insight, but that Hartz had got the mechanism of simplification wrong.[11] Ideas, I suggested, have been remarkably mobile, not only 'big' ideas about political life of the sort Hartz was after, but a host of more ordinary, everyday ideas and assumptions about social organization, work, and the details of daily life. Such ideas travelled in the thoughts and memories of travellers, part of their invisible baggage wherever they went. Any substantial group of people represented, at least in principle, an enormous capacity to transfer ways of life from one place to another because of the store of knowledge that accompanied them. On the other hand, not all, by any means, of this intellectual and cultural baggage was relevant to new settings. Ideas and cultures had been decontextualized. It availed little to remember how to build a particular roof if the materials were not at hand, or if others, previously unavailable, were now cheaper and better. It availed little to plan for a gentry life if the economy would not produce the revenue to sustain it. The paring back of former ways in immigrant settings had much less to do, I held, with the particular groups that came than with the conditions in which they found themselves.

I remain of the view that a Hartzian analysis does not begin to explain the social structure of immigrant societies, and still broadly agree with Wakefield and Turner that the interaction of people and environment in the New World has been a powerful source of social change. But I have increasingly realized that the Hartzian analysis is relevant in ways Hartz did not intend. It does not explain social structure, but it does bear on the transfer of regional cultures. In effect, two selective processes tended to affect different segments of the Old World heritage. A new environment shaped, first and foremost, a society's terms of access to land – its relationship with property. These changed relationships bore particularly on the *vertical* structure of Old World society. They tended to mean that some components of intricate Old World social hierarchies were favoured and that others were not. In settings, for example, where land was relatively cheap and markets poor, a relatively generous space was opened for the ordinary family, and relatively little space for the upper echelons of Old World society. Where markets were accessible and resources attractive, capital and labour rushed in. On the other hand, the selective migrations of people from Old World societies tended to affect the *horizontal* structure of Old World culture, representing different cultures quite unevenly, and mixing cultures up. Overall, such migration left behind a great deal of the regional cultural complexity of the Old World. It was never possible to reproduce a regional culture, much less anything like the intricate horizontal range of Old World cultures; one reason for this cultural attrition was a migratory process in which a few people were drawn out of a much larger society and relocated across an ocean. Simply put, selective emigration emphasized some Old World regional cultures more than others. This was the other basic way in which the sum of Old World societies was drastically pared back in their extensions overseas. Some ideas were lost because they did not fit, and others because they did not come.

In sum, these two processes of social and cultural change tended to work at right angles to each other; together, their capacity to eliminate large parts of immigrants' Old World backgrounds was enormous. Some clusters of ideas did not reestablish themselves because the context was wrong. Others were not established because they never came or because they came in so few individual memories that there was an insufficient critical mass for their social reproduction. Unfamiliar environments tended to rework social structures, and pare back many former regional cultural ways; selective migrations tended to transfer only fragments of the intricate cultural mosaic that was spread across the Old World.

Immigrant British Columbia was a recently depopulated land that the time-space compressions of the mid-late nineteenth century had suddenly brought within reach of world markets (see Chapter 6). Its minerals, forests, and fish were attractive, particularly to western American capital, which was close at hand and experienced in these resource industries. As British Columbian resources came within range, capital poured in, often building the systems of transportation and communication it required, and opening industrial work camps at favoured resource locations. Over the years, capital reached into ever-more-remote interstices of a vast, rugged land to develop resources and, inadvertently, to create new human geographies. With it, sometimes preceding it, came labour and particular techniques of resource exploitation, most of western American origin. In this, rather than in pioneer agriculture, was the principal momentum of settlement and economic growth in an emerging, immigrant British Columbia. A work camp in the 'wilderness' and a line of industrial transportation to the outside world, rather than a pioneer farm tucked in a clearing, was the more basic geography of the place.

This huge, ongoing effort of development created abundant space for, and emphasized the social importance of, capital and labour. There were investments to make; practical jobs to be done by hard-headed, practical people; and, especially in the earlier years, an enormous amount of backbreaking physical labour. The basic arteries, economies, and settlements of a new human geography were being constructed. This vast practical effort drew selectively on prior social structures, emphasizing some elements and discouraging others. A British miner, reflecting on the gold rush society he observed in the Cariboo in the 1860s, saw it this way.[12] Educated people, he said, should stay away. Their place was in 'polished appreciative communities.' Capital could take its chances. The real opportunity was for labour (he wrote about placer mining, which was not capital intensive). Old World societies were 'overburdened with men of muscle'; there, 'muscle bears so small an interest that the labourer cannot hope to attain a higher grade than that at which he started.' But new societies had reversed these conditions. In them 'life is simplified ... man is brought more directly in relation with mother earth ... and the only middlemen are traders and artisans [who] have no aristocracy of birth, wealth or position.' He was offering, crudely, an analysis of the relationship between social organization and the factors of production in new societies, and arguing approximately the same case as Wakefield and Turner.

The miner's analysis fits some parts of British Columbia better than others, but, overall, there was a tendency for the workplaces of the province to emphasize the values of the bourgeoisie and the working class. The cleavage between capital and labour became a dominant axis of the social structure of the immigrant society, leaving a lasting mark on the province's polarized political culture. In work camps, where labour

View of Nanaimo, c. 1914. An industrial town built around the colliery and the working-class mining family.

overwhelmingly predominated, the values and aspirations were those of the working class; in early elections, labour candidates expected to do well in such settings. In the small towns dominated by primary resource industries, capital and labour were both well represented. Shopkeepers, somewhat in the middle, sided with one or the other. Often the struggle between them was intense, as when mine owners' associations and militant unions battled in isolated mining towns (see Chapter 7). At stake was the apportionment of a great deal of new wealth. In the cities, where the occupational structure was much more varied, class alignments were less sharp. Yet the cities, Vancouver in particular, were essentially points of exceptional connectivity in the commercial-industrial economy. They organized the local primary resource economy, maintained external trading connections, and were enthusiastic boosters of their own progress and development. Their most successful citizens were entrepreneurs, speculators, or business managers; some had made fortunes in the real estate game. Such cities were not a world apart; they were another physical creation of capital and labour. They were spatially divided along class lines, and reflected, in only somewhat attenuated form, the class divisions that ran through much of the province.

If there were a haven from the dominance of capital and labour, it was in farming. Mountainous as it is, British Columbia admitted farming to many of its valleys, though farming neither had the economic momentum of the primary resource industries nor became a defining regional presence, as it had on the Prairies and in much of eastern Canada. Still, agrarian visions were strong, and farming was vigorously pursued, both where it was possible and where it was not (see Chapter 8). By and large, farmers struggled with problems common to much of North American agriculture of the day: farms that were too small for the economies of scale of increasingly mechanized production; a cost-price squeeze associated with declining agricultural prices and rising equipment costs; and inaccessible, distant markets. In these circumstances, most agriculture was not very profitable, and the characteristic farm had a high subsistent component. It was usually subsidized by the low cost of family labour – on Chinese market gardens, usually by male family or village labour. Except in ranching, capital was hardly interested in agricultural investments, and the few attempts to create landed estates and lives of gentlemanly ease foundered on economic realities. Compared to the primary resource industries, farming tended to produce weakly stratified societies in which the tensions between capital and labour were largely absent, and the values of the farm family and, to a degree, those of the local rural community tended to come to the fore. Essentially, farming provided a niche, somewhat apart from the modern commercial economy, for families.

In this, farming contrasted strikingly with the primary resource industries, which tended to extend the growing separation of place of work from place of residence in modernizing economies to the point of excluding families altogether.[13] Work in the resource industries was for men, with the exception of salmon canneries, which employed Native and Japanese women. The work was often temporary, in settings with few amenities for families or, because of the shifting location of work, little incentive to create them. In such circumstances, much of the labour in the resource industries was performed by single men, a mobile labour force moving among the camps, bunkhouses, and cheap hotels associated with a particular resource industry. The Chinese labourer, unmarried or with wife and family in a peasant village near Canton, was part of a larger pattern. Wives and families appeared in the larger camps, but many workers in the resource industries never married or, if they did, lived apart from their wives for much of the year. Working lives over, elderly bachelor men lived out their lives in cheap rooming houses at the dilapidated edge of downtown.

The brawny maleness of most work in the resource industries and the scarcity of outside work for white women probably tended to reinforce the gendered separation of workplace and residence associated with industrializing societies. For many men, the domestic values of home became a particular locus of civility, a retreat from a competitive, isolated, and often exceedingly dangerous workplace. Women, in this view, were identified with domestic virtues, an identification that contributed to their isolation from outside work.[14] On pioneer farms, the gendered separation of workplace and residence tended to break down, as it did for immigrant non-white women, for whom there was a variety of poorly paid outside employments.

The resource industries also excluded a huge variety of skills associated with former work, skills that could not be transferred to new industrial workplaces because the factors of production were differently arranged and technologies were unfamiliar. The resource industries in British Columbia tended to rely on skills and technologies that had evolved in analogous settings in the far western United States and had diffused rapidly northward. The axis of immigration crossed that of technological diffusion. This, coupled with the facts that the range of different employments was often greatly diminished and that many immigrants found themselves engaged in what, for them, were novel occupations, meant that a large part of the former ways associated with daily male work was suddenly irrelevant. New skills had to be learned, and in most of the resource industries they could be, to some acceptable level, fairly quickly. A strong back, confidence, and adaptability, rather than a prolonged apprenticeship, were required.[15] As men were reskilled, they tended to be identified with their occupations; they became miners, or loggers, or fishermen, occupational identifications that ignored the particular backgrounds from which they had come.

Each resource industry illustrates this. Technologies of placer mining came north from mining camps in California, as did the first miners. Later, more miners came from the east into what, for them, were extraordinary circumstances. There was very little work other than placer mining, very little society other than placer miners. The skills of placer mining, unfamiliar to many, could be learned fairly quickly: they had far more to do with hard work, practical ingenuity, and some experience than with science, engineering, or craftsmanship. To be a placer miner in

Logging camp no. 2, Chemainus, 1903. A West Coast example of the oldest type of European settlement in Canada, the male work camp.

a remote camp suddenly assembled in what miners took to be wilderness was to acquire a few new ways, and leave an enormous amount behind. So it was in hard-rock mining and logging. Much of the technology of hard-rock mining in the mountains of southeastern British Columbia had evolved in American hard-rock camps, just as much of the technology of coastal logging came from American redwood and Douglas-fir forests. Experienced miners and loggers moved north with these technologies, but more immigrants who eventually became loggers or miners had no previous experience with this work. The huge coastal forest, a double-bitted axe, a ten- or twelve-foot crosscut saw, wedges and screw jacks (the basic tools of logging in British Columbia until World War II), a bunkhouse, a few other loggers: this was a powerful new environment of work. It fashioned loggers and rendered prior occupations irrelevant. As an individual became a logger, or a miner, prior skills slipped away. Even agricultural skills changed, often drastically. Experienced farmers (most who tried to farm in British Columbia were not) found that the relative cost of land and labour had changed, and that familiar crops were unsuited to new environments. In the interior, horticulture required irrigation, and ranching depended on a Hispanic cattle culture of Mexican origin, both new to immigrants from more humid regions. Almost wherever practised, farming was an ongoing experiment with unfamiliar conditions. Such, perhaps, was the condition of agriculture in any modernizing society, but to the usual uncertainties were added those associated with pioneering in unfamiliar environments. In sum, a particular distribution of resources and relationships among the factors of production and with markets had created types of work in British Columbia that were new to many immigrants. To earn a living, they usually had little choice but to adopt these ways; by so doing, they discarded much of the work experience associated with their place of origin.

Outside (predominantly male) work was more affected by these changes than inside (predominantly female) work. The former was exposed to the competitive market economy, and conformed to its efficiencies; the latter, somewhat shielded from the market, could reflect other values. For this reason, domestic female work tended to be far more conservative than outside male work. The nature and arrangement of furniture, the pictures on the wall, the stories told to children, the garments knit or sewed, the meals prepared, perhaps the language spoken: all this could reflect a home elsewhere, and often did. On a farm, there were often two landscapes: the fields tended by the man and conforming to the common regional practices of commercial agriculture; and the kitchen garden, tended by the woman, and reflecting the preferred vegetables, flowers, and herbs from home. In the logging or mining camps that were big and permanent enough to admit families, a worker's cabin might have a tiny garden, with bits of lace from home in the windows: pinpoints of another place and culture in landscapes dominated by the terms and conditions of industrial work. A man would return from forest or mine not only to a family, but also to a few touches from another place once lived in. Often the touches were weak because the women were limited by what they could afford, what was available in the stores, the peer-group-dominated interests of their children, and the opinions of neighbours. Farming was culturally more conservative than the primary resource industries, due to the primacy of the nuclear family and the considerable place it accorded for domestic work.

Within this, values associated with gentility and refined living had a tough time. Such values found a certain amount of space, but generally around the margins of a society with another momentum. They had neither a local economy nor a local past to fall back on. And yet, the late-nineteenth-century to early-twentieth-century emigrations from the British Isles to British Columbia included a good number of educated, upper-class people. There was a fair share of Oxbridge educations and venerable family names. Some of these people brought money, but most came with little more than public school educations, well-developed imaginations, and an educated upper-class English civility. Such ways had little practical relevance in the primary resource industries and made little headway there. There was more opportunity for the genteel English in agriculture, a socially acceptable pursuit for this class, but their farms tended to be long on picturesque landscapes and short on practical experience. The few pioneers who became successful farmers and left an established commercial position to their progeny were rarely of this group. Overall, the educated English were perceived to be haughty and useless. Indeed, their record of practical achievement is not good; at one extreme, men listed in *Burke's Peerage* lived in shacks in the Cariboo; at the other, young English blue bloods played polo on a terrace overlooking the Thompson River while Chinese workers built an elaborate irrigation system and planted an ill-conceived orchard.[16] The lives of such people had been radically decontextualized; old meanings and ways had lost their social fit. The shock was less in Vancouver, Victoria, and some rural areas – the Cowichan and Coldstream valleys, a few enclaves in the Kootenays – where settlers with mannered English ways converged, but, overall, British Columbia provided little economic base or social context for imported gentility. It considerably accelerated a process of social change that was taking place in Britain.

Such were some of the pressures that new terms of land access and new work environments placed on the ways of life that immigrants had previously known. Overall, these pressures tended to emphasize the social relationships associated with industrial capital and to weaken other forms of sociability. On pioneer farms, however, they emphasized the nuclear family and tended to fend off capital. They favoured a few new, dominating technologies and discouraged others; inside work, shielded from these technologies, was culturally more conservative than outside work. These pressures were never very conducive to the social reproduction of gentility.

This was not the only axis of simplification. Immigrants came from many different cultural backgrounds in widely different parts of the world. No individual culture could be replicated in British Columbia. Invariably they were pared back, some much more drastically than others, but always to a fraction of what they had been. As this happened, ways that had survived the process of migration were recontextualized; their meanings changed. For many immigrants, their own ethnicity was being invented.

Before World War II, the great majority of immigrants were of British background, most coming directly from the British Isles, and most of the rest from eastern Canada. The considerable majority of those coming directly from Britain were English, unlike the predominantly Scottish and Irish migrations to early Ontario and the Maritimes. The eastern Canadians were usually two or more generations removed from the British Isles, as were the Americans of British background who entered the province. In 1931, these people – British born or of British background – were 73 per cent of the non-Native population of British Columbia, quite enough to ensure that English would be the province's predominant as well as official language. These 'British' people were, however, a culturally diverse collection. The British Isles were still a cultural mosaic, if one increasingly dominated by the English language and a standardizing national culture. Eastern Canadians brought different ways, bred of their North American years, from immigrants directly from Britain. The Scottishness of Cape Breton was not the refashioned Irishness (Catholic or Protestant) of much of southern Ontario, or the sixth-generation Loyalist culture of the St. John Valley of New Brunswick. Such, and more, was the regionally variegated Britishness that entered British Columbia.

Regional differences within the concept of British could hardly be sustained in British Columbia. People were mixed up; there was not a critical mass – whatever, precisely, it might be – of people from a particular regional background, and there was little will to maintain such differences. People of different backgrounds married; the census identified their progeny as British, but the connection with Yorkshire or the St. John Valley was gone. Differences in accent and dialect thinned out, not overnight and not entirely, but the drift was towards a regional English accent that combined eastern Canadian, English, and northwestern

American influences. A generalized British diet tended to survive; so, too, for the most part, a generalized enthusiasm for Britain and the empire. Expatriate Scots got together on Robbie Burns night to sing his songs, drink, and feel Scottish. Expatriate Irish did much the same on St. Patrick's Day. Anglicans built Gothic revival churches and, where they could, planted and tended English flowers in the churchyards, replicating patches of Ruskinesque England. This diverse group, which collectively comprised both the cultural majority and social elite within a British colony endowed with British institutions, gave British Columbian society a British tone. It was not, however, a particular cultural replication, rather an amalgam of different regional ways that omitted a great deal from any one of them.

In 1931, 27 per cent of the non-Native population of British Columbia was not of British origin. Some 19 per cent were from continental Europe, principally from Germany, Sweden, Norway, Italy, and Russia. Just over 7 per cent were from East Asia: China (4 per cent) and Japan (3 per cent). There was a sprinkling of others. These people found themselves as cultural minorities in a society dominated by the English-speaking and the reworked 'British' culture described above. Many had no intention of staying; they were in British Columbia to earn some money and return home. Whether or not they came to stay, a great many did, and their British Columbian lives unfolded in a place where migration had turned them into an identifiable cultural and, in some cases, racial minority. There were many coping strategies. Some tried to integrate as quickly as possible; as a group, the Germans were perhaps foremost in this approach. Most sought out people of their own kind, partly for the familiarity of language and culture, partly for security against the perceived and often real hostility of the larger society. Even in the resource industries, workers of particular regional backgrounds stuck together when and where they could. Italians lived in residential 'Little Italys' in the Kootenay mining towns. Swedes took over a corner of a bunkhouse. Societies and associations perpetuated various links with home. In some cases, children were sent to special classes after the public schools closed, to learn to read and write their parents' language. Such efforts to maintain links with home were always an uphill struggle; the assimilative pressures were enormous. The first generation of British Columbian-born could usually speak their parents' language, yet hardly read or write it; the second generation usually knew only a few words. The overall decline of many details of cultures rooted elsewhere may have been roughly in proportion to the decline in languages. Domestic ways always tended to be more resistant than those associated with the cash economy, but old ways were under assault everywhere. In time, they often survived only in special ceremonial occasions, such as weddings or national days, and perhaps in a few basic values, such as deference to parents. British Columbian Japanese could be embarrassed when presented to high-ranking Japanese officials visiting the province; they had forgotten the correct form of polite address because they no longer lived in a society in which such forms had social meaning.

There was always a small minority of immigrants who came to British Columbia to preserve an Old World social vision. Such were some of the upper-middle-class English, who no longer had the means to sustain their social pretensions in England, and considered a farm or ranch in a British settler colony a socially acceptable safety valve. Such, indirectly, were the missionary agendas for Christian utopias – European inspirations without European space – among Native people, whom they believed lived in darkness and sin, but who could be led to light and salvation in isolated settlements shielded from the nefarious influences of other whites.[17] The utopian impulse was expressed most directly in various communal settlements that sought, in some tucked-away corner in the mountains, a little space and isolation from the values and demands of an encroaching world. Of these, the most conspicuous were the Doukhobor settlements in the Kootenays. The Doukhobors, an ascetic, Christian-anarchist sect from the Caucasus, sought to live communally apart from the state, apart from the corrupt values of the larger society. As Hartz would have put it, they sought to make the ethos of a fragment – their peasant Doukhobor communities – their whole social circumference, an ambition they partly achieved in British Columbia for more than a generation. The Doukhobors are an idiosyncratic example of the common immigrant tendency, made almost inevitable in circumstances where comprehensive social reproduction was impossible, to focus on some parts of the former social whole and let the rest slip away. For the Doukhobors, as for others with an explicit utopian vision, the rest was a welcome riddance.

In all of this, former ways of life were being reproduced in increasingly abstract and symbolic form. To live in a village in County Armagh, Ireland, or in Guangdong Province, China, was to live in a regional culture that affected most details of daily life, yet was virtually invisible. Cultural assumptions were shared. The lifeworld was pervasive, enveloping, and apparent only when strangers came along or local people travelled and were reminded of their difference. *In situ*, the stranger seemed odd, but travel turned people into strangers who, as they moved away from the familiar, began to feel odd themselves. To settle down in another place, among different people and different ways, was constantly to be reminded of one's own difference. What was implicit had been made explicit. People discovered their own ethnicity. When, at the same time, there was a great deal of cultural loss, as invariably there was, this explicit identification focused on a declining number of markers. Increasingly, for those inside an expatriate culture, these markers became symbols of where one had come from and who one was. Such was the significance of the 'ethnic' wedding. Ethnicity was no longer invisible and implicit in a way of life. It had become spare, symbolic, and altogether explicit, and, so abstracted, it could be exceedingly powerful. It could be said that migrations tended to destroy cultures and invent ethnicities.

This change took place in different ways with different groups and individuals. The more centrally people were placed in the British migrations, the more of their own ways they were able to retain, and the less explicitly they were likely to be held. These people were least likely to discover their own ethnicity; they thought others were 'ethnics.' For cultural minorities, the process of explicit ethnic identification was very much to the fore. Some people fled it to assimilate as quickly as possible. Others did not have this option, or did not seek it. Ethnic definitions were strong, especially when reinforced by race. They defined many people to themselves and to each other, and comprised another basic axis of social differentiation in an immigrant society.

Recombinations

If one followed migration paths from their origin in the Old World to their destination overseas, and compared the ways of life in the two locations, one would often be struck by how little of the former lifeworld had been transferred to the latter. I have suggested what seem the basic reasons for these common, and frequently drastic, deletions. But migration paths originating in very different, geographically distant cultures converged in places like British Columbia. People who had lived apart, and had been aware of each other only in the most general terms, if at all, met abruptly on unfamiliar terrain. The land and the means of earning a living thereon, as well as the people around, were often exceedingly strange. Immigrant life was located at the intersection of what, for the people involved, were two radically novel circumstances: an attenuating connection with a distant home, and an expanding connection with the ingredients of a new setting. Immigrant society reflected both these sets of relationships.

People migrated to British Columbia, as elsewhere, for a great many reasons, most economic in one way or another. The few who came for cultural reasons did so to protect, or modify, some aspect of the culture they left behind. Almost no one was drawn to a new mix of cultures. Because it seemed the route to prosperity, some immigrants tried to assimilate quickly into what they perceived to be the dominant culture, but many were more wary. The common reaction was to fend off otherness as much as one reasonably could. People sought to get ahead and retain something of their own cultural identities. I have mentioned some of the strategies of cultural conservation, and their common result: an increasingly reified ethnicity based on a declining number of increasingly symbolic markers. But the success of immigrants' attempts to draw boundaries around their own ways of life and keep strangeness somewhat at bay varied with the size and power of the immigrant group. A small, non-English-speaking immigrant minority, with little access to government and not much capital, had little power – beyond an intense local struggle waged at the scale of the family and of community organizations – to defend its own cultural boundaries. Immigrants of British background, a solid majority with the levers of economic and political power at their disposal, were in an altogether different position to defend themselves and their way of life. They set out to define a territory in their terms and make it theirs, in the process creating boundaries that they used to fend off or control others.

British immigrants to British Columbia assumed what Edward Said, in *Orientalism*, has called an 'imaginative geography' of the world. In this geography, there was Europe, the centre of civilization, and there was the rest of the world, less civilized, less ordered, somewhat mysterious, essentially barbarous or savage. This divide was a cultural construction, not so much a geography of the world as of the European mind. Therein lay its power. It enabled Europeans to define and locate themselves in relation to the world in, for them, an altogether satisfactory way. They, more than any others, were the bearers of civilization and progress; the rest of the world was identified by stereotypes that served to emphasize the superiority of Europeans and hide the achievements and variety of non-Europeans. This imaginative geography underlay orientalism as a field of study, ran as a pervasive strand through European art and literature, and provided moral validation for European imperialism. It accompanied European technology and military might out into the world, discourse and physical power validating each other.[18] British immigrants to British Columbia, like Europeans elsewhere in various nineteenth-century empires, took the discourse entirely for granted; they knew they were among the civilized. But they were not in Europe, not even on the Atlantic Ocean, rather in a distant corner of the world with Asia beyond the horizon and a 'savage' population at hand. To the extent that their new location was on the wrong side of an imaginative geographical divide, it was a geography to be corrected. In September 1858, late in the first summer of the gold rush, Governor Douglas addressed a large congregation of miners at the foot of the Fraser Canyon, only weeks after miners and Natives had been fighting a few miles to the north. He welcomed them, assured them of the protection and value of British law, and then, addressing the British miners, said that he was 'Commanded to say to all Her Majesty's Native born subjects that this is their country.'[19] Considering where he was, and when, this was an extraordinary statement. It was not just that a new colony was being added to the empire; rather, settlers were welcomed to a colony that was to become 'their country' approximately as England or Scotland had been. British Columbia was to be added, in effect, to the geography of a greater Britain, part of a greater Europe, the locus of civilization.

Such a project could only involve keeping others out, or, if this could not be done, containing them in as little space as possible. Boundaries became exceedingly important: the boundary of a colony (later of Canada) could be used to exclude immigrants, and, internally, boundaries could be used to separate those who were welcome because they were civilized, and those who had to be put up with because they were not. In drawing these latter boundaries, it could easily seem a moral duty, from the perspective of the civilized, to be as parsimonious as possible with the uncivilized.

The drawing of boundaries was enormously facilitated by the idea of race, which gained in currency and, apparently, scientific foundation during the nineteenth century. The Enlightenment idea of the fundamental unity of all people still found expression in the British government's abolition of slavery in 1833 and in the Treaty of Waitangi with the Maori in New Zealand in 1840, but gave way, from the mid-nineteenth century on, to increasingly racial classifications of people. It was a relatively small step, especially in the light of Darwinian theories of selection and of the survival of the fittest, to identify advanced and backward races – different stages, apparently, of evolution.[20] This 'binary typology' of race, as Said has called it, readily complemented the far older European discourse about the location of civilization and savagery; it gave the discourse scientific validity, casting the difference between Europeans and non-Europeans into an immutable, biologically determined fact. Most late-nineteenth-century imperial discourses were racialized in this way, and a lively idea of race became part of the baggage of European emigrants. In British Columbia, such ideas, somewhat abstracted from Europe, encountered their object in a place where social and cultural change was the common lot and an immigrant society, of somewhat uncertain future, was being constructed. These encounters and uncertainties, superimposed on a broad background of racist opinion, generated a particularly virulent racism. The moral and physical failings of the 'yellow race,' considered the most threatening in British Columbia, were elaborated in detail, the dangers of contamination widely described. In a society given to increasingly symbolic social representation, race became the preeminent symbol. It defined simply and effectively, with no need to go into details, who was acceptable and who was not.

English reflections. Martell family home on Esplanade beach, Nanaimo, c. 1890. A transplanted middle-class English lifestyle.

So armed, a white and British majority population set out to police its boundaries. From its vantage point, the simplest solution was to keep other races out. The province's demands for exclusionary immigration policies, often more extreme than the federal government was prepared to go, steadily raised racial barriers. A head tax on Chinese immigrants set at $10 in 1884 became $50 the next year and $500 in 1904. Still the Chinese arrived, and in greater numbers than ever in the years just before World War I, when their labour was required to complete two new transcontinental railways. When the railways were built, the Chinese Exclusion Act (1923), supported by the overwhelming majority of voting British Columbians, stopped Chinese immigration. Restrictions on the Japanese were only slightly less severe. An agreement with Japan in 1908 allowed 400 Japanese men and their wives into Canada each year; in 1928, the number was reduced to 150. East Indians, almost all Jat Sikhs, faced another version of the same racial politics. More than 5,000 arrived between 1904 and 1908, anti-'Hindoo' sentiment intensified, and in 1908 the Canadian government, unable to ban immigration from another British colony, required that each East Indian immigrant have $200 on arrival. East Indian immigration virtually stopped. Combined, these measures had essentially sealed off British Columbia to non-whites by 1930.

Those who had entered before these barriers were erected, or had managed to cross them, faced other exclusions. People of Asian heritage could not vote. In most cases, they could not purchase Crown land or logging licences. In 1923, the number of fishing licences for 'orientals' was

Scene in Chinatown, Nanaimo. A ghetto for lonely men; perhaps a letter from home.

reduced sharply. Because they did not vote, they did not have access to the professions. They were excluded from most unions. Many found a little space in unorganized corners of the economy: as house boys, cooks, or gardeners; as launders or restauranteurs; as market gardeners. Others found wage work where reliable, inexpensive labour was required for work that whites would rarely perform. Some became fishermen or boat builders. A few became successful shopkeepers, importers, or labour brokers. All these activities faced the constant pressure of a white majority that assumed such people did not belong. At times prejudice turned into racial riots. More common were the ubiquitous boundaries that could not be crossed. 'Orientals' could not ride streetcars in New Westminster at one time; even the private land market often would not sell to them. The prejudice of the majority, coupled with the minority's protective response and tendency to gather together, created Chinatowns and Japtowns: racialized ghettos on cheap land at the least inviting edge of frontier towns. Kay Anderson, in her study of *Vancouver's Chinatown*, has shown how ideas of race and place were mutually reinforced within this geographic construction.[21] White racial discourse required Chinatown, a place apart for Chinese, and the social pathologies associated with a largely male population jammed into such a place only reinforced pejorative, racialized stereotypes. In British Columbia, the idea of race drew sharp boundaries.

In the eyes of most British Columbians, the other main racial minority was indigenous, but after the epidemics, Native peoples were perceived to be much less threatening. By 1900, perhaps much earlier, the white

No. 1 Indian Reserve, Nanaimo, c. 1885. Out of sight at an edge of town.

majority knew that it was well in control. There was no large Native population lurking elsewhere, as with the Asians. There was, rather, a remnant non-European people –'backward,' 'uncivilized,' and 'savage' – who, in the racialized discourse of the late nineteenth century, might be assimilated to a point, but could not become white, neither racially nor culturally. Even the missionaries, who considered all people equally precious in God's eyes and assumed that devout Christians would meet in heaven, hardly anticipated such equality on earth. For most British Columbians, Native people stood in the way of progress and development. The reserve was the solution, another place apart required by a white discourse of otherness. There the indigenous other would be tucked away, given as little land as possible, marginalized in its own territory. For most of the majority, this was entirely appropriate, not only because of the *realpolitik* of power, but because they were civilized and Natives were not. The civilized knew how to use land effectively. Another racialized space, the reserve, appeared as tiny patches across the map of British Columbia (see Figure 3.7).

Such boundary drawing was intended to deny the un-European complexities of a new place. The white British majority could cope with new technologies and terms of work: in them was change but also opportunity as the majority understood it. They could cope, with more or less grace, with other Europeans; despite lapses here and there, they too were among the civilized, and would be assimilated into an English-speaking society. They could cope, often with much regret, with the loss of ways from home. What they could not cope with – in this, they were prisoners of their own beliefs – was a drastic assertion of un-Europeanness, and they did what they could to keep the un-European out of a place that was thousands of miles from Europe.

Boundaries, of course, were never watertight; there was always seepage. There continued to be white-Native marriages, though not nearly as many as in the fur trade years. There were whites who learned Native languages fluently and devoted years to the study of Native cultures. One of them, James Teit of Spences Bridge, became a central, trusted adviser when, before World War I, chiefs of many Native groups began to forge a collective voice on the issue of land title.[22] There were missionaries who became absorbed in the lives of their Native congregations, creating complex, cross-cultural relationships with ramifications both ways. One of them, a young Englishman who arrived in Lytton in 1927 fresh from Canterbury, asked, years later, that his ashes be spread over the grave of the Nlha7kápmx woman who had taught him the language and something of Nlha7kápmx culture.[23] There were others, like Emily Carr, creative nonconformist souls who ventured some appreciative distance into Native worlds; and many other people, more ordinary and unremembered, whose lives overlapped with Native society in various ways. The Asian-European boundary was probably sharper, partly because there were few Asian women in British Columbia, partly because Asians were not a 'curiosity,' and were considered threatening. Before World War II, there were almost no white-Japanese or white-Chinese marriages in British Columbia. But even to have a Chinese cook in the house, a Chinese peddler delivering vegetables, or Chinese workers in a bunkhouse next door was to identify individuals in the mass and begin, however slightly, to weaken a stereotype and its boundary-making propensities.

Some seepage, certainly, but essentially the boundaries held. In the eyes of most of its white inhabitants, British Columbia had become what its name implied: an integrated part of the British empire within, as things had turned out, the Dominion of Canada. Its future was assumed to be white, English-speaking, and primarily British. By the early twentieth century, most British Columbians rarely saw a Native person. Asians and whites lived in closer proximity and their paths crossed more frequently, but interaction was almost always constrained by differences in language, culture, and social power, as well as by prejudice. Continental Europeans, especially the Protestants, were being drawn into the predominant culture. Their progeny and those of British immigrants increasingly intermarried. There were many interpersonal cultural exchanges, but as no one continental European nationality amounted to over 2 per cent of the population before World War II, none had much capacity to influence a derivative British culture. It could easily be said that British Columbia risked becoming a narrow, expatriate British society, shorn of much of its British background, increasingly attached to symbols or abstractions of itself (particularly its whiteness), and determined to fend off novel connections and complexities that offered, potentially, some of the more creative opportunities in its new setting.

And yet, for all the rigidities that many sought to impose, immigrant society in British Columbia was an evolving New World creation. In this chapter, I have discussed some general tendencies that shaped the province's composition. The salience of capital and labour – most starkly represented in the industrial work camps, but far more widely expressed – was undoubtedly crucial, as were their associated work environments, new to most immigrants. From this, agriculture stood apart, space primarily for nuclear families in weakly stratified societies. Mannered gentility found little space anywhere. None of the regional cultures from which immigrants had come could be reproduced *in toto*, though majorities transferred more than minorities. The primarily British migrations to British Columbia produced an English-speaking population that increasingly melded different regional shades of Britishness, in the process discarding many regional ways and creating a regional culture (in detail, several regional subcultures) with no precise antecedents. Minorities struggled to hold on to cultural fragments, in the process creating an increasingly symbolic ethnicity while, particularly among immigrants from continental Europe, ways of life merged more and more into an expanding majority culture adjusted only a little by their presence. The tendency to turn ways of life into symbols was pervasive, and when the racialized European colonial discourse of the late nineteenth century was superimposed on the uncertainties of an emerging immigrant society, race became an overriding symbol. Whiteness became the first and most essential marker of social respectability. From the idea of race followed a number of boundary operations intent on affixing space for insiders and outsiders, and ensuring that the former had most of it. While never entirely successful, they produced and sustained a powerful set of exclusions.

Out of these tendencies, with their myriad tensions and cross-currents, emerged an immigrant society. Robert Young, one of the best current analysts of colonial discourse, has remarked that a 'culture never repeats itself perfectly away from home.' Of this there is no doubt. However, when Young goes on to say that 'any exported culture will in some way run amok, go phut or threaten to turn into mumbo-jumbo as it dissolves in the heterogeneity of the elsewhere,'[24] one such as I, who lives in the mumbo-jumbo and the heterogeneity of the elsewhere, is suddenly uneasy. Such phrases are vivid but empty; they provide no analytical assistance and virtually deny the possibility of understanding. What, Young implies, can be made of mumbo-jumbo? Yet it *is* possible to identify some of the principal structuring tendencies in the disaggregated and dislocated societies that emerged overseas. I have tried to do this here, suggesting something of the overall shape of British Columbia's immigrant society and locating some of the lives that comprised it.

And so I am led back to the three lives with which I began. Topaz Edgeworth, who lived her British Columbian years amid respectable society within the domestic economy in the elite West End, was as insulated from social change as an immigrant life could be in British Columbia. She was largely oblivious to what was different in her new setting. She saw a lot of Yow, but as a cook with a remote culture. She admired the north shore mountains and the seagulls in the park, but knew next to nothing of this un-English nature. One night at the family cottage, Topaz decided to sleep on the porch, only to flee inside when the small noises of the night – island deer cropping the grass, a boom of logs squeaking rhythmically in the swell – took her back, terrified, to Mrs. Porter's School in Brighton and the Greek god Pan, whose fluting turned those who heard it mad. In this, as in so much else, her thought led back to England, an orientation that could just be maintained, in her comfortable circumstances, for the second half of a life. Nan Bourgon's life, on the other hand, had begun English but had become something else. An English social hierarchy was not in the Bulkley Valley; deprived of its social context, Milady's reference had lost its meaning. Nan lived there within a barely stratified local society tied to semi-commercial family farming. On the other hand, she was exposed to cultural differences, particularly in the person of her French Canadian husband, that she could not have encountered in England. Her family itself became a primary locus of cultural interaction and change. Her children grew up in a socio-cultural context and within a weakly developed social hierarchy that Nan, as a young girl, could not have begun to imagine. Leong May-ying was caught, partly by her own conservative assumptions drawn from peasant China, in a social world where such assumptions no longer quite fit. She struggled with this disjunction throughout her Canadian life, a talented soul tossed into extraordinary circumstances. The subsequent generations had changed. Hing, whose teachers thought she should be a doctor, had had no such opportunity; she trained to be a psychiatric nurse, then left the profession when she married. One of Hing's daughters became an economist and senior economic adviser in Ottawa, married a white man, and wrote a remarkable book about her grandmother. The processes of social change in an immigrant society work themselves out through the generations.

If one adds up such lives, and keeps adding, one returns, I think, to the patterns I have attempted to describe. An immigrant society has to be studied with immigration, and its effects, in mind. One should also remember that immigrants did not occupy a wilderness. In the background, nearer or farther, are those who were displaced by the resettlement of British Columbia, and for whom colonialism is not so much about events in the past as an ongoing engagement with an invasive society that imposed itself across their territories, then extolled its own energy while denying the destruction it wrought. For the May-yings,

Nans, and Aunt Topazes of this world, Native peoples were virtually invisible. Now many of us should be able to see our own circumstances more clearly. If we better understood the tensions inherent in an immigrant society, and realized that immigrant opportunities in this remarkable place have always rested, and continue to rest, on the displacement of Native peoples, we would, I think, live here more thoughtfully and much more gently.

Notes

Chapter 1: Voices of Smallpox

Earlier drafts of this chapter greatly benefitted from comments by Karl Butzer, Daniel Clayton, Julie Cruikshank, Jody Decker, Robert Galois, Averill Groeneveld-Meijer, Richard Inglis, Grant Keddie, Shirley Leon, George Lovell, Richard Mackie, Sonny McHalsie, Daniel Marshall, Bruce Miller, Gordon Mohs, Matthew Sparke, and Wayne Suttles. Republished with permission and with some additions from *Ethnohistory* 41, 4 (1994):593-626.

1 Jimmy Peters, interview by Gordon Mohs and Sonny McHalsie, 29 September 1986, Stó:lō Heritage, book 11(A), Oral History Stó:lō Tribal Council, Sardis. This study owes much of its initial impetus to comments by Ruben Ware in *A Stó:lō Bibliography* (Sardis 1983), and to the remarkable collection of research materials in the Coqualeetza Resource Centre.

2 Charles Hill-Tout, 'Ethnological Report on the Stseelis [Chehalis] and Skaulits [Scowlitz] Tribes of the Halkomelem Division of the Salish of British Columbia,' *Journal of the Royal Anthropological Institute* 34 (July-December 1904), reprinted in Ralph Maud, ed., *The Mainland Halkomelem*, vol. 3 of *The Salish People: The Local Contribution of Charles Hill-Tout* (Vancouver 1978), 100.

3 Karl W. Butzer, 'The Americas before and after 1492: An Introduction to Current Geographical Research,' *Annals, Association of American Geographers* 82, 3 (1992):352.

4 On the medical implications of genetic similarity, see Francis L. Black, 'Why Did They Die?' *Science* 258 (11 December 1992):1, 739-40.

5 For current estimates and reviews of estimates, see William Denevan, 'Native American Populations in 1492: Recent Research and Revised Hemispheric Estimate,' in William Denevan, ed., *The Native Population of the Americas in 1492*, 2nd ed. (Madison 1992), xvii-xxxviii, and Douglas H. Ubelaker, 'North American Indian Population Size: Changing Perspectives,' in J.W. Verano and D.H. Ubelaker, eds., *Disease and Demography in the Americas* (Washington 1992), 169-78.

6 The most contested judgment is *Delgamuukw et al.* v. *The Queen, Reasons for Judgment*, Supreme Court of British Columbia, 8 March 1991.

7 Glenn Trewartha, 'A Case for Population Geography,' *Annals, Association of American Geographers* 43 (June 1953):71-97.

8 Jan Vansina, *Oral Tradition as History* (Madison 1985), 83.

9 Erna Gunther, *Klallam Ethnology*, University of Washington Publications in Anthropology, vol. 1, no. 5 (Washington 1927), 171-314; Homer Barnett, *The Coast Salish of British Columbia* (Eugene 1955).

10 Wilson Duff, *The Upper Stalo Indians of the Fraser River of B.C.*, Anthropology in British Columbia, Memoir no. 1 (Victoria 1952).

11 W.W. Elmendorf, *The Structure of Twana Culture*, Washington State University Research Studies 28 (3), Monographic Supplement 2 (Pullman, WA, 1960), 272.

12 Wayne Suttles, 'Post-Contact Culture Change among the Lummi Indians,' *British Columbia Historical Quarterly* 18, 1-2 (1954):42.
13 By 'Hydahs' in this story, but Haida do not appear to have been on the south coast before 1853. These raiders were probably Lequiltok, southern Kwakwaka'wakw peoples.
14 E.C. Webber, 'An Old Kwanthum Village – Its People and Its Fall,' *American Antiquarian* 21 (September-October 1899):309-14. The dragon, presumably, is Ellen Webber's invention.
15 E.R. Webber, 'A Kwantlum Battle,' *Museum and Art Notes* 6, 3 (September 1931):119.
16 C. Hill-Tout, 'Notes on the Cosmogony and History of the Squamish Indians of British Columbia,' *Transactions, Royal Society of Canada* 2, 3 (1897): Section II, reprinted in R. Maud, ed., *The Squamish and the Lillooet*, vol. 2 of *The Salish People*, 22. Franz Boas collected a somewhat similar Squamish story about a sequence of disasters caused by fire, flood, and finally smallpox and winter: 'Later Qa' is sent the smallpox and one winter with deep snow to the people as punishment for their wickedness.' Cited in 'Indian Legends of the North Pacific Coast of America Collected by Franz Boas,' ts., translated by Deitrich Bertz for the BC Indian Languages Project, 1977, 92, Special Collections, UBC Library. T.P.O. Menzies, curator of the Vancouver City Museum, heard a version of Mulk's story from Chief George in North Vancouver in June 1934, folder 5, vol. 44, add. mss. 1,077, Newcombe Family Papers, BCARS.
17 Maud, *The Salish People*, vol. 2, 22.
18 Diamond Jenness, *The Faith of a Coast Salish Indian*, Anthropology in British Columbia, Memoir no. 3 (Victoria 1955).
19 Ibid., 34.
20 Albert Louie, interview by Oliver Wells, 28 July 1965, in 'Stó:lō Villages, Encampments and Settlements,' Stó:lō Tribal Council (1987), 160.
21 Oliver Wells, *The Chilliwack and Their Neighbours* (Vancouver 1987), 40. Albert Louie told much the same story (see previous note).
22 Wells, 'Stó:lō Villages, Encampments and Settlements.'
23 Patrick Charlie, interview by Wilson Duff, Yale, summer 1950, Stalo Notebook 1, BCARS.
24 Jimmy Peters, interview by Gordon Mohs and Sonny McHalsie, 29 September 1986, Stó:lō Heritage, book 11(A), Oral History Stó:lō Tribal Council, Sardis.
25 Series II, ethnological vol. 44, folder 1, add. mss. 1,077, Newcombe Family Papers, BCARS.
26 'Are All Fishermen Superstitious?' *Fisherman* (20 March 1964):15.
27 Martin Sampson, *Indians of Skagit County*, Skagit County Historical Series no. 2, Skagit County Historical Society (Mount Vernon, WA, 1972):25.
28 'Quimper's Journal,' in H.R. Wagner, ed., *Spanish Explorations in the Strait of Juan de Fuca* (Santa Ana 1933), 129-32.
29 'Extract of the Navigation Made by the Pilot Don Juan Pantoja,' in Wagner, ed., *Spanish Explorations*, 185-8.
30 'Voyage of the Sutil and Mexicana,' in Wagner, ed., *Spanish Explorations*, esp. 254, 289, 293. On the Spanish route through Johnstone Strait, see Robert Galois, *Kwakwaka'wakw Settlements 1775-1920: A Geographical Survey* (Vancouver 1995).
31 W. Kaye Lamb, ed., *A Voyage of Discovery to the North Pacific Ocean and Round the World, 1791-1795*, Hakluyt Society (London 1984), 2, 516-17, 538.
32 T. Manby Journal, December 1790-June 1793, 43, William Robertson Coe Collection, Yale University; photocopy in box 1, W. Kaye Lamb Papers, Special Collections, UBC Library.
33 Puget Journal, adm. 55, 27, 133-4, Public Record Office, London.
34 James Johnstone Log Book, 2 January 1792, 20 May 1792, 176, photocopy in box 4, W. Kaye Lamb Papers. This point was obviously discussed. Archibald Menzies, the expedition's botanist, put it this way: 'In this excursion ... we saw only the few natives I have already mentioned, silence and solitude seemed to prevail over this fine and extensive country, even the feathered race, as if unable to endure the stillness that pervaded everywhere had in great measure abandoned it and were therefore very scarce.' C.F. Newcombe, ed., *Menzies' Journal of Vancouver's Voyage, April-October, 1792* (Victoria 1923), 40.

35 Newcombe, ed., *Menzies' Journal*, 53.
36 T. Manby Journal, 12 June 1792.
37 Lamb, ed., *Voyage of Discovery*, 603-4.
38 Ibid., 613.
39 Ibid., 538.
40 Newcombe, ed., *Menzies' Journal*, 49.
41 Puget Journal, 133-4.
42 Lamb, ed., *Voyage of Discovery*, 540.
43 Ibid., 528.
44 Ibid., 559.
45 Puget Journal, 34.
46 R.G. Thwaites, ed., *Original Journals of the Lewis and Clark Expedition, 1804-1806*, vol. 4. (New York 1905), 240-1.
47 Barbara Belyea, ed., *Columbia Journals: David Thompson* (Montreal and Kingston 1994), 70.
48 Richard Glover, ed., *Thompson's Narrative, 1774-1812* (Toronto 1962), 367.
49 W. Kaye Lamb, ed., *The Letters and Journals of Simon Fraser, 1806-1808* (Toronto 1960), 94.
50 Ross Cox, *Adventures on the Columbia River*, vol. 1 (London 1831), 314.
51 John Work's Journal, 18 November 1824-30 December 1824, A/B/40/W89.2A, BCARS.
52 'Dr. John Scouler's Journal of a Voyage to N.W. America,' *Quarterly of the Oregon Historical Society* 6 (June 1905):303-4.
53 Fort Langley Journal, 27 June 1827-30 July 1830, BCARS.
54 Lamb, ed., *Voyage of Discovery*, 603. For example, Donald H. Mitchell, 'Excavations at Two Trench Embankments in the Gulf of Georgia Region,' *Syesis* 1, 1 and 2 (December 1968):29-46, and Gary Coupland, 'Warfare and Social Complexity on the Northwest Coast,' in D.C. Tkaczuk and B.C. Vivian, eds., *Cultures in Conflict: Current Archaeological Perspectives,* University of Calgary Archaeological Association (Calgary 1989), 205-41. Defensive sites began to be built around the Strait of Georgia about 1,000 years ago, and some were maintained into the nineteenth century; personal communication, Grant Keddie, archaeologist at the Royal British Columbia Museum.
55 Myron Eells, *The Indians of Puget Sound: The Notebooks of Myron Eells* (Seattle 1985), 24.
56 Erna Gunther, *Klallam Ethnology*, esp. 195, 196, 214; W.W. Elmendorf, *The Structure of Twana Culture*, esp. 260-4; Wayne Suttles, 'Post-Contact Culture,' esp. 53-4.
57 The ethnographic record has been taken to describe pre-contact patterns of settlement and seasonal migration. However, Richard Inglis and James Haggarty recently argued that on the west coast of Vancouver Island, the pre-contact settlement pattern was one of many small villages, each occupied by a house group that depended on very local resources; 'Pacific Rim National Park Ethnographic History,' microfiche report series 257, Parks, Environment Canada, 1986.
58 'Dr. John Scouler's Journal,' 198.
59 A tendency that can be observed from the earliest days of the St. Lawrence fur trade. See, for example, R. Cole Harris, ed., *From the Beginning to 1800*, vol. 1 of *Historical Atlas of Canada* (Toronto 1987), 84 and plate 35.
60 Ann F. Ramenofsky, *Vectors of Death: The Archaeology of European Contact* (Albuquerque 1987), 130; H.F. Dobyns, 'Estimating Aboriginal American Population: An Appraisal of Techniques with a New Hemispheric Estimate,' *Current Anthropology* 7 (1966):395-416.
61 W. George Lovell, *Conquest and Survival in Colonial Guatemala: A Historical Geography of the Cuchumatán Highlands, 1500-1821* (Montreal 1992), 154-7; Fernando Casanuava, 'Smallpox and War in Southern Chile in the Late 18th Century,' in N.D. Cook and W.G. Lovell, eds., *Secret Judgments of God* (Norman, OK, 1992), 183-212.
62 S.F. Cook, 'Smallpox in Spanish and Mexican California, 1770-1845,' *Bulletin of the History of Medicine* 7 (1939):153-94; Marc Simmons, 'New Mexico's Smallpox Epidemic of 1780-1781,' *New Mexico Historical Review* 41 (1966):319-26; Arthur J. Ray, *Indians in the Fur Trade: Their Role as Hunters, Trappers and Middlemen in the Lands Southwest of Hudson Bay, 1660-1870* (Toronto 1974), 105-8; Jody F. Decker, 'Tracing Historical Diffusion Patterns: The Case of the 1780-1782 Smallpox Epidemic among the Indians of

Western Canada,' *Native Studies Review* 4, 1 and 2 (1988):1-24; and Jody F. Decker, 'Depopulation of the Northern Plains Natives,' *Social Science and Medicine* 33, 4 (1991):381-96.

63 Glover, ed., *Thompson's Narrative*, 236.

64 Ibid, 235-6.

65 R.G. Thwaites, ed., *Original Journals*, vol. 1, 202; cited in Ramenofsky, *Vectors of Death*, 128-9. Lewis and Clark were told that 'smallpox destroyed the greater part of the [Mandan] nation and reduced them to one large village and Some Small ones, all the nations before this maladey was afraid of them, after they were reduced the Seaux and other Indians waged war, and Killed a great many, and they moved up the Missourie'; see Thwaites, ed., *Original Journals*, vol. 1, 220.

66 Glover, ed., *Thompson's Narrative*, 49.

67 Decker, 'Tracing Historical Diffusion Patterns,' 12.

68 William R. Swagerty, 'Indian Trade in the Trans-Mississippi West to 1870,' in Wilcomb E. Washburn, ed., *Handbook of North American Indians, Vol. 4, History of Indian-White Relations* (Washington, DC, 1988), 352.

69 Clark Wissler, 'Material Culture of the Blackfoot Indians,' *Anthropological Papers of the American Museum of Natural History* 5, 1 (1910):13.

70 The quotes from Smith and Work are cited in Robert Boyd, 'The Introduction of Infectious Diseases among the Indians of the Pacific Northwest, 1774-1874,' PhD diss., University of Washington, 1985, 78-80.

71 Gregory Mengarini, *Recollections of the Flathead Mission* (Glendale, CA, 1977), 193-4.

72 Cox, *Adventures on the Columbia*, vol. 1, 312-13.

73 John Dunn, *The Oregon Territory and the British North American Fur Trade* (Philadelphia 1845), 84-5.

74 Ibid.

75 James Mooney, 'Population,' *Bureau of American Ethnology Bulletin* 30 (1910).

76 Elmendorf was told that the disease came from the Lower Chehalis River via the Satsop people; see *The Structure of Twana Culture*, 272.

77 John Hoskins, 'John Hoskins' Narrative of the Second Voyage of the *Columbia*,' in F.W. Howay, ed., *Voyages of the 'Columbia' to the Northwest Coast, 1787-1790 and 1790-1793* (Boston 1941), 196; John Boit, 'John Boit's Log of the Second Voyage of the *Columbia*,' in Howay, ed., *Voyages of the 'Columbia,'* 371. The estimate of diffusion northward in the Strait of Georgia is approximate. It accords generally with Vancouver's observations in 1792 and with George Simpson's in 1841 that the Qwakeolths had never been affected by smallpox. Sir George Simpson, *Narrative of a Journey around the World during the Years 1841 and 1842*, 2 vols. (London 1847), 1, 189.

78 Decker, 'Tracing Historical Diffusion Patterns,' 16-17.

79 Robert Boyd, 'The Introduction of Infectious Diseases,' 71-111, and 'Demographic History, 1774-1874,' 137-8, in Wayne Suttles, ed., *Northwest Coast*, vol. 7 of *Handbook of North American Indians* (Washington, DC, 1990). Boyd has recently defended his interpretation against the argument presented here. See 'Commentary on Early Contact-Era Smallpox in the Pacific Northwest,' *Ethnohistory* 43, 2 (1996):307-28.

80 Cox, *Adventures on the Columbia*, vol. 1, 314.

81 Even on the Columbia as early as 1814, pockmarked faces were becoming uncommon; Ross Cox noted that 'the vestiges ... were still visible on the countenances of the elderly men and women.' Ibid., vol. 1, 312.

82 It was reported that Roman Catholic missionaries vaccinated 'upward of 12,000 Indians on the Lower Fraser' (see *New Westminster Columbian*, 29 April 1863), and that government officials vaccinated some 1,200 Natives at Lytton (*New Westminster Columbian*, 25 June 1862). A few Natives along the Harrison River and at Douglas contracted the disease, but there was no epidemic along the lower Fraser at this time. Beyond Lytton, the picture was very different.

83 Archibald McDonald to HBC Governor and Council, Northern Department of Rupert's Land, 25 February 1830, HBCA microfilm reel 3M53, D.4/123, fos. 66-72; and printed, with minor errors of transcription, in Mary K. Cullen, 'The History of Fort Langley, 1827-96,' *Canadian Historic Sites: Occasional Papers in Archaeology and History*, vol. 20 (Ottawa 1979), 82-9.

84 For a survey of methodologies of population reconstruction, see Noble David Cook, *Demographic Collapse, Indian Peru, 1520-1620*, vol. 1, (Cambridge 1981).
85 Ramenofsky, *Vectors of Death*, is a brave attempt. See also Cook, *Demographic Collapse*.
86 Fort Langley Journal, 20 and 27 July 1828.
87 John Work's Journal, 19 December 1824.
88 Such comments abound in the Fort Langley Journal.
89 McDonald to the HBC Governor and Council, 25 February 1830.
90 William F. Tolmie, *The Journals of William Fraser Tolmie, Physician and Fur Trader* (Vancouver 1963), 317-20.
91 Michael Kew, 'Salmon Availability, Technology, and Cultural Adaptation in the Fraser River Watershed,' in Brian Hayden, ed., *A Complex Culture of the British Columbia Plateau: Traditional Stl'atl'imx Resource Use* (Vancouver 1992).
92 This figure includes all coastal peoples listed south of the Fraser River around Puget Sound as far as, but not including, the Clallam. The census total is 570 men, a figure I have multiplied by five. This may be approximately the territory for which Puget and Menzies provided estimates.
93 Jenness, *The Faith of a Coast Salish Indian*, 33.
94 Bob Joe, interview by Oliver Wells, 8 February 1962, in Wells, *The Chilliwacks and Their Neighbours*, 54.
95 Agnes Kelly, interview by Gordon Mohs, 7 July 1986, Stó:lō Heritage, book 11(A), Oral History Stó:lō Tribal Council, Sardis.
96 The Southern Thompson villages (Tuckquiome to Spuzzum) are based largely on inventories compiled by James Teit, Charles Hill-Tout, and Gilbert M. Sproat. See Cole Harris, 'The Fraser Canyon Encountered,' *BC Studies* 94 (summer 1992):5-28. The Stó:lō villages are based on 'Stó:lō Villages, Encampments and Settlements' an inventory prepared by Gordon Mohs and Sonny McHalsie for the Stó:lō Tribal Council, and derived from site-by-site considerations of available ethnographic and archeological evidence.
97 A dense non-agricultural population living close to the technical/ecological limit of the food supply appears to be vulnerable to sudden catastrophes or 'die-offs.' See Ester Boserup, 'Environment, Population, and Technology in Primitive Societies,' in Donald Worster, ed., *The Ends of the Earth: Perspectives on Modern Environmental History* (New York 1988), and Ezra B.W. Zubrow, *Prehistoric Carrying Capacity: A Model* (Menlo Park, CA, 1975). The many stories about a succession of disasters and depopulations should not be dismissed as myth.
98 All these movements are poorly understood, and their connections to smallpox-related depopulations are open to debate. On the Katzie: Wayne Suttles, *Katzie Ethnographic Notes*, Anthropology in British Columbia, Memoir 2 (Victoria 1955), 8-11; on the Chilliwack: Wilson Duff, *The Upper Stalo Indians*, 43-5; on the Semiahmoo: Wayne Suttles, 'Economic Life of the Coast Salish of Haro and Rosario Straits,' PhD diss., University of Washington, 1951, 29.
99 Suttles, 'Post-Contact Culture Change,' 42-3.
100 Galois, *Kwakwa̱ka̱'wakw Settlement Sites*, Introduction and Section D. In the 1920s, Diamond Jenness learned that smallpox had decimated the Saanich Indians of southeastern Vancouver Island about 1780, and had crippled their resistance to enemy raids; see 'The Sanitch Indians of Vancouver Island,' ts., 56, n.d., BCARS. I thank Daniel Clayton for bringing this reference to my attention.
101 Sampson, *Indians of Skagit County*, 1.
102 James Mooney, *The Aboriginal Population of America North of Mexico*, Smithsonian Miscellaneous Collection, vol. 80, no.7 (Washington, DC, 1928). For a discussion of the basis of Mooney's calculations, see Douglas H. Ubelaker, 'The Sources and Methodology for Mooney's Estimates of North American Indian Populations,' in Denevan, ed., *The Native Population of the Americas*, 243-92.
103 Wilson Duff, *The Impact of the White Man*, vol. 1 of *The Indian History of British Columbia*, Anthropology in British Columbia, Memoir no. 5 (Victoria 1964), 39, 44.
104 Philip Drucker, *Cultures of the North Pacific Coast* (San Francisco 1965), 188-9.
105 Robin Fisher, *Contact and Conflict: Indian-European Relations in British Columbia, 1774-1890* (Vancouver 1977), 22-3.

106 James R. Gibson, 'Smallpox on the Northwest Coast, 1835-1838,' *BC Studies* 56 (winter 1982-3):61-81.
107 Except possibly in Quatsino Sound, where there is an enigmatic and isolated reference to disease and death. See E. Curtis, *The Kwakiutl*, vol. 10 of *The North American Indian* (Cambridge, MA, 1915; reprinted facs. ed., New York 1970), 305.
108 Simpson, *Narrative of a Journey*, 189; Galois, *Kwakwaka'wakw Settlements.*
109 Mooney, 'The Aboriginal Population,' 286-7.
110 Ibid.
111 A.L. Kroeber, *Cultural and Natural Areas of Native North America*, vol. 38, 4th ed. (Berkeley 1963 [1939]), 132, 134.
112 A good introduction to the literature on these questions is Daniel T. Reff, *Disease, Depopulation and Cultural Change in Northwestern New Spain, 1518-1764* (Salt Lake City 1991), ch. 1.
113 One example is the relationship between the striking work of the subaltern historians on the dispossessed in India and the spate of recent attempts to articulate Native voices in the Americas. See Ranajit Guha and Gayatri Chakravorty Spivak, eds., *Selected Subaltern Studies* (New York 1988).
114 The census of Canada lists the Native population of British Columbia as follows: 1881: 25,661; 1901: 25,488; 1911: 20,134; 1921: 22,377. None of these figures should be taken as more than a low-side approximation, but, altogether, they are the most accurate available representation of the Native population of the province a little more than a century after contact. If the population had declined by 90 to 95 per cent during these years, then its pre-contact level was in the 200,000 to 400,000 range. The estimate for the Coast Salish is derived from the nominal 1881 census, District 187, Division 7 and District 189, Division A2. Counting people on the non-Native as well as the Native rolls, there were 5,452 Coast Salish around the Strait of Georgia in 1881, a figure which is then assumed to be roughly 5 to 10 per cent of the pre-epidemic population.
115 Henry Dobyns, *Their Number Became Thinned: Native American Population Dynamics in Eastern North America* (Knoxville 1983), has argued for a hemispheric smallpox pandemic in the 1520s, but Reff's work (note 112) on northwestern Mexico and the southwestern US provides, I think, compelling evidence against a sixteenth-century pandemic in the northern Cordillera. However, the case has been argued; see Sarah Campbell, 'Post-Columbian Culture History in the Northern Columbia Plateau: AD 1500-1900,' PhD diss., University of Washington, 1989.

Chapter 2: Strategies of Power

This chapter has benefitted from comments by Noel Castree, Daniel Clayton, David Demeritt, Ken Favrholdt, Robert Galois, John Lutz, Richard Mackie, Susan Marsden, Dan Marshall, Jamie Morton, Ruth Sandwell, and Graeme Wynn. Part of it was published in the *Canadian Geographer* (39, 2 [1995]:131-40), and is republished here with permission.

1 H.R. Wagner, *Spanish Explorations in the Strait of Juan de Fuca* (Santa Ana 1933), 101-2.
2 W. Kaye Lamb, ed., *George Vancouver: A Voyage of Discovery to the North Pacific Ocean and Round the World, 1791-1795*, vol. 2 (London 1984), 569. For a similar possession-taking in Australia the year before, see vol. 1, 337.
3 Gabriel Franchère, *A Voyage on the Northwest Coast of North America during the Years 1811, 1812, 1813, and 1814*, W. Kaye Lamb, ed. (Toronto 1969), 133. Franchère explained what was taking place to the neighbouring chiefs. For a more modern version, see Barry M. Gough, *The Royal Navy and the Northwest Coast of North America 1810-1914: A Study of British Maritime Supremacy* (Vancouver 1971), ch. 1.
4 Malcolm McLeod, ed., *Peace River. A Canoe Voyage from Hudson's Bay to Pacific, by the late Sir George Simpson; (Governor, Hon. Hudson's Bay Company) in 1828 Journal of the Late Chief Factor, Archibald McDonald (Hon. Hudson's Bay Company), who Accompanied Him* (Ottawa 1872), 26-8.
5 By discourse I mean the interrelated ideas, assumptions, and practices associated with a particular configuration of social power. In this sense the discourse of the fur trade refers

to the accumulated practices – everything from the layout of forts to the disciplining of men to the conduct of brigades – by which the fur trade operated in the West.

6 This was the Clallam expedition. For more information, see Frank Ermatinger, 'Notes Connected with the Clallam Expedition Fitted out Under the Command of Alex. R. McLeod, Esquire, Chief Trader at Fort Vancouver on the 17th of June 1828,' *Washington Historical Quarterly* 1 (January 1907):16-29, and John McLoughlin to HBC Governor and Committee, 7 August 1828, in E.E. Rich, ed., *The Letters of John McLoughlin from Fort Vancouver to the Governor and Committee,* first series, 1825-38 (Toronto 1941), 63-7.

7 For example, in the summer of 1825, an American trader ordered Peter Skene Ogden of the HBC out of the Snake country because it was American territory. Ogden replied that he would only follow the orders of his own government. See Ogden to HBC Governor, Chief Factor, etc. Snake Plains, 27 June 1825, in E.E. Rich, *Letters of John McLoughlin,* first series, 296-9.

8 43 George III, c. 138; cited in J.P. Reid, 'The Hudson's Bay Company and Retaliation in Kind Against Indian Offenders in New Caledonia,' *Montana: The Magazine of Western History* 43 (winter 1993):6. See also J.P. Reid, 'Principles of Vengeance: Fur Trappers, Indians, and Retaliation for Homicide in the Transboundary North American West,' *Western Historical Quarterly* 24 (February 1993):21-43; Hamar Foster, 'Long-Distance Justice: The Criminal Jurisdiction of the Canadian Courts West of the Canadas, 1763-1859,' *American Journal of Legal History* 34 (1990):1-48; Hamar Foster, 'Sins Against the Great Spirit: The Law, the Hudson's Bay Company, and the Mackenzie's River Murders, 1835-1839,' *Criminal Justice History* 10 (1989):23-76; Hamar Foster, 'The Queen's Law Is Better than Yours: International Homicide in Early British Columbia,' in Jim Phillips et al., eds., *Essays in the History of Canadian Law: Crime and Criminal Justice* (Toronto 1994); Tina Loo, *Making Law, Order, and Authority in British Columbia, 1821-1871* (Toronto 1994), ch. 1.

9 For a considerable elaboration of this stark observation, see Jean and John Comaroff, *Of Revelation and Revolution: Christianity, Colonialism, and Consciousness in South Africa,* vol. 1 (Chicago 1991), ch. 3; see also Edward Said, *Orientalism* (New York 1979), ch. 1.

10 On economic aspects of the fur trade discourse along the Northwest Coast, see Richard Mackie, *Trading Beyond the Mountains: The British Fur Trade on the Pacific, 1793-1843* (Vancouver 1996), and Daniel Clayton, 'Geographies of the Lower Skeena,' *BC Studies* 94 (summer 1992):29-58.

11 On the taking of Fort Nelson on the Liard, see George Keith to Roderic Mackenzie, Forks Mackenzie's River Department, 15 January 1814, in L.F.R. Masson, *Les Bourgeois de la compagnie du Nord-Ouest,* vol. 2 (New York 1960), 125-7. On the taking of Read's House in Shoshone territory, see Ross Cox, *Adventures on the Columbia River,* vol. 1 (London 1831), 277-83.

12 Cox, *Adventures on the Columbia,* vol. 2, 80. See also William F. Tolmie, *The Journals of William Fraser Tolmie, Physician and Fur Trader* (Vancouver 1963), 195ff.

13 There are many descriptions of individual forts. The two best generic descriptions are J.W. McKay, 'The Fur Trading System,' in R.E. Gosnell, ed., *The Year Book of British Columbia* (Victoria 1897), 22-3, and P.N. Compton, 'Fort and Fort Life in New Caledonia,' Victoria, 1878, Bancroft Library, Berkeley; transcript in BCARS.

14 Archibald McDonald to Edwd Ermatinger, Fort Langley, 5 March 1831, in Archibald McDonald, Corr. Outward, 1830-1849, BCARS.

15 A. McDonald to Yale and Annance, Fort Langley, 13 September 1830, Fort Langley Correspondence, HBCA bk. B113/6/1, reel IM 183.

16 Peter Corney, *Voyage in the North Pacific* (Honolulu 1896), 56.

17 Cox, *Adventures on the Columbia,* vol. 1, 266.

18 John McDonald of Garth, 'Autobiographical Notes, 1791-1816,' in Masson, *Les Bourgeois,* vol. 2, 50.

19 The phrase is Anthony Giddens's, widely used in *The Constitution of Society: Outline of the Theory of Structuration* (Berkeley and Los Angeles 1984).

20 John Tod, Thompson River Journal, 4 August 1841-18 December 1843, HBCA. (Ts. in Legislative Library, Victoria, and in Special Collections, UBC Library).

21 For mention of this postal system as early as 1812, see W. Kaye Lamb, ed., *Sixteen Years in the Indian Country: The Journal of Daniel Williams Harmon 1800-1816* (Toronto 1957), 151-2. For more general descriptions, see Alexander Ross, *The Fur Hunters of the Far West: A Narrative of Adventures in the Oregon and Rocky Mountains* (London 1855), 107-8 (with comments about literacy), and Paul Kane, *Wanderings of an Artist among the Indians of North America* (Toronto 1925), 171-2.
22 William F. Tolmie, 'History of Puget Sound and the Northwest Coast,' Victoria, 1878, 11, Bancroft Library, Berkeley (ts. in BCARS).
23 The best general account, on which this paragraph is largely based, is by A.C. Anderson, 'History of the Northwest Coast,' Victoria, 1878, 41-3, original in the Bancroft Library, Berkeley (ts. in BCARS, and in Special Collections, UBC Library).
24 Anderson, 'History of the Northwest Coast,' 46.
25 Mackie, *Trading Beyond the Mountains,* ch. 7.
26 The best account of these expresses is in C.O. Ermatinger, ed. 'Edward Ermatinger's York Factory Express Journal, Being a Record of Journeys Made between Fort Vancouver and Hudson Bay in the Years 1827-1828,' *Transactions of the Royal Society of Canada* 6, 2 (Ottawa 1912).
27 See, for example, Servants' Contracts, HBCA-NAC MG20, reel 404A, and A32/37, fo. 52 (Charles LaFleur). These contracts are cited in full in Loo, *Making Law, Order, and Authority*, 163-4.
28 HBC, Standing Rules and Regulations, 1828, Minutes of Council, 230, in R.H. Fleming, ed., *Minutes of Council of the Northern Department, 1821-31* (Toronto 1940), 218-31.
29 Loo, *Making Law, Order, and Authority,* ch. 1.
30 Ibid., 31.
31 Cox, *Adventures on the Columbia*, vol. 2, 60.
32 Carol M. Judd, 'Mixed Bands of Many Nations, 1821-1870,' in C.M. Judd and A.J. Ray, eds., *Old Trails and New Directions: Papers of the Third North American Fur Trade Conference* (Toronto 1980), 127-46.
33 Simpson's Official Reports, 1827, HBCA D4/90,9. Cited in Judd, 'Mixed Bands of Many Nations,' 138-9.
34 Ross, *Fur Hunters of the Far West*, 109-10.
35 Hamar Foster, 'Killing Mr. John: Law and Jurisdiction at Fort Stikine, 1842-1846,' in J. McLaren, H. Foster, and C. Orloff, eds., *Law for the Elephant, Law for the Beaver: Essays in the Legal History of the North American West* (Regina 1992), 147-93, 175.
36 Cox, *Adventures on the Columbia,* 201.
37 Tolmie, *The Journals of William Fraser Tolmie*, 240, 246, 268-9.
38 A.G. Morice, *The History of the Northern Interior of British Columbia* (Smithers, BC, 1978; first published Toronto 1904), ch. 18.
39 H. Beaver to B. Harrison, Fort Vancouver, 10 March 1837, in T.E. Jessett, ed., *Reports and Letters of Herbert Beaver* (Portland 1959), 36-7.
40 William John Macdonald, 'British Columbia Sketches,' Victoria, 1878, 21-2, Bancroft Library, Berkeley (ts. in BCARS).
41 McLoughlin to HBC Governor and Committee, 26 October 1837, in Rich, *McLoughlin's Fort Vancouver Letters*, first series, vol. 1, 192.
42 Morice, *History of the Northern Interior*, 280.
43 Rich, *McLoughlin's Fort Vancouver Letters*, first series, vol. 1, 193.
44 Douglas to HBC Governor and Committee, 18 October 1838, in Rich, *McLoughlin's Fort Vancouver Letters*, first series, vol. 1, 247.
45 'Philip Turnor's Journal, 1790-92,' in J.B. Tyrrell, ed., *Journals of Samuel Hearne and Philip Turnor* (Toronto 1934), 447.
46 The killing provoked a protracted, bitter feud between McLoughlin and Simpson, and is analyzed by Hamar Foster, 'Killing Mr. John,' n. 35.
47 Morice, *History of the Northern Interior*, 280.
48 Foster, 'Killing Mr. John,' 176-7.
49 Ross, *Fur Hunters of the Far West*, 61-2.
50 Lamb, ed., *Sixteen Years in the Indian Country*; W.F. Wentzel to Mr. McKenzie, Mackenzie River, 30 April 1811, in Masson, *Les Bourgeois*, 106.

51 Men might go off to '*courir la marigot*' (take it easy for a time). Charles de la Morandière, *Histoire de la pêche française de la morue dans l'amérique septentrionale*, tome 1 (Paris 1962), 172.
52 J.A. Teit, 'Shuswap,' in *Memoir of the American Museum of Natural History*, vol. 4, no. 7 (New York 1909), 443-813. Reprinted as vol. 2, pt. 7, of the Jesup North Pacific Expedition (New York 1975).
53 Richard White, *The Middle Ground: Indians, Empires, and Republics in the Great Lakes Region, 1650-1815* (Cambridge 1991).
54 E.E. Rich, ed., *Peter Skene Ogden's Snake Country Journal, 1824-25 and 1825-26* (London 1950), 51-5, 73.
55 Ogden to HBC Governor, Snake Plains, 27 June 1825, in Rich, *McLoughlin's Fort Vancouver Letters,* first series, 297.
56 Mary Cullen, 'Outfitting New Caledonia, 1821-58,' in Judd and Ray, eds., *Old Trails and New Directions*, 239.
57 For example, see Cox, *Adventures on the Columbia*, vol. 1, 232-5. Cox reacted to Flathead tortures of captured Blackfeet, below Quebec in 1632, much as the Jesuit Father Le Jeune had reacted to Algonkian tortures of captured Iroquois. Cox threatened to 'quit the country forever' unless the torture of Blackfeet women stopped, though he was told, as Le Jeune had been, that their enemies treated them the same way, and 'that they could not think of giving up the gratification of their revenge to the foolish and womanish feelings of white men.'
58 These quotes are from Ogden (1826) and McLoughlin (1828), cited in Rich, and Cox (referring to 1813), all of a type that recurs widely in the fur trade records.
59 Reid, 'Principles of Vengeance.'
60 Cox, *Adventures on the Columbia*, vol. 1, 305.
61 Gabriel Franchère, *A Voyage on the Northwest Coast of North America during the Years 1811, 1812, 1813, and 1814*, W. Kaye Lamb, ed. (Toronto 1969), 107.
62 Ross, *Fur Hunters of the Far West*, 216.
63 Cox, *Adventures on the Columbia*, vol. 1, 214-18; see also Franchère, *A Voyage on the Northwest Coast,* 140-2.
64 Ross, *Fur Hunters of the Far West*, 32.
65 Corney, *Voyage in the North Pacific*, 42-3.
66 Cox, *Adventures on the Columbia*, 297-9.
67 Ross, *Fur Hunters of the Far West*, 130-3.
68 Lamb, ed., *Sixteen Years in the Indian Country*, 137-46.
69 K.G. Davies, ed., *Peter Skene Ogden's Snake Country Journal, 1826-27* (London 1961), 70-1. Also discussed in Reid, 'Principles of Vengeance,' 21-42.
70 Tolmie, 'History of Puget Sound.' See also McLoughlin to Blanchette et al., 19 August 1840, HBCA B.223/b/27, fo. 57, 60-8, and Mackie, *Trading Beyond the Mountains*.
71 William Yates, 'Reminiscences,' ts., n.d., BCARS.
72 John Tod, Thompson River Journal, 1 March 1843.
73 John Tod to Edward Ermatinger, New Caledonia, McLeods Lake, 14 February 1829, Ermatinger Papers, NAC.
74 Colvile to Sir J.H. Pelly, Fort Victoria, 15 October 1849, in E.E. Rich, ed., *London Correspondence Inward from Eden Colvile, 1849-52* (London 1956), 2; see also Morice, *History of the Northern Interior*, ch. 17. The affair is discussed in Foster, 'The Queen's Law' 58-60.
75 John Tod, 'History of New Caledonia and Northwest Coast,' Victoria, 1878, Bancroft Library, Berkeley (ts. in BCARS). Current discussions of this murder are in Reid, 'Principles of Vengeance,' 26-7, and Foster, 'The Queen's Law,' 56-8.
76 John Tod, Thompson River Journal, 6 October 1841. See also Tod, 'History of New Caledonia,' and Anderson, 'History of the Northwest Coast.'
77 Frank Ermatinger, 'Notes Connected with the Clallam Expedition,' 16.
78 McLoughlin to HBC Governor and Committee, 7 August 1828, in Rich, *McLoughlin's Fort Vancouver Letters,* first series, 65.
79 Ibid., 10 July 1828, 57.

80 The basic account is in the Fort Langley Journal, 27 August to 15 September 1830, HBCA, and copies in Special Collections at UBC Library and BCARS. Unless otherwise indicated, the quotations are from this source.
81 Arch. McDonald to Edwd. Ermatinger, Fort Langley, 5 March 1830, Archibald McDonald, Corr. Outward, 1830-9, BCARS.
82 A. McDonald to Yale and Annance, Fort Langley, 13 September 1830, Fort Langley Correspondence, bk. B113/b/1 reel IM 183.
83 J. Douglas to HBC Governor and Committee, Fort Victoria, 27 October 1849, in Hartwell Bowsfield, ed., *Fort Victoria Letters, 1846-1851* (Winnipeg 1979), 63.
84 See Reid, 'Principles of Vengeance,' 42-3; Foster, 'Sins against the Great Spirit,' and most recently, 'The Queen's Law,' 60.
85 The fullest expression of this position appears to be R.C. MacLeod, 'Law and Order on the Western-Canadian Frontier,' in McLaren et al., eds., *Law for the Elephant*. MacLeod writes about the Plains, not the Cordillera.
86 Ross, *Fur Hunters of the Far West*, 73-6.
87 Michel Foucault, *Discipline and Punish: The Birth of the Prison* (New York 1979), 57.
88 Along the Putumayo River in the upper Amazon basin, women were captured and then tortured or killed in order to force men, who did not need trade goods, to gather rubber; Michael Taussig, *Shamanism, Colonialism, and the Wild Man: A Study in Terror and Healing* (Chicago 1987), part 1. Taussig argues, however, that alongside and transcending this political economy was a pervasive culture of terror. Along the Mackenzie River at the end of the eighteenth century, North West Company traders seized Native women, but not so much to force their men to trade – the seizures had the opposite effect – as to claim them for debts, and sell them at a profit to company servants.
89 Fort Langley Journal, 24 September 1829.
90 Cuthbert Grant, Athabasca Fort, 5 April 1786, North West Company Journal, HBCA; cited in W.A. Sloan, 'The Native Response to the Extension of the European Traders into the Athabasca and Mackenzie Basin, 1770-1814, *Canadian Historical Review* 60 (September 1979):291.
91 James McKenzie, 'Journal, 1799-1800,' in Masson, *Les Bourgeois*, vol. 2, 387-8.
92 Cox, *Adventures on the Columbia*, vol. 1, ch. 8.
93 See Chapter 1. See also Robert Boyd, 'Demographic History, 1774-1874,' in Wayne Suttles, ed., *Northwest Coast*, vol. 7 of *Handbook of North American Indians* (Washington, DC, 1990); James R. Gibson, 'Smallpox on the Northwest Coast, 1835-1838,' *BC Studies* 56 (winter 1982-3):61-81.
94 Cox, *Adventures on the Columbia*, vol. 1, 314-15.
95 H.H. Bancroft, *History of British Columbia, 1792-1887* (San Francisco 1887), 142-52.
96 For example, see Ross, *Fur Hunters of the Far West*, 153; Bancroft, *History of British Columbia*, 155-6.
97 John McDonald of Garth, 'Autobiographical Notes 1791-1816,' in Masson, *Les Bourgeois*, vol. 2, 32-3.
98 Lamb, ed., *Sixteen Years in the Indian Country*, 139-40, 252.
99 Kane, *Wanderings of an Artist*, 171-2.
100 Discussed by Hamar Foster in 'The Queen's Law,' using Judge Begbie's Benchbook notes, reel B5085, vol. 4, 203, BCARS. See also Loo, *Making Law, Order, and Authority*, ch. 7. On the differences between intricate, experiential knowledge based on orality and knowledge based on literacy, see Jack Goody, *The Interface between the Written and the Oral* (Cambridge 1987).
101 Ross, *Fur Hunters of the Far West*, 223.
102 Fort Langley Journal, 13 November 1828.
103 For example, Cox, *Adventures on the Columbia*, vol. 1, 1, 235; *Journals of William Fraser Tolmie*, 238-9.
104 Cited in Georgiana Ball, 'The Monopoly System of Wildlife Management,' *BC Studies* 66 (summer 1985):51.
105 On the dynamics of power alignments, see particularly Thomas E. Wartenberg, 'Situated Social Power,' in T.E. Wartenberg, ed., *Rethinking Power* (Albany 1992), 79-101; see also T.E. Wartenberg, *Forms of Power: From Domination to Transformation* (Philadelphia 1990);

and Joseph Rouse, 'Power/Knowledge,' in Gary Gutting, ed., *The Cambridge Companion to Foucault* (Cambridge and New York 1994), 92-114.

106 Cox, *Adventures on the Columbia*, vol. 1, 345-6.

107 I am influenced by Jean and John Comaroff's discussion of conversion and cultural change, which, they suggest, had less to do with doctrine than with the encounters of everyday life. *Of Revelation and Revolution*, ch. 6.

108 Teit, 'Shuswap,' 564.

109 Nicholas Thomas, *Entangled Objects: Exchange, Material Culture, and Colonialism in the Pacific* (Cambridge, MA, 1991).

110 Mackie, *Trading Beyond the Mountains*.

111 J. Douglas to Archibald Barclay, Fort Victoria, 3 September 1849, in Bowsfield, ed., *Fort Victoria Letters*, 35-48.

112 Wentzel to Rod. McKenzie, Forks, Mackenzie River, 27 March 1807, in Masson, *Les Bourgeois*, vol. 1, 96.

113 For accounts of the Cowichan expedition, see Barry M. Gough, *Gunboat Frontier: British Maritime Authority and Northwest Coast Indians, 1846-1890* (Vancouver 1984), 51-6; and Foster, 'The Queen's Law,' 61-4.

114 This and, unless otherwise indicated, other quotations in this paragraph are from Douglas's diary, 3-11 January 1853, in J. Douglas, Private Papers, second series, reel 737A, BCARS.

115 John Moresby, *Two Admirals: Admiral of the Fleet Sir Fairfax Moresby (1786-1877) and His Son, John Moresby* (London 1913), 110; also cited in Gough, *Gunboat Frontier*, 53.

116 Vancouver Island, Colony Accounts, 1848-1860, HBCA E.22/2, fos. 56-7: 'Paid to Indians for secret service on the Cowitchin Expeditions: 20 blankets, 1 gun, 24 clay pipes, 70 lb tobacco.' I thank Dan Clayton for this reference.

117 Douglas C. Harris, 'The Nklka'pamux Meeting at Lytton, 1879, and the Rule of Law,' *BC Studies* 108 (winter 1995-6):5-28.

118 Sproat to Supt. Gen, 5 September 1879, RG 10, reel C-10,117, vol. 3669, file 10,691, DIA; also cited in Harris, 'The Nklka'pamux Meeting at Lytton.'

119 Petition to the Honourable G.A. Walkem, Attorney General and Premier of BC, from A.C. Anderson, W. Duncan, R. Finlayson, W.I. Macdonald, J.W. McKay, Archibald McKinlay, W.F. Tolmie, C.A. Vernon, and Admiral Prevost, 25 September 1879, RG 10, reel C-10,117, vol. 3,669, file 10,691, DIA; also cited in Harris, 'The Nklka'pamux Meeting at Lytton.'

Chapter 3: The Making of the Lower Mainland

I thank Daniel Clayton, David Demeritt, Donna Cook, Robert Galois, Robin Fisher, Edward Higginbottom, Michael Kew, Richard Mackie, Yasmeen Qureshi, Sharon Rempel, and Wayne Suttles, each of whom commented on an earlier draft or offered particular expertise. Republished considerably altered from Graeme Wynn and Timothy Oke, eds., *Vancouver and Its Region* (Vancouver 1992).

1 Homer G. Barnett, Field Notes, UBC, Special Collections, box 1.

2 The point of entry to modern studies of the Halkomelem-speaking peoples is Wayne Suttles, 'Central Coast Salish,' in Suttles, ed., *Handbook of North American Indians*, vol. 7, Northwest Coast (Washington, DC, 1990), 453-75. See also Suttles, *Coast Salish Essays* (Seattle 1987), and, more specifically, his *Katzie Ethnographic Notes*, Anthropology in British Columbia, Memoir 2 (Victoria 1955), as well as, in the same volume, Diamond Jenness, 'The Faith of a Coast Salish Indian.' The most careful general ethnographer is Homer G. Barnett, *The Coast Salish of British Columbia* (Eugene, OR, 1955 and reprinted Westport, CT, 1975). See also Barnett's field notes, mentioned above. Earlier and more idiosyncratic is Charles Hill-Tout, 'Ethnological Studies of the Mainland Halkome'lem, a Division of the Salish of British Columbia,' *Report of the British Association for the Advancement of Science* 72 (London 1902), 355-449, and reprinted with an introduction by Ralph Maud (Vancouver 1978). James A. Teit, a remarkable amateur ethnographer of the Interior Salish and associated with Franz Boas, wrote little on the Coast Salish, but his field notes in the Boas Collection in the American Philosophical Society in Philadelphia contain relevant material.

3 The maps of seasonal population distribution in the early 1820s give a highly schematic picture of a much more complex pattern of seasonal movement and resource use. They are largely based on the ethnographic and archival materials described above. The distributions indicated in Burrard Inlet are probably the most contentious. In the 1930s Chief Khatsahlano told Major J.S. Matthews, the city archivist, that the Squamish had always live there. On the other hand, Homer Barnett was told by his Squamish informants that the Squamish settled there in the winter only when the sawmills were built (Field Notes, box 1, folders 4-5). Gilbert Malcolm Sproat, who spent some time in Burrard Inlet in the late 1870s as Indian Reserve Commissioner, also reported this (e.g., Department of Indian Affairs, RG 10, reel C-10106, vol. 3611, file 3756-7; or reel C-101 13, vol. 3645, file 7936). I therefore adopt this position.

4 François-Noel Annance, Journal of Voyage from Fort George to Fraser River,1824-25, Hudson's Bay Company Archive (HBCA) B76/a/1, fos. 2-10 (microfilm reel IM55).

5 This number, indeed, was said to have passed in four days, September 22-5. Fort Langley Journal, 17 June 1827-30 July 1830, copies in UBC, Special Collections, the BC Archives and Record Service (BCARS), and in the HBCA.

6 The concept of lifeworld is taken from Jürgen Habermas, *The Theory of Communicative Action*, vol. 2 of *Lifeworld and System: A Critique of Functionalist Reason* (Boston 1987). Others, however, have argued similarly: for example, Claude Lévi-Strauss, *The Savage Mind* (Chicago 1966), ch. 1; and Robin Riddington, *Little Bit Know Something: Stories in a Language of Anthropology* (Vancouver 1990).

7 W. Kaye Lamb, ed., *The Letters and Journals of Simon Fraser, 1806-1808* (Toronto 1960), 103.

8 T.C. Elliot, ed., 'Journal of John Work, November and December, 1824,' *Washington Historical Quarterly* 3 (July 1912):198-228.

9 A vivid account of these raids, recorded by Ellen Webber and published in *American Antiquarian* in 1898, is quoted in Chapter 1. For a discussion of the background of the raids, see Robert Galois, *Kwakwaka'waka Settlements, 1775-1920: A Geographical Analysis and Gazetteer* (Vancouver 1994).

10 Only a small fraction of the Hudson's Bay Company records relating to Fort Langley has survived. The Fort Langley Journal, cited above, is invaluable, and is the basis of much of this section. Other important sources are the Correspondence Relating to Fort Langley, 1830-59 (A/B20, 1 3A) in BCARS; and the Fort Langley Correspondence Book, 1830-71 (B112/b/1-4), Correspondence Inward, 1844-70 (B113/c/1), and Miscellaneous Items, 1830-78 (B113/z/1-2) in the HBCA. The secondary literature on Fort Langley includes: Mary K. Cullen, 'The History of Fort Langley, 1827-96,' *Canadian Historic Sites: Occasional Papers in Archaeology and History* (Ottawa 1979), 5-122; and Jamie Morton, 'Fort Langley: An Overview of the Operations of a Diversified Fur Trade Post 1848 to 1858 and the Physical Context in 1858' (ms., prepared for Parks Canada, n.d.).

11 Fort Langley Journal, 11 August 1827.

12 Ibid., 26 November 1827.

13 Richard Mackie, 'Colonial Land, Indian Labour and Company Capital: The Economy of Vancouver Island, 1849-1858,' MA thesis, University of Victoria, 1984; also by Mackie, *Trading Beyond the Mountains: The British Fur Trade on the Pacific, 1793-1843* (Vancouver 1996). James R. Gibson, *Farming the Frontier: The Agricultural Opening of the Oregon Country, 1786-1846* (Vancouver 1985).

14 Fort Langley Journal, 1 April 1829.

15 Ibid., 3 July 1829.

16 Ibid., 29 July 1829.

17 For a fuller account of these events, see Barry M. Gough, *Gunboat Frontier: British Maritime Authority and Northwest Coast Indians, 1846-1890* (Vancouver 1984), ch. 4.

18 A.C. Anderson, 'Journal of an expedition under command of Alex C. Anderson of the Hudson's Bay Co, undertaken with the view of ascertaining the practicability of a communication with the interior, for the import of the annual supplies,' 1846, ADDMSS 559, vol. 2, file 1, BCARS.

19 Moody to Douglas, HMS Plumper, 28 January 1859, Colonial Correspondence, B-1 347, 1159, BCARS; cited in Margaret McDonald, 'New Westminster, 1858-1871,' MA thesis, University of British Columbia, 1947, 20.

20 Ibid.
21 Laura E. Scott, 'The Imposition of British Culture as Portrayed in the New Westminster Capital Plan of 1859 to 1862,' MA thesis, Simon Fraser University, 1983.
22 Moody to Douglas, 17 March 1859; cited in McDonald, 'New Westminster,' 25.
23 Census of Canada, 1880-1, 'Nominal Return of the Living,' NAC, microfilm reel C-13285. See also Chapter 5.
24 Kay J. Anderson, *Vancouver's Chinatown: Racial Discourse in Canada, 1875-1990* (Montreal 1991). See also Chapter 9.
25 Robert E. Cail, *Land, Man, and the Law: The Disposal of Crown Lands in British Columbia, 1871-1913* (Vancouver 1974), 9.
26 Douglas to Lytton, 19 February 1859. Cited in Phyllis Mikkelsen, 'Land Settlement Policy on the Mainland of British Columbia, 1858-1874,' MA thesis, University of British Columbia, 1950, 60; also Cail, ibid., 11.
27 Mikkelsen, ibid., 108.
28 On early agricultural settlement in the lower Fraser Valley, see John E. Gibbard, 'Early History of the Fraser Valley, 1808-1885,' MA thesis, University of British Columbia, 1937; Donna H. Cook, 'Early Settlement in the Chilliwack Valley,' MA research paper, University of British Columbia, 1979; and particularly an inventory meticulously prepared by F.W. Laing, 'Colonial Farm Settlers on the Mainland of British Columbia, 1858-1871,' BCARS. Also by Laing, 'Agricultural Notes from Records in the Provincial Archives,' Vancouver City Archives. The first somewhat systematic inventory of agriculture in the Fraser Valley is the 'Second Report of the Department of Agriculture of the Province of British Columbia,' *British Columbia Sessional Papers* (Victoria 1893).
29 'The McCleery Diary 1862-1866,' *Vancouver Historical Journal* 5 (August 1965).
30 There are two censuses of the Natives in the Lower Mainland in 1876-7 – one by James Lenihan, Indian Superintendent, taken in May and June 1877 (DIA, RG 10, reel C10114, vol. 3650, file 8302); and the other by George Blenkinsop, apparently taken at the beginning of December 1876 (NAC, RG 88, vol. 494). The map of 1877 and details in the text are based on these censuses and accompanying notes.
31 The general picture is described in Robin Fisher, *Contact and Conflict: Indian-European Relations in British Columbia, 1774-1890* (Vancouver 1977), ch. 5; and in Paul Tennant, *Aboriginal Peoples and Politics: The Indian Land Question in British Columbia, 1849-1989* (Vancouver 1990), ch. 4.
32 Barbara Weightman, 'The Musqueam Reserve: A Case Study of the Indian Social Milieu in an Urban Environment,' PhD diss., University of Washington, 1972, 90.
33 G.M. Sproat to Forbes Vernon, 12 April 1878, Energy, Mines, and Resources: Canada Land Survey Records, Vancouver Office, Sproat's Letterbook no. 2, 10-12.
34 Lenihan census, 1877. See note 30.
35 The basic secondary sources on the first decade of salmon canning are: Cicely Lyons, *Salmon Our Heritage: The Story of Province and an Industry* (Vancouver 1969); Keith Ralston, 'Patterns of Trade and Investment on the Pacific Coast, 1867-1892: The Case of the British Columbia Salmon Canning Industry,' *BC Studies* 1 (winter 1968-9):37-45; Edward N. Higginbottom, 'The Changing Geography of Salmon Canning in British Columbia, 1870-1931, MA thesis, Simon Fraser University, 1988; Duncan Stacey, 'Technological Change in the Fraser River Salmon Canning Industry, 1871-1912,' MA thesis, University of British Columbia, 1977. Details are more elusive as no company records survive for this period. The most precise annual information is in the 'Annual Report of the Ministers of Public Works' (or, after 1876, of the Department of Marine and Fisheries), *Sessional Papers, Parliament of Canada.*
36 A.C. Anderson, Inspector of Fisheries, *Sessional Papers of the Dominion of Canada* (Ottawa 1879), part 4, Appendix 17, 297.
37 For a general account of Native activity in the fishery in these years, see Diane Newell, *Tangled Webs of History: Indians and the Law in Canada's Pacific Coast Fisheries* (Toronto 1993).
38 The only information I have found on Native housing at the canneries is in the James Lenihan census. See note 30.

39 Edward Stamp to James Douglas, Victoria, 21 December 1859, Colonial Correspondence, B-1366, 1643, BCARS.
40 The secondary literature on logging and sawmilling in Burrard Inlet includes: F.W. Howay, 'Early Shipping on Burrard Inlet, 1863-1870,' *British Columbia Historical Quarterly* 1 (1937):3-20; James E. Flynn, 'Early Lumbering on Burrard Inlet, 1862-1891,' BSc thesis, University of British Columbia, 1942; James Morton, *The Enterprising Mr. Moody, the Bumptious Captain Stamp* (North Vancouver 1977); and, since I wrote this essay, Robert A.J. McDonald, *Making Vancouver, 1863-1913* (Vancouver 1996).
41 Douglas Cole and Bradley Lockner, eds., *The Journals of George M. Dawson, British Columbia, 1875-1878* (Vancouver 1989), 115.
42 Edward Stamp to Colonial Secretary, 17 May 1865, Colonial Correspondence, B-1366, 1643, BCARS.
43 The timber lease for Hastings Mill is published in the *British Columbia Sessional Papers* (Victoria 1885), 387-9.
44 Edward Stamp to Colonial Secretary, 4 April 1861, Colonial Correspondence, B-1366, 1643, BCARS.
45 Stamp's sawmill claim overlapped an Indian village, 'one of the oldest in the inlet.' J.B. Launders to Colonial Secretary, 3 June 1865, Colonial Correspondence, B-1343, 969, BCARS.
46 Chartres Brew to Colonial Secretary, 7 June 1865, Colonial Correspondence, B-1311, 194, BCARS.
47 S.P. Moody to J.W. Trutch, Burrard Inlet, 5 January 1870, and Moody to Robert Beaven, Burrard Inlet, 12 May 1873, Colonial Correspondence, B-1347, 1159, BCARS.
48 G.M. Sproat, letters of 7 December 1876, DIA, RG 10, reel C-10106, vol. 3611, file 3765-5; and of 24 November 1877, DIA, RG 10, reel C-10122, vol 3699, file 16665.
49 Calvert Simson, 'Hastings Saw Mill Store: Re start of store,' Vancouver City Archives, Additional Manuscript 170, vol. 1, file 7, 5.
50 On changing individual space-time geographies associated with industrial work, see Allan Pred, *Making Histories and Constructing Human Geographies: The Local Transformation of Practice, Power Relations, and Consciousness* (Boulder 1990), esp. ch. 3.
51 Census of Canada, 1800-81.
52 David Demeritt, 'Visions of Agriculture in British Columbia,' *BC Studies* 108 (winter 1995-6):29-59.
53 Alan Ryan, *Property and Political Theory* (Oxford 1984).
54 Tina Loo, *Making Law, Order, and Authority in British Columbia, 1821-1871* (Toronto 1994).
55 E.B. Lytton to Colonel Moody, Downing Street, 29 October 1858, Colonial Correspondence, B-1346, 1149b, BCARS.
56 Edward W. Said, *Orientalism* (New York 1979); Robert Young, *White Mythologies: Writing History and the West* (London 1990).
57 Michel Foucault, *Discipline and Punish: The Birth of the Prison* (New York 1979), and *The History of Sexuality Volume 1: An Introduction* (New York 1980).
58 Melanie Jones, 'The Ste-Marie Mission, 1860-1900,' MA thesis, University of British Columbia, 1992.

Chapter 4: The Fraser Canyon Encountered

This chapter grew, in good part, out of a considerable pool of interrelated graduate student work on aspects of the colonial world in the Fraser Canyon. I particularly acknowledge the work and guidance of Brett Christophers on Anglican missionary discourse; Averill Groeneveld-Meijer on the construction of gender during the gold rush; Daniel Marshall on miners' violence; and Nadine Schuurman on patterns of Native resistance during the McKenna-McBride hearings. Daniel Clayton and Lynn Stewart provided helpful general comments, as did Wendy Wickwire. A preliminary version of this chapter appeared in *BC Studies* 94 (summer 1992):5-28.

1 After fellow North Wester David Thompson who, Fraser thought, was then exploring the upper reaches of the river. W. Kaye Lamb, ed., *The Letters and Journals of Simon Fraser, 1806-1808* (Toronto 1960), 86-92.

2 Kokwe'la (Thq'w'q'wíle), the son of Carrotroot, trained in the mountains and became a magician with invincible powers. Pat Shaw and Dale Kinkade, Department of Linguistics, UBC, kindly provided this identification.
3 J.A. Teit, 'Mythology of the Thompson Indians,' in *The Jesup North Pacific Expedition: Memoirs of the American Museum of Natural History*, vol. 8, part 2 (New York 1912), 416. There are other versions of this account. Gold rush miner Edward Stout, for example, gave a short version in the 'Reminiscences' he recounted in Yale, 1908, E/E/St 71, BCARS. Also, see Wendy C. Wickwire, 'To See Ourselves as the Other's Other: Nlaka'pamux Contact Narratives,' *Canadian Historical Review* 75, 1 (1994):1-20.
4 J.A. Teit, 'Notes to the Maps of the Pacific Northwest,' 372, roll 4, map 4, Boas Collection, American Philosophical Society. Yet there was some trade. Up-river trade into Nlha7kápmx territory comprised canoes, abalone shells, dried dog salmon, sturgeon oil, and a few other items. Down-river trade into Stó:lō territory comprised a variety of roots, skins, berries, animal fat, dried goat meat, goat hair, and cedar-root blankets. J.A. Teit, 'The Thompson Indians of British Columbia,' in *The Jesup North Pacific Expedition: Memoirs of the American Museum of Natural*, vol. 1, part 4 (New York 1900), 259.
5 Teit, 'Thompson Indians,' 259.
6 Ibid., 343.
7 For some indication of the detail of Nlha7kápmx environmental knowledge, see N.J. Turner, L.C. Thompson, M.T. Thompson, and A.Z. York, *Thompson Ethnobotany: Knowledge and Usage of Plants by the Thompson Indians of British Columbia*, Memoir no. 3 (Victoria 1990).
8 On these matters, see Jürgen Habermas, *Lifeworld and System: A Critique of Functionalist Reason*, vol. 2 of *The Theory of Communicative Action* (Boston 1989), 153-98; and Claude Lévi-Strauss, *The Savage Mind* (Chicago 1966), ch. 1.
9 Robin Riddington, *Little Bit Know Something: Stories in a Language of Anthropology* (Vancouver and Toronto 1990).
10 Evidence is sparse, and some of this is inferred from Lillooet armament described by miner C.C. Gardiner, 'Fraser River of British Columbia. Michigan Bluffs, Cal., Nov. 17, 1858,' *British Columbia Historical Quarterly* (October 1937):243-53. See also William Yates, who said the canyon 'Indians had nothing but the old fashioned Hudsons Bay guns [in] those days,' 'Reminiscences,' ts., n.d., BCARS. Averill Groeneveld-Meijer kindly brought this to my attention.
11 Robert Galois, 'Measles, 1847-1850: The First Modern Epidemic in British Columbia,' *BC Studies* 109 (spring 1996):31-46.
12 Averill Groeneveld-Meijer, 'Manning the Fraser River Gold Rush,' MA thesis, University of British Columbia, 1994.
13 See, for example, many of the miners' letters in the *Victoria Gazette*. See also Tina Loo, *Making Law, Order, and Authority in British Columbia, 1821-1871* (Toronto 1994), 158.
14 Apparently some Native women lived happily with white miners and, as in the fur trade, warned them of impending attacks. See, for example, Edward Stout, Yale, BC, 14 May 1908, 'Reminiscences,' BCARS.
15 For example, J.C. Lual, 'A Trip to Fraser River in 1858,' Lytton, BC, 20 January 1911, BCARS.
16 This, and the account of the retreat from the Thompson River, are in Stout, 'Reminiscences.'
17 Doyce B. Nunis, Jr., ed., *The Golden Frontier: The Recollections of Herman Francis Reinhart, 1851-1869* (Austin 1962), 135; cited in Daniel P. Marshall, 'Claiming the Land: The Fraser River Gold Rush and the Conquest of Native Lands,' paper presented to the Annual Meeting of the Canadian Historical Association, Montreal, 1995.
18 John Callbreath to Mother, Bridge River, BC, 24 January 1859, Bancroft Library, Berkeley. Dan Marshall kindly brought this to my attention.
19 H.M. Snyder to James Douglas, Governor of Vancouver Island, Fort Yale, 28 August 1858, Colonial Correspondence, B-1364, 1617, BCARS. Again, Dan Marshall brought this important letter to my attention, and is publishing an annotated version in *Native Studies Review* (spring 1996).

20 On the nineteenth-century revolution in small arms, see Daniel R. Headrick, *The Tools of Empire: Technology and European Imperialism in the Nineteenth Century* (New York 1981), chs. 4 and 5; and for a dated discussion about the six-shooter, see Walter Prescott Webb, *The Great Plains* (Boston 1931), ch. 5.
21 For most of this paragraph, Snyder to Douglas, 28 August 1858.
22 Snyder said that after his interpreter had talked with a Native, the man gave a yell 'and then you could see the Indians coming in every direction, from the Mountains, gulches, Ravines, and bushes.' Snyder to Douglas, 28 August 1858.
23 Teit, 'Mythology of the Thompson Indians,' 410-14.
24 The Nlha7kápmx version, recounted by Teit, describes the events of 1858, but places Douglas in Lytton. Douglas was there in 1860 and in Yale in the fall of 1858, but neither visit fits the account, and it is likely that Douglas and Snyder were confused, whether at the time or later, in the telling.
25 For example, Callbreath, who camped at the mouth of the Bridge River in the winter of 1858-9.
26 Teit, 'Mythology of the Thompson Indians,' 412.
27 William Yates, n.d., 'Reminiscences.'
28 Address of His Excellence the Governor to the Inhabitants at Fort Yale, 12 September 1858, Colonial Correspondence.
29 James Douglas, 'Diary of Gold Discovery on Fraser's River in 1858,' James Douglas, Private Papers, first series, BCARS; see also Loo, *Making Law, Order, and Authority,* chs. 3 and 4.
30 George Hills, Diary, 12 June 1860, Archives, Vancouver School of Theology, UBC.
31 James Turnbull, R.E., 'Rough Sketch Showing Line of Wagon Road from Lytton in Direction of Boston Bar,' BCARS, 14T1 R & T, June 1860.
32 This paragraph and the next are derived from Hills's diary account of his tour through the canyon in June and July 1860.
33 On some of these matters, see Myra Rutherdale, 'Revisiting Colonization through Gender: Anglican Missionary Women in the Pacific Northwest and the Arctic, 1860-1945,' *BC Studies* 104 (winter 1994-5):3-24; and, more thoroughly, Brett Christophers, 'Time, Space and the Judgement of God: Anglican Missionary Discourse in British Columbia,' MA thesis, University of British Columbia, 1995.
34 This is not the relationship between power and normative and disciplinary knowledge that Michel Foucault explored in *Discipline and Punish: The Birth of the Prison* (New York 1979) and *The History of Sexuality* (New York 1980), and it may contradict Foucault's more basic assertion that knowledge and power were dynamic relationships, rather than things possessed. Missionaries like Hills thought they possessed a particular knowledge with a particular power to save souls, and understood that their social power lay in convincing Native people that this was so. Their influence varied in direct proportion to the Native conviction that the missionaries did indeed possess singular knowledge, and the spirit power associated with it. I would argue that, in the missionary sphere, knowledge and power were both dynamic relationships and things possessed. For an introduction to some of the theoretical issues involved, see Joseph Rouse, 'Power/Knowledge,' in Garry Gutting, ed., *The Cambridge Companion to Foucault* (Cambridge and New York 1994), ch. 4.
35 On the problems of communication in such situations, see Stephen Greenblatt, *Marvelous Possessions: The Wonder of the New World* (Chicago 1991).
36 G.M. Sproat to Superintendent General of Indian Affairs, Ottawa, 6 May 1878, Energy, Mines and Resources (EMR) Canada, Land Survey Records (CLSR), Vancouver Office, Sproat Letterbooks, no. 2, 75-9. EMR has collected the letters, field minutes, and minutes of decision associated with the Indian reserve commission. Much of this material is also available in RG 1O in the NAC (for example, Sproat's letters to Ottawa in vols. 1273-4).
37 This point is repeatedly made in the Sproat correspondence. See, for example, G.M. Sproat to Chief Commissioner of Lands and Works, 4 May 1878, Sproat Letterbooks, no. 2, 70-2.
38 G.M. Sproat to Forbes Vernon, 12 April 1878, Sproat Letterbooks 2, 10-12.

39 George Blenkinsop, 'Census of Indian Tribes, 1876-1878,' RG 88, vol. 494, NAC.
40 I base these remarks on James Teit's observations twenty years later.
41 'I did not find at Spapum Flats the Chinaman who can speak English (Ah Chung), and was therefore unable to explain the result of my inquiries as to the land question to Ah Yip whom I saw.' G.M. Sproat to J.C. Barnes, Nicola, BC, 26 August 1878, Sproat Letterbooks, no. 2, 245-6, CLSR.
42 These various details of settlement around Boothroyds are in G.M. Sproat, Field Minutes, Boothroyd Group, 8 June 1878, CLSR.
43 G.M. Sproat, Field Minutes, Boston Bar Group, 1 June 1878.
44 Ibid.
45 For example, see the photograph of Boothroyds by Frederick Dally, 10232, BCARS.
46 For a general account of Sproat's activities and views at this time, see Robin Fisher, *Contact and Conflict: Indian-European Relations in British Columbia, 1774-1890* (Vancouver 1977), 189-99.
47 Water Records, Lytton Area, list compiled by G.M. Sproat, Minutes of Decision, vol. 24, 101-3, CLSR.
48 Edward Mohun to G.M. Sproat, Lytton, 12 July 1878, Sproat, Minutes of Decision, vol. 24a, 128-39, CLSR; see also, in the same volume, G.M. Sproat, Extracted Field Minutes, 20 July 1878, 109-28, CLSR.
49 On these crucial elements of land policy, see Robert E. Cail, *Land, Man, and the Law* (Vancouver 1974).
50 Sproat's writings are filled with musings such as 'I do not know whether under the Old Colonial Regime persons holding free miner certificates could work on Indian Reserves: they certainly cannot do so under the very stringent Canadian Indian Act of 1876, and these Chinamen under that act would be liable to be summarily ejected and heavily fined. But on the other hand, if the Colonial government led these Chinamen to believe that they might work on the Reserve, and, if so, as appears to be the fact, the Prov. Gov't since 1870 have made water Records of these Chinamen at the Spot in question, it is possible that the Prov. Gov't might consider that these Chinamen had, in equity, some claim for compensation for the loss of their improvement and the disturbance of their business.' G.M. Sproat to Peter O'Reilly, Boston Bar, 3 June 1878, Sproat Letterbooks, no. 2, 140-1, CLSR.
51 Alan Ryan, *Property and Political Theory* (Oxford 1984), 8. This paragraph derives from Ryan.
52 G.M. Sproat to Superintendent General of Indian Affairs, Popkum, BC, 12 June 1879, Sproat Letterbooks, no. 3, 301-6, CLSR.
53 G.M. Sproat to E.A. Meredith, Department of the Minister of the Indians, Cook's Ferry, 30 July 1878, Sproat Letterbooks, no. 2, 193-7, CLSR.
54 G.M. Sproat to Superintendent General of Indian Affairs, near Hope, 6 November 1878, Sproat Letterbooks, no. 2, 324-8, CLSR.
55 I have adopted Habermas's language here, with some hesitation. In addition to Habermas, see S.K. White, *The Recent Work of Jürgen Habermas: Reason, Justice and Modernity* (Cambridge 1988), and S. Benhabib, *Critique, Norm, and Utopia: A Study of the Foundations of Critical Theory* (New York 1986).
56 Rules and Regulations Formed by the Nekla-Kap-a-muk Council, Lytton, BC, 17 July 1879, Sproat Letterbooks, no. 3, 347-51, 351-6, CLSR.
57 Sproat's response is summarized in two letters to the Superintendent General of Indian Affairs in Ottawa, both written in Lytton on 26 July 1879, Sproat Letterbooks, no. 3, 328-60, 361-2, CLSR.
58 Douglas Harris has recently argued that the Nlha7kápmx were operating within the rule of law, as whites would have understood the concept, and that the response of the provincial and federal governments was based on power rather than law. Douglas Harris, 'The Nlha7kápmx Meeting at Lytton in 1879 and the Rule of Law,' *BC Studies* 108 (1995):5-28.
59 Among Plateau peoples, the Interior tribes of British Columbia and, in the Lower Mainland and on Vancouver Island, the Indian Rights Association were sending delegations to Ottawa and Victoria, and preparing memorials (often translated by James Teit)

for visiting prime ministers. For an introduction to the McKenna-McBride Commission, see Paul Tennant, *Aboriginal Peoples and Politics: The Indian Land Question in British Columbia, 1849-1989* (Vancouver 1990), ch. 7.

60 For a map of the Lytton Agency, c. 1914, see *Report of the Royal Commission on Indian Affairs for the Province of British Columbia* (Victoria 1916).

61 'Almost the same, but not white,' in Homi K. Bhabha, *The Location of Culture* (London and New York 1994), 81.

62 Transcripts of the Royal Commission: Meeting at Spuzzum November 18, 1914, PAC, RG 10. Royal Commission on Indian Affairs for the Province of British Columbia, vol. 11025, file AH7, Lytton Agency, Evidence from the hearings, reel T-3963.

63 Foucault, *Discipline and Punish*, 139-41.

64 Meeting with the Boston Bar Band, 17 November 1914, 5.

65 These are contradictions that Bhabha, a theorist of colonial discourse, identifies as the 'ambivalence' of colonial texts. See *The Location of Culture*.

66 Meeting with the Lytton Band, 15 November 1914, 28.

67 Peter Hohohaush to the commission, Kanaka Bar, 14 November 1914.

68 Transcripts of the Royal Commission, Meeting at Boston Bar, 17 November 1914.

69 This paragraph is derived from Bhabha (*The Location of Culture*), for whom irony is one form of the 'sly civility' of the colonized's address to their colonizers. Melancholia, he also suggests, is one of the most pervasive of a colonized peoples' indictments of their colonizers. Nadine Schuurman suggested several of the examples used.

70 Billy Sigh to the commission, Boston Bar, 17 November 1914.

71 Chief George to the commission, Boston Bar, 17 November 1914.

72 Patrick to the commission, Boston Bar, 17 November 1914.

73 Ibid.

74 Frantz Fanon, *The Wretched of the Earth* (New York 1963), 37.

Chapter 5: A Population Geography of BC

This chapter benefitted from comments by Trevor Barnes, Daniel Clayton, David Demeritt, Dan Hiebert, Averill Groeneveld-Meijer, David Ley, Richard Mackie, Gerry Pratt, Peter Ward, and, especially, Ellen Pond. It was first published in the *Canadian Geographer* (38, 1 [1994]:43-60), and is republished here with permission.

1 Work on this topic was begun by Robert Galois for Volume 2 of the *Historical Atlas of Canada*, and continued by Galois and Cole Harris as part of the Historical Geography of BC Project. The essential tasks of establishing where, day by day, the enumerators were, of establishing a format for data retrieval, and then of transcribing the data have been primarily Galois's, while the writing has been primarily Harris's. After the initial work for the atlas, both have been involved throughout. Averill Groeneveld-Meijer assisted in data collection.

2 On the interrelations between society and space, see, among others, A. Giddens, *The Constitution of Society: Outline of the Theory of Structuration* (Berkeley and Los Angeles 1984), especially ch. 3, 355-68; H. Lefebvre, *The Production of Space* (Oxford 1991); and, less explicitly, Michel Foucault, *Discipline and Punish: The Birth of the Prison* (New York 1979).

3 *Census of Canada, 1880-1881*, 4 vols. (Ottawa 1882). The nominal census (districts 187-191) is at NAC, microfilm reels C-13284-5. The Vancouver Island divisions of the nominal census have been coded and published in P. Baskerville, E. Sager, et al., *1881 Canadian Census: Vancouver Island* (Victoria 1990). However, by listing people alphabetically within districts, this publication removes them from their local contexts, which, to be sure, can be retrieved from the computer files.

4 These other records include voters' lists, city and regional directories, assessment rolls, and gold commissioners' records. Historic maps and the published reports of the minister of mines also provide valuable information, as does F.W. Laing, 'Colonial farm settlers on the mainland of British Columbia, 1858-1871,' UBC Special Collections; copy also at BCARS. Using such data, it is possible to trace the route taken by the census enumerators, thus locating individuals much more precisely than the nominal census itself allows, and making possible the type of analysis attempted in this paper.

5 Figure 5.1 includes the populations that were neither estimated nor enumerated in the census. The sources we have used to fill in these gaps are: Father Jean-Marie Lejacq, in NAC, RG 10, vol. 3,639, file 7,381; Father Fréderic Guertin, in Oblate Papers, 3,695, microfilm reel M707, UBC Library; G.M. Dawson, diary, 21 June 1879, Rare Book Room, McGill University; G.M. Dawson, 1888, 'Report on an exploration in the Yukon District, Canadian Geological Survey, N.W.T., and adjacent northern portions of British Columbia,' *Geological Survey of Canada, Annual Report, 1887* (Montreal), 200B; Canada, Department of Indian Affairs, *Annual Report* (Ottawa 1883), 188 (Klahoose); J. Helm, ed., *Subarctic*, vol. 6 of *Handbook of North American Indians* (Washington 1981), see articles by MacLachlan (p. 460), Asch (p. 347), and Riddington (p. 351). Our estimate does not address the question of under-enumeration.

6 Estimates of the contact population range from about 80,000 to more than 300,000. See Chapter 1.

7 Until 1862, emigration was organized by the Hudson's Bay Company, thereafter by the Vancouver Coal Mining and Land Company.

8 This probably does not include half-breed wives who, given their father's ethnicity in the census, rarely can be identified. Partners were usually listed in the census as concubines.

9 On J.W. McKay, see entry in *Dictionary of Canadian Biography*, vol. 12 (Toronto 1990), 641-3. George Blenkinsop, former HBC officer at Fort Rupert and Fort Colvile, acted as enumerator for District 187 subdistrict D, division 4.

10 D.C. Lai, 'Home County and Clan Origins of Overseas Chinese in Canada in the early 1880s,' *BC Studies* 27 (1975):3-29.

11 Most were wives, the others likely prostitutes.

12 D.C. Lai, *Chinatowns: Towns within Cities in Canada* (Vancouver 1988).

13 For a summary of the demographic history of the coast, see Robert T. Boyd, 'Demographic History, 1774-1874,' in W. Suttles, ed., *Handbook of North American Indians*, vol. 7 (Washington, DC, 1990), 135-48.

14 G.M. Dawson, 'Report on the Queen Charlotte Islands,' *Report of Progress, Geological Survey of Canada, 1878-79* (Montreal 1881), 173B.

15 See, for example, J.A. Teit, 'The Thompson Indians of British Columbia,' in *The Jesup North Pacific Expedition: Memoirs of the American Museum of Natural History*, vol. 1, part 4 (New York 1900), 321-2.

16 The best-known example is Metlakatla, near present-day Prince Rupert, established by William Duncan in 1862. See I. Usher, 'William Duncan of Metlakatla: A Victorian Missionary in British Columbia,' vol. 5 of *Publications in History* (Ottawa 1974).

17 For the impact of wars on the Kwakwaka'wakw, see H. Codere, *Fighting with Property: A Study of Kwakiutl Potlatching and Warfare, 1792-1930*, American Ethnological Society, Monograph 18 (Washington 1950); and R.P. Rohner, *The People of Gilford Island*, Bulletin 225 (Ottawa 1967). For descriptions of the 1862 smallpox epidemic and the general health conditions in the 1860s, see Log of the *Hecate*, 11 September 1863, reel 447A, BCARS; and E. Begg, Log of the *Beaver*, fo. 16, adm. 101/276, NAC.

18 D. Clayton, 'Geographies of the Lower Skeena,' *BC Studies* 94 (1992):29-58.

19 Douglas Papers, B/20 1853, BCARS. The journal for Fort Simpson indicates that the HBC census was undertaken on 21 and 22 February 1842, HBCA B201/a/6. All these sites had been used prior to contact.

20 'Northern Indians' began substantial seasonal migrations to southern Vancouver Island and Puget Sound in 1853; see Douglas to Barclay, HBCA B226/b/11. For information on the northern canneries, see *Daily Colonist* (Victoria) 16 July 1881 and 1 September 1881; Department of Marine and Fisheries, *Annual Report* (Ottawa 1881), 224-5.

21 On Duncan's activities at Metlakatla, see Usher, 'William Duncan of Metlakatla,' and P. Murray, *The Devil and Mr Duncan* (Victoria 1985). On the cannery, see W.H. Collison, *In the Wake of the War Canoe*, C. Lilliard, ed. (Victoria 1981), 32.

22 Duncan to Attorney-General of BC, 24 September 1877, BCARS, GR 429, Attorney-General Correspondence Inward. Attorney-General to Duncan, 8 October 1877, Duncan Papers, 4,729. On Native protests about the 'Land Question' in the 1870s, see 'Letter from the Missionary Society of the Methodist Church to the Superintendent-General of

Indian Affairs,' RG 10, vol. 3,818, file 57,837, v, 3, 14-15, NAC; RG 10, vol. 3,700, file 16,686, NAC; and see also R. Galois, 'The Burning of Kitsegukla, 1872,' *BC Studies* 94 (1992):59-81.

23 There are many ethnographic references to high population densities. The first census of the lower canyon, compiled at Fort Langley in 1830 by Archibald McDonald, gives high populations even after at least one smallpox epidemic. See Chapter 5.

24 On the other hand, most canyon people were vaccinated before the smallpox epidemic of 1862-3. Some groups that were not, such as the Canyon Shuswap, off the map to the north, virtually died out.

25 Canada, Department of Indian Affairs, *Annual Report* (Ottawa 1881).

26 In 1877, G.M. Sproat, Indian Reserve Commissioner, was horrified to find that the provincial government had granted Natives in the canyon few reserves and, in this dry area, no water rights. See Chapter 4.

27 In Thompson society, parents commonly arranged marriages of young women with considerably older men, who also had a great deal of authority over their wives. See Teit, *Thompson Indians of British Columbia*, vol. 1, pt. 4, 321-2.

28 E. Wickberg, ed., *From China to Canada: A History of the Chinese Communities in Canada* (Toronto 1982), ch. 2.

29 On the Chinese in the canyon, see Chapter 5. J.B. Good, the Anglican priest who enumerated the canyon population in 1881, identified a few Chinese by regional origin in China before giving up on such detail.

30 This was a competition that Natives would eventually lose, although, according to Rolf Knight, there were still substantial Native ranches in the Nicola Valley in 1900. See Knight's *Indians at Work* (Vancouver 1978), 74.

31 If the father stayed around, the census considered the children of these marriages to be whites. Some, like Joe Coutlee, cowboss at Douglas Lake, apparently lived between white and Native worlds. See N.G. Wolliams, *Cattle Ranch* (Vancouver 1979), 81-2ff.

32 W.P. Ward, *White Canada Forever* (Montreal and Kingston 1978). On opium dens in Victoria, see *Daily Colonist*, 15 February 1881. On the other hand, there was a wariness about the dependence upon Chinese labour, especially in the canning industry; see *Daily Colonist*, 30 July 1881.

33 They came for many years, but had stopped coming to the canneries sometime before the McKenna-McBride Commission toured the canyon in 1914. The Royal Commission on Indian Affairs for the Province of British Columbia, Meeting with the Spuzzum Band, 18 November 1914. RG 10, vol. 11,025, file AH7, reel T-3963, NAC.

34 At Comox, farther up island, most settlers came from the Maritimes and belonged to the Church of Scotland.

35 Sproat received many complaints from Natives in the lower Fraser Valley about lack of land. See Chapter 3 and, for another example, Canada, Indian and Northern Affairs, Letter to Forbes Vernon, 12 April 1878, Sproat Letterbooks, no. 2, 10-12.

36 Information about Native housing at the canneries is in a census taken by James Lenihen, Indian Superintendent, May-June 1877, RG 10, reel C-10114, vol. 3,650, file 8,302, DIA. See also *Daily Colonist*, 28, 29, and 30 July 1881.

37 See Chapter 3.

38 H. Barnett, 'Field Notes,' n.d., box 1, folders 4-5, UBC, Special Collections.

39 Canada, Department of Indian Affairs, *Annual Report*, DIARR (Ottawa 1881).

40 A. Giddens, *The Nation-State and Violence*, vol. 2 of *A Contemporary Critique of Historical Materialism* (Berkeley 1987), chs. 6 and 7.

41 K.J. Anderson, *Vancouver's Chinatown: Racial Discourse in Canada, 1875-1990* (Montreal and Kingston 1991).

42 See Teit, *Thompson Indians of British Columbia*, vol. 1, pt. 4, 321-2, and Robin Fisher, *Contact and Conflict: Indian-European Relations in British Columbia, 1774-1890* (Vancouver 1977), 90-1.

43 For an example of the range of Native feelings towards William Duncan, see W. Clah, 'How Tamks saved William Duncan's Life' in *Trade and Warfare*, vol. 2 of G. McDonald and J. Cove, eds., *Tsimshian Narratives*, Mercury Series, directorate paper no. 3,210-12 (Ottawa). For a more generalized Native reaction to whites, see Teit, *Thompson Indians of British Columbia*, 366.

44 For information on strikes at Nanaimo and the neighbouring town of Wellington, see L. Bowen, *Three Dollar Dreams* (Lantzville 1987).

45 Our discussion somewhat overlaps claims made by both W. Peter Ward and Rennie Warburton. W.P. Ward, 'Class and Race in the Social Structure of British Columbia, 1870-1939,' *BC Studies* 45 (1980):17-35, and R. Warburton, 'Race and Class in British Columbia: A Comment,' *BC Studies* 49 (spring 1981):79-85.

46 C. Harris, 'The Simplification of Europe Overseas,' *Annals, Association of American Geographers* 67 (1977):469-83, and C. Harris, 'European Beginnings in the Northwest Atlantic: A Comparative View,' in David D. Hall and David G. Allen, eds., *Seventeenth-Century New England* (Boston 1984), 119-52.

47 For an outline of the general picture, see B. Laslett, 'Gender and Social Production: Historical Perspectives,' *Annual Review of Sociology* 15 (1989):381-404.

48 This relationship recurs in much British Columbian literature, for example, in the conclusion of M.A. Grainger, *Woodsmen of the West* (London 1908; reprinted Toronto 1964), or in the attitudes revealed in Gordon Gibson, *Bull of the Woods* (Vancouver 1980), ch. 1. There are also other accounts, such as D. Marlatt, 'Subverting the Heroic: Recent Feminist Writing on the West Coast,' in G. Creese and V. Strong-Boag, eds., *British Columbia Reconsidered: Essays on Women* (Vancouver 1992), 296-308.

49 Such women in British Columbia did not have access to jobs as factory operatives or, in most cases, as domestic servants. The only jobs of the former type (in the salmon canneries) were taken by Native women, and most of the jobs of the latter type were taken by Chinese men.

50 M.G. Cohen, *Women's Work, Markets, and Economic Development in Nineteenth-Century Ontario* (Toronto 1988).

51 T. Hagerstrand's time geographies would be revealing. For examples of their applications, see A. Pred, *Making Histories and Constructing Human Geographies* (Boulder, San Francisco, and Oxford 1990).

52 Consider, for example, S.J. Hornsby, *Nineteenth Century Cape Breton: A Historical Geography* (Montreal and Kingston 1992), especially ch. 9.

Chapter 6: The Struggle with Distance

This chapter has benefitted from comments by Daniel Clayton, David Demeritt, Ken Favrholdt, Robert Galois, R.C. (Bob) Harris, and Nadine Schuurman.

1 Among the most imposing of this literature are: Edward Said, *Orientalism* (New York 1979); Edward Said, *Culture and Imperialism* (New York 1994); Homi K. Bhabha, ed., *Nation and Narration* (London 1990); Homi K. Bhabha, *The Location of Culture* (London 1994); Gayatri Chakravorty Spivak, *In Other Worlds: Essays in Cultural Politics* (London 1988); Gayatri Chakravorty Spivak, *The Post-Colonial Critic* (London 1990); Robert Young, *White Mythologies: Writing History and the West* (London 1990). A striking engagement with some of these ideas in British Columbia is Daniel Clayton's 'Islands of Truth: Vancouver Island from Captain Cook to the Beginning of Colonialism,' PhD diss., University of British Columbia, 1995.

2 Innis's main writing is collected and his thought summarized in Daniel Drache, ed., *Staples, Markets, and Cultural Change: Selected Essays: Harold Innis* (Montreal and Kingston 1995).

3 J. Despard Pemberton, *Facts and Figures Relating to Vancouver Island and British Columbia, Showing What to Expect and How to Get There* (London 1860), 84.

4 Richard Mackie, *Trading Beyond the Mountains: The British Fur Trade on the Pacific* (Vancouver 1996).

5 For the British side of this, see Barry M. Gough, *The Royal Navy and the Northwest Coast of North America, 1810-1914: A Study of British Maritime Ascendency* (Vancouver 1971).

6 *Lieutenant Matthew Fontain Maury's Explanations and Sailing Directions to Accompany the Wind and Current Charts*, 7th ed. (Philadelphia 1855); cited in Raymond A. Rydell, *Cape Horn to the Pacific: The Rise and Decline of an Ocean Highway* (Berkeley 1952), 127ff.

7 Rydell, *Cape Horn to the Pacific*, 139.

8 A.S. Deaville, *The Colonial Postal Systems and Postage Stamps of Vancouver Island and British Columbia, 1849-1871* (Victoria 1928), 36.
9 Pemberton, *Facts and Figures*, 86-91.
10 *British Columbian*; cited in Corday MacKay, 'The Collins Overland Telegraph,' *British Columbia Historical Quarterly* 10 (July 1946): 200.
11 Cited in MacKay, 'The Collins Overland Telegraph,' 192-3.
12 Ed. Conway to Col. C. Bulkeley, San Francisco, 19 February 1867, 159-60, Bulkeley Papers, Special Collections, UBC Library.
13 Messages were retransmitted between relay stations across the continent, and backlogs built up; a telegram from Montreal or New York to New Westminster might take several days, much more if the line were down.
14 That is, about $3.00 per 100 miles, when $3.00 was a good daily wage.
15 H.A. Innis, *A History of the Canadian Pacific Railway* (London and Toronto 1923), 138-9.
16 Ken Favrholdt, 'Hudson's Bay Company's Cordilleran Communications,' MA thesis, University of British Columbia, 1996.
17 This was the Dewdney Trail built from Hope on the lower Fraser to Wild Horse Creek in the Rocky Mountain Trench in 1864, abandoned in its eastern half in the early 1870s.
18 Despatches from Governor Frederick Seymour to the Secretary of State for the Colonies, the Duke of Newcastle, 30 August and 9 September 1864.
19 'The Telegraph,' *Cariboo Sentinel*, 1 October 1870.
20 William Cronon, *Nature's Metropolis: Chicago and the Great West* (New York 1991), 63-81.
21 For a somewhat fuller account of the evolving pattern of railways in southern British Columbia, see my earlier essay 'Moving amid the Mountains, 1870-1930,' *BC Studies* 58 (summer 1983):3-39.
22 Again, see Harris, 'Moving amid the Mountains'; or, for more detail, E.L. Affleck, *Sternwheelers, Sandbars and Switchbacks* (Vancouver 1973). There are many detailed local accounts, a good recent example of which is David L. Davies, 'Sternwheelers on the Thompson,' in Wayne Norton and Wilf Schmidt, eds., *Reflections: Thompson Valley Histories* (Kamloops 1994).
23 Fondly remembered by Andy Craig in a lively collection of reminiscences: *Trucking: A History of Trucking in British Columbia since 1900* (Saanichton 1977). A more analytical account is in Rhys Evans, 'Looking at the World through a Windshield: A Historical Geography of Trucking in British Columbia,' MA thesis, University of British Columbia, 1995.
24 Gerald A. Rushton, *Whistle up the Inlet: The Union Steamship Story* (Vancouver 1974).
25 For a comprehensive list of BC post offices, including date of establishment and closure, see William Topping, *A Checklist of British Columbia Post Offices* (Vancouver 1983); copy in Special Collections, UBC Library. See also George H. Melvin, *The Post Offices of British Columbia, 1858-1970* (Vernon 1962).
26 There is no good study of the introduction, diffusion, and impact of the telephone in British Columbia, but some of the picture can be gleaned from *Telephone Talk*, a newsletter published by the BC Telephone Company: 1, nos. 1, 2, 3, 8, and 12 (1911); 9, 3 (1919); 10, 12 (1920); 12, 1 and 2 (1922); and 29, 1 and 2 (1939); see also Edmond B. Ogle, *Long Distance Please: The Story of the Trans-Canada Telephone System* (Don Mills 1979).
27 Margaret Prang suggests that most of the BC interior, including the Peace River, was outside the range of any Canadian radio stations. 'The Origins of Public Broadcasting in Canada,' *Canadian Historical Review* 46 (March 1965):4.
28 There is a large, lively popular literature on these matters. I also recommend Richard White, *Land Use, Environment and Social Change: The Shaping of Island County, Washington* (Seattle 1980), particularly on logging with oxen; Roderick Haig-Brown, *Timber* (Toronto and London 1946), particularly on patterns of logging with logging railways and donkey engines; and Gabrielle Kahrer, 'Logging and Landscape Change on the North Arm of Burrard Inlet, 1860s to 1930s,' MA thesis, University of British Columbia, 1988, particularly on the conveyances and contraptions that brought logs and shake bolts from the north shore mountains to mills around Burrard Inlet.

29 Among the considerable literature on the salmon fishery, the work most closely focused on these matters is Edward Higginbottom, 'The Changing Geography of Salmon Canning in British Columbia, 1870-1931,' MA thesis, Simon Fraser University, 1989.
30 Daniel R. Headrick, *The Tools of Empire: Technology and European Imperialism in the Nineteenth Century* (New York 1981); Daniel R. Headrick, *The Tentacles of Progress: Technology Transfer in the Age of Imperialism, 1850-1940* (New York 1988).
31 Among the large literature on this topic, see particularly Stephen Kern, *The Culture of Time and Space, 1880-1918* (Cambridge, MA, 1983), chs. 8 and 9, and Said, *Orientalism*, particularly ch. 1, pts. 1 and 2.
32 See Neil Smith, *Uneven Development: Nature, Capital and the Production of Space* (Oxford 1984), 102-5.
33 Innis, *Canadian Pacific Railway*, 139; J.H. Hamilton, 'The "All-Red Route," 1893-1953: A History of the Trans-Pacific Mail Service between British Columbia, Australia, and New Zealand,' *British Columbia Historical Quarterly* 20 (January-April 1956).
34 Said, *Orientalism*, 92.
35 See, particularly, Michel Foucault, *Discipline and Punish: The Birth of the Prison* (New York 1979).
36 Gilles Deleuze and Félix Guattari, *Anti-Oedipus: Capitalism and Schizophrenia*, trans. Robert Hurley, Mark Seem, and Helen R. Lane (New York 1977).
37 David Harvey, *The Limits to Capital* (Oxford 1982).
38 David Harvey, *The Condition of Postmodernity: An Enquiry into the Origins of Cultural Change* (Oxford 1989), 238.
39 For a fuller summary of Deleuze and Guattari's thinking about desire, capitalism, and spatiality, see Robert J.C. Young, *Colonial Desire: Hybridity in Theory, Culture, and Race* (London 1995), especially 166-74.
40 Jean and John Comaroff, *Of Revelation and Revolution: Christianity, Colonialism, and Consciousness in South Africa*, vol. 1 (Chicago 1991), 309-14.
41 In some cases, Native people adapted very quickly. In 1866, less than two years after the telegraph arrived, Nlha7kápmx people sent a telegram in Chinook to the Anglican missionary J.B. Good at Yale, inviting him to establish a mission at Lytton. Good went, interpreting the telegram as a call from God. Brett Christophers, 'Time, Space and the People of God: Anglican Colonialism in Nineteenth Century British Columbia,' MA thesis, University of British Columbia, 1995.
42 Mackie, *Trading Beyond the Mountains*.
43 Consider the analogous relationship of St. Louis and Chicago, admirably described by Cronon, *Nature's Metropolis*, 295-309.
44 As subsequent events in BC have shown, colonial theorist Robert Young is correct in saying that prior cultures were not so much destroyed as layered over, and the layers increasingly imbricated with each other. See Young, *Colonial Desire*, 174.
45 Kay Anderson, *Vancouver's Chinatown: Racial Discourse in Canada, 1875-1990* (Montreal and Kingston 1991).
46 Said, *Orientalism*, 93.

Chapter 7: Industry and the Good Life

1 'Map of Northern Rocky Mountains and Plateau,' c. 1842-8, De Smetiana Collection, Jesuit Missouri Province Archives, St. Louis; and published in Jacqueline Peterson and Laura Peers, *Sacred Encounters: Father De Smet and the Indians of the Rocky Mountain West* (Norman, OK, 1993), 118-19.
2 James A. Teit, *The Salishan Tribes of the Western Plateaus* (Washington, DC, 1930), 210-12.
3 Ibid., 212-13.
4 It is not known when whites first saw Slocan Lake and the surrounding mountains. The lake was mentioned by G.M. Sproat, retired commissioner of Indian lands, in early 1884; see 'Mr. Sproat's Report on Kootenay,' British Columbia, *Sessional Papers 1883-4* (Victoria 1885), 310-23. It was visited later that year and again in 1886 by prospectors looking for placer gold, *New Denver Ledge*, 5 November 1896. The lake was also known

by a trapper who lived to the south along the Slocan River. R.H. Kemp, 'Early Days in Kootenay,' *BC Mining Record* III (January 1897):14. It first appeared on a map in 1890.

5 There is archeological evidence of Indian settlement (Interior Salish) along the Slocan River, but not around Idaho Peak.

6 This discovery was to become the Payne Mine. The story survives that an old forge and wedge were found at the site, also lumps of ore on tree stumps. The unlikely inference has been that Hudson's Bay Company men made lead bullets there.

7 On this American background, see particularly Richard E. Lingenfelter, *The Hardrock Miners: A History of the Mining Labor Movement in the American West, 1863-1893* (Berkley 1974), and Mark Wyman, *Hard Rock Epic: Western Miners and the Industrial Revolution, 1860-1910* (Berkeley 1979). The geographical development of a proximate American region is treated by D.W. Meinig, *The Great Columbia Plain: A Historical Geography, 1805-1910* (Seattle 1968), especially ch. 9. On the general development of mining in the Kootenays, H.A. Innis's worst book, written too quickly and without a clear mastery of the intricacies of the Kootenays, is the best analytical treatment: *Settlement and the Forest and Mining Frontiers*, part 2 of W.A. Mackintosh and W.L. Joerg, eds., *Settlement and the Mining Frontier*, Canadian Frontiers of Settlement, vol. 9 (Toronto 1936).

8 The almost 4,500 tons of ore shipped from the Slocan in 1894 averaged 138 ounces of silver per ton. British Columbia, *Sessional Papers*, Annual Reports, Minister of Mines, 1895 and subsequent years (Victoria 1896, and subsequently). Apparently some small, individual shipments contained several thousand ounces of silver per ton. For example, shipments from the Arlington Mine as reported in *New Denver Ledge*, 22 August 1895.

9 Old-timers in the Slocan maintain that prospectors never set fires deliberately, but many people in the early Slocan certainly thought they did. See, for example, *Nakusp Ledge*, 23 August 1894; and J.D. Kendall, 'Southern British Columbia,' *BC Mining Record* IV (October 1898):29.

10 This may not have been a recent occurrence. G.M. Sproat reported in 1883 that much Kootenay timber had been burned, and that he had difficulty seeing the country for smoke haze. Indian legend, as remembered by Chief Louis Joseph of the Burton Reserve, held that many years ago a vindictive chief had set fire to much of the west Kootenays. Mrs. E.C. Johnson Scrapbook, Selkirk College Archives, Castlegar, BC.

11 Incorporated about a year after the first Slocan discoveries, the Kaslo and Slocan Railway was a measure of the speculative energy of early British Columbian industrialists and of governmental support for their efforts. The line's principal backer, John Hendry, was a prominent lumberman in New Westminster and Vancouver. The provincial government provided a land grant of 250,022 acres, and the federal government provided a subsidy of $3,200 per mile. See R.E. Cail, *Land, Man, and the Law* (Vancouver 1974), 159, 163.

12 *Mining Review*, Sandon, 15 January 1898.

13 'This camp has been no exception to almost all new mining camps, which have sprung up in the last few years, since the railroad has made almost all the big mineral belts accessible or easy to get at. As soon as a new camp is struck, a class of "sharks" with the cry of "boom," "boom," rush in, and before the honest prospector has time to look around, they have staked all the surrounding country, regardless of whether it is mineral or not; then sit around, talk big, and try to sell their claims.' Views of 'an old-time prospector,' *Silvertonian*, 15 January 1898.

14 Bunkhouse food was generally preferred to bunkhouse lodging: a lot of pork, potatoes, rolled oats, bread, beans, turnips, cabbage, carrots, canned tomatoes, tapioca pudding, dried fruit, Eagle brand canned milk, eggs perhaps twice a week, and occasionally fresh fruit and vegetables.

15 Mine Mill Papers [MMP], vols. 156-7, Sandon Union Hospital Reports, Special Collections, UBC Library. Lingenfelter, *Hardrock Miners*, 7, suggests that the average age of a Comstock miner was thirty-six; this figure could not be far from the Slocan average.

16 Lingenfelter, *Hardrock Miners*, ch. 1; Wyman, *Hard Rock Epic*, ch. 9.

17 Royal Commission Re Miners and Mine Owners in the Province of BC, Report and Evidence, 1900, microfilm misc. 92, 115, 260, 318, Department of Labour Library, Ottawa.

18 The Chinese cook for the CPR train crew would not leave the car in Sandon for fear of his life. There were unsubstantiated reports of Oriental workers who got on the steamboat at Slocan City at the foot of Slocan Lake and did not get off (having been pushed overboard at night). For the general picture, see W. Peter Ward, *White Canada Forever: Popular Attitudes and Public Policy toward Orientals in British Columbia* (Montreal 1978).

19 In 1899, provincial legislation reduced the working day underground to eight hours. When the Slocan mine owners proposed a reduction in wages from $3.50 to $3.00, the miners struck. The $3.50 wage had long been a standard throughout the western hard-rock mines. After almost a year, a compromise settlement produced a $3.25 wage, but the eight-hour day underground remained. In the crushing mills and smelters (the nearest smelter was on Kootenay Lake), the working day was usually twelve hours.

20 None of the Slocan mines worked year round. Moreover, it was 'almost a physical impossibility for a miner to endure a year's steady work in a lead mine. Some few might stand it but with the average it would break down the constitution or dull the intellect.' *Paystreak*, Sandon, 25 November 1899. In a statement before a board of conciliation investigating a wage dispute in 1913, one young miner said that seven months was 'as long as he could stand it, day in and day out,' in the mines. Certified Copy of Report and Findings of the Board of Conciliation and Investigation, Ottawa, 25 February 1913, MMP, vol. 156. An average working year of 200 days (six to eight months) is only an estimate. It is important to emphasize that work was irregular; voluntary or forced unemployment was part of the hard-rock mining life, at least in the Slocan.

21 Wyman, *Hard Rock Epic*, ch. 4

22 Interview with Dick Avison, son of an early Slocan miner, Silverton, BC, June 1976.

23 Lingenfelter, *Hardrock Miners*, 219.

24 The common ailments treated in the Union Hospital in Sandon were rheumatism and pneumonia, products of wet mines and inadequate bunkhouses. The mines were a good deal safer than many contemporary workplaces. Apparently a Nelson doctor routinely told men who had worked for more than eight months in the lead smelter that 'if they don't quit they will die shortly as the Lead is Killing them.' Frank Phillips, secretary, Local 96, Western Federation of Miners [WFM] to A. Shilland, Nelson, 19 February 1905, MMP, vol. 158. The union sought to reduce the working day in the smelter to ten hours; no one argued that it should be closed.

25 Most shows were American, but Pauline Johnson came to read her poems, and Walter McRae to impersonate Drummond's habitant characters. After 1902 or 1903, as the market contracted, there were few shows of any sort.

26 J.C. Bruce to A. Shilland, New York, 3 December 1903, MMP, vol. 157.

27 Walter Joy to Shilland, Silverton, 21 November 1900; Alex Smith to Shilland, Kaslo, 8 January 1903; Val Klemm to Shilland, Seattle, 15 January 1902; Archie McLeod to Shilland, Atlin, 10 December 1901; J. Dempsey to Shilland, Tonopah, 16 June 1904: all correspondence from MMP, vols. 157-8.

28 Jack Macdonald to Shilland, Ottawa Mine, 29 October 1905, MMP, vol. 156.

29 In the Pennsylvania coal mines, a good daily wage was $2.25.

30 Certified Copy of Report and Findings of the Board of Conciliation and Investigation, Ottawa, 25 February 1913, MMP, vol. 156.

31 Royal Commission Re Miners and Mine Owners in the Province of BC, Report and Evidence, 1900, microfilm misc. 86, Department of Labour Library, Ottawa.

32 Financial Statement of the Estate of the late Wm. T. Douglas, September 1902, MMP, vol. 157.

33 From time to time, the union took up a collection to support a miner crippled by silicosis. The recipients' simple, appreciative letters are in the Mine Mill Papers. There was little enough that the union could do; the miners could not afford many such collections.

34 In 1896, J.M. Harris, owner of the Reco Mine near Sandon, ordered the machinery for a 100-ton concentrating mill from a firm in Milwaukee. The price was $7,232 plus $375 for a pelton wheel. The price for a 7,000-foot aerial tramway was $11,500 (uninstalled). N.L. Barlee Collection, *Canada West Magazine*, Aldergrove, BC; R.J. Cory, Mgr Edward P. Allis Co, Machinists and Founders, to Harris, Milwaukee, 20 August 1896, J.M. Harris Papers, BCARS.

35 *Mining Review*, 12 June 1897.
36 *Paystreak*, 4 September 1897.
37 'The miners and the citizens held a football tussle the other day on the Cody grounds.' *Mining Review*, Sandon, June 1899. Although loosely used, the term 'citizen' referred to acceptable people who had settled in the valley. Mining promoters briefly in the Slocan were hardly citizens, nor were prostitutes or Chinese laundrymen.
38 'In a staid old Mining country like the Slocan has grown to be, there is nothing very startling or strange to be chronicled ... Pat Burns and Co closed up their shop here some time ago. J.R. Cameron, the Tailor – though still Mayor of Sandon – moved his business down to Kaslo last Summer. J.W. Power, Hardware Merchant and Packer forsook the town about the same time. Jim McKinnon sold his Cows and although the Creek is still running past his door, quit selling milk last Fall. Dan Hurley sold out his Drayage business to McKinnon and moved to the Coast. Ed Atherton closed up in January last and has gone to look for pastures new. The Grocery and Dry Goods trade is in the hands of Johnnie Black and Howard Cameron, who bought out Jalland Bros up the Gulch but proposes moving down to Atherton's Store ... Liquid and solid refreshments are still dispensed by Bennett at the Reco Hotel, Bob Cumming at the Sandon House, Jim Thompson at the Exchange.' Shilland to J.C. Bell, Sandon, 2 March 1908, MMP, vol. 156.
39 A good miner might become a foreman and earn $5 a day. A few acquired a bit of land and quit mining. Jack Price, an Englishman of some education, left mining to live as a hermit on two or three cleared acres across Slocan Lake, and to appear now and then in Silverton to peddle eggs and goat's milk. A very few managed to get into small business. Neil Tattrie left home on a farm near Pugwash at twelve, worked around Nova Scotia until he came west in 1904 to follow the harvest train, cut cord wood near Portage la Prairie, came to the Slocan because cousins were there, worked in the Slocan mines to become an expert miner, and, by 1914, a foreman. Eventually he left mining to work for a small retail chain, and when the firm went into receivership he bought its Sandon store. After dozens of labouring jobs scattered across a continent and a decade of Slocan mining, Tattrie, then in his mid-thirties, had left the mining ranks. Interview with Neil Tattrie, New Denver, BC, July 1976.
40 Most notably J.M. Harris, a Virginian, who owned the Reco Mine, the Reco Hotel, and, for a time, most of the townsite of Sandon. In 1897, Harris became a member of the Spokane Stock Exchange, and in 1900, he was trying to sell the Reco Mine in New York, asking $1 million for it. His broker in New York was enthusiastic, not only about the Reco: 'I would like for us to do some business together John, whether it is with the Reco or some other property. Of course, what we all want is to make money and in order to do that we will have to keep working. I am almost positive you can get some development property outside of the Reco, that we might be able to make a good turn on. There is plenty of Mining money in the East for good development properties and it is not very hard to get, when you are in good shape to go after it.' W. Alperson, vice-president, Richmond Mining Co, 39 Broadway, New York, to Harris, Sandon, 17 November 1900, J.M. Harris Papers.
41 Bylaws of the Silver-Lead Mines Association of BC, n.d., J.M. Harris Papers.
42 Minutes of a Conference held at Rossland, BC, between representatives from the Mine Owners and Managers Association of Boundary Creek District, the Nelson District Mines Association, and from the Silver-Lead Mines Association of Sandon, BC, and the Mine Owners and Managers of the Rossland District, 9 December 1899, J.M. Harris Papers.
43 The lists included the names of those who reported and did not report for work on the days of riots in the mines and mills nearby. J.M. Harris Papers.
44 Reports of both Thiel and Pinkerton agents are in the J.M. Harris Papers, all prepared in a form for circulation to mine owners. Most of these reports deal with the activities of 'operatives' in the United States. The union instructed members in 'secret work' of its own, but the extent of the mine owners' penetration of the union perhaps is indicated by the fact that the Minute Book of the Sandon Union through most of the 1899-1900 strike is among the papers of J.M. Harris, the principal mine owner in Sandon.

45 Minutes of a Conference held at Rossland, BC, J.M. Harris Papers. It is not my purpose, here, to assess these views. Of course, then as now, the concept of freedom in the workplace was most attractive to those who wielded most power there.

46 On the WFM, see Lingenfelter, *Hardrock Miners*, ch. 9; Vernon H. Jensen, *Heritage of Conflict: Labor Relations in the Nonferrous Metals Industry up to 1930* (Ithaca 1950); J.H.M. Laslett, *Labor and the Left: A Study of Socialist and Radical Influences in the American Labor Movement, 1881-1924* (New York 1970), ch. 7; Melvyn Dubofsky, *We Shall Be All: A History of the Industrial Workers of the World* (Chicago 1969), 19-87. D.J. Bercuson, 'Labour Radicalism and the Western Industrial Frontier: 1897-1919,' *Canadian Historical Review* LVIII (June 1977):154-75, describes the Canadian setting.

47 The one policeman had nothing to do. Royal Commission Re Miners and Mine Owners in the Province of BC, Report and Evidence, 1900, microfilm misc. 373, Department of Labour Library, Ottawa.

48 On 29 April 1899, the Old Jonah mill in Wardner, Idaho, was blown up, and troops were eventually sent in. An account of earlier violence in the Coeur d'Alene is in R.W. Smith, *The Coeur d'Alene Mining War of 1892* (Corvallis 1961). This background of conflict charged the ideological air in the Slocan.

49 However differently expressed, brotherhood was a common goal. Union leaders raised on the Shorter Presbyterian Catechism could remind men that 'the Bible says, "He that gives to the poor lends to the Lord"'; and the union, too, could embrace a vision of a better world: 'Although the phrase is hackneyed, it is increasingly true that in union is strength, and not alone strength itself but the last and only power we possess to successfully wage the battle that started with the Creation, and – saving the advent of the Co-operative Commonwealth – cannot end while this Earth exists.' Shilland to members of Sandon Miners Union, 20 November 1910, MMP, vol. 156.

50 If there were great men in the early Slocan valley, one of them was Andrew Shilland, secretary for years of the Sandon local of the WFM. Judging by the surviving fragments of his correspondence, Shilland, an educated Scot, understood full well the broken social circumstances and largely unregulated industrial environment in which the miners lived, and did what he could to mitigate the effects. He became a close friend of many a lonely, virtually illiterate miner.

51 Union leaders considered their Sandon hospital to be the embodiment of the principle of fellowship on which, they thought, a more just society should rest. During the long strike of 1899-1900, Dr. Gomm, a Californian, and Nurse Chisholm donated their services. Both remained in Sandon as the camp declined, providing a high standard of medical service for very little remuneration. With such support the hospital struggled on, its symbolic value heightened by the mine owners' hostility. It was a sad day early in the Depression when, after more than thirty years, the hospital was finally forced to close.

52 Five miners at the Rambler Mine to Shilland, 8 July 1903, MMP, vol. 158.

53 John Cameron to Shilland, Rambler Mine, 28 February 1902, MMP, vol. 157.

54 In January 1900, during the strike, some mine owners imported Finnish and Swedish miners from Minnesota. The union, furious, described such men as 'foreigners of the lowest sort'; from the owners' perspective, one of their advantages was that they did not speak English and, therefore, could not easily find out what was going on in the camp.

55 C.H. Green to Shilland, Trout Lake, BC, 29 December 1903, MMP, vol. 156.

56 *Henderson's British Columbia Gazetteer and Directory* (Victoria 1900).

57 Based on names listed in *Henderson's British Columbia Gazetteer and Directory* (Victoria 1894, 1901, 1910, and 1921).

58 Hubert Charbonneau and his colleagues in demography at the Université de Montréal are able to identify the precise origins of immigrants to Canada in the seventeenth century much more accurately than I can identify immigrants to New Denver in the twentieth century. There were no marriage contracts. Informants who were alive in New Denver in 1910 give the origins of people named in the directory of that year as follows: eastern Canada 39, England 17, Scotland and Wales 5, Ireland 6, continental Europe 10, United States 2, Orient 2, unknown 96. Interviews conducted with Dick Avison, Turk

Avison, Lindsay Carter, Edith Greer, Dick Harris, Sandy Harris, and Gertrude Watney in 1976.

59 This map and most of my remarks about the structure of New Denver before 1914 rest on the memories of people who were children in the village then. Such a source is easily warped, particularly when some informants are relatives, but there is no alternative. The tentative pasts of incipient places like New Denver have left few records. My interviews were conducted in 1976 (see note 57).

60 Minutes of the New Denver Brass Band, Selkirk College Archives.

61 To the Electors of the Slocan District (handbill), New Denver, BC, 1 November 1909, J.C. Harris Papers, BCARS. This was my grandfather, one of the many across the breadth of the North American frontier who thought that old ways could be rectified in new, God-given places. At the end of a life that had brought some mixture of the Webbs, Christian conviction, and Eeyore to a British Columbia mountainside, he thought he had failed. His ranch, which became an internment home for Japanese evacuees from the coast during World War II, has posed many of the questions about this country that, over the years, I have tried to answer.

62 *Sandon Mining Standard*, 26 November 1904.

63 Ibid., 10 June 1905.

64 This is now made clear in R. Cole Harris, ed., *From the Beginning to 1800*, vol. 1 of *Historical Atlas of Canada* (Toronto 1987). The pattern also emerges clearly in works such as C. Grant Head, *Eighteenth Century Newfoundland: A Geographer's Perspective* (Toronto 1976), and Graeme Wynn, *Timber Colony: A Historical Geography of Early 19th Century New Brunswick* (Toronto 1981).

65 I.M. Robinson, 'New Industrial Towns in Canada's Resource Frontier,' Department of Geography, Research Paper No. 73, University of Chicago, 1962; R.A. Lucas, *Minetown, Milltown and Railtown: Life in Canadian Communities of Single Industry* (Toronto 1971); J.H. Bradbury, 'Towards an Alternative Theory of Resource-Based Town Development in Canada,' *Economic Geography* 55 (1979):147-66.

66 I am not saying, of course, that Acadian and Canadian agricultural economies were closed and subsistent. Clearly they were not. Recent excavations of an early eighteenth-century house near Port-Royal reveal many imported ceramics and metal goods in a simple, timber-frame house that was built on a fieldstone sill and thatched. The people who lived in such a house farmed for their own needs and produced modest quantities for sale. David Christianson, 'Acadian Archaeological Research at Belleisle, Nova Scotia,' *The Occasional* 8 (spring 1984):16-22. Along the lower St. Lawrence, where agricultural exports were largest during the 1730s and early 1740s, agriculture was never detached from a market economy. But there were degrees of connection; Acadian or Canadian farmers directed less of their labour towards the market than did most fishermen in Newfoundland. This relative difference is important and is my point.

67 The term 'staple trade,' well established in the literature since the early work of Harold Innis, is perhaps misleading. Only the fur trade was a trade per se; fishing, lumbering, and mining were resource industries that produced export staples.

68 Often long before they were mechanized, as in the early fishery.

69 Such migrations, of course, were not confined to the European outreach to the New World or to staple trades. See Olwen H. Hufton, *The Poor of Eighteenth-Century France, 1750-1789* (Oxford 1974), ch. 3.

70 I have argued some of these matters in other contexts: 'The Simplification of Europe Overseas,' *Annals, Association of American Geographers*, 67 (December 1977):469-83, and 'European Beginnings in the Northwestern Atlantic: A Comparative View,' in David D. Hall and David G. Allen, eds., *Seventeenth-Century New England* (Boston 1984), 119-52.

Chapter 8: Farming and Rural Life

Earlier drafts of this chapter benefitted from comments by John Chapman, Richard Mackie, Sharon Rempel, Ruth Sandwell, and Graeme Wynn.

1 Peter Hulme, 'The Spontaneous Hand of Nature: Savagery, Colonialism, and the Enlightenment,' in P. Hulme and L. Jordanova, eds., *The Enlightenment and Its Shadows* (New York 1990), 18-34.

2 This general picture of agriculture in British Columbia in 1891 is worked out largely from the 'First Report of the Department of Agriculture of the Province of British Columbia,' *British Columbia Sessional Papers* (Victoria 1891), and the 'Second Report' in 1893.

3 'Pests,' wrote a rancher near Clinton, 'consist of wild horses, of which there are probably 1000 head between this place and Big Bar and Bridge Creek.' 'Second Report of the Department of Agriculture,' *British Columbia Sessional Papers* (Victoria 1893), 776.

4 William Cronon, *Nature's Metropolis: Chicago and the Great West* (New York 1991), 266-7.

5 Among the general literature on these points, see especially Walter Goldschmidt, *As You Sow* (New York 1947), and Mark Kramer, *Three Farms: Making Milk, Meat, and Money from the American Soil* (Cambridge, MA, 1980). Sociologists have vigorously debated when and to what extent agriculture was subsumed in capitalist relations of production, a discussion summarized by Susan Archer Mann, *Agrarian Capitalism in Theory and Practice* (Chapel Hill 1990). For other views, see Frederick Buttel, Olaf Larson, and Gilbert Gillespie, *The Sociology of Agriculture* (Westport 1989).

6 Marjorie Griffin Cohen, *Women's Work: Markets and Economic Development in Nineteenth Century Ontario* (Toronto 1988), note 15.

7 The classic statement is James A. Henretta, 'Families and Farms: Mentalité in Pre-Industrial America,' *William and Mary Quarterly*, third series, 35 (1978):3-32; see also David Vickers, 'Competency and Competition: Economic Culture in Early America,' *William and Mary Quarterly*, third series, 47 (1990):3-29.

8 Arthur Meighen, quoted in Paul M. Koroscil, 'Soldiers, Settlement, and Development in British Columbia, 1915-1930,' *BC Studies* 54 (1982):69.

9 On the English background of these values, see Denis E. Cosgrove, *Social Formation and Symbolic Landscape* (London 1984), ch. 8; more generally, David Demeritt, 'Visions of Agriculture in British Columbia,' *BC Studies* 108 (winter 1995-6):29-59.

10 Alice Ravenhill, *Some Labour-Saving Devices in the Home*, Bulletin 41 (Victoria 1912). Her other bulletins are *The Place and Purpose of Family Life*, *The Preparation of Food*, *The Preservation of Food*, *Food and Diet*, and *The Art of Right Living*.

11 The English sociologist Anthony Giddens argues that in modern societies, the nation-state itself, rather than town or countryside, has become the 'power container' of society. *The Nation-State and Violence*, vol. 2 of *A Contemporary Critique of Historical Materialism* (Berkeley 1987); see also Stephen Kern, *The Culture of Time and Space, 1880-1918* (Cambridge, MA, 1983), especially ch. 8.

12 This sketch from R. Cole Harris and Elizabeth Phillips, eds., *Letters from Windermere, 1912-1914* (Vancouver 1984).

13 Nan Bourgon, *Rubber Boots for Dancing and Other Memories of Pioneer Life in the Bulkley Valley* (Cloverdale, BC, 1979).

14 Rose Hill Farmers' Institute, Heritage Committee, *Bunch Grass to Barbed Wire* (Cloverdale, BC, 1984), 107-9.

15 G.M. Dawson and R.W. Murchie, *The Settlement of the Peace River Country: A Study of a Pioneer Area*, vol. 4 of the Canadian Frontiers of Settlement Series, W.A. Mackintosh and W.L.G. Joerg, eds. (Toronto 1934), 236-40.

16 Ibid., 251.

17 Paul M. Koroscil, 'Boosterism and the Settlement Process in the Okanagan Valley, British Columbia,' in *Canadian Papers in Rural History*, vol. 5 (Gananoque, ON, 1986), 73-103; David Dendy, 'The Development of the Orchard Industry in the Okanagan Valley, 1890-1914,' in *Okanagan Historical Society Report*, vol. 3 (Vernon 1974), 68-73; Colin M. Reeves, 'The Establishment of the Kelowna Orcharding Area: A Study of Accommodation to Site and Situation,' MA thesis, University of British Columbia, 1973.

18 Wayne Wilson, 'Irrigating the Okanagan: 1860-1920,' MA thesis, University of British Columbia, 1989.

19 Reeves, 'The Establishment of the Kelowna Orcharding Area,' ch. 3.

20 Ibid., ch. 4; Margaret Ormsby, 'Fruit Marketing in the Okanagan Valley of British Columbia,' *Agricultural History* 9 (1935):80-97; Ian MacPherson, 'Creating Order amid Degrees of Marginality: Divisions in the Struggle for Orderly Marketing in British Columbia, 1900-1940,' *Canadian Papers in Rural History* 7 (1990):309-34.

21 Robert E. Cail, *Land, Man, and the Law: The Disposal of Crown Lands in British Columbia, 1871-1913* (Vancouver 1974), chs. 1-3.
22 G.E.G. Thomas, 'The British Columbia Ranching Frontier, 1858-1896,' MA thesis, University of British Columbia, 1976.
23 Thomas R. Weir, *Ranching in the Southern Interior Plateau of British Columbia*, 2nd ed. (Ottawa 1964), 125.
24 Ibid., 42. For a more detailed analysis, see M. Allan MacDonald, 'Overgrazing on Western Rangelands with Special Reference to Those of British Columbia,' MSc thesis, University of British Columbia, 1949.
25 Weir, *Ranching in the Southern Interior*, ch. 6.
26 Nina G. Woolliams, *Cattle Ranch: The Story of the Douglas Lake Cattle Company* (Vancouver 1979).
27 Cronon, *Nature's Metropolis*, ch. 5.
28 H. Thomas Johnson, *Agricultural Depression in the 1920's: Fact or Statistical Artifact?* (New York 1985), and James H. Shideler, *Farm Crisis 1919-1923* (Berkeley 1957).
29 According to Doris E. Lee, there was no central stockyard in BC in the 1920s because of the opposition of the meat packers. 'Some Factors Making for the Success or Failure of Agriculture in B.C.,' MA thesis, University of British Columbia, 1925.
30 MacDonald, 'Overgrazing on Western Rangelands,' 138-9.
31 'First Report of the Department of Agriculture of the Province of British Columbia,' *British Columbia Sessional Papers* (Victoria 1891), 733, 946-8.
32 Their effect was to favour the larger, more mechanized producers. For example, when it became illegal to sell unpasteurized milk (1928), the smaller producers, who could ill afford the cans and other sanitary facilities needed to deal with a creamery, were the most affected.
33 H.R. Dare, *Dairy-Farming in British Columbia: An Economic Study of Seven Hundred and Twenty-Six Farms*, Bulletin 103 (Victoria 1928), 79-80. If anything, Dare's sample is biased towards the bigger producers.
34 Marjorie Griffin Cohen, 'The Decline of Women in Canadian Dairying,' *Histoire Sociale/Social History* 27, 34 (1984):307-34.
35 Morag E. Maclachlan, 'The Fraser Valley Milk Producers' Association: Successful Cooperative,' MA thesis, University of British Columbia, 1972; see also her article 'The Success of the Fraser Valley Milk Producers' Association,' *BC Studies* 24 (1974-5):52-64. For similar battles elsewhere, see Linda G. Ford, 'Another Double Burden: Farm Women and Agrarian Activism in Depression Era New York State,' *New York History* 75 (1994):373-98.
36 This was the Dairy Products Sales Adjustment Act. It required 66 per cent compliance to be put into effect.
37 Also, a white one. Few if any commercial dairies were run by Chinese, Japanese, or East Indians. The concern, ostensibly, was public health, but the inspiration was racist. In 1918, the Richmond Local of the FVMPA reported as follows: 'Our association notify Head Office that a Jap is shipping milk ... and that our association is decidedly opposed to this.' Cited in Maclachlan, 'The Fraser Valley Milk Producers' Association,' 34.
38 E.D. Barrows, FVMPA Minutes, 9 February 1918; cited in Maclachlan, 'The Fraser Valley Milk Producers' Association,' 64.
39 Testimony of A.W. Wells to British Columbia Royal Commission on Agriculture at Chilliwack, BC, 6 May 1913, GR 324, box 2, vol. 1, 139, BCARS.
40 Dare, *Dairy-Farming*.
41 See, for example, Testimony to the Royal Commission on Agriculture, 26 April 1913 and 5 May 1913, GR 324, box 1, vol. 4, 283, BCARS; and box 2, vol. 1, 119, BCARS.
42 For example, the agreement of the Delta Co-operative Growers' Association that banned members from 'selling, renting, leasing ... all or any of the Grower's lands ... (to) persons of East Indian or Asiatic birth or origin other than the white race.' Quoted in W.G. Donley, 'The Oriental Agriculturalist in British Columbia,' BA honour's essay, University of British Columbia, 1928, 13.

43 This is well described in California by Sucheng Chan, *This Bittersweet Soil: The Chinese in California Agriculture, 1860-1910* (Berkeley 1986), 386-402. We assume a similar situation in British Columbia.
44 John M. Read, 'The Pre-war Japanese Canadians of Maple Ridge: Land Ownerships and the Ken Tie,' MA thesis, University of British Columbia, 1975.
45 For example, remarks by E.A. Manor, MP from Fraser Valley, quoted in Donley, 'The Oriental Agriculturalist,' 19.
46 Yamaga Yasataro, the director in question, was a pillar of the Japanese community at Maple Ridge. His papers, from which this information is taken, are in Special Collections, UBC Library.
47 Hulbert Family Papers, Add. Mss. 285, BCARS.
48 H.N. Whitford and Roland D. Craig, *Forests of British Columbia* (Ottawa 1918).

Chapter 9: Making an Immigrant Society

An earlier draft of this chapter benefitted from comments by Brett Christophers, Daniel Clayton, Jeanne Kay, Audrey Kobayashi, Nadine Schuurman, and Graeme Wynn.

1 Derived from Ethel Wilson, *The Innocent Traveller* (Toronto 1949).
2 Derived from Nan Bourgon, *Rubber Boots for Dancing and Other Memories of Pioneer Life in the Bulkley Valley* (Cloverdale, BC, 1979).
3 Derived from Denise Chong, *The Concubine's Children* (Toronto 1994).
4 This literature focuses on the colonized and on European attitudes towards them, and seldom deals with the most successful of all colonizing strategies: the creation of new societies made up of the colonizers. For an anthropological response to these issues, see Ann Laura Stoler, 'Rethinking Colonial Categories: European Communities and the Boundaries of Rule,' *Comparative Studies in Society and History* 31, 1 (1989):134-61. The geographer Derek Gregory provides a broad discussion of current orientations in the literature on colonialism/resistance in *Geographical Imaginations* (Cambridge, MA, and Oxford 1994), particularly 168-203.
5 For example, Jack Hodgins, *The Invention of the World* (Toronto 1977).
6 This terminology is from Gilles Deleuze and Félix Guattari, *Anti-Oedipus: Capitalism and Schizophrenia*, trans. Robert Hurley, Mark Seem, and Helen R. Lane (New York 1977).
7 For a fairly straightforward elaboration of this position, see Anthony Giddens, *The Constitution of Society: Outline of the Theory of Structuration* (Berkeley and Los Angeles 1984).
8 The word 'simplification' has caused problems in the past, but I cannot find an acceptable alternative. I do not mean that New World societies were somehow simpler than Old World societies, a proposition that can hardly be analyzed and that is intuitively implausible. I use the word to refer to the paring back of, or the deletions from, particular Old World traditions that occurred with migration and resettlement. Only elements of the ways of one setting were reproduced in another. Against this 'simplification' of particular traditions were the many new experiences and relationships that immigrants encountered in new settings. In short order, an immigrant society became another creation, probably neither simpler nor more complex than its Old World antecedents, but clearly different. I suggest that the character of such societies had a good deal to do with the loss (simplification) of a great many Old World ways, and the incorporation of many new ways associated with a new setting broadly conceived.
9 Edward Gibbon Wakefield, *A view of the art of colonization, with present reference to the British Empire; in letters between a statesman and a colonist* (London 1849). Among the most astute comments on Wakefield are those by his near- contemporary Herman Merivale, *Lectures on Colonization and the Colonies* (London 1861). Turner's famous article on 'The Significance of the Frontier in American History', published in 1893, dominated two generations of American historiography. Turner's frontier was a complex, somewhat mystical space where, following one of his most central metaphors, free land emphasized a changed and far more accessible relationship with property.
10 Louis Hartz, *The Founding of New Societies* (New York 1964).
11 Cole Harris, 'The Simplification of Europe Overseas,' *Annals, Association of American Geographers* 67, 4 (December 1977):469-83; and 'European Beginnings in the

Northwestern Atlantic: A Comparative View,' in David D. Hall and David G. Allen, eds., *Seventeenth-Century New England* (Boston 1984), 119-52.

12 R.B. Johnson, *Very Far West Indeed: a few rough experiences in the northwest Pacific Coast* (London 1872), ch. 9.

13 For general accounts of the changed gendering of places of work and residence, see Barbara Laslett, 'Gender and Social Production: Historical Perspectives,' *Annual Review of Sociology* 15 (1989):381-404; and Gillian Rose, *Feminism and Geography: The Limits of Geographical Knowledge* (Minneapolis 1993), ch. 2.

14 On the domestic image of women in the imperial imagination, see Anna Davin, 'Imperialism and Motherhood,' in Raphael Samuel, ed., *Patriotism: The Making and Unmaking of British National Identity,* vol. 1 (London and New York 1989); Anne McClintock, *Imperial Leather: Race, Gender and Sexuality in the Colonial Context* (New York and London 1995); and, more specifically on British Columbia, Adele Perry, ' "Oh I'm Just Sick of the Faces of Men:" Gender Imbalance, Race, Sexuality, and Sociability in Nineteenth-Century British Columbia,' *BC Studies* 105-6 (spring/summer 1995):27-45. For an example of the frontier male tendency to put women on a pedestal of civility, see Gordon Gibson, *Bull of the Woods* (Vancouver 1980), esp. ch. 1.

15 In his novel *Woodsmen of the West* (London 1908, repub. Toronto 1964), M.A. Grainger describes the confident, never-say-can't attitude of western labour, what he calls 'Western Spirit,' an attitude formed where extended apprenticeships and close surveillance were out of the question.

16 Nelson Riis, 'The Walhachin Myth: A Study of Settlement Abandonment,' *BC Studies* 17 (1973):3-25.

17 On the missionary politics of space, see Jean and John Comaroff, *Of Revelation and Revolution: Christianity, Colonialism, and Consciousness in South Africa* (Chicago 1991), ch. 6. More specifically, Jean Usher, *William Duncan of Metlakatla: A Victorian Missionary in British Columbia* (Ottawa 1974); and Brett Christophers, 'Time, Space, and the Judgement of God: Anglican Missionary Discourse in British Columbia,' MA thesis, University of British Columbia, 1995.

18 'Imaginative geography of the "our land-barbarian land" variety does not require that the barbarians acknowledge the distinction. It is enough for "us" to set up these boundaries in our own minds; "they" become "they" accordingly, both their territory and their mentality are designated as different from "ours."' Edward Said, *Orientalism* (New York 1979), 54. Said suggests that the power of this simple 'imaginative geography and of the dramatic boundaries it draws' has been enormous.

19 Address of His Excellency the Governor to the Inhabitants at Fort Yale, Sept. 12 1858, Douglas Papers, BCARS.

20 For an admirable discussion of this evolution, see Catherine Hall, 'Imperial Man: Edward Eyre in Australasia and the West Indies 1833-66,' in Bill Schwartz, ed., *The Expansion of England: Race, Ethnicity and Cultural History* (London and New York 1996). Also, J. and J. Comaroff, *Of Revelation and Revolution*, ch. 3; Young, *Colonial Desire*, ch. 2.

21 Kay Anderson, *Vancouver's Chinatown: Racial Discourse in Canada, 1875-1980* (Montreal and Kingston 1991). Anderson is right about the territorial ambitions of white racist attitudes, but she discounts Chinese agency, which may have been more active than she allows in the making of Chinatowns.

22 As a young man, Teit became an associate of Franz Boas; out of this association, plus his marriage to a Nlha7kápmx woman, came a series of magnificent ethnographies of the Interior Salish, still the standard works. Teit, a Shetland Islander and a socialist, never identified with mainstream white British Columbia and, fluent in several Interior Salish languages, admired Native societies and was a confidante of many Native people.

23 G. Bramhall, 'That They Might Have Life: An Autobiography of the Late Stanley E. Higgs,' BCARS, AMS 1332.

24 Young, *Colonial Desire*, 174. As I pointed out above, the post-colonial literature largely ignores European settlement overseas; as a result, the literature is prone to statements such as Young's, which, for all their authors' intentions to the contrary, embody a form of orientalism.

Index